The Lily Theatre

'One of the most wonderful books that I have read for years . . . written in a beautiful, restrained but powerful style . . . the theme is authentic, and Wang knows how to conjure up an enormous wealth of images'
NRC Handelsblad

'An original and strongly affecting book . . . a roaring success'
Gotlands Allehanda

'Spellbinding and stirring . . . an honest picture which does not accuse blindly, but depicts, reveals facts and inquires . . . a precious piece of contemporary history'
Hessiche Allgemeine

'A wonderful evocation of freedom and the human spirit'
Canberra Times

'A frankly autobiographical story in which the heroine, Lian, joins the tradition of the wise child. To call her a Mandarin Huck Finn may be a bit of a reach, but it makes the point, which is that sometimes it takes an innocent to see society's hypocrisies . . . an intimate and unexpectedly salty illustration of that old Chinese curse, "May you live in interesting times"'
Time

'A successful combination of personal experience, painfully gained maturity and writing talent . . . Lulu Wang's strength is her fresh and sensitive style, her sharp observation and the mix of experience and fictive plot'
Aachener Zeitung

'An exciting and fascinating story . . . the author knows exactly how to move the story forward. The insight into a historically significant period in a culture and a society we in the Western world have little experience of is both rewarding and frightening'

Nya Ludvika Tidning

'It is universal in that it is about a little girl who grows up under difficult circumstances . . . Wang writes in detailed, beautifully wrought language'

Laholms Tidning

'A very exciting and gripping novel. What gives Lulu Wang's book an extra dimension is the involving story about Lian and Kim . . . about spring friendship and two teenage girls and their development into women'

Hudiksvalls Tidning

'Lulu Wang, a personal witness of the Cultural Revolution, not only knows how to narrate in a very original and gripping way, but with her subjective point of view also shows aspects of Chinese daily life under Mao which the European reader is not likely to have known before . . . With her very elastic, direct and descriptive language, Lulu Wang succeeds in making Chinese life and thought palpable for Europeans who want to learn more'

Rheinischer Merkur

'This is the story of a woman's struggle during the Chinese cultural revolution but fear not. It is not told in flashbacks, it doesn't cover three generations, it does not end happily ever after in America. This is a raw story, unspoiled by any sentimental varnish'

The Age, Melbourne

THE *lily* THEATRE

Lulu Wang

TRANSLATED BY HESTER VELMANS

SCEPTRE

First published by Vassallucci, Amsterdam, in 1997
First published in the UK in 2000 by Hodder and Stoughton
A division of Hodder Headline
A Sceptre Paperback

The English language edition has been rearranged
and partially revised and rewritten from the original
Dutch novel, *Het Lelietheater*.

A CIP catalogue record for this title is available
from the British Library

ISBN 0 340 69667 2

Typeset by Palimpsest Book Production Limited,
Polmont, Stirlingshire
Printed and bound in Great Britain by
Mackays of Chatham plc, Chatham, Kent

Hodder and Stoughton
A division of Hodder Headline
338 Euston Road
London NW1 3BH

AUTHOR'S NOTE

This is the story of a young girl growing up in China. Even though the events described in this book are based on my own personal experiences, the details don't always coincide with the facts, and are, with regard to the players – except in the case of Mao Zedong – totally fictitious.

The names of the main characters have been transcribed according to Western usage – with the last name last and the first name first. The other names are written in the Chinese way, with the first name last and the last name first.

In Chinese, the Q is pronounced *tch*, and the X is pronounced *szh*. The translations of passages from the *Little Red Book*, as well as the Chinese poetry quotations, are my own.

TRANSLATOR'S NOTE

The novelty of a book written in Dutch by a young Chinese immigrant who had only just mastered that tongue took the Netherlands by storm in 1997, catapulting *The Lily Theatre* to an almost permanent place at the top of Holland's bestseller list. The liberties Lulu Wang took with her adopted language entranced the Dutch, who immediately embraced her as one of the most original voices to have come along in years.

One of the most distinctive characteristics of that voice is the preference for concrete imagery and colloquial idioms; Ms Wang was able to commandeer common Dutch words and phrases and turn them into something distinctly Chinese. Onomatopoeic transcriptions, such as *Cttch!* or *Trieee!* are an oral storytelling device to catch the audience's attention. Flowery language is juxtaposed with the coarsest of obscenities; a cliché seen through Chinese eyes acquires a new and often startling significance. As Lulu Wang says, 'I want to *shock* people with my language.'

In order to preserve the special flavour of this style, she and I worked closely together to find a similar balance of familiar and foreign-sounding turns of phrase in English.

Some of the idioms, Chinese words and a few hysterically convoluted expressions are explained by the author in the Glossary.

The sea
of sorrow
stretches
into infinity

But
turn around:
at your feet
lies the safe shore

Buddhist saying

苦海無邊
回頭是岸

'Which basket of toys do you want? You choose.'

Lian nodded. The pigtail that poked up into the air like a little chili pepper went up and down, and her face lit up, like a water lily unfurling, bashful and serene.

'Which basket do you want? The jimus, or the one with the dolls and the stuffed animals?'

Lian crossed her arms over her chest and rocked her upper body from side to side.

'The dolls then. Just a minute, Lian.'

Father got on a step stool. She opened her eyes wide and followed every movement of his arms. He set the basket down, tipped the thing over and dumped the contents on to the floor. Greedily Lian threw herself on the mountain of dolls and animals. Squatting down beside her, Father reached out to stroke her back. Lian picked up a blind teddy bear, pressed it against her face, shut her eyes and waited for him to be done with his cuddling.

As soon as she heard him close the door behind him, Lian poked a finger into one of the doll's empty eye sockets. Does it hurt? she asked silently, with her eyes. Oh, of course not, you're just a doll. Lian inspected her brood, checking to see if any of them had any eyes left. Some were still in treatment: their eyes hung down on either side of their noses. The yarn with which they were attached had been stretched so that the glass beads looked like big fat tears rolling down their cheeks. She stroked an eye with her finger, thinking it was a shame to pull it out, then leaned over anyway and bit at the yarn with her teeth. Cttch! The eye skittered over the concrete floor. Ting-ting-ting-ting . . .

Now the legs. These she bent until they snapped. The giraffe's neck was difficult though – it was so sturdy that it took a long time to get a proper kink in it. 'Ehnnnn' – it took all her strength to fold the neck in two. Lian pursed her lips resolutely. She did manage to crack it in the end. Not all the way through, but it came close – it was good and floppy now, anyway. Lian pressed the giraffe against her face and kissed him over and over again, stroking his soft, light brown fur.

PART ONE

1972

I cannot tell
What Mount Lu looks like
From where I sit, inside

Su Shi, 1084

MAMA'S JEST

Trees were in full bloom, birds were busy courting, and the funny blotches were spreading all up and down my arms. I got up and rubbed the affected areas with the sticky, smelly brown ointment, just as I did every day. I felt lonely and sad. Never again would I have clean sheets and clean underwear like other children – the ointment made everything filthy.

That morning, at the start of her weekend home leave, Mother took a bath, then put on her best clothes, the ones she used to wear before she was detained. How different she looked, suddenly, after months of slouching around in nothing but rags! I couldn't believe my eyes.

Mother drew a fine leather handbag from the wardrobe and filled it with delicacies that she had bought for a song from the peasants who lived around the labour camp. We were going to visit a former colleague of Father's, a dermatologist. He was retired, so when the rest of the hospital staff were evacuated he had been allowed to stay home. Unlike Father, who had been exiled to the far-off province of the Gansu desert for six months now.

The dermatologist's wife was ecstatic when she saw the chestnuts and the pickled eggs. 'We haven't tasted those in years! What are you bringing us this kind of extravagant present for? Aren't Lian's father and my husband good friends?'

The specialist examined me and then had a talk with Mother, in private. Half an hour later Mother dragged me back home. Her eyes shone with unusual determination and her feet smacked boldly on the pavement.

For weeks now Mother had been writing letters of petition to the various leaders of her university – the Teachers' University of Beijing – in the hope of persuading them that it was essential to have me live close by, so that she could keep an eye on my rapidly worsening condition.

Chemistry class was interrupted by a knock on the door. I was called out and saw Mother standing in the corridor. I was going to ask her how she had managed to return from the re-education camp again so soon, but on seeing her tense face I decided to keep the question to myself. I had to run to keep up with her as she strode to the office of the director of the Teachers' University.

'Well, well, little Wine-Cup, in the six months since I saw you last, you have grown from a cheeky little girl into a charming young lady!'

I blushed. I wasn't sure how to behave in his presence. I knew him quite well, because he had supervised the project Mother had been working on for the past five years – the *Textbook of the Modern History of China*. I had often visited Mother's office after school. The Director was usually there. He used to tease me about the dimple in my right cheek: 'Well, well, if that little Wine-Cup were full of wine, and you were to drink from it until it was all gone, you'd have to ask your neighbours, "Remind me, what's my name again?" That's how deep that dimple of yours is, did you know that?' He was friendly towards me.

Mother nudged me forward. 'Say good afternoon to the venerable Head of the Party Committee of the University!'

Shyly I stepped forward to greet him. But the Director had taken a pile of papers out of a drawer in his desk and was reading intently. He looked very stern. The mood in the room had suddenly turned sombre; I hardly dared breathe. Without raising his eyes from the papers, he motioned us to two posh leather chairs. Gingerly we sat down.

After a few anxious minutes, he gathered up the papers and said in a hushed voice: 'Revolutionary comrade Yang, your dozen or so petitions demand the impossible of me. How on earth can I cut short your detention? Just because you want to take care of your ailing daughter! In the five years since our university's re-education camp was founded, fourteen hundred people have been sent there, and every single one has had to complete his sentence in full. Even if one falls seriously ill oneself during that time, one has to stay there. Professor Wu – don't you remember? One of the physics faculty, died in camp of liver cancer. What's a little skin condition compared to that?' His face softened; he sent me a tender look. 'Besides, who says that our little Wine-Cup is disfigured by this vitiligo? I only wish my own Laihui were half as pretty . . .' Laihui was his only daughter. She was four years older than I and in the fifth year of my former school.

The compliment did not sit well with Mother, apparently, because she was fidgeting nervously with her handbag. 'Most highly respected leader, it is true that the patches have not yet appeared on any exposed areas, such as the hands or the face. But should the poor child be left to her lot much longer and her physical and psychological state continue to deteriorate, then it won't be long before the spots start appearing there as well. I have spoken with a prominent dermatologist, and he tells me that this is a psychosomatic condition. Only with loving care is there any hope of halting the progression of the disease.'

The Director shrugged.

'Merciful head of the Party Committee, if the illness continues to develop at this rate, Lian will soon find herself shunned by society, stigmatised by her appearance. You yourself are a father. If something like this were to happen to Laihui, how would you feel? Would you not move Heaven and Earth to save her from such a horrible fate?' She took out a handkerchief to dab at her tears.

'Oh, Yunxiang . . .' Suddenly he was addressing Mother by her first name. 'Aren't you exaggerating just a little? A few spots on one's body, what difference does it make?'

'A *few* spots?' Mother's voice had gone hoarse.

After a pregnant pause, Mother stood up and said, 'Lian, take your clothes off so the Director can judge for himself whether I am exaggerating or not.'

I almost burst out laughing at Mother's hilarious jest. Until I noticed the fierce, determined look on Mother's face. Her expression warned me that I had better not even *think* of ignoring her command. My eyes swivelled from one to the other: from Mother, who was forcing me to do something that made my flesh crawl – just thinking about it made me wilt with shame – to the man who was sitting there with an indifferent expression on his face. Evidently he thought Mother was creating a mountain out of a molehill. I hesitated, then reluctantly unhooked my belt and eased my trousers down, inch by inch.

When the Director saw my skin mottled with unsightly, overlapping white blemishes, he blanched and started combing jittery fingers through his bristly grey hair. Mother, noticing that he was wavering, snatched the opportunity of finishing the business of convincing him. With a hand coarsened by hard labour, she smacked me so hard that I lost my balance and fell down. Without a moment's hesitation, she pounced again, pulling my underpants down below my ankles. Numb with shame, I just lay there whimpering softly. I was afraid the Director would get angry with me if I started bawling out loud.

'Lian, child, don't cry,' he said, rushing to my side and helping me to my feet. I was choking on my tears and completely forgot to pull my pants back up. 'Yunxiang, I never knew you to be so rough with your daughter!'

But Mother was still seething. She gave me a firm kick in the bare backside, grabbed me by my plaits and started dragging me around the office. 'You ungrateful brat! What are you snivelling for? Don't you see that I'm doing it for *you*?'

'*Stop it!*' the man bellowed, quite unhinged at the sight of my bleached skin and at Mother's hysterical, barbaric behaviour. His booming voice brought Mother back to her senses. She put her arms around me, full of self-reproach.

'Yunxiang—' He did not bother to hide his tears. 'Here, behind closed doors, I will let you in on my dilemma. If it were up to me, I would have let you come home the day before yesterday for the sake of this child . . . I can't believe my eyes! It's appalling, to think that little Lian can have been so mucked up by this goddamn disease in just a matter of half a year . . .' Mother held her breath so she wouldn't miss a single word. 'But . . . I cannot propose something that the university's Revolutionary Committee is certain to reject.'

Besides students, Red Guards, campus janitors and furnace stokers, the Committee was composed of second-rate teachers who had nothing better to do than to torment their more successful colleagues in the name of the Revolution. Driven by revenge, ambition and, in some cases, ignorance, they had sold their consciences to the Father, Mother, Lover and Mistress All-Rolled-Into-One. They would not hesitate to dismiss the Director from his post and throw him in jail if he dared to show any bleeding-heart concern over some bourgeois intellectual.

'You don't have to revoke my detention. Yesterday I came up with a much better idea. Please give me permission to take Lian with me to my camp.'

'Are you out of your mind? What is she to do in such a depressing place? How is she going to go to school?'

'I myself can teach her the basics. And you know as well as I do that my fellow detainees include some of the most brilliant teachers and professors in the country. My daughter will receive a much better education there. And when she is with me, she will feel better and calmer. I swear by Mao the Saviour Star that her condition will not spread as quickly as it is doing now.'

Helplessly, he shook his head and wrote a note, which he handed over to his secretary.

'Make a *kowtow* to the gentleman and thank him for his mercy,' Mother commanded me. I just stared out of the window, stubbornly mute.

It was close to six o'clock when Mother returned to the Director's office a second time to pick up a typed document which stated that as of 28th May, I had permission to stay in Mother's camp for an indeterminate period of time.

*   *   *

When Mother, singing, served up the evening meal, I refused to eat. I loathed myself. I had taken off my clothes in front of a man who was not a doctor; who, to make it worse, had known me well for four years and had often joked around with me. I would never forgive Mother for making me do such a scandalous thing.

At night, safe in bed, where I had nothing to fear by way of insult or humiliation, I fantasised I was someone else. Someone who was free as a bird, happy as a little pink cloud in the sky, with normal-looking skin, just like other children. To keep my dream perfect, I decided to smash the mirror in the bathroom – 'by accident'.

SHARING THE MISERY FAIRLY AND SQUARELY

When I arrived back at the Accommodation Centre at seven a.m., I found all the other children green with envy. In their eyes, the prospect of leaving the Accommodation Centre was tantamount to entering Nirvana. My hatred of Mother evaporated in an instant. It was Mother, after all, who was making it possible for me to leave this wretched place; and I was sure that I would get better once I was with Mother again. For the first time in weeks I found myself cracking a smile. But even in that split second of glee, I was haunted by the mental picture of myself standing in the Director's office naked from the waist down. What a mortifying price I had paid for my freedom! Should I hate Mother for being such a mean witch, or should I be grateful to her for rescuing me from the sickening loneliness and the lonely sickness that had held me captive until now?

In the afternoon, I strode cheerfully down the corridor of the Western-Capitalists-Are-Grasshoppers-After-The-Harvest-Is-Over Building. Now that I could look forward to leaving, relief settled over me. It had been a long time since I had felt so relaxed. Only now did I realise how little notice I had taken of what was going on with the other students around me over the past months – my affliction had sucked up all my attention. I suddenly realised that Qiuju, who used to look like a sturdy little peasant, was weak and pallid. Qiuju had all sorts of big and little paper bags lying next to her pillow. They were full of pills. I waited patiently until Qiuju was out of the room and then asked Zhuoyue what was the matter with her.

'Didn't you know? She's had nephritis for a month now. Didn't you notice her eyelids? As swollen as two walnuts! If you didn't know better, you'd think she was constantly bawling her eyes out. It's because of the oedema, it's a symptom of her kidney infection, says Mrs Liu. Want me to tell you how many times she gets up to go to the toilet at night? Eight times. I swear on the *Little Red Book*, it's true! I counted, once. Mrs Liu takes her to the hospital once a week. She has to pee in a little bottle.' She pointed to a fiery-red scarf and whispered in my ear, 'Grandpa Heaven! It's *that* colour!'

I looked at Zhuoyue. I'm sorry, but you don't look all that well yourself, I thought to myself. Zhuoyue's cheeks were sunken; her face was more yellow than saffron.

'Oh, don't worry!' Zhuoyue, noticing my piercing look, slapped her cheeks to splash some colour into them and raked her fingers through her lusterless hair. 'I don't have jaundice, you mustn't think that. It's just that I'm beginning to look more like my father. He has naturally yellow skin. Mrs Liu has taken me to the clinic to have me checked at least five times. It's only that my CT-count is a little high. The doctor says most patients suffering from hepatitis have high cholesterol, but the opposite doesn't necessarily hold true ... What, don't you believe me? If a single word is a lie, may Buddha reward me with a cold sore on my lip!'

However strenuously Zhuoyue might protest that she wasn't as sick as Qiuju, it was as clear as daylight to me that Zhuoyue's health, too, left a lot to be desired. Only Qianru, the precious 'little princess', still seemed fit as a fiddle. I would never have thought it of her. For Ru had always been the skinny one, as washed-out as an anaemic. How in Heaven's name could it be that all of us, who had seemed so much more robust, were laid low by illness, and not she?

After dinner I called Zhuoyue and Qiuju to a meeting. We locked ourselves in the toilet, where we sat and venomously deplored Qianru's luck. After a heated debate, we arrived at the conclusion that Ru, for some reason or other, was immune to the miserable plight in which the rest of us 'orphaned' children found ourselves. Nothing seemed to get to her, not the homesickness, not the inadequate food – she hardly ate a thing anyway – nor the constant snarling of the adults in charge. 'It isn't fair!' we complained in unison – under our breath of course, because we couldn't afford to have anyone overhear our secret pow-wow. Qiuju was passing blood when she urinated and suffered chronic back pain and a constant bellyache; Zhuoyue ran a fever every afternoon and often had to throw up; I was covered with blotches; of the boys in the room next door, Fangguo could boast of circular bald patches all over his scalp and Dong was dogged by eczema. But Ru had nothing. Could anyone with even the trace of a sense of justice accept this?

We gnashed our teeth and racked our brains: 'How can we make Ru pay for staying as healthy as a ... as a ...' – for a moment we couldn't come up with a word strong enough to express our indignation – '. . . as a *sow*?'

During the course of our plotting it occurred to me that just three hours earlier, Zhuoyue had been gloating about Qiuju's kidney infection; Qiuju in turn had hailed my skin condition as good news. How was it then that we were suddenly the best of friends?

'Just wait,' we vowed, 'Ru has had all the luck. It's time for a payback!'

'The little wool blanket!' Zhuoyue's eyes shone as she made the pronouncement.

'Damn!' I clapped my palms together. 'That's the ticket. What a grandmother of a goose I am, not to have thought of it myself! Qiuju, don't you remember, Ru told us that whenever she feels bad she sniffs and cuddles her little woollen blanket? She's had that grubby rag since she was a baby, it's a kind of good-luck charm for the little brat. Have you ever seen her go to bed without that blanket clutched to her nose?'

Qiuju pugnaciously punched her fist into the air: 'Tomorrow we'll steal that mascot of hers and then we'll see how long she can stay hardy as a weed!'

The next day, just before naptime, we hid the little blanket behind a garbage pail in the hall and waited impatiently to see how Ru would react. Sure enough, Ru couldn't get to sleep and paced back and forth restlessly. She searched every corner of our dorm, the bathroom and the communal sitting room. Then she came back and crawled under her bed. When we saw her re-emerge, all red in the face, we saw that she, too, had finally lost her cool.

'Have any of you seen my blanket?' asked Ru in despair.

'Blanket? What blanket? *We* haven't hidden it,' announced Qiuju, much too promptly, with a pout. I itched to box Ju on the ears: now she had gone and spilled the beans.

And sure enough, before the curtain of the night fell, we were summoned to Mrs Xu's office. Xu banged her fist on the desk and threatened to send a Black Report on all three of us to our school unless we returned Ru's blanket.

I stuck to my guns. So did the other two. We pulled our most pitiful faces and acted like innocents unjustly accused. 'Of course, Ma'am,' we sighed, poker-faced, 'if you *do* decide to report us and ruin our political reputations, there is nothing we can do to stop you. But we can assure you we haven't touched that, what did you say, quilt – or was it a blanket or something . . . ? Anyway, what would we want with it? That thing stinks of Ru's spit and snot . . .'

'Ah-ha!' Xu shook her forefinger at us. 'How did you know it smells if you didn't take it?'

At last we cracked. 'Please, Ma'am – if you promise not to tell on us to our teachers, the blanket will be back on Ru's bed in five minutes.'

That is how the plan to take revenge on Ru ended up down the toilet. However, the three conspirators could note with some satisfaction that from that fateful afternoon on, Ru did not seem as placid and content as before. She had come to understand that she was both envied and shunned by us, and the realisation clearly hurt.

～

I said goodbye to my classmates and companions from the Accommodation Centre. They were practically dying of envy. Zhuoyue finally admitted that her tummy, the area around her liver to be precise, often hurt, and she was going to use that pretext to persuade her parents to rescue her from the Centre. Qianru, who had never shown her feelings before, looked extremely down in the dumps. Her eyes were red, not because she had been crying but because she had an infection. I knew about this because I had seen Ru running to Mrs Liu the day before to have her sore eyes checked. It was a start, at least; she too would have her fair share of misery.

FREEDOM

At home, Mother and I went about stuffing a couple of duffel bags with clothing, schoolbooks and other necessities. I was so happy I could have burst into song. To be with Mother again, finally! The fact that it was in a prison camp didn't matter.

It was with mixed feelings that I thought back on the time I had spent in the Accommodation Centre. Now that my homesickness was a thing of the past, I could even begin to feel somewhat nostalgic about that sorry episode. I had heard that in the West, people visiting another country would often buy a postcard or something similar as a reminder of their trip. I had no need for that sort of memento. The white patches stamped all over my body were something I would probably carry with me my entire life, a souvenir of my 'Sojourn in the Isle of Loneliness'.

When the morning of the departure came with its typical scene of deportee parents saying goodbye to their weeping children, it didn't rattle me as much as usual. It felt as if I were watching a movie: the anger and sadness provoked by the spectacle remained at a bearable remove. It was easy for me to feel that way of course, because *I* was standing in the packed dump truck, sardined between Mother and her fellow prisoners; *I* wasn't being torn from my mother's arms. It wasn't that I lacked compassion for my peers – it was just the way it was. The intense grief with which the haggard children watched their father or mother, or both, get sent away, didn't register under the circumstances.

The dump truck in which we were standing, creaking on all sides, stuttered its way from the stuffy grey city to the freshly-scented, verdant countryside. The sky seemed bluer and purer here, and the heavy air hanging over the metropolis lightened noticeably. Inhaling deeply, I considered myself lucky to be going to prison in the wide-open, liberating countryside – a place that would set me free.

THE CAMP

The dump truck stopped in front of some row-houses. Could this be a prison camp? No high walls, no barbed wire nor armed guards. The buildings were surrounded by emerald-green fields that went on for ever and were strewn with buttercups, poppies and daisies. The flowers picked up their heads as if to bid them welcome. The open air and the invigorating rhapsody of fresh colours made me think of a holiday resort rather than a prison camp. But, of course, the barracks didn't need to be fenced in – even if they'd had any thought of escaping, there was nowhere for the detainees to go. A slogan popped into my head unbidden, one that I had had to learn by heart when I was little: The Judicial Net of the Dictatorship of the People Encloses All Heaven and All Earth.

I followed my mother to one of the huts in the third row of the compound. *Yecch!* My nose wrinkled convulsively as a musty smell rose to greet me. I could hardly make out anything in the room; the curtains

13

must not have been opened yet. Groping in the dark, I trailed Mother inside, trusting the sound of her footsteps.

Someone turned on the light. I looked around: it was a dormitory with no windows. There were just two openings for ventilation. The iron grates over these squares were the first explicit evidence of our incarceration. I estimated the room to measure 350 square feet, about twenty-five by forty. There were twenty-five bunk beds all told, crammed so close together that you had to shuffle in sideways to reach your bed. Forty-nine women slept here.

With a thud, Mother let my bags flop on to the bare plank of one of the beds. A plump old woman squeezed through a narrow slot between the bunks: 'This must be our little Lian, the camp's youngest inmate!' She wrapped her arms around me, firmly and warmly. 'Welcome to our midst.' Then she hoisted her own bedroll on to the top bunk, drawing a hailstorm of protest-cries out of Mother's mouth: 'Maly, you are *not* sleeping up on top! With your rheumatism, it's too hard for you to climb up and down. Let the child do that – her legs are still strong and supple.'

The old lady shook her head so violently that her glasses almost slid off her nose. 'No, Yunxiang, the most tender morsel must be saved for the young. We may well rot in prison, but our children will see better things.'

I opened my eyes wide in astonishment. How did this old lady have the nerve to say such negative things about the glorious Proletarian Cultural Revolution? Wouldn't she get into even deeper trouble?

A weather-beaten and obviously ailing face rose from one of the other bunks. 'Yunxiang, just accept Maly's offer. She is right. Let us serve as fertile ground for the budding blooms of the next generation.'

My jaw dropped: weren't they afraid that their cryptic, yet none the less audacious criticism of government policies might be overheard and reported to the camp authorities? Wasn't it a well-known fact that prison snitching was one of the chief methods the Party had for keeping covert tabs on people?

But then, the name 'Maly' struck a bell. . . . Of course, *that* was it – it was the name on the cover of the textbook *English with No Trouble!* Could this grey, haggard, shrivelled old woman in beggars' rags, with hair like a worn scrubbing brush, be the author of the famous self-study series?

Tchttt-tchttt . . . Mother had gathered an armful of straw green with mould from a corner of the room, and was spreading it out over the wooden plank that was my bed. From the looks of it, this was supposed to be my mattress.

'Can't I just do without?' I asked quickly, because the sight of the stuff turned my stomach.

'No. It's very humid in here – just look at the floor. At least the straw acts as a buffer. You don't want to be saddled with rheumatism at your age, do you?'

I looked down. The ground was sweating like someone running in a marathon.

After I had made my bed and unpacked my bags, I heard my stomach growl. 'When do we eat?' I asked.

'Shhh!' Mother warned me. 'Don't talk so loud!'

I looked around. Most of our room-mates were squatting by the water basins at the foot of their beds, washing their faces or doing laundry. No one was asleep. Why shouldn't I speak out loud?

'Mama, I'm not disturbing anyone, am I?'

'Stop your jabbering!' Mother hissed in my ear. 'It is bourgeois to mention bodily needs such as eating or drinking. Understand? Suppose one of my room-mates wanted to ruin me! She might repeat what you said to the camp authorities and then I'd be left having to pay royally for your Capitalistic cravings, wouldn't I!'

I clammed up at once. But my head was spinning with questions. I didn't understand a thing any more. Just a minute ago, Maly and her neighbour had had the nerve to say bad things about the Cultural Revolution, and no one even squawked. Yet here was Mother suddenly shaking in her boots because I had asked her when the canteen would be dishing out food! If you went by common logic, my words had been completely innocent, politically speaking, compared with what Maly had said. 'I *used* to think grown-ups made sense,' I muttered to myself. But from the nervous look on Mother's face, I saw that her fear of being denounced was real. I was forced, in the end, to drop the subject.

From this moment on, I began to have doubts about my own judgement. In this forest of imposing adults – every one a member of the intelligentsia, yet behaving in baffling, contradictory ways – a sense of inferiority began twining itself around me, like a vine. Any time I did not understand something, I would blame it on myself: You idiot, you'd better lie low and not make waves – your very presence here is a blot on this illustrious company . . .

At five o'clock, the canteen bell rang. I grabbed the floral terrycloth sack containing my eating utensils – two enamel bowls and a pair of chopsticks – and flew out the door. As soon as I received my rations I tore into a huge

15

piece of steamed cornbread about as big as my head and bolted it down in just a couple of bites. Suddenly I realised my throat hurt. The coarse grains had scoured my gullet going down.

I wanted Mother to have my rice porridge and pickled bok choy, because she had the stomach for that kind of delicacy and I didn't. But Mother pushed my nose into the gruel and said, 'Finish everything in your bowl. It's the only way your body will ever build up any resistance to the vitiligo.'

Ruff-ruff. Greedily I gobbled everything down and then patted my bloated tummy with both hands. I got up, darting happily around Mother, and began serenading her with the song 'The Red Lantern Shows Us The Way To The Communist Paradise'.

Abruptly the noisy dining hall went quiet. My voice came through loud and clear. Seeing Mother's approving look, I went on singing.

Suddenly I heard *tick-tick-tick-tick*. A man wearing a worn straw hat was tapping his chopsticks against his bowl to mark the rhythm. Emboldened, I began another tune:

> *To sail, you need a compass*
> *To grow crops, you need the sun*
> *To live, you need Chairman Mao . . .*

Now some more chopsticks took up the beat. There was clapping, and other voices chiming in: it was quite a concert.

I received a deafening ovation when, my entire repertory exhausted, I finally returned to my spot. One man was clapping particularly hard, and continued for a while even when the general applause had died down. He was sitting towards the back, but stood out because of his gleaming bald pate. I would not easily forget his eyes: they radiated virility and strength, softened by something very tender. When I looked at him I felt I was being sucked in by the light.

I pressed the nail of my thumb hard into the soft middle belly of my index finger: don't be such a sentimental hamster!

At six o'clock the camp Director, Wanli Gao, knocked on the door.

We all sat up in our beds – since there were no tables or chairs in the room, you either sat or lounged on your bed. Everyone was wondering: whose turn was it today for a surprise interrogation?

'Comrade Yunxiang Yang! Please step outside and bring your daughter with you,' he commanded.

Everyone, including Mother, breathed a sigh of relief, because we knew that if he prefaced it with the word 'comrade', it meant nothing ominous was hanging over our heads. I jumped up and opened the door. The dazzling light of the spring day almost blinded me, used as I was to the gloomy dormitory. I grimaced.

The Director saw my wrinkled nose and clenched lips, and laughed, 'Come on, you little comedian. Let's go for a little stroll.'

I skipped alongside him and peered into his long, lean and rather refined face. Mother hovered a few steps behind, following our conversation closely.

'Lian Shui, the youngest guest in this establishment!' As he pronounced the words he twisted his head from left to right, his arms crossed behind his back, his slow and dignified pace that of a respected traditional Chinese teacher.

What a nice man! I hopped even more friskily beside him and admitted: 'Dui! That's right!'

'At school, were you a member of the song-and-dance-propaganda-brigade?'

I was flattered that he seemed to think me worthy of that position. 'No, Sir, but my uncle is a well-known amateur opera singer.'

'Would you like to sing in the canteen more often? It would be an ideal distraction for the aunts and uncles who work in the fields all day and are tired from their labours. Besides, the Revolutionary Comrade, Sister-in-Arms, Pupil and Spouse of the Great Helmsman Mao – Madame Mao – has said: "It is more enlightening for the People to hear just *one* Socialist song, than to repeat a Party slogan a hundred times over."'

He was saying this to rule out any chance that I might some day, on an impulse, be prompted to burst into some bourgeois-leaning song. He knew that children my age were taught just the four strictly-censored model Beijing operas – that is, *The Story of the Red Lantern*, *The Fisherman's Village Shajiabang*, *The Ambush on Mount Weihu* and *The Battle of Shanghai Harbour*.

Why not? I thought. That way I'll be doing something meaningful for the grown-ups here, who have to slog so hard in the fields and who are constantly forced to criticise themselves for their reactionary thoughts. I answered politely, 'I would love to.'

Pleased, he patted me on the shoulder, and continued tapping me there as if he had more to discuss. 'What grade were you in, again?'

'In the first year of secondary school, Sir.'

'Then you are the same age as my daughter Chunhua.'

'Is she at the Youth Accommodation Centre, too?' I asked.

17

'No, she is with my wife's oldest sister. In a village in the province Shangxi.'

'Do you miss her?'

Abruptly he turned to face me, gazing at me with surprise but also tenderness. Then he said to my mother: 'This little girl has guts. Nobody in this camp would dare to talk to me like that.'

I ran to the edge of the path and picked a pink daisy for him: 'Look, here's your daughter. Now you can have her with you. Her name means "Spring Flower", doesn't it? When you look at this, it'll be as if you're seeing her.'

Mother drew back her arm and let fly, giving me a stinging slap on the cheek. 'Lian, you have no concept how high is Heaven and how wide the earth, do you! What have you been up to that's given you the *gall* to speak so disrespectfully to Director Gao?'

But the camp Director pulled me under his armpit to shield me from Mother's blows. Only then did he accept the daisy from me and thank me, visibly moved.

After this conversation, the Director was especially nice to me. I was the only one in the camp who was allowed to go anywhere I wanted – into the cavernous kitchen, the pigsty, the small transistor factory, the workshop of Laifu the carpenter, even the Director's office. I was also given permission to attend the prisoners' self-criticism and denunciation meetings.

Later I found out from others that the Director was himself a detainee: a Party official who had fallen out of favour, to be precise. By appointing him to this hated post in the labour camp, his political opponents had seen to it that he would lose his former job without too much loss of face.

THE WINE OF REGRET

When Mother and I returned to the dormitory after our walk, I noticed several of the women balancing notebooks on their knees in order to write letters. Others were reading bits of the *People's Daily*, which had been torn into quarters. These women kept having to shoo away their impatient neighbours: 'Tsssk, can't you wait your turn? I only just got it myself.' There was one newspaper for fifty inmates. Not that it contained very much of interest: every last word had been gone over with a fine-tooth comb by the Party censors. The reason the newspaper was so popular was that it was the only specimen of the printed word to be permitted here. Being caught reading a textbook, novel or magazine was an offence that carried with it a mandatory prolongation of one's sentence.

Maly was talking to her neighbour Luosha in hushed tones: 'When was the last time you received a letter from abroad?'

After peering around furtively, Luosha whispered: 'Two years ago, but you never know, with this sort of thing. Jinlan, of the Economics Faculty, remember her? The one with the sporty hairdo, that swings as she walks? Well, she had news of her brother in Australia not two months ago.'

Maly and Luosha were among the few who had family living in 'parts of the world infected by the cancer of Capitalism'.

In 1949, on the eve of the Communist takeover, Maly's father, who owned a chain of hotels, decided to flee to Hong Kong. He wanted to take all his possessions with him, including his gold, his wife, eight concubines and a dozen children. His eldest daughter Maly was a student at the university, where the underground Communists wielded much influence. She believed fervently in the dazzling future of the dawning Red China and refused to leave. 'He who pins his hopes on the rotting West is a chicken without a head,' she said, repeating the propagandist line. As Mao's army approached Beijing, Papa's concubines wet their pants . . . out of fear this time. They were scared that the People's Liberation Army would rape them and then skin them alive, under the banner of 'eliminating capitalist parasites'. There was nothing to do but to say goodbye to Maly.

Maly laughed at them and later told the Communists, 'You are such great guys. Would you *believe* those silly geese were convinced you would be ruthless red dictators?' But her rosy outlook did not last long. Starting in 1953, Maly's 'complex, suspicious and bourgeois' family background became grounds for a never-ending barrage of persecution, harassment and discrimination against her.

Five years ago she had received a letter that had been hand-carried by the captain of a foreign cargo ship. She read that her parents were very happy in Hong Kong. Since 1950 they had built four modern hotels which had, as in the past, turned into gold mines. Recently her father had sold the hotels; now he was living off the income. Enclosed in the letter were two photographs. They showed her parents living – just the two of them, mind – in a white house five times as large as our barracks, big enough to house two hundred and fifty prisoners. And that wasn't the end of it: each of her father's other wives had her own villa, and these were situated in all eight directions of the wind, so that Pa might indulge his appetites anywhere he turned. Wenshan, her eldest brother, who when he was young had been not half as good a student as Maly, now had his own law firm in the US.

As fate would have it, his daughter, named Caroline, was the same age as Maly's son Jingdong (*jing* for 'reverence' and *dong* for 'Mao Zedong'). The only difference was that Jingdong washed his face with tears every day at the Youth Accommodation Centre, whereas Caroline holidayed in Europe with her parents at least twice a year.

'Well, we shouldn't compare a doomed Capitalistic colony with our own Communist Paradise.' Sternly, Maly put Western decadence in its place. It is best never to taste the wine of regret.

THE ROOF GENT

At nine o'clock precisely the power was turned off and the light in the dormitories flickered out. After all the excitement of my first day in the camp, I fell asleep, exhausted.

Bong-bong-bong. In the middle of the night, a noise on the roof woke me with a start. I held my breath and tried to figure out the source of the sound. To judge from the racket it made, the thing that was stumbling around up there was pretty heavy, but the impact it made caused a soft, muffled thud, like that of bare feet ... Footsteps? Listen! They sounded measured and cautious. Was it a *liangshang junzi*, a 'roof gent', waiting to rob us – or a murderer? What or whom was he looking for here? Overcome with fear, I couldn't move a muscle.

When I opened my eyes the next morning, I remembered the incident of the night before. Had the thief stolen anything? I was waiting for someone to start screaming, 'I've been robbed!' But nothing happened.

On the way to the canteen I noticed some gross brown animals shuffling around the felled logs and tree stumps. They had black eyes, pointy snouts, round ears and long tails. They looked exactly like rats, but then at least ten times the size!

'Mama, what are those?'

'Don't you know? Rats.'

'But they are bigger than cats!'

'Yes, Lian. It's a giant kind of rat that is common in wetlands like these. The climate is mild here, and there's lots for them to eat.'

Trrriiieeeee! After breakfast, a shrill whistle summoned the detainees to assemble in a central courtyard. They marched off in four neat columns, two hundred and fifty slave labourers under the surveillance of eight guards, on their way to the rice paddies, two miles from the camp. On foot.

I stayed behind, prowling around the canteen in search of a cat. Wherever there is food, there must be cats. So I asked a balding cook to direct me to the storeroom, where I found a whole family of cats purring in a corner. I picked up the father, a tabby-cat, and carried him over to the rats' turf, hoping he would frighten them away. I put the cat down on a log and waited for the showdown between two natural enemies.

The overgrown rat threw a lazy glance at the vain, striped, whiskered creature, and shut his eyes, bored. I picked up the cowardly cat and flung him at the rat. The cat made a menacing sound – directed not at his natural foe, but at me. He even scratched me! After ten minutes or so, I gave up. It was obvious the cat would never attack the rat.

The cook said, 'Just wait till you hear one of those rats on the roof at night. It sounds just as if some big lug of a fellow is pacing around up there.'

A STRANGE KIND OF SCHOOL

At half past twelve, Mother and her fellow workers staggered into the canteen. The sweat had carved little runnels down the thick yellow dust on their faces and they looked totally worn out. After lunch, however, Mother perked up visibly. Grabbing my left arm, she dragged me across the canteen, coming to a stop in front of a wafer-thin little woman. Mother pushed my head down so that it almost banged into my knees, and commanded, 'Bow to Madam Professor Dr Bao!' She might as well have told a corpse to fall down dead – pinned in Mother's headlock, my spine was already as bowed as a prawn's. All I could make out was two pairs of muddy shoes. The strain on my neck muscles was excruciating, and I tried to straighten up, one vertebra at a time.

Pang! Mother rammed my chin back down into my bony chest and screeched, 'Hey! Have the bats bitten your ears off? I *told* you to bow to your new mathematics teacher, didn't you hear me?'

The other woman's feet took a step forward and I was finally freed from Mother's grip. With my face burning red, I looked up gratefully at my deliverer. Sure enough, she had a kind face – shiny black eyes that rolled around in their sockets like well-oiled steel ball-bearings, and even when she wasn't smiling, her mouth turned up at the corners, so that she always made a cheerful impression.

She stroked my head and said, 'Child, your mother thinks I am doing you a big favour if I give you lessons. Little does she know! By being allowed to instruct you, I get permission (a) to read my textbooks here in camp, and (b) to shorten my workday by one hour every other day. Where else can one possibly find such heavenly good fortune nowadays?' Then she turned to Mother and confided: 'Yunxiang, wouldn't *your* stomach get all in a twist if you finally got a chance to practise your profession, after all those years of being called a cow-devil and snake-demon, and having to grub in the fields like an earthworm?'

Mother rolled her tense shoulders and said, 'Professor Dr Bao, you don't take it as an insult, then, that you are to instruct a mere schoolgirl? You of all people, who took the National Science Prize eight years ago, you who are one of the most successful mathematicians in the land . . .'

'Oh stop it, Yunxiang! Why do you have to pick the only kettle on the stove that isn't on the boil? Want to know why I have been here longer than just about anyone else? Seven whole years? It's because of my "enormous" contribution to the progress of Capitalist knowledge!'

Opening her mouth, she displayed a wide toothless gap. 'See? The Red Guards knocked three of my teeth out – it was their way of paying homage to my devotion to the cause of licking science and technology's bourgeois arse. If only I had sat on my lazy bum before the Revolution and had achieved nothing useful! Then I would never have been punished as severely as I am being punished now.' She drew my head under her armpit and sighed, 'Oh well, once a counter-revolutionary scholar, always a counter-revolutionary scholar. If someone gives me the opportunity to teach, I'll take it!'

'Is it all right with you, then, if the lessons start tomorrow? At half past five in your room?' asked Mother.

'Fine. Lian, please lend me the textbooks you've been using, if you can. I have never taught children your age and must prepare myself.'

After this, I had to make kowtows to the Reverend Professors Drs Yu, Fang and Shi, and Madam Professor Dr Zhao. These were, respectively, my teachers in physics, chemistry, biology, and Chinese language and literature. I didn't have to go far to find an English teacher, of course: my bunkmate Professor Maly was the perfect candidate for the job. Mother counted them off on her fingers one by one and told me: 'Now all you're missing is a Chinese history teacher.'

With bated breath I waited for Mother's decision. It stood to reason that Mother herself would instruct me in this subject. Mother was, after all, a college history lecturer, and more than qualified at that. Still . . .

I kicked at an imaginary pebble. I refused to be the first to broach the subject.

'Don't worry.' Mother tapped me on the nose, grinning at me slyly. 'I was actually planning to teach you myself at first, but Buddhist texts do sound better when chanted by monks from the next monastery. I know you'd rather be taught by a stranger – your mother couldn't possibly be as good a teacher as her colleagues, surely? Ha! You are right, for once. Here in this camp you have the cream of the crop, the best historians in the entire country. I would be ashamed to utter even a single word on the topic of history in their presence. Professor Dr Qin, author of the classic *Concise History of China from the Time of the Ming Dynasty*, is one of them. It would be an unsurpassed honour if you could be his pupil. You might as well start singing the praises of the Cultural Revolution, my dear, because if it weren't for the political maelstrom we're in, you'd never even get *close* to so many famous intellectuals. Did you know that at one time, even important professors, who would come from far and near to see Qin, had to wait *months* for an appointment?'

She led me to the farthest corner of the canteen, which seemed to be empty except for some sacks of potatoes and dried corn kernels. 'Bow down before Professor Dr Qin,' she ordered. I peered around: where was he? Then I saw something greyish emerging from among the potato sacks. Something – a creature dressed in rags that had been squatting there – was getting to its feet. Next I was standing nose to nose with what seemed the shadow of a man: the crooked back, sallow skin and sunken cheeks all in startling contrast to the piercing light shining from his eyes. I hastened to help him to his feet and nearly fell backwards when he pushed me away roughly with his withered yet surprisingly strong arms.

'Yunxiang, save your spit and don't ask me. I'm done with teaching.'

'But Professor Qin . . .'

'Get lost, both of you, before my patience runs out!' He waved his hands savagely, as if shooing away a cloud of flies swarming around his rice bowl, studiously keeping his eyes averted.

Why wouldn't he look us in the eye? Suddenly it occurred to me there was something familiar about him. Didn't I know him from somewhere? My memory creaked into gear.

With her head bowed, Mother left Qin's territory with me in tow. I turned back to stare at the famous historian who looked like a tramp and – *Kwalá!* – suddenly the dam restraining my memories spilled open . . . I had met this man once, five years ago.

QIN'S VISIT

One night there had been a knock on the door, and a smartly dressed gentleman had entered. He shook Father's and Mother's hands and stared at me as if he had never seen a girl of seven. A puzzled look appeared on his face and he spread his legs wide, until he looked like an open compass set to draw a huge circle. He pressed a finger to the tip of my nose, furrowed his brow and asked, in all seriousness, 'How come you are so small?'

I had never heard a question like it. I stuck a finger in my mouth and tried to help him come up with the answer . . .

He sat down on the living-room sofa with his legs crossed in the lotus position and said: 'Where do you keep the beds?'

I immediately fell under the spell of this gentleman, particularly since his strange remarks did not seem to suit his advanced years. Thanks to his intercession, I was allowed to stay up late that night.

After his visit, Mother explained that the gentleman had only just been released from the highest-security State prison a week earlier. In the ten years that he had been locked up, he had seen neither children nor living rooms; that was why he had asked such bizarre questions.

⌒

When Mother returned to the dormitory, she consoled me: 'It isn't the end of the world if Professor Qin refuses to be your teacher. It looks as if it may be Buddha's will that I be the one to teach you history. Don't hold it against Mr Qin. He has suffered so many disappointments, he probably just wants to cut himself off from the world entirely.'

My dejection suddenly turned to curiosity: 'What kind of disappointments?'

Using a grubby shawl, Mother was slapping the wilted grass and yellow dust out of her tousled hair. She plopped on to the bed like a bag full of potting soil, sighing, 'I'll tell you another time. I'm tired, and need to rest up a bit before I have to go back to the fields . . . Ggrrrrr . . .'

She was already snoring.

24

THE DREADFUL PAST

The next morning, Mother claimed to have too many important things on her mind to tell me stories about Qin. But I was beginning to learn, and decided to try a compromise.

Ever since I could remember, one of my chores had been to clean my canvas shoes. For some reason I seriously hated this job. That morning, however, I said, as sweetly as I could, 'Mama, I'm going to shampoo my shoes.'

Mother, chalking this up as a victory for her child-rearing methods, beamed and said, 'Now *that's* what I like to hear.' As a reward, she would keep her word. After lunch she would tell me about Qin.

After the midday nap, Mother took me with her to the rice fields. Since we didn't run into a soul on the way there, we were able to speak freely.

'Professor Shunxing Qin, also known as Wenting Qin, was born at the turn of the century into a well-to-do peasant family.'

I looked up and frowned. 'What do you mean? Does Qin have *two* names?'

'That's right. He uses the first one in his everyday life; the other is his academic name, the one he uses to sign his poems or articles, or when he corresponds with other distinguished intellectuals. It's an ancient Chinese tradition.

'Anyway, when he was six, he attended a village school, and when he was twelve he went to secondary school in the nearby town. Thanks to his outstanding grades, he was accepted at Yanjing University, which was then the pre-eminent institution of higher learning in China. He decided to study history . . .'

'Isn't it confusing, to have two names? Suppose I said, "Yesterday I met Shunxing," while you know him only by his scholarly name of Wenting.'

'First of all, it is most unusual for someone to be known only by his academic name; secondly, you yourself would probably have been thrilled to have been born before the People's Republic was established and to have had two names. Don't look so puzzled, I was trying to explain it to you! The first, everyday name, always expresses some sort of earthly desire. "Shunxing", for instance, means "to lead a prosperous life". The second name expresses a more exalted wish. So, "Wenting" means "literary pavilion". Isn't that a poetic image? The old way of giving people two names, then, provided them with two aspects of their being: the desire for material things on the one hand, and the striving for spiritual perfection on the other.'

'So when Qin calls himself Shunxing, what he's thinking about is wealth and fame; and when he calls himself Wenting, he fancies himself meditating in a Taoist monastery, floating away on little white clouds into a pure blue sky . . .'

'You could put it that way, I suppose. The reality and the ideal are like the sun and the moon, fated never to meet. Perhaps that is why we like to have two names.'

'But—'

'Do you want to hear Qin's story, or do you want to philosophise about names?'

I made an effort to keep my questions to myself henceforth, so that Mother might continue her tale uninterrupted.

'While he was still a student, Qin published books and articles comparing Chinese and European history. As soon as he graduated, he was given a teaching post at his faculty. In 1934 he became the youngest professor to be appointed since the university was founded.'

'Cool.'

'That's no way to talk, Lian. Say "super" instead, or something.'

'You don't know what you're talking about! *Cool*, that's the way we all say it in our . . . in my old class . . .' Nostalgia stung me – Oh, how I suddenly missed the pandemonium of morning recess at my school!

Noticing my long face, Mother tried to console me. 'Aren't you happy to be here? Tell me, who else among your classmates has the opportunity you have, to be surrounded and taught by such a distinguished group of teachers and professors? Soon you will be the most highly-educated girl in your entire class.'

Yes, I definitely wanted that, to be highly educated. Not so much because I was interested in knowledge for itself, but because I wanted to be able to join in the adults' conversation around here. For the past few days, living among these prisoners had unleashed in me an inferiority complex. The conversation always went over my head, and however hard I tried to come up with questions that I considered to be 'intellectual, stimulating and deep', I couldn't help feeling I didn't really count.

Mother interpreted my silence as agreement, and went on with her story: 'China's Communist Party, which back then was still outlawed and had no real power, was setting up underground cells all over the country. Of course there was one of these cells at Yanjing University as well. The Communists could use a young professor like Qin – prominent in his field, easy to influence. In the beginning they called it "an exchange of ideas with Professor Qin regarding China's recent history as well as the most profitable political direction the current government might take", but it quickly turned into an exposé of the corruption and chaos rife throughout the country. It was to be expected that the more he thought about it, the more Qin would become disenchanted with the ruling regime of the CNP, or Chinese Nationalist Party. Before he realised what was happening, he had been hitched to the Communist bandwagon.

'In 1938, the Japanese invaded Beijing. Now Qin finally made the leap. The CPC underground had been trying to persuade him to move to the district of Yanan, which was the Communists' headquarters. Qin had lost all confidence in the Nationalist regime and considered the ideals of the CPC the only hope for a decent future remaining to China.'

'What were those ideals, then?'

'Oh Lian! Isn't that the very first thing they teach you to repeat over and over again in nursery school?'

'Yes, I know, but I thought it was just propaganda. We don't talk that kind of rot when we're alone, do we!'

'It was precisely those slogans that made Qin seek solace in the CPC: equal rights for everyone, an equitable distribution of wealth; a leadership that serves the masses. In other words, the absolute antithesis of corruption, which was at the root of all of China's problems according to the CPC.'

I chuckled and sang:

> *Starving from hunger is easy to bear, la-lala*
> *Unless the others out there don't care, tra-lala*
> *Death to fat-cat landlords everywhere, bum-tada, bum-tada*

Mother shook her head and went on, unperturbed: 'In the Red District, Qin worked first for the Ministry of Culture and Propaganda, but was soon appointed private secretary to W., the Foreign Minister. In 1949 the CPC set up 'the only government on earth representing the interests of the People', and all the party bosses moved into the former imperial palace. Qin went with them, was appointed head of the Foreign Ministry's Secretariat and had twenty high-level officials working under him. Top-secret documents crossed his desk every day, documents that revealed the lethal truth behind the back-to-back political movements. He was appalled, but kept his mouth shut, clinging to the conviction that the Leader responsible for the murder of tens of thousands – millions – no, tens of millions – was doing it all for the general good. His conscience gnawed at him, but he suppressed his discomfort by working extra hard. He spent his free time reading to keep

27

up in his field, and he produced one academic paper after another. Where would he find the time for a normal life? It's no wonder that he remained celibate until 1954.

'It was in the summer of that year that Feilan Zhu, that legendary siren, set her almond eyes on the successful and important official Professor Qin who, it must be said, was still handsome for his age. Feilan was the belle of the palace, a star in her own right. A journalist attached to the party organ *The Red Star*, she was pursued left, right and centre by a swarm of younger swains.

'In 1957, at the height of the political witch hunts, Qin finally expressed some mildly-worded positive criticism of the Party. His immediate superior, Minister W., was not inclined to come down hard on him for this, but one of Qin's rivals leapt at the opportunity to make him pay. The man's name was Xiangmin Bai and he was an editor at *The Red Star*: whenever Feilan was around he practically drowned in his own drool. Xiangmin wrote an anonymous letter to Mao's Secretary Tong, who in turn saw to it that Qin was apprehended while W. was on a State Visit to the Soviet Union. Even though W. soon learned of Qin's arrest, he didn't lift a finger to save his loyal and worthy associate. After all, criticising the government was tantamount to blasphemy. Whoever dared to stick his neck out for such a sinner would be condemned as a sinner himself.

'And so Qin landed in China's highest-security jail for élite prisoners. It was where you were sent when you were found guilty of heretical thought about the Party. These men and women had held too high a post in the government and knew too many Party secrets to be mixed in with your run-of-the-mill felons, such as common murderers or rapists. From his prison cell, Qin wrote hundreds of letters to his fiancée Feilan, and never received one word in reply.

'Eventually, the former dissidents lost all interest in anything but their next meal and their next shit. There was no reason for the authorities to keep them locked up any longer. Meanwhile, new batches of political prisoners kept streaming into the prisons, washed up by the relentless tidal wave of the Cultural Revolution. In 1967, in the wake of serious prison overcrowding, Qin was finally released.

'Minister W. invited him to the palace for a meeting. Feeling a little guilty over Qin's ten-year ordeal, W. promised that Qin would be spared any further persecution. Moreover, W. would help Qin any way he could to rebuild his life and his career. But the disillusioned and embittered sixty-year-old, wearing the sick grin of a peasant who has accidentally swallowed one of his own teeth after mistaking it for a clove of garlic, expressed just one wish: to leave politics and resume his first profession – teaching. His number one choice was the Teachers' University of Beijing.

'Well, that's settled then,' said W. 'May that be where you spend the remainder of your life, with my blessing.'

'Via the rumour-mill, many of us at the university got to hear the story of Qin's life. Thanks to his unique political background, he enjoyed a position of privilege from the start, which made him all but untouchable. He could grumble about the regime all he wanted; he could talk back to the university authorities, and carry out all sorts of other death-defying stunts.

'The story everyone in the school has heard about Qin became known as the "pink incident".

'It was 1969. One day, Qin was quietly reading in his room in the Residence for Bachelors. Suddenly there was a knock at the door. Guess who sashayed in? It was the former girl of his dreams, Feilan Zhu, coyly wiggling her shapely behind. Her heavily made-up face scattered clouds of white around, like a fully-laden powder-puff. Yet Qin still discerned her soft, invitingly blushing skin beneath the layers of make-up. To judge from her slender figure – a young fawn's – she was still capable of setting battalions of men's heads spinning, like a row of weathercocks in a storm. That must mean, Qin decided, that her husband – the architect of Qin's ruin and the man into whose arms Feilan had thrown herself just two weeks into Qin's incarceration – had been frugal in his use of her.

'But now she would have to find another pair of arms to throw herself into. Her husband had been dragged away by the Red Guards the previous month, for being a "Capitalist roader". She wiggled her hips and pouted, bitch in heat that she was, and said "Wenting, I see now that I married the wrong man . . . !"

'Qin slammed his book down on the bed, picked her up bodily and threw her, kicking and screaming, out into the hall. You have already seen how strong he is.

'He has practically no friends now, and doesn't want any. He never asks for help, nor will he ever offer any to others. He wasn't like this yet five years ago, when he had just been released from prison and visited us at home that one time. But then former colleagues, classmates and so-called friends who were being hounded by the Cultural Revolution began coming to see him in droves. With a crafty look and humble grin, they would try to wriggle their way into his good books because they knew that if he chose to, he could get them out of the trouble they were in, in two shakes – just one note from him to Minister W.'s secretary and their worries were behind them. But where had *they* been when Qin had been behind bars? Soon after the incident with Feilan, Qin cut himself off from everyone and everything and he has been leading a hermit's existence ever since, similar to the one he got used to in prison.'

'And then?' I didn't want this fascinating story ever to end.

'And then what? That's all I can tell you about Professor Qin . . . No wait, there *is* something else. Do you know what his motto is?'

'No.'

'Wangshi bukan huishou.'

'Oh! I know that expression. I've often seen it in the novels we're not really supposed to read because they are moving and affecting and therefore bourgeois. It means, Don't turn around, because behind you lies the dreadful past.'

'Well done!' said Mother.

THE USES OF MATHEMATICS

After breakfast at seven thirty, I went to my maths teacher Dr Bao's dormitory. We sat down on stools drawn up to the bed, which served as the desk. I opened my textbook. Bao explained the first chapter using diagrams and examples, and then gave me some homework problems to do.

'It's too bad we have to share one book between us, that means I can't prepare the lessons,' she said.

'When Mother and I go on weekend leave five days from now, we'll buy you another copy in Beijing.'

'Please do! Oh dear, I have so many maths texts at home, child, but unfortunately those are much too advanced . . .'

A little shutter opened in my mind and a fresh wind blew in, rousing my brain from its slumber: there was more to learning, evidently, than could be found in my schoolbooks. The idea intrigued me, and I decided to explore uncharted territory under the guidance of these first-rate teachers . . . Back in my own dorm, I not only finished my homework but also read the chapter we were to cover in two days' time. I had never tried studying anything by myself before, but I managed to get through it pretty well. Up until then I had always learned in a passive way; the teacher would explain the formula to me, and I would apply it. There! But studying by myself meant I had to start thinking for myself. I discovered a hidden logic and connection behind theories that used to seem arbitrary. I made note of the things I didn't understand: I would ask Bao about them later. Strange, the more I exercised my brain, the more active it became. I realised I was capable of reasoning just like an adult.

Outside the crickets chirped. The leaves on the trees winked at me. The blushing sun fondled the flowers and the animals until they wilted as if swooning in ecstasy. Normally I would have thrown myself into nature's alluring arms at once, to bask in the bounty of this spring day. But now I had better things to do. I opened my physics textbook and started on a new chapter. I had a physics lesson coming up with Professor Yu before dinnertime. I couldn't wait to see him opening his eyes as wide as two saucers and to hear him ask: 'Did you learn this *all* by yourself, without any help?'

One by one, I met with each of my instructors for my lessons. It turned out to be something of an anti-climax, in the end. I had plenty of time to prepare my lessons ahead of time. Since there wasn't much left for the teachers to explain, nor anything new to go over, teacher and pupil would end up sitting there looking at one another, with no idea how to fill the remaining half-hour. The teachers were granted a sixty-minute reprieve from their work in the fields. If they cut short the lesson, they would have to return to work at once, and that, apparently, was a less attractive alternative than to be saddled with a dim-witted child. Anyway, whatever their motive, the instructors stuck it out, yawning with pure boredom. So I would ransack my brain for a topic, preferably something relating to the teacher's realm of expertise, though that nearly always led to disaster. To their overdeveloped tastes, the few crumbs of knowledge I possessed of their subject amounted to little more than a half-chewed crust of mouldy bread, whereas the things that interested them were inevitably way over my head. My inferiority complex drove me to desperate measures. I decided to read as much as possible, to devour books in order to make myself a worthy interlocutor of these super-intellects.

⌒

Mrs Bao finished the lesson in less than fifteen minutes. It was time for a dose of shock therapy. I admonished the little chicks chirping excitedly in my stomach to be quiet, and said, as calmly as I could: 'Mrs Bao, *I* believe that the answer to many political problems can be found in mathematics.'

Mrs Bao peered not at me, but at a spot beyond me, as if she were trying to catch a glimpse of the philosopher hiding behind the girl.

'With the numerical sequence, for instance, we can strip the class struggle naked, and expose it for what it is: nothing but a rip-off . . .'

Mrs Bao turned pale and looked around nervously. But her mind, dulled by years of imprisonment, was pricked by an irrepressible curiosity. Clapping both hands over my mouth, she whispered, 'Watch out, or you'll be arrested for your counter-revolutionary thoughts, just like me! But tell me, what on earth can numerical sequencing have to do with the class struggle?'

How could I be expected to answer, with Bao's bony but steely fingers pinching my lips together? I blinked rapidly and made throaty sounds of protest.

'All right, you are a minor and you still have the right to speak your mind, but just do it quietly . . .! To tell you the truth, I have always found it fascinating to search for parallels between the natural and the social sciences.'

I tried to keep my voice low, and Bao shifted around so that she could keep one eye on the door while reading my lips with the other.

'The numerical sequence, a concept that you have just begun teaching me, is like a balance-beam that is divided into tenths. Every part has a number assigned to it. The difference between the numbers gives you the distance between the parts. Therefore between one and two it's only one step, while one and nine are separated by eight steps. Suppose we advance each number by one step, so that one becomes two, two becomes three, eight becomes nine, et cetera . . .'

'Okay, but what are you driving at?'

'This is what I mean: what we see in considering the numerical sequence is that the *starting point* of a number plays an important role in its ability to move forward. Thus even if one takes a step towards two, it remains inferior to the original number two, because the latter will have moved forward as well. In order to overtake two, number one must take *two* steps, assuming of course that number two takes just one step. On the other hand, even if the number one were to overtake number two, he is still miles away from, for example, seven. In order to catch up with seven, he'd have to take seven steps forward . . .'

'So?' Bao had to be wondering whether I was an imbecile or a genius, since only someone at either extreme of the spectrum would take it into her head to mess with something that was as self-evident as a water buffalo in a rice paddy.

'It means that it would take a tremendous effort for the one to overtake the seven, for example. And that is the way it *should* be, if we are talking pure mathematics. But if we try to adapt this very straightforward rule to politics, we see at once that we can now unmask the class struggle – a concept so desirable to most people that they'll stake their own lives, or better, the lives of others on it – for what it truly is. Suppose the numbers stand for the social classes, as follows: one – vagrants; two – landless serfs; three – sharecroppers; four – small holders; five – landlords; six – agricultural landlords; seven – industrialists; eight – overlords; nine – syndicate-bosses with strong political connections; ten – politicians who have syndicates of their own. 'The gap between numbers one and ten is so big that a vagrant would have to move up NINE steps to become a politician, provided that the politician does not move another step forward himself. But suppose this vagabond is too impatient to toil for years and years to get there, what does he do? He picks up a cleaver and summons his fellow outcasts to a meeting: "Haven't we had enough of suffering, of not having a roof over our heads, while the fat cats in their palaces hold orgies in their carved ivory beds?" So they form a Red army, they bash in the rich men's brains and confiscate their possessions. And, hey presto, number one has overtaken number ten in a single bound. *That* is the essence of the class struggle.'

'But . . . well – the homeless vagrants and the sharecroppers can't really get ahead, can they, without *some* kind of assistance from the government, and thus from the politicians?'

Not only is she *not* laughing at me, she's even willing to discuss the finer points of my logic! I was thinking to myself excitedly. 'I grant you that some measures would have to be taken to deliver numbers one and two from their backwardness. But what I really meant to show with the numerical sequence was that by slaughtering people who are better off than they are, and then confiscating their wealth, the poor have managed to bypass the natural laws of advancement.'

Bao's face clouded over. 'I warn you: don't you *ever* dare talk in this kind of vein in front of the Director or the guards. Minor or not, you will surely be punished for your dangerous reactionary ideas!'

MOTHER'S FANCY HOME

The first time I was granted a weekend pass from the camp I burst into song on our dump-truck transport like a nightingale gone crazy.

When Mother opened the front door, I couldn't believe my eyes. There were windows, large windows even, in our apartment. The sun poured its delicious warm light into the rooms. There were no worms crawling anywhere and everything was clean and neat as a pin, dry as a bone. The place was even furnished with tables, chairs and sofas, so that I didn't have to squat or sit cross-legged.

I ran up to Mother, gratefully pressed my hand in hers and said, 'Mama, what a fancy house you have!'

For a moment Mother did not understand what I was talking about. She looked into my eyes and realised that, intoxicated by this unexpected good fortune, I didn't quite know where I was.

'Yes indeed, we *both* have a very nice home. Just try to make the most of it, now that we have a day and a half to enjoy it.'

In spite of Mother's words, I just could not get used to the idea that this dream house belonged to me. I suddenly understood how impressed Kim must have been the first time she came over.

A BOND

It was only a year ago that I had to use the ploy of offering to let Kim borrow some books to persuade her to come home with me; reading books for pleasure was a novelty to Kim. After leaving school, I led Kim to my neighbourhood, where the streets were paved. Few peasants ever set foot there.

Uh . . . Where had Kim gone?

I looked around. Kim was walking about ten feet behind me. I tried to catch her eye, but Kim pretended she didn't know me.

I halted.

Kim promptly slowed her pace.

When the distance between us had narrowed unavoidably, Kim spun around.

'Hey! Where are you going?' I cried, flabbergasted.

'Shhht . . . !' Kim frowned and hissed, 'You walk in front. I'll follow you. Don't you see we're nearly at the gate?'

'So what?' I was talking loudly on purpose, to let Kim know that I didn't give a fig what others thought of us.

'Do you really want people to start harassing us?' Even though it was spoken in a whisper, I could hardly miss the anxiety in Kim's tone. I looked around. It was true, we were surrounded by first-casters, whose flickering eagle eyes took in the most minute infraction. There was no doubt they

34

would look askance if they saw me walking alongside a third-caster. First they would throw disapproving looks my way, and if that didn't do the trick, they'd start calling both of us names, enlisting the support of the bystanders, putting up a united front against the pair who had the nerve to overstep the boundaries of caste. Meekly, I went up ahead.

At the entrance to my apartment complex I told the guard, 'This is my classmate Kim Zhang. She is coming to do her homework with me. She's leaving by six o'clock at the latest.'

In order to give the guard the impression that it was the most natural thing in the world for me to bring home a third-caster, I gave Kim's arm a friendly tug. I could feel Kim trembling. This must be the first time that Kim had been in this neighbourhood in broad daylight. I imagined she felt naked, exposed to the scandalised, hostile eyes of the first-casters. Knowing Kim, I knew better than to try to put her at ease; that was bound to backfire. All I could think of, for the moment, was to set as relaxed an example as possible. I donned a mask of perky cheerfulness and greeted almost everyone we encountered.

'Auntie Qian, have you eaten?'

'Yes, surely, child.'

'Older sister Yunping, are you going to start studying for your February exam?'

'Ah-ha.'

'Grandpa Gao, where're you going?'

'Outside.'

'Uncle Song, what are you doing?'

'Oh, doing something.'

Each in turn stared at me in surprise. They must have been wondering at how I, usually such a shy, quiet girl, had suddenly turned into such a friendly chatterbox.

It seemed to do the trick: Kim was visibly buoyed by my mood. She caught up with me and gazed up at the rows of apartment buildings. She gaped at all the glass windows. The window-panes in our classroom were also made of real glass, but that didn't count because no one lived there. This was the real thing.

'Now I see why you first-casters bloom before the rest of us. You have such an abundance of sunlight and warmth,' decided Kim.

I broke into her musings. 'Come on, you can see one of those apartments from the inside, at my house.'

Kim shook herself and followed me.

My flat was in Building Number 23, on the third floor. When I opened the door, Mother came out of her room. She was home even though it wasn't three thirty yet. As a university teacher, she had to be at work only when she had classes or meetings.

'So! This must be Kimmy.' That was typical of Mother: when meeting my friends for the first time, she'd always come up with some kind of pet-name, as if they were still waddling around with dummies in their mouths.

Kim ducked behind me.

'Are you reading dissertations?' I asked.

Mother sent me an understanding look, as if to say, I guess that means you two want to be alone. She went to go back into her room, saying, 'There's a pot of jasmine tea under the tea cosy. You know where the sweets and fruit are kept.' She turned to Kim and stroked her over the head. 'Child, enjoy yourself in our home.'

I led Kim into the living room. Awed, Kim took in the three-seater sofa and easy chairs. She stared at the wall-unit, with its bowls filled with sweets and apples displayed behind glass doors. Then her gaze wandered to the opposite wall, where two metal pipes attracted her attention. She walked over and touched them. 'Auwa!' she yelled, 'they're hot!'

'Yes,' I said dryly, 'fortunately. It wouldn't be central *heating* otherwise, would it!'

'What?' Kim jumped up and down like a frog. 'Do you really have central heating?'

I had never known anything else. It had never occurred to me that there were people who had never experienced a thing I took for granted.

Kim was examining the ribs on the radiator. 'How do you get the coal in there?'

'We don't have to do it ourselves. It's done centrally, at our complex's main furnace.'

'So you don't stoke it yourselves? The warm air just comes up those white pipes, like running water?' Kim's gaze followed the pipes upward. Her eyes shone with awe and amazement.

She pulled her sleeves over her hands. I saw why: she was trying to cover up her chilblains. In winter, Kim's hands looked like raisin-buns: all swollen, speckled with burgundy open sores. I quickly walked over to the dresser and set the sweets and fruit out on the table.

'Just take as much as you want,' I told Kim, as if to redeem the guilt I was feeling.

Kim took a toffee and twisted it around in her hands.

'Why don't you eat it? Don't you like it?'

'Of course, only . . . Jiening has never tasted anything like this before . . .'

'Then take some for her!' I emptied the entire bowl into her jacket pocket and pressed more into her hands. Kim hesitated a moment, then stuffed those in her pockets too. Buddha Almighty! Was she intending to save the entire lot for her little sister?

'Want to see the other rooms?'

Kim nodded.

I knocked on a door.

'Come in.'

'This is where my parents work and sleep,' I explained.

'If you don't mind, I'll just continue reading,' Mother excused herself, pointing to a pile of papers on the desk before her.

'We don't mind, Mama. Right, Kim?' I looked at my friend. Kim's eyes swivelled from one bookcase to the next, taking in the entire wall of volumes. She walked over to the bookcases, then ran back to where she'd been standing. We had just started taking English at school, and Kim was having a hard time making head or tail of the foreign writing.

Kim was now staring, fascinated, at the double bed by the window. There were no trunks on top of this strange piece of furniture, nor did she see a chest of drawers. The bedding wasn't rolled up at one end, the way it was on the *kang* at Kim's house, and instead of a straw mat, an immaculately-white embroidered sheet was spread over the entire thing, hiding something lumpy underneath. Kim made a beeline for it. Before Mother and I knew what she was doing, Kim had jumped on to the bed, and tried to sit down on it cross-legged.

'Buddha have mercy!' she screeched, as if she were being lynched.

I tried to see where she'd gone, but nothing of Kim was visible except for a pair of flailing arms. The rest of her was totally engulfed in the rumpled bedding. I ran over to the bed and grabbed her by the hands. Kim sat up with some difficulty. Her face was whiter than the sheet. She wiped the cold sweat from her forehead and looked at me in utter bewilderment.

'I thought I'd landed in a cesspit,' Kim stammered. 'Sanniu, a boy in Jiening's class, fell into one of those pits . . . last summer, and . . . he suffocated to death . . .'

'Oh, child,' said Mother, hugging Kim's head to her breast, 'don't worry. This is a bed with a mattress, with inner springs. Do you know what springs are? They're these little metal spirals.' Always the teacher. My mother never could pass up the opportunity of explaining something.

Kim, having regained her composure, said, 'Oh, I see . . . That bed really is pretty comfortable, soft as a haystack.' With those words, she climbed back on to the bed. Regally crossing her legs, she patted the mattress next to her, inviting me with a look that said: Come on, let's have a nice little chat up here.

Mother's mouth fell open in dismay.

It took several seconds for Kim to notice there was something wrong. She climbed off the bed and rushed over to my side.

I said, as nonchalantly as possible, 'Oh yeah, I forgot to tell you, we prefer to sit on a sofa or a chair. The bed's just for sleeping. Weird, huh?'

But of course Kim could see that she'd made a fool of herself. She stared down at the floor. Had she detected even the tiniest crack there, she'd have sunk right down through it.

'Let's go to my room, shall we?' I suggested.

My room was at the far end of the corridor. On the way there Kim peeked through the half-open doors to the kitchen and the bathroom.

'You're allowed to *sit* on *my* bed,' I said in a conspiratorial tone as soon as I had shut the door behind Kim.

But Kim steered clear of the bed as if it were a scalding iron. She sat down on a chair and spread her hands on the desk. 'Shall we do our homework here from now on?' Not waiting for an answer, she pointed to an easy chair: 'Does that one have inner springs too?' Then she walked to the chest of drawers. This time she had a real question. 'Who's that?' She was pointing to an old man in a family photograph.

'That's my grandpa on Father's side.'

Kim examined the picture narrowly and shook her head. 'That's impossible. He's just like my grandpa. He looks like a farmer.'

Grandpa had a white sweatband tied around his head, just like the picture of turbaned Mohammedans that I had once seen in a magazine. His jacket was fastened in the traditional way, with braided loops, and he was wearing short baggy trousers – the traditional dress of a peasant.

I said proudly, 'Grandpa *was* a farmer. He lived in a village on the outskirts of Beijing. He worked hard all his life to send his children to school. My father, who was the youngest son, went to earn a living as a teacher after passing his finals. Six years later, he had enough money saved to go study medicine.'

Kim looked dubiously from me to Father, who was also in the photograph, and finally at Grandpa. She touched the picture frame with her clammy palm, causing it to mist up. I put my hand on the frame too. Our fingers entwined and our eyes spoke a language only we understood.

Remembering how I felt a year ago, I only now realised that friendship was a luxury item. A luxury one could afford only when basic needs, such as food, drink and safety, were taken care of.

On the last day of our weekend leave, Mother sent me to the university store to pick up our meat rations. It was 86°F in the shade and I was wearing a short-sleeved blouse. I kept glancing around skittishly, because I wanted to be able to hide my arms quickly if anybody came near, in case they jeered or cursed at me when they noticed the blotches on my elbows.

The queue for the meat commissary snaked out into the alley, all the way to the post office. I got in line and promptly began nodding off on my feet, overcome by the heat and the prospect of having to wait at least an hour for my turn.

Khenn-khen, Khenn-khen . . . A dry, persistent cough awoke me from my little snooze, not so much because the sound disturbed me but because I realised someone was attempting to start a conversation. I turned around and saw Yuejiao, a classmate from secondary school. It had been a long time since I had been with anyone my own age. In the camp I had started identifying with the old, grey-haired, worn-out prisoners. I reacted enthusiastically: 'Hey, Yue, it's great to see you!'

Yue looked me over from head to toe, frowned, but then managed a somewhat forced grin. 'Uh . . . sure, same here.'

I immediately understood what was bothering Yue: the disgusting blotches on my arms. I took a few steps backwards.

'I haven't seen you in a long time. Where've you been?'

'Hadn't you heard? It's been over six months since they moved me to the Accommodation Centre at the University for Industrial Technology. My mother was sent to prison camp. But for the last two weeks I've been living in the camp with her.'

'Yuck, you poor thing! You get nothing to eat but pigswill there, you sleep in a slimy, drafty dorm and you have to slave from early in the morning until late at night, with nasty guards armed with clubs watching your every move . . .'

'Not true. *I* don't have to work. I'm not a political felon . . . it's only my mother who is—'

'But you have no friends there, no school, no movies, no public transportation. Who would want to live there?'

I peeked at my arms and debated with myself whether I should tell Yue the true reason for my stay in the prison camp. But luckily Yue broached the difficult subject herself.

'What are those spots?'

I answered, relieved, 'Vitiligo. A skin disease.'

'Oh, I see . . . Does it hurt, or itch or anything?'

'No, I don't feel a thing.'

The conversation came to a dead end. Yue seemed lost in thought and

I decided I had weathered the confrontation over my humiliating disease pretty well . . .

But suddenly, when it was almost her turn to be served, Yue cried out, 'Say, Lian, are you contagious?'

I just stood there, speechless. I felt sorry for Yue, who was keeping her distance from me, just to be on the safe side, and so was shouting in order to make herself heard. The people stuck behind Yue in line cleared their throats impatiently.

I gazed at the sky, sighed, and said slowly, 'Yue, it would be wonderful if it were contagious. Then there would be medicine to cure it and I would get better soon.'

Yue drew a deep breath, took one cautious step closer and seemed quite reassured.

I paid for the meat rations hastily and was glad to get away from the crowd. Every time I had to apologise, to reassure others that I posed no danger to their health, I died a little, inside.

GOOD FORTUNE FROM MISFORTUNE

Back at camp Mother and I were sitting on our haunches in the canteen, eating our lunch. Suddenly we noticed Professor Qin approaching. A rare smile hovered on his face, investing his whole being with an aura of amiability. He said, 'Mrs Yang – or may I call you Yunxiang? – this morning I spoke with Director Wanli Gao. He says it's fine if I return from the fields an hour earlier every other day so that I may give Lian a lesson in modern Chinese history.' Then he turned to me. 'My child, can you come to my room at five o'clock tomorrow?'

Mother and I looked up at Qin, speechless. Had we heard him right? What had prompted his 180-degree about-turn?

Qin, squatting down in front of us, said, 'Finish your meal first, then we'll go for a little walk.'

As if we had rehearsed it together beforehand, we threw our half-finished corn breads into one bowl, raced to the tap to rinse our chopsticks and the other bowl, and in less than two minutes we were at the door.

Once outside, Qin said, 'Yunxiang, the day before yesterday, in Beijing, I went to the campus store to buy some ground pork. As I was standing in line, I overheard a conversation between your daughter and one of her classmates . . .' He went on to repeat word for word what Yue and I had said to each other. I was amazed at the accuracy of his report. '. . . And then I realised what a fine girl Lian is. For a child of thirteen, she was able to come up with a most ingenious answer to the humiliating question, "Are you contagious?" Not only did she manage to reassure the other girl, but she also saw to it that the girl was not unduly embarrassed. Her answer was to the point, but courteous; her behaviour correct yet at the same time considerate . . .'

Mother looked at me as if I were a total stranger.

Qin went on: 'Your daughter not only has a heart of gold, she also has tact. Kindness and intelligence. The two qualities that will save the world.'

Mother squeezed my hand while looking into Qin's eyes.

Qin took Mother's hand and said, 'I don't know you well. If I had to give myself a grade, I would give myself a four out of ten. I think that at heart I am pretty good-natured and I certainly *try* to be fair, but I am too direct. People like me may want to achieve great things for our country, but we don't always succeed. Let us try to teach the younger generation to have more sense, so that theirs will be a better world than the world in which we live now. In the years remaining to me, I would like to see Lian succeed in the path that she chooses.'

I wormed myself in between the two of them, grabbed their arms and scrunched myself up into a ball. I swung myself up into the air and chortled like a baby that's being tickled.

So you see, I thought, my blotches bring me misery, but they also bring me blessings.

A HISTORY LESSON

The very next afternoon I walked over to the first row of buildings, where Professor Qin shared a room with forty-eight other men. It was only ten to five – the door was still locked. At five o'clock on the dot I heard a familiar din. Skipping, I went to look for the source of the racket. Qin was dragging his wrought-iron shovel behind him over the dirt road that was strewn with pebbles as big as duck eggs. The shovel bounced from one stone to the next, setting off a little ditty in my ears:

> Tjing-tjang-tjay,
> *The toiling of today*
> *Is done, thank God, I say*

41

Except that in this case it was a solo performance, since the rest of the prisoners were still at work in the rice fields. Qin had come home an hour early to give me my lesson.

With furrowed brow, the professor thumbed through my textbook, *The Modern History of China: 1910 until the present day*. He looked just like a Buddhist monk who has accidentally picked up a piece of pornographic trash.

Pow! He hurled the textbook on to his bed – our desk – and thundered angrily, 'Lian, it's up to you: I can either read you the lies in this textbook, or we can throw it on the dung-heap!'

Trembling, I had to grab hold of the edge of the 'table' to steady myself. I looked at Qin bug-eyed. Even though I knew he wasn't angry with *me*, I couldn't help cringing.

But Qin did not notice. He picked up the textbook, shaking it so that it quivered like a piece of tofu. 'What do you need *me* for? Just memorise the contents of every chapter and copy it on your test paper. You'll sail through the exam next summer with one hand tied behind your back, guaranteed.'

'I do need you,' I said. 'Mother says that history holds up a mirror to the present. Maybe, by looking back at the past, I'll find answers to my questions about our current government.'

Qin nodded, and the muscles in his face relaxed. 'Okay, then we'll just consider the textbook a necessary evil. You can study it by yourself, and learn just the "important" bits by heart. Just for the test, mind you. I'll highlight the most crucial parts in red tomorrow. But what I am going to teach you is to look at history as an honest human being, and a circumspect and wise historian. Agreed?'

I felt that Qin wasn't treating me like a silly girl, but as an equal. I laughed and forgot I had been quaking in fear a few minutes ago.

'But before I begin with the modern period, I should like to find out what you know about ancient history, the period from 345 BC to 1910.'

I got up from my little stool and folded my hands behind my back, as I had been taught to do whenever called on to answer a teacher's question. Looking up at the ceiling, I parroted, virtually word for word, a paragraph from last year's textbook:

'China's two-thousand-year-old feudal system miraculously brought to light the Truth which Mao, the Peerless Leader, describes on page 129 of His *Little Red Book*: "The oppressed masses push forward the wagon of history." In their never-ending bloody strife against the oppressor-class, the people overthrew one dynasty after another, building up new ones in their place time and again.'

Qin's eyes flickered – he must be very impressed by my performance. I looked even more intently at the ceiling, as if my text were being projected up there by a light-box:

'The class struggle, unfortunately, never came to anything. Despite periodic peasant uprisings, the ruling classes continued to exploit the masses and the people lived on the skids, in boiling oil and hell fire. The cause of this tragic state of affairs, of course, was the fact that Mao had not yet been born.

'Our native land's dark days finally came to an end in 1893 when Mao, the "Saviour Star", appeared on the horizon. The mountains and the valleys cried out, "Long live the Heavenly Son of the True Dragon!" Suddenly China was given a brand-new future. Mao sowed the seeds of Communism in all corners of the land. And after their two thousand years of blind and impotent struggle against the exploiters, He finally showed the masses the way to paradise. This is where the Modern History of China, the MHC, begins, which can be summed up in a single phrase: the MHC is the period during which Mao, the Greatest Prophet of the Universe, battled a series of constantly resurgent counter-revolutionary devils, in order to found, in 1949, the Blessed State – the People's Republic of China.'

I took a deep breath, feeling like a pop star with another major hit on her hands, and sat down on my little stool like a good girl. Impatiently I waited for a pat on the back from Qin, because last year, in my history orals, I had been awarded full marks for the exact same feat.

The professor looked at me severely and asked, 'Did you mean what you were saying or were you pulling my leg?'

I shook my head, to clear my ears. How could Qin doubt that I was sincere in what I had said?

'I swear, Mr Qin, that's all I know about ancient history.'

'In that case we'll have to start at the very beginning. Naturally, I will emphasise the modern period, but I *must* devote three or four lessons to what came before. Be that as it may, what you *should* have said is: "That's all they *told* me about ancient history." There is a big difference between what you have been *told* and what you *know*.'

'But to be told something, isn't that the only way to find out anything about history? I can't very well turn back the clock to see for myself what actually happened a long time ago, can I?'

'What you *can* do is gather information about a certain event from a variety of sources, and then draw your own conclusion. Only then can you say, "That's all I know about that history." That is how scientific investigation is born.'

This was getting interesting, and exciting too. It suddenly hit me that words and their meanings can be different things.

'If you genuinely want to understand my teachings, there is one condition: you must tune out the propaganda, stop thinking dogmatically and learn to think for yourself. Everything that Mao says isn't necessarily a truth engraved in stone, you know, and, besides . . .'

He stopped abruptly, because, with an *ee-ouw!* the door of the room was opening. Stiffening, Qin stared straight ahead. I glanced at Qin's watch: it was only five thirty.

The man who came shuffling in said, 'Officer Feng let me go home early because – look . . .' He lifted his right foot, which was as swollen as a steamed bun and as purple as a piece of calf's liver, '. . . I drove my shovel into my foot by accident . . .'

Qin, still staring straight ahead woodenly, failed to show the sympathy common courtesy demanded. His tense posture slackened only a little when his wounded room-mate climbed up on to his bed and joked, 'When all's said and done, it's worth injuring oneself a little once in a while . . . It hurts, of course, but this way at least I escape being sworn at some more by the guards in the rice field. I am coming round to the idea that physical pain is preferable to psychological abuse. The Eskimos have thirty-six words for "snow"; soon I will be able to come up with seventy-two words for "torment"!'

I saw Qin's intent stare, and it began to dawn on me what it was that was alarming him so. He was afraid his room-mate might have overheard his blasphemous remarks about Mao, and, if that was the case, was wondering whether the fellow would denounce him to the camp authorities.

I skipped over to the injured man's bed and simpered, like a foolish little child, 'Well, Uncle Yu, what did you think of my history lesson? Probably much too simple for a grown-up, right?'

Yu was a teacher of psychology. He closed his eyes, bored, and said, 'What lesson, child?'

I glanced at Qin and sent him a wink of relief. He smiled back, but then his face once more assumed a frown.

I hopped from one foot to the other and, humming an irrelevant little tune, remarked breezily, 'Didn't you hear what Mr Qin was talking about, then, when you walked in?'

But Yu snapped at me: 'Enough, Lian! Leave me alone. My goddamn foot is really hurting now. Auuwah! Want to know the only thing I've heard so far? Your jibber-jabbering!'

Concealing my delight, I looked at Qin again. My suppressed grin touched the smile on Qin's face. Suddenly, a bridge grew up between the two of us, like a rainbow. The closer he got to my side of the bridge, the lighter his burden of misery, and the closer I came to his side, the more grown-up I felt.

The second time we met for a lesson, Qin spoke much more softly. Just as Bao had been doing, he positioned his stool so that he could see the door. I copied him instinctively. Whenever Qin was immersed in his notes, unable to keep an eye on the door, I would take over the watch; like a couple of guard dogs we pricked up our ears and took note of the slightest movement outside.

THE SACRIFICE

Mother and I were on home leave. We were sitting in the apartment, blissfully reading.

Tock, tock at the door. I stood up and exchanged a quick glance with Mother. Who could it be?

Ever since Mother's banishment, we hardly ever had visitors. To have dealings with a convicted bourgeois would besmirch your name. Even fellow camp mates did not visit each other, although one would have thought that they had nothing to lose. There are no walls that will not let in some air. One way or another, the camp authorities always managed to find out if any prisoners had met privately in each other's homes – for that you could count on your politically-correct neighbours – and then you were in deep shit. The authorities would interrogate the prisoners: 'What were you talking about? Just idle chat? Surely you don't expect us to believe that! If that's the case, then why didn't you just do it in the camp, instead of behind our backs, at home?' One had to heed the proverb,

> *Good things can be said openly*
> *Bad things are best kept to oneself*

According to this logic, 'privacy' – a foreign concept imported from abroad – was tantamount to 'sin'. That was why Mother's fellow inmates, even when they were home on their Sundays off, hundreds of miles from prison, avoided any sort of contact with each other.

At the tenth knock, Mother nodded at me. I went and carefully opened the door.

Kim! Suddenly I was standing face to face with my best friend.

It was as if time had stood still, as if it were about a half year earlier, when Kim used to come by my house every afternoon. There was something so familiar about this scene – it was as if Kim had come over so that we could do our homework together.

Hurriedly I pulled Kim inside. In my astonishment and delight, I had totally forgotten how one receives a guest. I just stood there in the hallway staring at her, with Kim staring back at me. One of us took a step to the left; the other followed. Without realising what we were doing, we made four complete circles around each other clockwise. Memories from the past flooded us with emotion, and we raked each other hungrily with our eyes, waiting for the familiar click with which, months ago, our hearts would fuse into one.

Mother, still holding her book, stared at us, too astonished at the fact that we had a visitor to think of anything to say.

Pok-pokpokpok! A new sound broke the silence. It came from the bag hanging from Kim's right arm. I noticed something floundering around in there wildly; the bag lunged and emitted a squawk of protest. My eyes began to gleam: it was Whitey!

I scratched Whitey's belly through the bag and exclaimed, 'Oh, Kim, you brought our little friend along! I've missed *both* of you so much!' Only now did I realise how empty my life had been without them. I silently sent Mother a pleading look: couldn't we let Whitey run around, just this once? Mother nodded.

Whitey's carrier bag was nothing but a rag; Kim had simply tied the four corners of the flowered fabric into a knot, with Whitey, as good as folded in half, stuffed inside.

I began fumbling with the bag hanging from Kim's arm, trying to untie the knot. But to my consternation, Kim shrugged me off violently. I almost lost my balance, and gazed at Kim in astonishment. Kim's lips were pursed and her eyes were red. Tears rolled down her cheeks. I had never seen Kim cry. I did not know what to do.

Kim turned her eyes away from me and stared at the wall. We were still standing in the hallway. Whitey, meanwhile, never stopped her tireless cackling. Kim banged on the bag brutally, uttering the first words she had spoken since entering: 'Just shut up, you cluckhead!' Tears cascaded from her eyes faster and faster, and a muffled wail, shrill and quavering, broke from her throat.

'What . . . what's the matter?' I asked and started to cry too, even though I didn't know why.

'I . . . I heard you were ill. Vi-whatever-it-is-ligo, that's what you have. At first I didn't have the guts to come and see you . . . because I didn't do what

46

I'd promised . . . I didn't take part in the Autumn Games . . . Later I found out what kind of disease that ligo is. I couldn't believe you had white spots on you just like the White Ghost . . . I mean Jiangying . . . So I made up my mind to come to see you after all . . . But I never imagined that the blotches would have crept all over . . . even your arms, even your hands!' She slapped herself on the cheeks and went on in a rush, 'What a retarded pig I am! I must have shit for brains. Jiangying has had white spots since she was two years old, and you've only had them for a few months . . . Yet only Buddha knows how that crummy mess manages to spread so quickly!'

Of course! I forgot I didn't look the same any more, the way Kim remembered me. Whenever I took the time to examine my blotches, I realised, naturally, that I looked different. But when I was distracted by other things, I still felt the same as before, free of disease and free of worries . . . The last thing in the world I wanted was to cause Kim any pain. I was used to helping Kim, making her see the bright side – and now here was Kim crying about me!

I hid my arms behind my back and forced a smile. 'Come on, Kim, they're not *that* bad, my spots.' I had a lump in my throat but did my best not to look glum.

Kim turned towards me, and stared at me for a long-drawn-out minute. Her attempts to stifle her sobs only made it worse. She threw down the bag that had Whitey in it, grabbed my hands and brusquely pulled me towards her, wrapping me in a big bear hug.

'*Lia-a-an!*' she moaned.

Now it was my turn to blubber. Mother walked up to us, patted us and tried to console us: 'Children, that's just the way life is. When you get to be older, you will know there's lots of suffering in the world, and you just have to learn to live with it.'

Kim struggled free from my arms and cried: 'It's not fair! Just nine months ago Lian was still . . . the prettiest girl I ever saw, and now she's covered in blotches, and, and, she's just as skinny and scrawny as . . . as I am!' She bent down and in one deft motion untied the knot. Picking Whitey up by the wings, she said, 'Here. For you. I bet all you've had to eat in the camp is pickles and cornbread. Tell me something about the chow in prison! Erwazi, our neighbour's number-two son, was locked up there for two years. That's probably why you look so unhealthy. Mrs Yang, I'm going to prepare a big pot of chicken soup for Lian. It will do her good . . .'

What the . . . ?! Had she brought Whitey not to play with but . . . to eat? I put my hands on my hips and stamped my feet. My tears dried up immediately.

'But that's murder! Why – Whitey is your bread and butter! Where else

47

will you get the money for salt, soap, matches or writing paper? How could you even *think* of putting her on the chopping-board!'

Kim bit her lip and screeched, in a voice so shrill that the ceiling lamp vibrated, 'What's the big deal? What's it to you anyway? Just look at that skinny sliver of dried-out flesh of yours! Call that a face? Unless you get better things to eat, you'll soon go to pot completely and the blotches will spread all over your whole body!' She bolted into the kitchen, grabbed a cleaver hanging on the wall and . . . *Cetcchh!* I heard a loud commotion, ending in a loud *Dong!*

I was shaking all over. Mother had run after Kim, but I was paralysed with fear. Finally I managed to bring myself under control. Once inside the kitchen, I could see it was just as I'd feared: Whitey's head, chopped off in one stroke, had toppled into the tin sink.

Kim was holding the chicken carcass upside down, so that Whitey's blood could drip into a large rice bowl. Round robin-red drops of blood were spilling from the poor creature's neck and into the dish.

I leaned back against the wall, my eyes shut tight. But I couldn't shut my ears. They kept meticulous track of each pearl of blood, as it hit the side of the bowl and shattered into a thousand pieces.

After what seemed like forever, I heard Kim open one of the kitchen cabinets – she knew her way around my flat as if it were her own. Kim shook a little salt into the bowl, to make the blood clot faster. She said, 'See, Mrs Yang? You can use this to prepare the gourmet delicacy Fried Wine-red Playing-Dice.'

Without saying a word, Mother handed Kim a cake of soap to wash her bloodstained hands.

Watching Kim scrub every finger and every fingernail as thoroughly as a surgeon felt like having a fine yet brutal needle lance my heart. The cold-blooded manner in which Kim had been able to finish off Whitey sent a shiver up my spine. Suddenly it dawned on me that Kim might kill a human being just as easily, coolly and efficiently . . .

When Kim had dried her hands, she fumbled in her trouser pocket and pulled out something that looked like a little piece of wood: 'This is the root of the Hesong tree. It doesn't grow here. Mama and I found it on Mount Qingcheng. According to Great-Grandmother on Father's side, the juice of this root purifies the blood and heals both blue and white blemishes.'

'But Kim, that's in the province of Sichuan, hundreds of miles away. How on earth did you get there?'

'I have my ways.' Her eyes sparkled wickedly – Kim loved to cook up schemes that didn't exactly follow the letter of the law.

'Did you ride the rails again?'

'No. We bought train tickets, legit as anything.'

'I don't believe you.'

'Then why ask?' Grinning, she went on, 'We snuck on board in the town of Tongxian, where the trains stop for water and coal . . . Oh yes, before I forget, Mrs Yang, you must cut the root into ten pieces, that way you'll have enough for ten weeks. Every week you'll boil a piece of root in a pot of water and let Lian drink the tea twice a day. You'll see, Lian, before you've finished the entire root, all your blotches will be gone, I guarantee it.'

Mother and I both smiled from ear to ear; we did not for one minute doubt the magical properties of a recipe that had been passed on from generation to generation.

I broke the silence. 'Let's go to my room. We've got lots to talk about.'

Kim took a step backwards. 'I can't. I can't leave my mother waiting for me that long.'

'What do you mean?'

'My mother came with me, because I was afraid the gatekeeper wouldn't let me in. But he'd never turn away a white-haired old lady, now would he, even a third-caster? She's here, at the entrance. I really just wanted to deliver the chicken and the medicine and then I was going to go back . . .'

Mother ran outside, and within two minutes Kim's mother, with much pushing and pulling, was dragged into the flat. Even then she did not stop protesting: 'Buddha, please open Your eyes. Don't You see how improper it is for me, a poor, humble worm of the lowliest caste, covered in dirt, to set my muddy feet inside the home of a doctor and a university lecturer? Dear, dear Buddha, please forgive my impertinence . . .'

I rushed to her side: 'Mrs Mother-of-Kim, what's all this bashfulness? Your daughter is my best friend! Of course you are welcome in our home!'

Kim's mother was trying to smooth down her untidy salt-and-pepper hair with her fingers. 'No, that's different. Poor-folks' kids are entitled to forget their place once in a while to play with the children of rich folks. But grown-ups must follow the laws of their caste. Otherwise there can be no order in society.'

My mother had to laugh. 'You know, Mrs—'

Kim's mother interrupted her abruptly. 'Oh, my, but this poor back of mine, this pathetic pauper's spine, is too feeble to carry such an honour!'

Mother took a step back and asked, surprised, 'What honour?'

'Don't you see? The honour of being called "Mrs" by an illustrious university lecturer such as yourself!'

My mother shook her head. 'How can you even think that? It is I who am honoured, because you and your daughter have chosen to visit . . . political prisoners like us.'

Kim's mother looked up at the ceiling. 'Ancient and Most Wise Heavens, only You with Your all-seeing eyes can see what a piece of crap it is to lock up such important intellectuals in a prison camp. What does he expect, the Emperor – oh no, sorry, the Party Chairman? Does he want everyone to be as dumb as a pig's butt, as illiterate as Kim's father and me? See, *we* are the hopeless cases, because *we* never got an education. Mrs Yang, just believe me, this so-called, uh . . . Cultural Revolution is like a rabbit's tail – it never grows to be very long; and it won't last long, either.' With this, she grabbed my arms and held them up, grumbling, 'Missie, you don't deserve these spots. Drink the root-tea every day. You'll see, the blotches will slink off with their tails between their legs!'

Kim began to sob again. This time, my eyes remained dry – I had had enough. I didn't want Kim and her mother to be worrying about me: it certainly was an upside-down world! I ran into the living room, opened the drawer where we kept the sweets and filled a big bag with toffees and chocolates. Mother went to the bedroom, where she kept a cardboard box filled with walnuts and chestnuts stowed under the bed. On our return we plied Kim and her mother with bags of goodies.

'We can't accept a thing! Else the medicine won't work!'

That stopped Mother and me in our tracks. They were right – you weren't suppose to show gratitude before the illness was cured; otherwise the remedy would seem to have been prescribed for material gain alone. Obediently, we put the sweets away. When it came to a cure for my affliction, Mother had no qualms about kowtowing to this superstitious dogma, despite the fact that she was a scholar and researcher who taught her students to think rationally and whose husband, moreover, was a doctor of modern medicine.

Kim turned to her mother and apologised, 'I'm sorry, Mama, to have left you waiting outside so long. I wasted a lot of time trying to convince them to eat Whitey.'

'It doesn't matter, my child. Your mother's tough old hide can take it. Let's go home. Your father is fixing the roof, he can use our help. Mrs Yang, just give us a shout when the root is all gone. But I'm sure the spots will have disappeared by then.'

I accompanied them to the gate of my sector and stood staring at their receding backs until they had dwindled to two pinpricks in the distant green.

CRIME STOPPERS

I couldn't help thinking of the flap when Whitey went missing one time. Kim and I had been doing our homework at my house, and Kim had been acting strangely. She couldn't stop squirming and stared into the distance, preoccupied.

'What's the matter?' I asked.

'Whitey didn't come home last night.'

I looked at her in consternation. I knew how much that old hen meant to Kim's family. Whitey was the family's piggy bank. The inadequate salary that Kim's father brought home and the few fen that her mother scraped together with her little jobs amounted to just enough to buy a little cornmeal. All other expenses – salt, vinegar, detergent, books and notebooks for Kim and Jiening, as well as tobacco for their father – were paid for from the income from Whitey's eggs.

'Where did she go?' I asked, like a dolt.

'If only I knew! In the five years we've had her, she's never been lost. The weasels that live in the hills behind our house don't usually come out at this time of year. The only explanation we can think of is . . .' She didn't finish the sentence.

A shudder crawled up my spine. I knew what Kim was getting at: one of the neighbours must have stolen the hen.

'Maybe Whitey just got confused and lost her way this time. Well, I'm sure you'll find her. I bet she's cackling her little heart out in the chicken coop by the time you get home,' I tried by way of reassurance.

Kim's face lit up. 'Just you wait, Whitey. When you get home tonight, I'll shake you so hard the sawdust will scatter from your head! My parents didn't sleep a wink last night. How can Father ever pull a full load today? Oh, Whitey, just you wait: there's such a spanking in store for you!'

Two days later Whitey was still missing. After school, Kim and I shuffled to the mud-quarter with lead in our shoes. Today, we claimed, we felt like doing our homework at Kim's house, but we both knew darn well what we were up to, and why.

The mood at the house was tense. Kim's mother was pacing back and forth in the courtyard like a caged bear. She greeted me politely but distractedly.

I concealed my nervousness and tried to act normal. I settled on the kang with my books and notebooks.

'Puh, puh.'

I jumped. Now I could make out the shadow that was Kim's father sitting in the remotest corner of the kang. He was calmly smoking his pipe. Why? Had he not gone to work today?

'Eldest daughter, go make me a pot of tea! And Kim's father, stop moping! Bring me the longest ladder and put it up against the outside wall. Help me climb up on the roof.'

Silence. No one moved a muscle.

'Quick! Soon the sun will go down behind the Western Mountains.'

I looked at the sky. It was unusually fine out. Silver clouds were waltzing around the pure blue dome above. There wasn't a breath of wind to stir the tree branches in the sun-drenched courtyard. The neighbours were hanging their linens out to dry, or were sitting in their courtyards enjoying the last rays of sun . . .

The water for tea hissed in the kettle. Kim's mother was already seated on the flat roof of the mud hut. Besides being used as a place to dry sweet-potato slices and pickled vegetables, the roof also served as a broadcast station. Since it was up high, sound could travel a long way unhindered. If a mud house inhabitant had something to announce to the entire neighbourhood, he could literally shout it from the rooftops. Kim's mother had chosen a good day for her transmission: everyone was out of doors.

A few minutes later, Kim, too, climbed on to the roof, setting down a pot of tea and a cup before her mother. The mother gulped down some tea to lubricate her throat, which was dry with agitation. The moment had come to declare war on the enemy.

'Where is the one who let a vulture peck out his heart, and was cold-blooded enough to nick our Whitey with his thieving claws?' she thundered.

Suddenly the whole neighbourhood went still. Women gossiping at full throttle, quarrelling children, men who had been taking advantage of the fine weather to do repairs around the house – they all instantly dropped what they were doing. Everyone was all ears.

'What have we ever done to you, bastard offspring of a rabbit and an owl, to make you steal our Whitey?'

No reaction. The neighbourhood was quiet as a tomb.

Now the mother began to rage in earnest: 'Prick up those flop-ears of yours, you gutless chicken thief, and listen to me good. Do you think I don't know who pinched Whitey? Hey, you, slanty-eyed, yellow-toothed, bow-legged turtle-egg, I see you!'

I couldn't help laughing. It was inspired guesswork. Pretty much everyone in China had slanty eyes. Thanks to the mud-dwellers' abysmal hygienic conditions, most of them had yellow teeth. The extreme parsimony of vitamins and minerals in the diet ensured that at least half the neighbourhood was bow-legged. With that broad a description, Kim's mother could hardly miss.

She swallowed another gulp of tea and waited for the culprit to step forward to confess his guilt, his tail between his legs.

Still nothing. You could have heard a pin drop.

'So! You won't admit it, eh? That's too bad, because then I'll just have to leave it to the devil to punish you . . .

'Whoo-hoo-ah-whoo-hoo, Devil-king from Suloo! Put aside Your work in purgatory for a minute and rise up out of hell! There's a chicken thief up here who refuses to confess his crime; come help me please!

'If the wretch has already eaten my poor Whitey, let him puke until his stomach, gallbladder and intestines get retched right out of his despicable carcass!

'If he's keeping my hen for her eggs, then let all his animals croak! May all his cows come down with foot-and-mouth disease, may his goats miscarry endlessly and his pigs all die of the swine fever!

'Whoo-ah-whoo-hoo, thank You very much, Mr Devil!'

Her voice had gone completely hoarse. She drained her cup and glared at the people below. The mud dwellers seemed frozen to stone. Nobody did, or said, anything.

It was time to bring out the heavy artillery. 'Still refusing to come forward, are you?

'Foohrooh-whoo-moorooh, Lord of all devils Lackadooboo! Please punish this stubborn chicken thief. Let his wife bring forth nothing but cheap goods, so there will be no one to carry on the ancestral line!'

It wasn't even dark before Whitey was heard cackling down in the courtyard. The culprit must have been seriously worried that the Devil would hear Kim's mother's last curse. One paltry chicken wasn't worth the disaster of his wife's giving birth to nothing but 'cheap goods' – in other words, girls – from now on . . .

I said goodbye to Kim at a quarter to six. On my way home I noticed the neighbourhood was all abuzz with noise again.

Ting-tong-ting. The men hammered the last nail into their houses, children were back up to no good, plumes of smoke eddied from the chimneys and the air was heavy with wonderful cooking smells.

And now Whitey was gone, sacrificed for my sake. After seeing Kim and her mother off, I ran home and went straight to the mirror in Mother's wardrobe – the only one I hadn't smashed to pieces 'accidentally on purpose' yet – and gave the Lian who was staring back at me in the glass a withering scrutiny. My skinny face looked dark green and my lips had a bluish tint. My cheekbones stuck out from my face like two mountain peaks and my skin was as creased as parchment.

Without making a sound, Mother had slipped into the room and was standing behind me. She said, 'Kim is right. The canteen food is not the right thing for a growing teenager like you. I'm going to do something about it, I promise.'

CHILD LABOUR

We were back from our weekend leave, and I was starting to get used to my new surroundings. But Mother continued to worry about my health.

At lunchtime, Mother brought me over to where Professor Qin was hunkered down. She said to him, 'The less teeth a man has, the more wisdom he possesses. That is why I am coming to you for advice. Just look at my daughter's skinny little arms and legs: she looks like a child of nine. I'm worried she may never grow . . .'

Qin put his cornbread back in his bowl, stopped chewing and listened attentively.

Mother went on, 'I don't need a doctor for the diagnosis. The child is obviously undernourished . . . Ah, me, how can I ever face her father again, when he discovers how poorly I have taken care of her!'

Qin waited patiently for Mother's litany to end. He knew that Mother had enough common sense to realise my poor health was not her fault.

'Mr Qin, fair's fair. *I* am the prisoner here, not my daughter. If the authorities decree that I must wither and starve, then I'll accept that. But Lian doesn't deserve it. Is it asking too much to request better nourishment for her?'

'The answer is: yes, it is too much to ask. Your case is already creating headaches for the Director. I have heard that some of the detainees have gone to him to complain about Lian's "élitist" private lessons. The camp authorities have dismissed the complaints by arguing that it is appropriate for a member of the younger generation to receive an education, so that she may become a valuable revolutionary. But if you now go and make more demands, I'm afraid that you'll come back with a flattened nose.'

Mother's grip on me grew even tighter, as if I were growing thinner, so thin that I might drift away on the next breath of air.

Qin picked his bowl off the floor and said, 'But I do have an idea. This morning the head guard asked us which of us sexagenarians was interested in working in the flourmill. Now that I hear Lian is undernourished, I think perhaps I'll take the job. What do you think?'

His meaning was clear. He wanted me to petition the Director and ask if I could help Qin in the mill. I suddenly remembered that the mill-house workers were served an extra supper. This meal did not consist of ordinary prison swill, but of food deemed good enough for Party officials. I bopped up and down around Qin and Mother and cheered, 'Hurray, soon I'll be eating like an emperor! Meat, fresh vegetables, nothing pickled, and, best of all, white rice!' I had to stop talking to swallow my saliva before it choked me.

Auwa! My left arm suddenly stung painfully. In one split second, I fell from my cloud of euphoria back down to a sobering earth. I looked down at my arm, on which a star-shaped bruise was forming. Mother had *'ninged'* me. Whenever Mother was angry with me, she would pinch a fold of my skin between her thumb and index finger. Then she would twist the skin until, reeling with pain, I hopped up and down like a drop of water skittering around a red-hot frying pan.

Tears blinded me. But I should have known better. Any happiness in my life was always nipped in the bud by searing pain. In the thirteen years of my short life, I had never failed to pay dearly for any joy that might, for an instant, light up my dark world.

'*Chihuo!* The only brains *you* have are in your stomach!' Mother gave me a box on the ears for good measure and snarled,' All you can think of are the advantages of working in the mill. Don't you realise how hard you'll have to work for that paltry ration of fresh greens, those few miserable strips of meat and the one little bowl of white rice? Ten hours a day, non-stop! That electrified machine doesn't understand fatigue. Besides, the air in there is suffocating: flour muffling everything like a blanket. You'll end up satisfying your appetite at the expense of your lungs, which will start looking like two breaded chicken patties in no time!'

Qin could hardly deny that what Mother was saying was true, and he shook his head helplessly.

I had to use both hands to shield my head from the torrent of Mother's blows. I didn't dare blubber openly, for fear that it would only make Mother hit me harder . . .

It had been at least a minute since I had felt any blows. I looked up, puzzled.

Mother's eyes were red. In a flash I saw what it was that had caused Mother's bloodthirsty mood to evaporate – the sight of my arms, as shrivelled as dried-out bamboo sticks. And my knees sticking out from my skinny legs like giant lumps.

'Mr Qin, if my daughter weren't so severely undernourished, I would never have the heart to allow her to slave ten hours a day in that kind of polluted atmosphere. But, well, the mill workers' nutritious food really *is* indispensable to Lian's health. I will ask to see the Director this afternoon . . .'

Qin said, 'Yunxiang, don't worry. I will do my utmost to see to it that Lian gets better. But make sure she is punctual, that she is there promptly, at one o'clock sharp, so that everyone will see that she is a good worker, capable of earning her supper. As soon as it gets quiet around the mill, say five o'clock, I'll send her home. Then she can come back at ten, in time for the eleven o'clock supper.'

I was thinking about the flour mill's non-stop, deafening drone, and suddenly an idea occurred to me. 'Mr Qin can give me a history lesson while we work! That way,' I whispered, first into Mother's and then the professor's ears, 'no one can overhear the counter-revolutionary ideas Mr Qin teaches me.'

He tapped his index finger against my brow. 'Well! I see that that cheeky, clever little brain of yours hasn't suffered any lethal effects from starvation!' From his radiant smile, I could tell he thought it was a good idea.

Later, Mother told me that the Director had agreed to her request.

That night, I could not fall asleep.

LABOUR COMPENSATION

At the stroke of one, I entered the mill. My heart was pounding wildly, not only because it was my first day at the mill and I was nervous, but also because the whole building was shaking, up and down and from side to side, like a ship on a raging sea. The giant electric-powered machine was roaring like a lunatic. Qin was already there. He pressed a cap and overalls into my hands. The uniform was made of the same stuff as the burlap flour bags. I inspected first Qin and then myself: we looked like two flour sacks with legs.

The mill, which was the prison camp's showpiece, was made up of three parts. The first was a huge vat the shape of the rear of a pickup truck.

It contained the yellow-brown mass of raw grain that was bubbling like a volcano about to erupt. The second component was a heavy pipe of polished aluminum snaking its way through the mill's interior and ending up in the room-sized engine – the third part. This machinery was connected to another pipe as big as a trough, to which was tied a flour sack about two feet by three feet wide. The air blowing out of the pipe puffed up the flour sack like a balloon. The balloon was hung in front of the window, and the sunshine streaming in allowed me to see right through it. I noticed it wasn't filled solely with air, but also with flour, which was accumulating at an alarming rate with every passing second . . .

'Hurry up!' shouted Qin and threw an empty sack at me. 'Take one end, and hold on tight.'

I ran to him and tried to do as he ordered. But in vain, because the sack came up to my chin and I wasn't tall enough to hold it up to the balloon. Qin flew to a corner of the room and grabbed a stool for me to stand on. This time we managed to hold up the empty sack at the same height.

In the meantime, the balloon had filled to bursting with freshly-ground flour. Qin untied a knot in the bottom. *Hrrruuuff!* In a rush of deafening noise and flour, the white mass thundered into the empty bag we were holding. It was raining flour particles, blinding me and making me choke.

Qin pulled a piece of string from a box on the window-sill and tied the sack shut. *'Wu-eiow!'* he grunted like a giant about to shoulder a mountain, picked up the heavy load and dragged it to the other side of the workshop. Dear Buddha, there I saw hundreds of flour sacks, a skyscraper of them, all neatly stacked, like giant bricks.

'Quick!' Qin shouted in my ear. 'The balloon is half full already. We've got to stand by with the next sack.' His shouting made me jump, and I picked up a new bag. Inside the furiously roaring mill, shouting was a necessary evil.

Like two speeding bullets, Qin and I ricocheted back and forth between the storage area and the balloon, which, goddamn bastard son of an unwed mother, seemed to keep filling up faster and faster. We were soon out of breath and dripping with sweat.

It was only half past one. How was I going to keep this up day in, day out? I'd never manage it! But I didn't have time to worry about it, because the sack and the pipe took all my attention and strength.

After three hours of working and running as hard as I could, I had grown used to it. The balloon now seemed to be filling up at a slower rate, fortunately, and there was a longer wait before the balloon needed emptying again. I looked at Qin, who looked like the abominable snowman. He was standing next to me with his eyes fixed attentively on the sack tied to the pipe. Putting my mouth up close to his ear, I yelled, 'Aren't you tired?'

He scratched at his ears as if trying to dislodge my words, and said, 'Child, there's no need to shout. I can hear you.'

I tilted my head sideways and listened for the noise. Strangely enough, it did seem much less loud. With some practice at lip reading, I was now able to understand Qin's words even when spoken at a normal pitch. I asked again, 'Aren't you tired?'

'Tired?' laughed Qin. 'Compared with slaving in the fields, this is a job for a lazybones.' Even though it was hard to believe – how could anything be more exhausting than this? – I knew he must be right. For it was true that Qin looked happy. His stance was relaxed, his eyes were glistening merrily and his head was nodding back and forth to some internal beat. He was humming a little tune as he looked out the window. 'See now – was I right, or what? After five p.m. there isn't a soul around here any more. Upsy-daisy, Lian, run off home now! Go finish your homework, and study for tomorrow's lessons.'

'I already did it this morning. I can't leave you here to finish this heavy work all by yourself!'

'It is *meant* to be done by one person! I really don't need anyone to help me. You are here for the sole purpose of showing the others that you are not getting your midnight supper for nothing.'

It was not very nice to hear I wasn't indispensable. But Qin's patience was wearing thin. 'Go! It'll be dinnertime in less than an hour. The people coming from the fields have to pass this way on their way to the canteen. If you drag your feet, everyone will see that you are not working here full time.'

Reluctantly I took my leave. 'See you tonight then, Mr Qin – ten o'clock.'

When it was time to return to work, Mother gave me a flashlight to carry and said, 'Watch out for puddles on the road – they may be deeper than you expect. I don't want you breaking an ankle.'

Going out at night by yourself in the camp was very different from going out in the city. Here the only dangers lurking for the night-time stroller were the treacherous potholes that, once filled with water, were impossible to spot. Following the flashlight's yellow beam, I stepped into the cool embrace of summer's night. The night sky was transparent yet inky, like a black lace curtain stretched across Heaven. Stars were twinkling through the lace, attesting wordlessly to the celestial goings-on up there. The dormitory lights had been extinguished, and so too had the sounds. There was a deep hush everywhere, broken only by the chirping of the crickets and the croaking of the frogs perched on their reeds and water-lily pads at the lake behind the camp, who were still busily chattering about the long hot summer day that had just flown by.

The flourmill, which never tired, ground on relentlessly.

Qin's face lit up with a smile when I reappeared at the plant. He did not look quite as sprightly as he had that afternoon – he had been working without a break. I insisted that he let me drag the flour sacks to the storage area by myself, an offer he now accepted without protest.

At eleven he finally shut off the machinery. I promptly felt as if I were inside a sound vacuum. Never before had I appreciated peace and quiet as I did now. I picked up my bowl and chopsticks and skipped alongside Qin as we made our way to the canteen's VIP-lounge. It was a five-minute walk. Not a word was exchanged between us, but I was certain that he knew that we were, at that moment, the two happiest people on earth.

A garish light illuminated the room where the special meal was being prepared for the camp administrators – whose meetings ostensibly continued late into the night – as well as for the night guards and mill workers. The cook was dishing out food from an unusually small wok no larger than a washbasin; the wok normally used during the day was bigger than a bathtub. A smaller wok was associated with tastier food, and not without justification.

I held my bowl against the side of the wok, my heart thumping in my chest at the thought of a dish fit for an emperor. I closed my eyes in delicious anticipation. Sautéed spring onions with crispy deep-fried pork! I hadn't had anything like it in months – I just about went out of my mind with joy.

I did not know what possessed me, but I refused to move along and held out my bowl again, hoping that the cook would give me another dollop. My eyes must have held an extremely greedy expression, because the cook burst out laughing and said to the female cook standing next to him, 'This little creature sure knows every trick in the book! Look, she wants some more,' and with that, he granted my wish. I blushed, ashamed of my own gluttony, but the temptingly fragrant dish and the steaming, dazzlingly white rice soon made me forget everything else. I ran to a corner of the kitchen, hunkered down and started wolfing down my meal.

Qin came up to me and said, 'Lian, look, this room is different from the canteen. Don't you see those tables and chairs, all empty, over there? Come, we can go and sit down to eat, like civilised people.'

I arched my back and a growl came out of the back of my throat, like a stray dog that has found a bone in the garbage which he is prepared to defend to the death from the ravenous jaws of his famished cohorts. I just went on stuffing spring onions into my mouth, the food bulging from my lips – my eyes were practically popping out of my head, it was that bad. Qin's eyes misted over, and he crouched down beside me. He watched as I guzzled down my food in a most uncivilised way; he himself was shovelling plain rice into his mouth only. Using his chopsticks, he began picking the strips of meat out of his bowl and placing them on top of my rice.

Surprised, I jumped to my feet, but Qin said, 'Sit, sit. Go on, eat. Uncle Qin is old. The eyes of an old nag are bigger than its stomach. Anyway, I don't seem to digest meat very well any more. Why shouldn't I give it to you, my child? You are still growing.'

With trembling chopsticks, I crammed the meat into my mouth. Qin's eyes glistened with emotion. I felt pampered and consoled.

After dinner, Qin dropped me off at my dorm. Quietly I crawled into bed, but I couldn't get to sleep because I was so happy. First I thought of Kim, who had risked her own neck by jumping on to a moving train in search of medicinal herbs high on the mountaintops, and had even sacrificed her pet and dearest comrade Whitey for my sake. The face of Kim's mother swam before my eyes as well. Then I thought of Qin. He was my mentor and my protector, and he sacrificed his own food for me. I knew myself to be safe and secure. My nerves, which had been on edge ever since Father's departure, were starting to unwind, filament by filament.

THE LILY THEATRE

Just as Qin and I had hoped and anticipated, we were able to continue the history lessons while working in the mill, during the grace periods between the stacking of the last sack and the filling of the next. Qin did not have to worry that someone might overhear his counter-revolutionary ideas, since the droning engine provided a perfect sound-camouflage. He could therefore give free rein to his idiosyncratic views of China's ancient past. He formulated his ideas in such a coherent and fascinating manner that, for the first time in my life, I found listening to a teacher a pleasure rather than an obligation. I followed his lectures with great attention and, spellbound, relived my country's ups and downs in the same way that, as a three-year-old, I used to listen to my nurse's stories, cheering when the good fairy restored the injured fawn to life and returned it to its mother, distressed when the wicked witch turned the little princess into an owl. As far as I was concerned, Qin could go on and on – I would never tire of it.

I was as proud as a peacock of my new-won knowledge and was dying to show it off. But . . . to whom? The adults around me were all convicts, 'undesirable human weeds', who worked at forced labour during the day and were too exhausted at night to do anything but doze off; there were no other children in the camp. Still, I was dying to share what I had learned – with the very walls even, if it were to come to that.

On the morning of my third day at work, after getting up and having breakfast an hour later than the others, I walked down to the little lake behind the barracks. Sitting on the grass, I spun a flat stone over the water and convinced myself that the noise the pebble made – *ting-ting-tong* – was the pond bidding me a warm welcome. So I started telling what I had learned to the plants and the frogs hopping from one lily pad to the next.

Every time I looked at the glassy surface, it seemed to me that I saw Qin's wrinkled old face reflected there. He listened attentively and put up with my audacious, often silly remarks, my childish interpretations of all sorts of historic events, with tender benevolence. His patience, his understanding and his uncritical acceptance of my naïveté caused something inside my heart to stir . . .

The next morning I wandered down to the lake again. I had by that time baptised it the 'Lily Theatre', a name that tickled my fancy and reinforced my notion that the frogs and the crickets were listening to me. Here I discussed the things Qin had taught me. I folded my hands behind my back and, leaning forward, strolled at a slow, deliberate pace, the way a highly revered teacher is supposed to do. I rubbed the bridge of my nose with the thumb and index finger of my right hand, as if I were pushing up my spectacles, the mark of learnedness.

Addressing the natural surroundings, I demanded: 'Do you, spectators of the Lily Theatre, know anything of the glory of the Chinese Empire? No? Well then, listen to me closely,' and I pointed my finger up in the air, just like a real teacher.

The crickets didn't give a fig for my oratory and chirped as if their mouths had been muzzled shut for a million years. The frogs pumped their elastic bellies up with air and went on croaking, demonstratively ignoring my hissed *'Shhhhh!'* But that did not quell my enthusiasm.

'Very, *very* long ago, when the Europeans were still swinging from the trees, the Chinese Empire was already in full bloom. And what an empire it was! Well, it was almost thirty times the size of England, for example, a little country somewhere in western Europe . . .

'Chinese society was organised in the most orderly way. At the top was the Emperor, who levied taxes from his vassals, who in turn levied their underlings. At the bottom of the ladder crawled the peasants, who supplied the entire country with foodstuffs and tools, and who were served up as cannon fodder whenever the country was at war.

'It was a perfect world: everybody knew their place, obeyed their superiors and did what they were supposed to do. The peasants toiled, the lords exploited the peasants – only to be sucked dry in turn by the "Son of the Dragon", as our Emperor was known. No one could wish for a neater formula for making the world of man turn round.

'The young "reptile" was taught how to make sure he would remain on his throne – by poisoning, mutilating or, at a pinch, assassinating any rivals. Towards the time that the little dragon reached manhood, he was given another task, one that he fulfilled with great gusto: that of producing more little reptiles. It was the only way the empire could acquire suitable future rulers.

'Uniformity was essential to the governance of such a large nation, otherwise it would have been impossible for the Emperor's might to reach into the most distant corners of the land. Seeing that every region or district had its own language, it would have been an impossible task to translate the imperial orders into all those hundreds of dialects. Therefore a single written language was invented, called Wenyan. Everyone who wanted to get ahead in life had to master this language, because all regional officials had to be able to read the government's directives. They had to see to it that the illiterate peasants danced to the tune of the overlords.

'In those times, there were no telephones and you couldn't send a telegram; even letters, in the modern sense of the word, did not yet exist. The problem was how to make the Emperor's decrees reach the isolated villages. This was done by means of special mail-coaches. Since the roads in some regions were not as wide as others, the carriages were sometimes unable to make it through. So the head of state dictated that all the roads in the empire had to conform to a set width.

'Even more important was uniformity of thought. It was necessary that everyone stand behind the government's policies, heart and soul. Imagine what would happen if, say, some idiot of a peasant or some drunken minister told the Emperor he was doing the wrong thing! That would certainly lead to a holy mess. For word of such bad-mouthing was sure to get around, and who could deny that even the Emperor was sometimes wrong? Since our nation had no official forum for criticising authority, that kind of potshot would have worked like a spark in a tinder-dry haystack! An uprising could happen at any time; civil war would be inevitable. Local warlords would muster their armies: they would jump at the chance of increasing their own power by driving neighbouring lords from their lands. The land would drown in blood and the peasants would have no time to till the earth. Even if you managed to escape death by the sword, you would end up starving to death anyhow. So you see, permitting criticism of the Emperor would lead to a national catastrophe. As a safeguard, a unique judicial system was set up.

'Do you know which was the most capital crime? Not murder; not treason, nor theft. No, the worst crime was harbouring any sort of doubt that any political decision of the Emperor's might not be a stroke of genius, one hundred per cent. If anybody dared to question him, the scum would get the ultimate penalty. Someone like that didn't deserve to be hanged or to have his head chopped off, no, that was way too good for him. He'd get pitched into an enormous frying pan, to be fished out only once he was fried to a crispy turn.

'Thanks to this kind of policy, the empire's stability was assured, and the economy flourished. At a time when the Europeans were still climbing trees and picking fruit to fill their hairy bellies, the Chinese already knew how to pack their barns to the rafters with grain. Improved farming methods kept increasing production. Irrigation lessened the farmers' dependence on the weather, and with their iron tools they were able to till the soil more deeply, faster and more efficiently. At a time when the Europeans were still chomping on fruit skin, pith and all, and scratching their heads in amazement when an apple tree happened to shoot up out of the ground in the very spot where they had emptied their bowels, the Chinese invented the magnetic compass. Now wagons could make a beeline for their destination without getting lost. To top it all, gunpowder was developed. Cultural and scientific milestones multiplied at a dizzying rate. A magnificent civilisation was born.

'Alas, that's where all that can be said about our nation's glory, ends. The rest of China's history was marked by conservatism, envy and sneaky subterfuge . . .'

At this point the stream of words dried up. Qin's face in the lake seemed more and more defined and lifelike. It was as if he were standing right there, patiently listening to my lecture. He encouraged me to continue my story, occasionally guiding me back to the straight and narrow when I made statements that were a little far-fetched.

I realised that, ever since Qin's first lesson, I had been longing for a chance to speak out freely. Now that I had found what I had been looking for here at the lake, I yearned for some kind of supervision of my words and my thoughts. Surely there must be a border somewhere, a dividing line between truth and nonsense? I yearned for a friendly crossing guard with an open mind, who would listen sympathetically to my unorthodox ideas while pointing out which of my crazier notions was totally off the wall. Now that I had the freedom to say whatever I wanted, I felt in urgent need of restraint. How I wished Qin were here!

Whenever I made some profound observation about life, Mother tended to give me such a strange look – full of scorn and disapproval. Mother wasn't ready to acknowledge that I was growing up, and ruthlessly pruned back every tendril she noticed emerging from my maturing consciousness. And Father was so far away, out there in Gansu: I had even forgotten what he looked like. Besides, even if he were here, I would not choose to expose, nakedly, my philosophical notions to his scrutiny. He was always so absent-minded, too preoccupied with his work and his concern for his patients.

I did not know why, but I had become very sensitive of late. One impatient gesture, one harsh word from Mother and my heart would shrivel up.

Qin was never impatient. The lines on his face were testimonials to the generosity of his intellect and his gentleness of spirit. His voice was always so calm and so kind . . .

Should I try to persuade him to come down to the lake to attend one of my lectures? I gave myself little hope of succeeding, since between the hours of midnight and one o'clock in the afternoon, he needed all the time he had to snatch a few winks, so that by the next day he would be rested enough to return to work. He was sixty-five years old, and had to conserve his energy prudently if he was to keep slaving at the mill for ten laborious hours a day.

⌒

The question was burning in my throat, but I was terrified of being refused. I couldn't concentrate on my work, and had already let one heavy flour sack slip out of my hands. That had shaken me up, but the prospect of the 'no' that was bound to come once I finally summoned the courage to cough up my request, was much scarier. In the end I decided to broach the subject in a roundabout way, coming at it slowly, in ever-decreasing circles . . .

'Mr Qin, there are some people my age who have interesting things to say too, you know.'

He looked back at me over his shoulder – we were dragging a sack of flour to the storage area, with Qin in front and me behind – and smiled, 'Young people your age have many fascinating things to tell. We adults think we know everything so much better, but if that were so, wouldn't you expect there to be less suffering and discord?'

Elated, I nearly dropped the sack again. I blurted out, 'So you don't think that what I have to say is necessarily *always* childish?'

He stood still, holding on to his side of the sack with one hand and wagging the index finger of the other hand at my nose: 'Lian, remember this: "to be grown-up" is not the same as "to be wise". We grown-ups are adept at concealing our true natures, and, as if that's not enough, we like to make sure others will feel ashamed of their own true natures as well.'

'So I don't have to be ashamed of my ideas?'

'Why should you be?' He gave the flour sack a few smart raps, so that the next sack would fit on top better. 'Shame ought to be banished from the earth. It's a totally useless thing. Shame paralyses you until you can't move forwards or backwards.'

I positioned myself in front of the flour sack and let the burning question catapult out of my throat like a fireball: 'I have come up with my own version of the story of China's past. Won't you come and hear it some time? But you mustn't make fun of me, promise?' As I was speaking I was thumping on the flour sack energetically, so I wouldn't have to look into Qin's eyes.

He tapped me on the shoulder and asked, 'What are you talking about? So you want to have a turn at giving history lessons? To me?'

I jumped up. 'Uh . . . no, Sir, no, I have only been repeating what you taught me, to the frogs and the crickets at the pond behind our sleeping quarters.'

'Oh, pity! I thought that my lessons might have helped you to form your own opinions.'

'Would that please you?'

'It would be evidence of your developing wisdom, at any rate.'

'But – then I *am* wise! I've already given one lecture in the Lily Theatre on Chinese history. Please, won't you come?'

'Where? Were you talking about going to the theatre?'

'Oh, I meant the pond behind the barracks.'

'What a lovely name!'

Qin laughed and pulled me towards him.

AN AUDIENCE OF ONE

I searched the field by the lake, hoping to find a piece of ground without
nettles and thorns, with some soft turf for Qin to sit on. My movements
disturbed the frogs, which threw hostile looks at me out of their bulging
eyes and jumped up, annoyed, from the peaceful lily pads studded with
pearly drops of dew. Qin said he didn't need to sit down, but I saw that
his back was crooked from lack of sleep. Yawning, he went and sat down in
the spot that I had carefully chosen for him and rubbed his red, tired eyes
until they cleared a little. I averted my face to hide my tears. How deeply
Qin must care for me to be willing to sacrifice his much-needed rest!

Trying to rectify what I thought had been wrong with my previous lecture,
I decided on a more succinct version for today . . .

'Most esteemed audience! What follows is my lecture on the history of
ancient China. When the Europeans were still swinging from the trees, the
Chinese Empire was already in full bloom . . .'

'Whoa, whoa, what did you say?' Qin was suddenly wide-awake. 'When
the Europeans were still swinging from trees? What gives you the right to
speak about other races in such an insulting manner? How would you like
it if today's Europeans, the ones building the fastest rockets and the highest
skyscrapers in the world, said about us, "While the slit-eyed Chinese still
plod along behind a buffalo's behind, ploughing their rice paddies in the
most prehistoric manner, we in our part of the globe are riding the world's
most modern tractors, cutting down the farmers' work to the mere push of
a button?"'

'Would I like it? No, I would call them racist.'

'What are *you* then? If you denigrate Westerners, then they will denigrate you.'

I went silent, to let Qin's words sink in. After a while I said, 'Mr Qin, I
understand that I shouldn't talk that way about the Europeans, but would
it be all right with you if I didn't focus on that right now? Otherwise I shall
get all in a muddle and won't know how to explain the differences between
China and the West.'

'Go ahead. Just as long as you are prepared to face the consequences.'

'What consequences?'

'Well, if for instance Westerners were to call you a "yellow-skinned guttersnipe", you would have to accept that you might have done something to deserve it.'

I swallowed hard. But I needed to get rid of my story so badly that I could not take all this into account, for the moment. I went and stood on a large flat rock, facing the water, and went on with my disquisition.

'—The agricultural production methods, which had previously lifted our nation to the apex of civilisation, were exhausted. With the population explosion and the demand for food constantly snowballing, agricultural production, which was the only source of sustenance, stagnated. Add to that the fact that the Emperor's and his vassals' appetite for luxury was ever increasing. The first Emperor had been content with two palaces, one juicy cutlet on his plate a day, and ten women in his harem; a later emperor considered suicide because he had only ten palaces, twenty chicken breasts per meal and a couple of thousand concubines . . . Lords and other important pooh-bahs followed his example and put the peasants through the wringer in order to squeeze them for their very last drop of blood.

'Food shortages caused by the population explosion on the one hand and large-scale extravagance by the top echelons of society on the other, created anger and unrest among the people. Peasant uprisings became as predictable as the four seasons, despite the harshness of the penalty. Because – what did the peasants care? Either they croaked of starvation, since pretty much their entire harvest was confiscated by their overlords; or they were cut down by the imperial army, standing shoulder to shoulder with their revolutionary comrades. Marx was right: The People have nothing to lose except their chains.

'The Emperor, in any case, had too much to think about – after all, he had to deliberate with himself every night over the choice of sleeping partner, no easy task when there are three thousand candidates to choose from. And then there was the supreme problem of that little thing dangling between his imperial legs and why it simply refused to subscribe to the holy omnipotence of the Son of the Dragon. Finally there was the troublesome question of how to keep the peasants in check.

'Political, judicial and administrative laws were rewritten every other day; scholars, philosophers and artists were charged with spending every waking hour dreaming up new ideas on how to keep the populace firmly under the Emperor's thumb.

'Nothing helped. The peasants continued to revolt and the Emperor went on putting down rebellions with the same bloody methods. Neither side would give up. It became an obsession: both parties solemnly believed that grabbing power was the only way to obtain the necessities or luxuries they needed. The never-abating war blinded people to the fact that prosperity for all could be found elsewhere than on the battlefield: for example, by inventing and developing new production methods, or by voluntary rationing to build up food reserves . . . No, no one had time for that kind of lame idea. The swords had to keep hacking, the heads had to keep rolling. It was the Chinese way: one person's happiness and fortune was to be made only by robbing another of his livelihood and life.

'Envy rooted itself deeply into the Chinese psyche and spurred people to attack those richer than themselves. The rich retaliated by nursing an innate grudge towards the poor, excited by fear, loathing and cruelty. The destructive strife that came out of all this siphoned off all available energy that might have led to progress.

'At the time when the Europeans started climbing down from the trees to stand with their two feet on the ground, and began reinventing themselves as farmers, potters, iron-smiths and shopkeepers, China's scholars and scientists were busy scribbling articles suggesting how the government could squeeze ever more labour out of the peasants, rob them of their harvest and still keep them in check. At the time when London was opening the first financial exchange, our ministers were debating which organ should be cut off if someone slighted the Emperor or led a rebellion: should it be the organ responsible for sowing the unrest – the tongue – or should it be the organ responsible for sowing new little rebels?

'Gradually the conflict between the Emperor and his underlings boiled over into a conflict among the underlings themselves. They were mad at the people in power, who were swimming in material wealth, while they themselves were starving to death like mosquitoes in winter. Meanwhile, however, one segment of the populace would turn green if another group happened to have one spoonful more of porridge to eat. Envy undermined the people and drove a wedge between them, a state of affairs voraciously exploited by the government to keep them all under control; it was a policy of divide and conquer. A system was set up whereby informers were royally rewarded. Pissed-off peasants turned in their neighbours as "rebellious elements", and were praised as "loyal subjects of the Emperor". Because of this, the battle between the peasants and the Emperor could never be won by the people, even if they had every reason in the world to kick the parasites out. War and intrigue, hate and envy, betrayal and violence – all combined to bring China's development to a screeching halt.

'When Europe began to set her sights on other parts of the world, sent out explorers to discover new continents and struck it rich with bottomless sources of wealth, the Chinese were busy quarrelling among themselves over who had one grain of rice more or one grain less. The outside world and its new pathways to abundance left us cold. The thinking went as follows: if only I can snatch my neighbour's food out of his mouth, whether by political or military means, then I'll end up rich and happy.

'Despite the never-ending bloodletting and suffering, the Chinese were still managing to hold their heads above water. Until the day, that is, that the European colonials arrived with their cannons and smashed their way through the iron gates of our "Eternal Empire", occupied a portion of the land and trampled our "Divine" superiority under their hairy feet . . . We now realised with a shock that we Chinese were not the only inhabitants of the earth and that there were nations who were stronger than our own, both economically and militarily. This traumatic discovery plunged China into a swamp of confusion. We ultimately found solace in raking up the glorious past of our ancient civilisation. Foaming at the mouth with rage and shame, we called the Europeans "blond apes with the stench of foxes wafting from their armpits". A sick sense of national pride kept us going during this humiliating period. But it did not prevent the Westerners' jeeps, which could easily outrace the Emperor's noblest and fleetest steeds, from rolling right over our self-esteem.

'Now what? Our former government, which was inherently predisposed to despise anything that was new and unfamiliar, finally realised that it was essential to modernise. Our most promising young people were sent abroad to study Western science and culture. When they returned to China, they tried to make reforms, following European models. That, however, was something our traditional leadership could not stomach. They would not stand for their monopoly to be shattered by a bunch of pompous snot-noses who had spent a few years eating raw meat and stinky stuff (by this they meant cheese), and had forgotten their place. And so the conflict between the old guard and the reformers trained in the West flared up . . . flared up . . . flared up . . .'

Like a broken record I was stuck on the last words, repeating them over and over again. I did not know how to go on, because this was the point at which Qin's last lesson had ended.

Qin flung the branch he had been using to make notes in the dirt away from him and got up with difficulty, supporting his back with his hand. He shook his legs, and looked down at his feet.

I waited for his reaction, my heart racing . . .

'You know, Lian, I haven't been giving you history lessons in order to teach you to think so derisively about China's past, nor about Europe's. Your outlook is alarmingly negative and it saddens me greatly . . .'

My nose began to glow. Tears ran down my face. It was true. Ever since Father had left for Gansu, the light in my life had gone out. Qin had listened intently to everything I had to say; he did not seem to have the slightest intention of punishing me, no matter how faulty my interpretation of history might be.

I looked at the long, narrow shadow cast by Qin on to the grass behind him, and an irresistible longing rose in me to call him 'Father'.

Qin shook his head and murmured, 'Lian, I must admit that I don't know what to tell you either. I don't know what attitude you should take. Rationally speaking, I'd say that a pessimistic view of the world is probably unhealthy and wrong-headed, but how can one remain cheerful and optimistic in light of China's recent history? Even I find it a puzzle . . .'

❧

It was only two p.m., but the prisoners had already been excused from their work. In my dormitory everyone was stuffing hessian sacks with dirty laundry and nuts and fruits bought from the peasants. There was singing and exuberant chattering. The atmosphere was festive: they were going home soon.

The happy hum was rudely interrupted by a sudden banging on the door. The voice of a guard was heard: 'Yunxiang Yang, go to the Director's office! At once!'

Suddenly the room was silent as a tomb. All the women stopped what they were doing.

I looked at Mother and wanted to run to her, but my legs would not comply.

Mother, letting her bag tumble to the floor, came over to where I stood rooted to the floor. Making a show of being calm, she patted me on the shoulder, then left without a word.

The noise in the room returned, hesitantly, but this time no one was singing and there was no laughter. Like me, they all shuddered to think what kind of disaster might be hanging over Mother's head.

After a while, she returned. She closed the door behind her and went back to her packing. But seeing the fearful eyes of her room-mates, she reassured them, 'It was nothing, not to worry. A routine check-up. Concerning the visitors we had during our last weekend leave. All I have to do is write down word for word what was said that Sunday, and hand in my report to the authorities.'

The room cheered up again immediately. There was even some joking and ribbing.

I was the only one who did not join in. I understood that the camp authorities were forbidding me from having any further contact with Kim or Kim's mother.

Mother tried to reason with me. 'Lian, they told me that we detainees do not have the right to infect the child of Red proletarian peasant workers with our bourgeois ideas.'

'Mama, I am only thirteen years old. Kim is fifteen. We *never* discuss politics. Can't we just play together?'

I swallowed the rest of what I was going to say, which was: what possible good could it do for the Party to interfere with the most trivial, innocent and personal aspects of our lives, which could never in a million years damage the Dictatorship of the People? The Cultural Revolution was responsible for sending Father away. Now my dearest friend too would vanish from my life. Besides Mother, the only one I had left was Qin.

KIM

My heart had been pounding when I walked into Middle School Number 58 for the very first time last year. In the noisy halls, I made my way through the running boys and giggling girls, hunting for Room 005. That was the classroom assigned to Group 3, Year One – my class.

From one of the rooms came a high-pitched screech.

'I fuck your mother!'

I was involuntarily drawn to the open door from which the cursing was issuing. On the door was the number I was looking for: 005. Inside, something was writhing on the floor, close to the dais. It turned out to be a girl, lying flat on her face. The seat of her raggedy trousers was marked with the dusty imprint of a shoe. She picked herself up almost immediately, her face twisted with pain, wiped some blood from her upper lip and dusted her trousers off as well as she could. Not a trace of tears in her eyes. And yet this was a girl!

Everyone in the classroom was staring, eyes wide as saucers. I could hear their brains working: What more perfect target could we possibly find to piss on?

A short, athletic son-of-a-bitch in a Mao suit leaped high into the air like a master of Kung Fu and delivered a second bone-crushing kick. This time the girl banged her head against the wooden rim of the blackboard as she fell. A shiny lump bulged almost immediately from her forehead.

'I fuck your grandmother on your father's side!' Spitefully, hysterically, without the least sign of vulnerability, she spat the curse at her tormentor.

I remained stock still, as if turned to stone. I had heard how, in secondary school, certain 'class scapegoats' became the designated butts of merciless teasing, but I hadn't expected it to be this bad.

As the little girl shuffled to her chair, another mean brat emptied a wastebasket over her head. She shook the rubbish out of her bird's-nest shock of hair, and scolded, 'I fuck your whole entire family tree all in one go!'

Ppfft . . . It cracked me up. Hats off to her! I was hugely impressed with the verbal inventiveness of a girl who, in the depths of her misery, was still capable of taking a run-of-the-mill curse and giving it such an apt and sweeping twist.

'Hee-hee, ha-ha-ha!' The entire classroom, prostrate with glee, cheered the bullies on. I balled my fists. I'd have liked to yell at my classmates: You sadistic devils, what's the matter with you, did you flush your consciences down the toilet with your shit? But I knew all too well that that was not a wise thing to do.

～

The scapegoat's name was Kim Zhang. Not a day went by that she wasn't tormented. One wise guy would sharpen his pencil and then calmly sprinkle the shavings over her head; another hid her textbooks in the boys' toilets. But Kim stood her ground. She did not cry, nor did she surrender. The one thing she did do was to keep up a constant string of curses. She knew that tears would not soften her fiendish torturers' granite hearts.

Teasing her became the class obsession. The goal, of course, was to bring her to her knees and make her beg them to stop. But she refused to give them that: capitulation was out of the question. There was nothing for it but to continue to pester her, which they did, teeth clenched, with grim determination.

I gradually came to discover the 'reason' for this abuse, or what Kim had done to 'earn' her mistreatment. The class was composed of a mix of the three social castes, trapped in a pecking-order which ordained that its members must despise, humiliate and oppress each other. This kind of arrangement cries out for a victim, someone who can be singled out as the general scapegoat, thus providing a common exhaust-vent for all the envy, prejudice, frustration and vindictiveness arising out of the caste system, allowing everyone to let off a little steam.

Kim fit all the requirements of 'class scapegoat'. First of all, her father was a peasant worker, which classified her as a member of the lowest caste; and, second, he performed the most menial, low-paid, dirty and demeaning work you could get.

THE BLACK SNOWMAN

I had met Kim's father once. It had been two years beforehand, on a cold winter afternoon. The biting wind whistling through the bare tree branches whipped my face with sharp, icy smacks. I was walking along a street that climbed uphill steeply. Suddenly a lumbering mountain of coal loomed up ahead of me. I jumped back, and looked at the black mound with interest. It appeared to be composed of hundreds of stacked 'beehives', the kind of coal used in cooking. The rickshaw's wheels were almost squashed flat by the enormous load. I peered left and right, but couldn't see a driver. The mountain of coal blocked my line of sight completely.

What was I waiting for? I slapped myself on both cheeks, for being such a cretin. Tossing my satchel over my shoulder, I leaned forward and began to push. At first no matter how hard I pushed, the cart plodded forward at the same steady pace, just like in a nightmare when you are trying to run away but you don't get anywhere. Only the drops of sweat plopping on to my quilted jacket were proof that I wasn't dreaming.

The street was deserted. The wind had died down suddenly. The only thing I could hear was someone panting and the creaking of the pushcart's shaft. I braced my back and calf muscles and planted my feet more firmly on the ground. The mound of coal began moving a little faster as the road started dipping down. At last the cart rolled along smoothly. I quickly walked around to the front, and there I saw the driver. He wasn't sitting down. It was he who had been pulling the cart the whole way.

Now that he didn't have to work quite so hard, he turned to me. Something white slashed across his coal-black face – he was smiling at me. His teeth contrasted starkly with his black skin.

I had to suppress the urge to run. I could never bear it when people tried to thank me for something; a terrible shyness would come over me and I wouldn't know where to look. But I couldn't just walk away. I looked at him without blinking. His head was like a steamer: perspiration created a halo of hot air around his face. He took a rag the colour of anthracite from his neck and used it to wipe away the sweat pouring down. One, two, three light-brown streaks now appeared on his face. His real skin colour was now visible. It was tan, not black.

To conceal my amazement I started kicking at a few pebbles that were suddenly in my way. Again I peeked at the man inquisitively. He was very small for a grown-up, not much over five foot. His chest was concave, his torso hollow. I looked at his emaciated limbs and wondered where he got the brute strength to pull such a massive load. I didn't dare ask: Why do you accept such a crummy job? I knew you weren't supposed to be that direct.

The thing that made it even worse was that he had to do his work in public, in full sight of the pedestrians, the bicyclists and the people riding by in buses, his back bowed like a prawn, smothered in coal-dust from head to toe, like a black version of the abominable snowman.

> *If you're starving, smack your cheeks until they puff up*
> *Then no one will see how skinny you are*

It was a piece of wisdom no self-respecting Chinese could afford to ignore: any hardship is bearable as long as others don't find out about it. People despised Kim's father mainly because he was unable to avoid the biggest disgrace of all: he was obliged to endure his miserable lot in the open, for all to see.

THE PROPAGANDA BOARD

At ten o'clock the school bell clanged its promise of reprieve. The students flew out of the classroom like birds out of an opened cage, the girls twittering with the latest gossip, the boys hurtling head over heels down the corridor like rockets in flight. Two girls stayed behind in the classroom: Kim and me.

Over this past week, Kim had been learning the hard way how risky it was for her to find herself within range of her fellow students. The moment she had set foot in the hallway five days earlier, she had given them the inspiration for a whole new contest: to see who could aim the most kicks at Kim's backside within a set timespan.

The girls turned their noses up at this game – but not because they disapproved of the abuse, not that: on the contrary, they felt Kim was asking for it. If she weren't so pitiful and repulsive, the boys wouldn't feel so obliged to beat her up. Be that as it may, it was a good idea for Kim to stay out of their way during recess.

I had twisted my ankle in gym; today I too remained behind in the classroom. My desk was three rows behind Kim's.

Kim looked over her shoulder, and stared at the brightly painted notice board hanging on the back wall. She hesitated, then stood up cautiously and shuffled towards it, one step at a time.

The notice board was the same size as the blackboard at the front of the classroom. Its official name was 'the Political Battlefield', but it had been dubbed the 'propaganda board' by the students. It boasted an artful patchwork of articles and political commentaries, written in coloured chalk, extolling the *Father Who Is More Dear Than Our Biological Fahter, Who At The Same Time Is The Mother Who Is More Caring Than Our Real Mother, Who Is, Besides, The Lover Who Is More Passionate Than All Lovers Of The World Combined, And Who Above All Is The Mistress More Tender Than All The Mistresses Of The World Rolled Into One.* Here for instance one might learn which political campaign was in full swing at that moment, or what new slogan Mao had concocted; Mao's most recent decrees were set out in language plain enough for children to understand. Thus one might learn that Mao's order to smash Confucius really meant that 'we must cook the Foreign Minister's goose'. What exactly the connection was between the great philosopher who had had the wisdom to go to his grave a good two thousand years before Mao's reign and the Minister alive today, was never fully explained. Other articles dealt with the behaviour of individual students. Revolutionary elements were extolled; bourgeois-minded individuals were condemned. For example, our classmate Shunzi was singled out one time for washing the classroom windows 'on the quiet'. Apparently, this was proof of his proletarian belief in Mao's creed:

> *Serve the people industriously,*
> *Like a water buffalo ploughing the rice field*

Around the strips of text, there were usually drawings of a red sun – symbolising the Great Helmsman – encircled by sunflowers, representing a docile populace. Here or there a stem of roses or a nosegay of violets had been added by way of decoration. The colourful bulletin board was a feast for the eye, and therefore always a big attraction.

The board had just been revised; Kim wanted to read what it said now. I wiggled my ankle left to right to see if it still hurt. Not too bad, fortunately. Struggling to my feet, I had started to limp over to the board, when I saw the muscles in Kim's neck tense up; she sidled from the lead article she had been perusing to the right-hand side. My heart shrank: was Kim really *that* scared of me? I was within fifteen feet of the board, and halted. Suddenly I didn't feel like reading it any more.

Kim was rooted to the spot. I could tell from her tense posture that she was in a turmoil. She did not seem to know what to do. To show Kim there was nothing to worry about, I walked up to the board. But before I knew it Kim had already scooted over to the far right edge, where there was nothing to read but the wooden frame.

I moved to the other end of the board, to show there was no need to duck out of my way. But my gesture was pointless. She stayed put, as if her feet were nailed to the floor. There was only one thing to do: I would have to say something.

But fear pinched my throat shut. I had never seen anyone address a word to Kim – unless screams and curses counted as words. If I talked to Kim, I would be alienating myself from my classmates. They would start avoiding me as a traitor to my own caste. On the other hand – and for once I had something to thank the Party for – I could stick it to them with a dose of their own medicine: after all, the Wisest Leader of All Time was always insisting that it was the peasant workers who were the superior class, and that all other classes were to be re-educated by them. Mao's teachings were one thing, but real life was another matter – the peasants were still regarded as doormats for the other castes to wipe their feet on. However, no one could get away with openly berating me for showing compassion for the lowlifes. The classmates could gossip and criticise me to their hearts' content, but they would have to keep it under their hats, even if it was hard to imagine why I would want to befriend a peasant. Only a show-off would do such a thing, in the hope of convincing the Leader that he – or she – was following His words to the letter. Someone like that was obviously a stinking hypocrite, an arse-licker! And if that wasn't a motivation, well then, I *had* to be a complete imbecile. And yet I wasn't deterred, not even by these rules of etiquette. My privileged position as a first-caster, the only child of a university lecturer and a cardiologist, made me so sure of myself that I felt I could afford to stick my neck out a little. And, besides, I would see to it that my sympathy for Kim remained a secret.

The coast was clear. There was no one else in the classroom. 'Come on over here, Kim,' I said as nonchalantly as I could, 'let's read the lead article together' – as if it were the most normal thing in the world for me to be talking to a third-caster.

Kim jerked her head round like a stalked deer, and stared at me. Deep wrinkles scurried across her face. What the hell was this? A first-caster talking to her, and in such a friendly tone too?

In order to convince Kim that my intentions were strictly on the level, I took a few steps forward, with a smile on my face. But Kim, in a panic, pushing tables and chairs out of her way, ran to safety – her seat in the front row, by the dais. The teachers made her sit there, right under their noses, so that no one would dare pester her during the lesson.

A THIRD-CASTE CITIZEN

Even though there were only two children in Kim's family – Kim herself and her little sister Jiening – their per capita income was only eleven yuan per month, or less than half that of a first-caster. Kim's mother did not have a steady job. Sometimes she found a little something on the side that let her chip in towards the family's livelihood. One of the few ways in which the unemployed like herself could earn a few coins was by making matchboxes. First she would have to go fetch a stack of pre-printed three-by-five-feet cardboard sheets. The printed shapes had to be cut out, folded into little box-shapes, and then glued in place. For every one hundred matchboxes she was paid a mao, or ten fen. If she worked at it from early in the morning until late at night, she could get five hundred done. That meant a day's earnings of fifty fen. Thirty days times fifty fen was fifteen yuan, or half of what her husband made. Not bad for a 'piece of cheap goods', as women were generally called.

Unfortunately, she was unable to fold matchboxes for fourteen hours a day straight; she suffered from dizzy spells. According to her sister Xiuhua, she suffered from a lack of red blood cells. If you asked me, she was just suffering from a lack of food.

As for Kim herself, she was quite a case. She simply looked a fright. Her face resembled a kiwi-fruit – not a regular kiwi, but one that's accidentally been stepped on. It was sunken, gaunt, with a greenish-yellow cast. She had the figure of a ten-year-old, whereas she was actually two years older than the rest of the class, having been kept back a year. Her hair was an angry jungle; it got washed and combed once a year if it was lucky. When I was up close enough, I'd nearly throw up from the smell. Two muddy rivulets oozed from Kim's nostrils to her mouth. When – *chaaachch!* – she snorted, the stream returned to the source; but if she was concentrating on something else and wasn't careful, it would drip on to her notebook. Since she could not afford gloves, in the winter her hands turned into beet-red, puffy claws with purple welts on them. These boils would erupt eventually, disgorging blood and pus. Her hands smelled like putrid rats.

Her clothes were a horror, men's hand-me-downs. I didn't need to be a rocket scientist to guess they had been cut down from the overalls her father was issued with once a year. Her father knew how to make one pair of overalls last three years, thus saving the other two for his family. Kim's mother did the alterations, turning the overalls into two jackets and two pairs of trousers. There was nothing to be done about the trousers' flies, of course. Kim looked ridiculous: what kind of girl wore trousers that had an opening in the front?

In fact, it was hard to tell Kim was a girl. She did not behave like one. Women might be treated like dirt, but if they didn't act feminine, their lives were not worth living. If a girl needed to move a table – no matter how light it was – she would pretend she didn't have the strength to pick it up. She was then supposed to utter a plaintive sigh loud enough to attract the attention of a boy standing as far as thirty feet away. The boy, his male ego inflamed, would snarl at the girl to get lost and proceed to lift the table with one hand. A man who treated a woman with deference was accused of being a faggot or a spineless dick.

Kim never asked a boy for help. She steered clear of getting snubbed that way, since no self-respecting boy would have lifted a finger for her in any case. But Kim could easily lift two tables at the same time, and plonk them down wherever they were needed. That was how she got the moniker 'wild boar'. I was surprised to observe that skinny little Kim seemed to have inherited her father's bear-strength.

No one had ever seen Kim cry. It was hard to believe: who had ever heard of a woman who did not have it in her to dab away a few tears? Especially a girl like Kim, who had all the reason in the world to weep.

The last, but certainly not the least important reason that Kim had been designated class scapegoat, was that she was a bad student. Hadn't she been made to repeat a year? Ninety-nine per cent of the students passed effortlessly up to the next level. The educational institutions were bursting at the seams. The teachers, turning a blind eye, usually promoted even the most indifferent students to the next year. Only those who truly could not get a handle on the material were singled out.

Kim did not create any extra work for the teachers; they did not even bother to read her homework or tests. They would give her a thirty per cent without looking – and even that was considered generous. She never asked any questions in class, even when she understood nothing. She would just gaze at the teacher with a thoughtful expression. And so she spared him the trouble of having to explain all over again the basic principles that she ought to have mastered a year ago. Kim refused to grant her classmates the pernicious pleasure they were after. Just think how those scoundrels would hoot and honk if Kim admitted she could not follow the lesson!

Yet she still came to school faithfully, every day. Staying home would only mean having to construct matchboxes; and she already had too many chores to do after school as it was.

THE THREE VIRTUES

Three days had passed since Kim had panicked and fled from me at the propaganda board. I had thought up a strategy to rescue Kim from her status as the scapegoat: I would help her get voted Student of the Three Virtues.

The Three Virtues were:

1. Harbouring proletarian, in other words progressive, sentiments
2. Passing with high marks in all subjects
3. Possessing good athletic skills and enjoying excellent health

The election was held twice a year: in February, before the Chinese New Year, and in July, before the summer holiday. Out of every hundred students, four were ordained to be chosen. In a class of sixty, therefore, one or two students possessed the necessary virtues to qualify. In theory, everyone could aspire to this distinction, irrespective of class or caste. If Kim were to become one of the chosen few, then her classmates would definitely have to think twice before kicking her in the shins.

Kim automatically fit the first criterion. As the daughter of a peasant worker, her sentiments had to be, by definition, proletarian. In practice, being proletarian meant being enthusiastic about hard, dirty labour, and not giving a damn about any sort of physical or mental hardship. Above all, you had to prove that you would blindly follow the Party's decrees.

The second criterion posed somewhat more of a challenge. In order to score high marks in her studies, Kim had some serious catching up to do, so I decided I would help Kim with her homework, and would tutor her as well. It would probably take a while, and some doing, but it offered the hope that Kim might some day be accepted as a respected member of the class.

In the third category Kim was a natural. Small and skinny as she was,

Kim was as strong as an ox. With regular training and workouts, she stood a good chance of coming first in several of the Autumn Games. That would clinch the third of the Three Virtues.

The mill that was my brain stopped grinding for a moment. It suddenly occurred to me that I was making plans for someone I had never even exchanged a word with. Something had to be done about that – but what? I did not dare speak to her openly in school. After school, then? I could go to Kim's house. But that would mean crossing the caste barriers. The very idea sent shivers down my spine.

THE PROPOSAL

Was I willing to defy the unspoken rule that peasants and intellectuals must not associate? That went without saying. Once I got an idea in my head, I didn't let the grass grow under my feet.

At two o'clock the school bell rang. It was a Saturday, when school finished an hour earlier. The students fought their way out of the classroom as if there were man-eating sharks snapping at their heels. Kim remained seated, patiently waiting her turn to leave the room – last. I looked out the window. The ripe autumn sun spread its arms out wide, and a comforting warmth poured from its breast; it told me to take heart and not be nervous. This is *the* moment to make my proposal to Kim, I told myself. I took out a notebook from my bag, studied it intently, then put it back, only to take it out again – so that it wouldn't look as if I was deliberately stalling.

The classroom was now empty, except for Kim and me. Outside the sun shone so fiercely on the trees that you'd have thought the leaves were made of crystal.

'Kim, I was thinking, the Autumn Games are in one month's time. You are such a good long-distance runner, so I . . .'

Kim looked at me in astonishment and puckered her face so that in the sunlight it looked like a pressed-out orange.

I went on unperturbed: 'With regular training, you might even finish first in the fifteen hundred metres. Do you feel like working out for it, with me as your partner? We could do it every morning, before school starts.' I'd blurted out my pre-rehearsed monologue in one breath. It had also taken every ounce of energy I possessed. Leaning heavily on a table, I waited nervously for Kim's reply.

Kim's little-old-man's features were knitted into a thin-lipped frown. The rest of her body was as rigid as a broomstick. I bit my lip to hold back the flood of words welling up out of my heart: Kim, please believe me, I am not your enemy, but your 'sister'. But my tongue was twisted into a knot.

Outside the crickets' chirping continued unabated; sparrows were idly nattering away, and raucous crows were making an ear-splitting racket. But inside, it was ominously quiet. Finally I could not stand it any longer – I *had* to break the silence.

'Kim, maybe you think I'm not good enough to train with you? I can run too, you know. Want to see how fast I am?'

Kim was standing with her back to the window. The sun had sketchily outlined her silhouette on the floor. A few seconds had elapsed since my outburst. Suddenly the shadow sprang to life. *Dongg!* Kim flipped her satchel on to her bony back, pounded her fist on the table and screeched, 'You rich parasite! Just *fuck* off!'

Unnerved, I took a step backwards, banging my legs against the table I had been leaning on.

Outside, the sparrows had meanwhile switched from idle gossip to professing their love for each other. Inside you could have heard a pin drop.

SWEET POTATOES

The clear blue sky was festooned with fleecy clouds; a sweet smell hovered in the air. I sniffed deeply and tried to figure out where it was coming from. It was drifting from the apartment kitchen windows, redolent of . . . Of course! Sweet potato season had arrived! My nostrils twitched; the heavenly aroma sent me dreaming . . .

The saying 'Baked sweet potatoes are just as delicious as roasted chestnuts' twanged like music in my ears. All the children were crazy about them, and I was no exception, especially since the strictly rationed sugar was sampled by the granule, so that I was always on the lookout for something sweet to eat. The yams were a delightfully welcome supplement to the monotonous diet.

But when I thought of the endless queues of people meandering outside the stores, I lost heart. Even if I mustered the stamina to wait it out with the others, I didn't see how it would pay off. Even with the best will in the world you were lucky if even half of your family's ten-pound ration could be declared edible. The rest you might as well throw out on the spot. Some of the tubers had bruises all over, oozing a slimy, smelly fluid; others were flecked with black spots, and, once cooked, they tasted of sawdust. The store clerks who unloaded the trucks always selected the best specimens for themselves first; then the driver would be told to dump the rest of the perishable shipment on to the bare ground. So the foodstuff of my dreams was left to rot out in the open, with nothing to shield it from frost or wet snow.

Kim's mother grew her own sweet potatoes. Since as third-casters they were not entitled to a State-owned apartment, Kim's parents had decided ten years ago to build their own house of mud. The only land they could find to build on was on the outskirts of the city, next to a muddy swamp that was used by the locals as a place to empty their chamber pots. Since most people were afraid of the water rats that terrorised that neighbourhood, this particular lot was still vacant. Kim's parents were elated. They built a little house, with a kitchen garden around it, where Kim's mother grew vegetables and grain. That was how Kim's home came to be stocked with dozens of pounds of delicious sweet potatoes every year. And she made sure her drooling classmates knew it, too.

One day Kim came to school with her trouser pockets stuffed with yams. At recess she took one out. First she peeled it with her teeth. Quite a bit of flesh still clung to the peel, but she just calmly spat it out – *poo-ah!* Her classmates stared at the floor, only barely managing to restrain themselves.

Kim closed her eyes deliberately and moaned, 'Mmmmm . . .' with her mouth full, just to annoy them. As she chewed, the others masticated right along with her; when she swallowed, they gulped too. The climax was reached when she decided she had had her fill and threw the half-eaten potato – *pjah!* – on to the dusty floor. It took an iron will not to give in to the urge to kneel down and wolf down Kim's leftovers.

Those few days when the sweet potatoes were harvested in her mother's vegetable garden were the only yearly island of happiness in Kim's otherwise mongrel existence. The potatoes were her sweet revenge.

I was so deeply engrossed in thought that I hadn't even noticed that I had reached the school gate. The sweet potatoes had given me an idea, but I needed time to work out my plan in peace. There would be ample opportunity for that in political education class, during Mr Kong's routine sermon on the importance of the class struggle.

At a quarter past four, I was waiting for Kim at the exit. As soon as Kim appeared, I began whirling my satchel around like a windmill run amuck. Pens, pencils, erasers, books and notebooks rained down on my head. My bag must not have been fastened properly. I must have presented a ridiculous sight, but I didn't care, as long as I got Kim's attention.

Kim paused for a moment, then gave me a wide berth. I cried, 'Yippee – my aunt from Qingdao is coming for a visit! She's bringing us a whole bag full of sweet potatoes!'

Kim spat on the ground and mocked, 'Oh dear, such a sad case. And she doesn't even realise *how* tragic she is!'

The fish was nibbling at the hook.

I threw down my satchel and snapped, indignantly: 'What do you mean?'

'*I* don't need any uncles or aunties to bring me sweet potatoes. In our vegetable garden, even the rats have had their fill of that garbage!'

I held my stomach as if my sides would split with laughter. 'It's only four o'clock. Don't you see that it's still light out? Yet it's clear you are already in the land of nod! Who would allow sweet potatoes to rot in their beds? Next you'll have me believe the sun's going to come up in the West tomorrow!'

'Come see for yourself! Our vegetable garden is a treasure trove.' Kim grabbed me by my left wrist. It was like being caught in a monkey-wrench. After putting up a half-hearted struggle, I meekly allowed myself to be towed to Kim's house.

After a few steps, Kim let go of my wrist. The indignant expression on her face had made way for the hooded caution that was the secret of her survival. To the right of the school gate there was a wide asphalt road leading to the 'row-house quarter' of the second-casters. Behind it lay the third-casters' 'mud-hut quarter'. The road narrowed as the row-house barracks came into sight.

Kim walked quickly, looking neither right nor left. With Kim at my side, I felt safe. The black-topped road became a path of cracked, chipped concrete blocks. Barely a yard back from the path, the row-house barracks began. Each consisted of a single room that housed an entire family, no matter how large. In most cases, eight or so family members were squeezed into a room twelve-foot square. There was a puddle of greenish-yellow ice in front of every door.

Pooff! I slipped and fell headlong on the ice. Kim, noting my clumsiness with disdain, never slackened her pace. I scrambled to my feet as fast as I could and ran to catch up with Kim.

Tyaaaah . . . Right in front of us, a ramshackle door creaked open. 'Watch your clothes!' A woman of about forty stepped outside with a slop bucket. Kim hauled me back three steps just in time and – *huaah!* – a sheet of light-green liquid waste splashed on to the ground. So *that* was where the green ice came from!

The smell of a public latrine, some one hundred and fifty yards further on, wafted out to greet us. There was one such facility for every four blocks of dwellings, which meant that it served forty families, or over three hundred people. But who in his right mind braved the cold in the middle of the night to make that long trip just to pee? Twenty yards further on there was a cement water trough; the spout was wrapped in straw. This was where all the inhabitants within a two-hundred-yard radius came to fetch their drinking water.

A young boy ran out of one of the rooms to my left. Someone shouted after him, 'Shut the door!'

These dwellings had no entry porches; most of the doors had quilted blankets hanging over them to keep out the cold.

The cement path became a dirt road. I could feel the frozen wagon ruts through my soles. The colour of the houses changed from rusty brick to yellow mud. Bits of straw stuck out of the walls. We had arrived in the mud-hut quarter.

The road zig-zagged here, since the dwellings were not State-built, but cobbled together by the peasant workers themselves, without planning ordinances. Most of the houses were encircled by high walls. The traditional Chinese building style had been preserved here: this was one place where the government had nothing to say.

Tyeeee! creaked the cornstalk gate. We were in the courtyard of Kim's house.

'Mama, a visitor!'

Gruuhn, gruuhn, snorted two coal-black pigs waddling across my path. A white hen flapped its wings and jumped on to the window-sill. From the mud kitchen that was just big enough to stand up in, a wafer-thin, wrinkled woman appeared. She wiped her hands on her apron and hurried towards me. Greeting me with a nod, she puffed at the wisps of hair that dangled over her eyes like a feather duster, allowing me a glimpse of what lurked underneath. Awe and deference gave the creased face a somewhat comic aspect.

'Oh dear Grandpa Heaven, what an auspicious wind we must be having today, that brings such an azalea of a young lady to our humble slum! Come in, come in please. Careful, don't step in the pig's droppings. Sorry about the mess. Oh, I ought to hide my old face in shame! I didn't get around to sweeping out the yard yet. You see, Miss,' – she pointed at a large wooden tub in the kitchen, 'I've been doing laundry all day.' Craning her neck, she shouted at a shadow inside the room, 'Kim's father, we have a distinguished visitor.'

I made to step inside, but Kim's mother slipped in ahead of me like an eel.

'Kim's father, here, cover your knees with this coat,' she ordered, all the while grinning shyly at her guest.

My pupils had to dilate as wide as they could. The room's sole window had no glass, only a piece of yellowed rice paper. I could barely make out the furnishings: a kang and a wooden stand with a washbasin.

'Please sit down,' said the shadow sitting on the kang. That must be Kim's father. From the sound of his voice I could tell he had a pipe clenched between his teeth. He moved over to make room for me on the bed.

'Good afternoon, Uncle Zhang,' I said shyly.

'Please don't laugh at Kim's father.' The mother did not know what to do with her hands. 'He's a bit of a sight today, because he's wearing an old pair of trousers of mine. You see, I was just washing his clothes.'

'Shut your damn snout, woman!' The man, raising his voice, snatched a blanket and covered his – or, to be precise, his wife's – trousers with it.

'You don't have to feel ashamed in front of this young lady, Kim's father. All these many years of mine, worn-out mule that I am, have taught me how to read people. See, she has a nice face, she could be one of us.' Smiling, she bustled over to me and went on, 'Tomorrow my husband is going to a wedding – the wedding of the youngest nephew of Kim's aunt's brother-in-law on the father's side. He should look neat, don't you agree? That's why I decided to give his clothes a good soak, for once. Hey, old man, what do you think, will they be dry by tomorrow afternoon?'

'Mama, do you think my classmate has come to listen to your stories?' Kim complained.

'Now that you mention it – you're right! Girl, go get some firewood. We must make a pot of tea for our guest.' She pulled her jacket up, puckering her eyes shut in concentration; she was fumbling for something hanging from her cloth belt. Finally she had it: it was a little key. She crawled to a wooden box on the kang, pried it open and took out a jar of tealeaves, still completely sealed.

I hesitated. Then I said, 'Aunt Zhang, I don't need any tea.'

'Don't you like tea? Shall I make you some egg-drop soup?' She bent down to take an earthenware bowl filled with rice from under the kang. She put her hand inside and stirred around in the rice. Her cheeks were flushed. She was muttering. 'Where did they get to? Whatever happened to them? Oh, of course, I nearly forgot . . . Jiening got the last egg last week, when she had the flu.' Peering outside, she fluted, 'Ko-o-o-kokoko! Whitey! Come here!'

The designated chicken ignored the summons. Kim's mother ran outside to try to catch her. Whitey flapped her wings. Feathers scattered into the air, drifting down to earth again like snow. The mother picked up a straw basket and pitched it neatly over the recalcitrant chicken. Holding the animal tightly under her arm, she skilfully pressed her thumb and index finger down on its posterior. After a minute she said, disappointed, 'I don't feel a lump inside her. No eggs today.'

'*Mo-o-o-ther!*' Kim stamped her feet and said, 'Lian came to look at the sweet potatoes in the vegetable garden. She doesn't need egg-drop soup.'

'Oh, you like sweet potatoes? Oh, you should have said that at once!' Her face lit up at once. 'Kim, take a shovel from the kitchen and dig up as many potatoes as the young lady desires.' Visibly relieved, she walked to the kitchen, sat down on a stool, pulled the wooden tub towards her and went back to scouring the clothes against the washboard.

We were about to go into the garden when a fragile little voice piped up out of the darkness. 'So – does this elegant young lady run out of food towards the end of the month, same as us?'

I peered at the kang. Sure enough, there was someone else sitting there: Kim's little sister Jiening, who had kept quiet until now. Kim pretended not to hear and gestured to me that I should just ignore her. The mother lifted her hands, which had turned purple in the ice-cold water, from the washtub and bellowed in the direction of the voice, 'Jiening! Don't talk such rot! The young lady is in the mood for sweet potatoes because she's getting sick of that expensive wheat flour and rice that she has to eat *all* the time.'

Something hanging down from the roof caught my eye: sweet-potato rings braided into strips, at least twenty of them. Of course! The peasant workers probably hoarded this food as emergency rations for the end of the month, when all the housekeeping money had run out. What a spoiled, greedy sow I was – how could I even *think* of making off with their rainy-day supplies!

As soon as Kim had planted her shovel in the earth, I blurted out, 'There *is* no aunt from Qingdao who brings us sweet potatoes. I made it up, just so I could talk to you. See, otherwise you'd never have let me come home with you.' Kim left the shovel parked right where it was. I could tell, from the square set of her jaw, that she was gritting her teeth; I expected a furious outburst.

There was a long silence. No reaction. I hardly dared look at Kim. Was Kim speechless with emotion, perhaps, over my attempt to make friends with her?

Another minute went by. Still no reaction. Kim yanked the shovel out of the ground and walked back inside. She knelt down by the stove and pulled out three sweet potatoes from a hole underneath, where they had been roasted to perfection in the hot ashes. Mmm, they smell of honey, I thought. Kim stuffed the treats into my jacket pockets and dragged me into the kitchen: 'Mama, Lian prefers roasted sweet potatoes. I've given her three of them. Now she has to go home.'

Kim pushed me out the door. 'Just say you're lost, if our neighbours ask what you're doing around here.' She shut the door on me.

All the way home, I tried to figure it out. Was Kim angry because I had lied? Or was she happy that I was trying to be her friend . . . ?

A PALE ATHLETE

At five minutes to eight the next morning I was seated at my desk. I craned my neck to spy the arrival of my 'friend'. Two endless minutes later, Kim finally slunk in. As was her wont, she hung her head and avoided eye contact with her classmates. When she was still quite a distance from her seat, she bent her legs and upper body, as if about to sit down – trying to make herself small, and a less obvious target of her classmates' mischief.

Until that moment, I had hoped that Kim would look my way and give me some secret signal. How naïve of me! Whatever made me think I had the right to expect anything like that? Never looking round, Kim flopped down in her seat and gazed blankly at the teacher, as usual.

$\sim$

I fumbled in my satchel, waiting for the classroom to empty. I didn't have the guts to talk to Kim again: it might be misconstrued. But what was I doing there, then? My desire to be Kim's friend overrode my common sense. I believed in miracles.

In the meantime, the classroom had emptied. I was alone with Kim once again. My nerves were wound so tight that they set off a loud din inside my head.

Kim got up and walked to the door. The cacophony in my head got worse, it sounded like a hurricane bellowing in there.

Kim turned towards me. It was like watching a silent movie – I couldn't hear a thing, but I could see Kim's lips move. The monotone ringing in my ears cut out all other sounds. *Wohwohwohwhooon* . . . It took all my courage to stand up and ask, 'What was that you said, Kim?'

Kim frowned, sent me a puzzled look, and repeated, 'Tomorrow morning, at six thirty, at your gate'. Then she ran off as fast as she could.

It couldn't be true! Not only had Kim spoken to me, she was apparently going along with my suggestion of training for the Autumn Games together. She had even given me a time to meet!

At six twenty-five, I was waiting at the gate of the enclave in which I lived. In the presence of the first-caste host, there was generally no need for the extremely thorough and demeaning grilling to which the sentries routinely subjected third-caste citizens like Kim. To get warm, I stamped my feet on the frozen ground. The sky was a thick black sheet. If I hadn't been standing under the gatehouse lamp, I would have been unable to make out my ten fingers held up in front of me.

Kim arrived at six thirty on the dot.

'Good morning!' I said.

No greeting in reply.

I fumbled for a topic of conversation. 'Cold, isn't it!'

Kim had no opinion on the subject.

'Our campus athletics field is a ten-minute walk from here. Let's run there, shall we?'

I took off on the double and Kim followed in silence. Soon we arrived at the athletics field, which was already crowded with people exercising. The earth droned under our feet. The wind battered my cheeks and made my skin tingle. 'Let's warm up first,' I suggested.

After warming up, I said, 'Shall we practise for the fifteen hundred metres?'

To my surprise, this time Kim had something to say.

'I'd rather do the two thousand,' she said.

At the starting line, Kim halted. She picked up her shabbily shod right foot and put it down behind her left. I had already crossed the line, but Kim caught up with me within fractions of a second.

At the end of the first four-hundred-metre lap, my legs were rubbery with fatigue. I collapsed on to the ground beside the track. The frost had turned the grass into a carpet of needles. Good enough for a first try, anyway, I consoled myself.

The black sheet in the sky was turning light grey. I could now make out the silhouettes of the other runners. Kim's skinny form was approaching the starting line. She was about to finish her second lap.

The sheet became translucent. I could now clearly distinguish Kim as she raced by. And I noticed something strange: unlike the other runners, who were all red in the face, Kim's face was as white as wax. The other runners' forms were all outlined in a halo of steaming sweat, but Kim was as dry as cork. The thing that alarmed me most was that the longer Kim ran, the more ashen she seemed to get. Yet she was still overtaking the others one by one, at breakneck speed. She wasn't even panting; her face remained expressionless. She looked like a running cadaver!

For some reason, I couldn't help being in awe of this odd, tight-lipped girl. Her whole being radiated a determination so intense it was almost scary. Kim's fierce willpower pushed her to completing a third, fourth, fifth and sixth lap, and still she showed no sign of quitting. She had now covered two thousand eight hundred metres . . .

After a while she rejoined me. She was holding her sides, as if trying to make more room for air. But soon she got her breath back. 'I must say there are a lot of people out, so early in the morning,' was her attempt at conversation.

This time the roles were reversed. I could think of nothing to say.

'If I train every day, I should have a chance of coming in first in the Autumn Games, don't you think?'

It was the first time I had heard her speak with confidence. I wanted to say, 'You bet!', but my voice refused to co-operate. I grabbed Kim's arm to convince myself I wasn't dreaming, that it really was Kim standing there. This morning I had seen quite a different Kim. This Kim was indefatigable, and made straight for her goal.

CAUGHT IN THE ACT

Too-woooo! A whistle announced the imminent departure of the dump trucks. I raced from the barracks to the convoy that would take us away from the camp. Home! That prospect made me so happy that I tossed all my worries over my shoulder.

In my dash to the trucks, I caught a glimpse out of the corner of my eye of Mrs Tang, looking very glum. She looked like she had been crying. And just before home-leave, too! On board the truck, I kept an eye out for her – but Mrs Tang was nowhere to be seen, on any of the four vehicles.

'Mama, isn't Mrs Tang going home?'

Mother pressed her knuckles hard against my lips. An icy shudder ran down my spine, for suddenly all the other passengers were looking at me.

As soon as we were home, I demanded: 'Come on, Mama, please tell me what was the matter with Mrs Tang.'

Mother's eyes narrowed so dangerously that they resembled a pair of razorblades.

'Okay, if you don't want to tell me, I'll just ask the others, back in camp.'

That certainly was the way to rile Mother. She flung her hessian sack at the wall and screeched, 'If you even dare to do that, I'll rip your mouth open from ear to ear!'

This was getting exciting. It must be something serious, to make Mother react like this. I ignored the threat and began to unpack my bag, with exaggerated calmness.

Mother stomped up to me and declared, 'Lian, if you want to be released from camp someday all in one piece, you've got to get out of the habit of sticking your nose into other people's business.'

I kept my mouth shut. I knew that if I did not respond, Mother wouldn't know what to do. Mother was obviously scared to death that I might start asking questions about Mrs Tang.

'Okay, Lian, you little pest. I'll tell you what's the matter with Mrs Tang. On one condition: you must *promise* you'll never discuss it with anyone.'

I pulled Mother over to the sofa in the living room. We sat down, our clothes still dusty from the trip, our hands and faces crusty with sand. Mother said, 'Eight days ago, in the middle of the night – you were asleep – the Tangs were caught in the act. In a cave, at the back of the lake.'

Shocked, I asked, 'Did they murder someone?'

'No . . . You are too young to understand . . . They were just . . . they were making love.'

'Is that all?'

'It is one of the most serious counter-revolutionary crimes!'

'The Director and the guards do it with their wives, don't they? What *is* this? Doesn't everyone do it? Where do all those millions of Chinese come from, otherwise?'

'See, that's exactly what I was afraid of. Lian, I'm warning you, don't you *ever* mention this subject to *anyone*. Your right-wing ideas are as dangerous as a keg of dynamite! Look, you can't compare bourgeois worms like us to true revolutionaries. Camp inmates in particular are not allowed, under any circumstance whatsoever, to indulge in sexual intercourse.'

'But the Tangs are husband and wife! I always thought it was pretty odd that the authorities didn't allow the couples that live in our camp to meet in private sometimes, or for that matter sleep together in the same room.'

'On page forty-five of the *Little Red Book* it says: "Revolution means repudiation of all human emotion. Whosoever is unable to comply is our enemy."'

'Oh, I see. We are not allowed to enjoy life. They are. The guards and the Director can take the jeep home every third day, to lie with their wives in their comfy beds and have a great time doing the business of the rain and the clouds. Meanwhile bourgeois teachers like yourself get dragged through the mud if they can't resist the urge to cuddle in a damp cave, just once.'

Mother shook her head. 'Because of the crime they have committed, the Tangs have been forbidden to leave the camp for the next six months; no weekend leave for them in the foreseeable future.'

It made me sick to my stomach.

PINK PIG

I had developed a tic. Without meaning to, my stomach muscles would contract every thirty seconds, then relax. One moment my tummy looked like a crater and the next it looked like a volleyball.

As if that wasn't bad enough, Mother was constantly on my back about it – 'Knock it off! Your stomach isn't a bicycle tyre – you don't have to pump it up all the time!' As if I could help it! The more I realised how beyond the pale my behaviour was, the less I could control it.

The sick urge kept getting worse, and I couldn't concentrate on anything else. Even my lessons went to pieces. How could I pay attention when my teachers tried to explain something to me? No matter how hard I argued with my stomach, in the hope that it would leave me alone, it made not the slightest difference.

At lunchtime, seated on our haunches, Mother and I were bolting down our meal when I saw three of my teachers approaching. I stopped chewing my corn bread long enough to listen to their complaint: 'Yunxiang, we might as well suspend the lessons; the child hasn't been taking in a single word . . .'

Great – I was sitting right there, yet they talked about me as if I were a hamster who was unable to make head or tail of their conversation.

At four thirty, Mother unexpectedly walked into the mill. Taking over Professor Qin's end at the sack-filling, she wailed, 'When is it going to end? Now Lian has a new disease. It's embarrassing and ridiculous. Her stomach looks like the lid on a boiling cooking pot.'

As Mother was saying this, I suddenly discovered that my stomach muscles had forgotten to contract for the past half hour. Qin took a step back, looked at me from a distance like an art connoisseur examining a calligraphy from the Tang dynasty, and said, amused, 'Well, Lian, your Mother claims you do something funny with your stomach. Strange, I never noticed it.'

I turned to him to try to show him that there was indeed something wrong with me. But this time the tensing and releasing of my stomach muscles did not give me the same secret thrill . . .

Qin said to Mother, 'Just leave her be, it will go away by itself.'

Mother almost went to pieces with despair. 'Professor, please help Lian,' she begged. 'The child already has so much to bear . . .' She interrupted herself to call me to order: 'Lian! Spare me – don't you go taking advantage of my fretting and start doing that thing with your belly again!'

Qin patted her back, relenting: 'Don't look so sad, Yunxiang. If you don't believe it will go away by itself, I will do something to make sure that it does.'

I held my breath, wondering how Qin would help me get over my problem.

Qin, studiedly avoiding Mother's gaze, said, 'Don't you think it might be a good idea to send her to Dr Fu? He used to be one of the top psychiatrists in Beijing.'

Mother blushed, and fumbled for the right words, 'Uh, well . . . of course! Why didn't I think of that myself!'

'Who is that?' I asked. I knew just about every inmate, but I had never heard of a psychiatrist named Fu.

Mother explained. 'The uncle who is a little plump, you know him. The guards call him Pink Pig.'

The first time I had set eyes on Dr Fu had been around a month ago. One morning after breakfast, when the prisoners were drawn up in rows four abreast, one of the guards had opened the barn door and dragged out five large bags of fertiliser. They had been piled on top of each other for months, and the manure had been compressed into a rock-hard cake. 'Pink Pig, come over here and break up this manure with your feet,' the guard barked.

A fat man with unusually smooth white skin stepped forward from the third row. Blushing like a ripe tomato, he peeked at the guard warily, hoping it was just a joke and that he wasn't really about to be humiliated in such a degrading manner in front of two hundred and fifty prisoners.

'Hurry up!'

Reluctantly, he climbed up on the sacks and began to stomp on the manure with his feet. The spectacle attracted the interest of some of the other guards. They laughed themselves blue in the face. The impresario, emboldened by the favourable reception of his farce, smirked, 'Hee, hee! The pig's weight is coming in handy! Faster, fatso! We're going to be needing that manure for the fields!'

Doctor Fu increased the tempo. His double chin, undulating gut and massive legs quivered and his eyes glittered with shame and sadness.

'Are you deaf? *Faster*, I said!' the guard screamed.

This seemed to electrify Fu. His whole body jiggled up and down like the vent-flap of a steam engine. The female detainees covered their eyes with their hands. I fancied I could hear their teeth chattering. My own stomach was spinning like the drum of a washing machine and I was afraid I was going to faint.

'Hee-hee-hee, ha-ha-ha! I fuck your great-grandmother! It's been ages since we've had such a good laugh. Who would ever have thought that Pink Pig was such an excellent tap dancer!' The guards were hugging their own stomachs, whooping like hyenas.

At rest time Mother and I followed Qin to his dormitory, which was also Dr Fu's sleeping quarters. The doctor bade us welcome with a shy smile and invited us to sit on his bed. Mother opened her mouth to speak but Fu put his finger to his lips. Suddenly he didn't seem so timid any more; he had put on a real doctor's face.

Fu said to me, 'Little girl, before we begin I must tell you a secret: I know quite a bit about you. For example, I know that you want to be a historian when you grow up and that you pay regular visits to the Lily Theatre . . .'

'How do *you* know that?'

'I have my informants.' He threw a meaningful look at Qin.

Mother blushed again.

What is going on? I wondered.

Abruptly the doctor asked, 'Now tell me honestly, Lian, what do you need that tic for?'

'*What?*' I had sprung to my feet. 'What gave you that idea? I *hate* my tic, from the pit of my gallbladder. What makes you think I'm looking for anything useful in it?'

'If that were so, then I think you'd have put a stop to it yourself long ago, and you would already be cured.' He threw me a probing glance, and was silent.

'Uncle Fu, I *do* want to get rid of my tic.'

'Why? As long as you are getting pleasure from this little handicap of yours, and you can feel sorry for yourself and moan about your lot, you should do so, by all means. For—'

Mother interrupted him. 'But doctor—'

Fu went on undeterred. 'Lian, there is just one thing you must learn to do from now on: to feel free to do what *you* want to do. Everything else will simply fall into place.'

TONGXINGLIAN

Mother and I had picked buttercups, dandelions and poppies for Dr Fu, to thank him. I considered him a magician, and was constantly finding excuses to go and talk to him. I suddenly changed my mind about wanting to be a historian, and decided to become a psychologist instead. Surely psychology was the best profession of all – it would teach me to probe the mysteries of the human mind.

I was on my way to Dr Fu to ask him how you can guess what someone else is thinking. Once I had that technique off pat – the very essence of the practice of psychology, I figured – I should be able to read the Chairman's thoughts and predict when he'd finally decide he had had enough of that masterpiece of his, the Cultural Revolution. Then my parents and I could go back to leading a normal life.

The pavement under my feet felt like glue – the summer sun had cooked the asphalt to jelly. It was three in the afternoon; on weekdays the prisoners were still slogging away in the fields at this time, but on Saturdays they stopped working at two. It was quiet in the camp. Everybody who wasn't confined to bed was at the market.

I knew that Dr Fu would be at home, because he was famous for his dislike of 'energy-sapping physical movement'. That was why he was also known as *Zuojia*, or 'Homebody'.

When I walked into the dormitory, I saw two men sitting on a bed. They had slung their arms around each other's shoulders and were mumbling something I couldn't understand because I was too far away. I had never seen such intimacy – even Father and Mother never touched each other in my presence. My first thought was to slip out quietly; three suddenly felt like a crowd. But before I could make myself scarce, I heard a rustling of clothes. The two gentlemen had discovered me and stood up, alarmed.

After a long, strained silence, Fu said hoarsely, 'Good afternoon, Lian. Sit down.'

One foot at a time I shuffled towards them, not daring to look up.

Qin laughed, 'I thought you were a ghost. All our room-mates are out at the market. I was wondering who it could be who was returning so soon . . . And now it appears that it was our little nymph Lian!'

His wisecrack helped to ease my embarrassment, and I finally made myself look up. The old gentlemen's cheeks were bright red, like four ripe peaches, something I had never noticed in either one of them before.

At night, in bed, I thought about Qin and Fu. How was it that they had looked so handsome and so happy? Was it 'Le Grand Amour', as it was called in bourgeois novels for grown-ups . . . ?

━

As soon as I set foot inside the mill, I said to Qin, 'Sorry, Uncle, for giving you such a fright last Saturday.'

He tottered backwards a few steps, shook his head and opened his mouth. But no words came out. Beneath his darkly tanned skin lurked a deep flush. I wasn't born yesterday: as far as blushes went, this was in quite a different category from the blush of two days ago. That blush had been one of pure bliss; this was one of embarrassment. Qin's composure was obviously shaken. I felt guilty.

He came up to me and whispered in my ear – as if that was necessary inside the growling and rattling mill! – 'Child, I cannot keep this secret from you, though it may be difficult for you to understand: Fu and I love each other. Shhh! Don't tell anybody – ever!'

I nearly hit the ceiling. 'But that's wonderful! *Finally* I meet someone who actually admits to being in love! All I ever hear, day in and day out until I'm sick of it, is about people wanting to make mincemeat of each other. And then they have to go and give it a fancy name too – *Class Struggle!*'

He stared at me wide-eyed and stammered, 'But do you realise . . . well, that Fu and I . . . two men . . . so . . .'

I interrupted him excitedly. 'Well then, we're the same, you and I: I love Kim, and we are both girls . . . ! So – is that why you are locked up here, in camp? Because you don't *have* to be, do you? Didn't the Foreign Minister promise you that you'd be spared further political persecution for the rest of your life?'

Qin sighed, as if he were a concert pianist asked to give a performance for an ox. 'Uh . . . eh . . . well, yes, in a way . . . Fu was almost tormented to death two years ago by left-wing extremists at the university. I got to know him during that time, and found out that he had tried to commit suicide more than once. I vowed I would save him from the tiger's maw. Thanks to my intervention, Fu was offered the golden opportunity of being sent to prison camp. At least here there are rules as to the kinds of corporal punishment that are permissible.'

'So you volunteered to become a prisoner too? To give Fu moral and emotional support?'

'That's it, more or less.'

'Is his love worth that much to you, then?'

'To me it is.' His eyes went misty and sad.

In a flash of whirling thoughts, I remembered Feilan, Qin's former girlfriend. She had dumped him at the most critical time of his life. Was it his disappointment in women that had made Qin turn to male affection? Yet none of the boys I knew had ever done anything to hurt me, and I too loved someone of my own sex.

'Homosexuality, *tongxinglian*, is officially taboo in our country, didn't you know that? So please don't ever breathe a word about this to anyone, in any language. Promise?'

'What do you mean, *tongxinglian* – you mean it's taboo for people with the same surname to love each other?'

'Oh Lian, Lian, whatever was I thinking of, to talk about this to you!'

I could have smacked myself until I was black and blue. What a bonehead I was! Such an ignoramus! An utter dimwit! I really understood bugger-all.

But I did give my word that I would tell no one about Qin and Fu's relationship. With that, the subject was closed.

━━━━

Even though I kept my promise and didn't breathe a word about Qin and Fu, I couldn't help sending Mother meaningful looks whenever their names came up. I was so enchanted with the idea that Qin and Fu were in love that whenever I thought of them, words would well up in my mouth. I wanted to share with Mother my joyous discovery that the world was a much nicer, gentler place when there was love in the air instead of hate.

If I was reading her correctly, it amused Mother to see my significant glances. But neither of us had the guts to broach the delicate subject first. It was as if we were sitting on either side of a thin paper screen; each was aware the other knew a secret about Qin and Fu, but neither wanted to be the first to lick her forefinger and dissolve a little peephole with her spit.

The day came when I couldn't keep it to myself any longer. I dragged Mother to a quiet corner behind the barracks and whispered, 'Does the Party know about Qin's and Fu's . . . uh, friendship?'

'Child, how do you think Qin got here in the first place? Don't you think the camp authorities would find it strange, if someone decides to go to prison of his own free will? It's just that this sort of love doesn't conflict with Mao's command to love the Father, Mother, Lover and Mistress All-Rolled-Into-One. It is not considered dangerous, because they figure it's less satisfying.'

'Are there others we know of who love each other like that?'

'Always the Nosy Parker, aren't you! That is none of your business. You are much too young to think about things like that.'

FUMBLING IN THE DARK

When Qin and I arrived at the lake, a bright sun was lighting up the water. There was a breeze and the surface looked exactly like the scaly skin of a golden carp. Qin went to sit in his usual spot and I stepped up to my small podium. It was so gorgeous out that we were both silent for a while. When Qin finally cleared his throat ostentatiously, I began my lecture.

I talked about the influence the October Revolution had had on Chinese society, about the May Fourth Movement, about the ascendancy of the Nationalist Party, and the conflict between the ruling Nationalists and the Communist Party.

Qin listened intently to my story, but his face was like a sky overcast with black storm clouds . . .

And indeed, he had good reason to scowl: my narrative was a litany of unpleasant historical facts – military conflicts, political intrigue, mass-murder, and cunningly refined violence.

As I stepped down off the flat rock, I had a ghastly vision. Two hungry bears – Cynicism and Pessimism – were snapping at my legs, trying to drag me down out of the tree that was Love of Life.

I went and sat down next to Qin in the grass and asked him what I should do about it. He was holding a round pebble between his fingers and was pinching it hard, his teeth clenched, as if it were a duck egg that he was trying to crush. He scooted away from me demonstratively and said coldly, 'What did you expect, Lian? A positive view of China's past and her historical figures? How can one be an optimist, given the present circumstances?' He got up suddenly, and hugged me tightly. I could hear his brain searching for words of consolation, but it could not find any . . .

I ducked out from under his arms. I could not believe things were really as black as he painted them. Or, rather, I *would* not believe it. Qin had been splashing about in the slough of despond for so long that he didn't have the energy to crawl out of it any more. Even though I felt for him, I was only thirteen years old, and I simply could not believe that what he was suggesting was true . . . But then, where *was* the truth?

A HUNGER STRIKER

It was six p.m. I was waiting at the prison gate for Mother and my fellow inmates. The iron shovels scraped over the path, which was as cracked and grooved by the summer's drought as a turtle-shell. The familiar cacophony announced the return of the labourers and, with it, dinnertime.

As soon as they reached the entrance, their guard, Kong, shouted, 'Halt! Revolutionary Prayer number 459!'

The slave labourers immediately put down their tools, and, like automatons, they took a deep breath, piously turning their eyes towards the east, there where the sun rises and the Sun That Never Sets is enthroned. Shouting in unison, they intoned:

> Mao, Merciful Saviour Star,
> please forgive our bourgeois sins of today
> and help us rinse the poop-reeking thoughts
> out of our Capitalist viper-heads
> Thank you most sincerely!

When it was over, Kong said, 'Dismissed!'

Like frisky dogs that are finally let off the leash, they disentangled themselves from their orderly column, and soon there was an eager din of jabbering voices.

'Lian, just look at what Uncle has brought you!' A tall, cadaverous and swarthy man who made me think of a dried piece of straw was hurrying towards me. Something was moving under his sweat-stained blue jacket.

My face lit up and I ran up to him. 'Uncle Yie, what's that you have there?'

He rummaged inside his jacket, his lips pressed together with the effort, and pulled out . . . a bird!

'Heavens, what a beauty!' I cried. The bird had shiny tar-black feathers, twinkly eyes and a bright orange beak, which contrasted beautifully with its stark black body.

Yie held the animal up by the legs and explained, 'This is a crow. I saw it in the rice paddy. It wasn't too hard for me to catch it.'

'A crow!' I said, repeating the name of this wondrous creature, the likes of which I had never seen up close before. 'Mama, may I keep it?' I begged.

Mother looked at us and said, 'All right then, but it's only because we are here in the camp, that I'll allow it.'

'That's right,' Yie advocated on my behalf, 'since the poor child has no other playmates here.'

I stroked the crow's head. How warm its feathers were, and how soft!

Yie offered to try to find a cage for the bird, which was now using every ounce of strength in an attempt to squirm out of his grip. After some hunting around, we found a giant basket of woven bamboo that was used for carrying potatoes and sugar beet.

I put my smallest enamel bowl under the overturned basket to serve as a feeding dish, and an old jam jar for water. There. The crow was duly deposited under the basket. I sat by my pet's little home for the next few hours, lost in wonder. The crow kept flapping its wings, which worried me a little: wasn't he happy now that he had food and drink set out for him gratis, and a new friend into the bargain? My joy won out over my concern, however. I felt I had finally found a soul mate, a creature vibrating to the same rhythms as myself. I felt closer to this bird than to Mother, closer even than to Qin.

At dinnertime I put aside four spoonfuls of porridge and two bites of cornbread: for my crow.

Carefully I lifted the basket off the floor, only to see my black buddy sitting there motionless. He hadn't touched his food from yesterday – not even a crumb. The water jar was as full as it had been when I had left it. It had been the same thing two days running. What could be the matter? Didn't he like this kind of food? Getting down on my knees, I pleaded with him to eat something. I whispered secrets in his ear that I wouldn't have dreamed of confiding to anyone else in camp, but he just stared ahead stonily, totally apathetic.

I ran to the kitchen to ask the cooks what to do. They told me crows usually prefer uncooked grain or seeds. 'All right then,' they nodded. 'Just this once, mind, we'll let you grab a handful of raw brown rice from the store room.'

I didn't have to be told twice. I hurried back to my bird with the special crow-feed, and dribbled it carefully under his beak, one grain at a time.

* * *

It took much fawning and cajoling to get the cooks to part with some more raw rice grains the next day. I rushed back with it to my playmate.

But I found the crow lying motionless under the basket, dead – every morsel of the food that I had worked so hard to collect lying untouched next to his lifeless head.

I sank to my knees; it was the first time that I could caress the bird lengthily and at leisure, now that he was no longer capable of putting up a struggle. The feathers were still beautiful, like a piece of rich black velvet. The beak too, resting gently on the ground, still looked the same, a bright orange gem. But there was no *ki* coursing through his body any more. His soul had flown. To Heaven.

I felt wretched. Was I a murderer? I attempted to jump up, to race to the canteen, but my courage plummeted into my shoes, turning my feet to lead.

When I finally dragged myself to the kitchen, an ominous silence greeted me there. That gave me pause. I walked slowly over to the galley of stoves, but there wasn't a soul to be seen. A vague murmuring reached me: it had all the hallmarks of a denunciation meeting. I ran to the dining hall, which was where the sound seemed to be coming from. How strange, I thought, the cooks don't usually hold this sort of gathering.

But yes, indeed, that's what it was: a real denunciation meeting. Someone was being forced into the 'aeroplane position'. Two sturdy fellows were pushing the man's head down to the ground with one hand while twisting the poor wretch's arms behind his back with the other, as if wringing out a floor mop.

Snippets reached my eardrums: '—Think it over – try using what's between your ears just this once in a million years, even if all you have for brains is a bowl-full of rotten eggs! Come on, give us an answer: who do you love more, the Father, the Mother, the Lover and Mistress All-Rolled-Into-One, or the Capitalist bitch out of whose belly you plopped fifty-one years ago—?'

Ordinarily, this kind of scene would have roused my indignation, but I wasn't interested in politics today. I sneaked silently from the room, realising I had no business being there. To interrupt such a serious occasion with news of the death of a bird would be nothing less than counter-revolutionary sabotage.

Not knowing what to do, I trailed around the camp. All the detainees had left for the fields, and the only ones left were the cooks. The image of the dead crow hovered before my eyes, and all sorts of painful questions haunted me. At my wits' end, I finally thought of Director Gao. Of course! *He* didn't have to work, and the cooks' meeting was not important enough for him to attend. Propelled by despair, I knocked on the Director's door.

'Come in.'

'Sir, my crow is dead!' I stormed into his office and promptly burst into tears.

The Director put down the newspaper he had been unhurriedly perusing next to his steaming pot of tea, and tried to console me: 'Oh, that's terrible! It's dead? And you've only had it three days!'

'He starved to death, I'm sure of it, because he wouldn't eat or drink a thing . . .'

The Director went to fetch a bamboo fan from his bed – his office also served as his bedroom – to cool off my tear-stained, sweaty face. 'Come on, my child. It isn't *that* bad now, is it! Do you want another bird? I'll ask the guards to catch one for you.'

'*Never* again!' I pushed the Director's fan away and stamped my foot. 'All birds do is die when I'm around . . . Oh, oh, what did I do to my poor crow to kill him? I gave him the wrong kind of food. I murdered him!'

The Director, who was usually so strict, did not lose his patience. On the contrary, he squatted down in front of me, wringing his hands, trying to find a way to get me to calm down. He started rummaging for his keys in the pockets of his trousers, in his desk drawers and under his pillow, but could not find them. 'Come, Lian. I think I won't lock the door, just this once. Let us go find your crow. I will examine it to see what caused its death.' Obediently I trotted along behind him.

After giving the crow a thorough examination, the Director declared, 'Child, it wasn't the feed . . . This crow died of grief and loneliness.'

'Can you tell what the crow was feeling, then?'

'No, little girl, but that's just the way it is. The crow felt rotten because it was imprisoned, far from its family, perhaps there was a nest full of baby birds. It was cut off from the green meadow where it used to fly to its heart's content. It's as plain as the nose on your face that it was feeling sad and angry: that's why it would not eat, no matter how delicious its food. Lian, don't you know the word "heartbroken"? The crow died, literally and figuratively, of a broken heart.'

'Really?'

'Would I kid about something as serious as that? Birds love freedom. Unfettered nature is where they belong. Catching them and keeping them in a cage usually means death to them.'

I opened my eyes wide: how strange that *people* don't die when they are imprisoned, I thought. I had been in prison camp two whole months, and

I had yet to see someone carried out in a coffin, even though it should have been obvious that people couldn't do without their freedom either. I longed to tell the Director to his face what I was thinking, and to see his reaction. As if he had read my mind, he suddenly turned around. His shoulders, usually so proudly squared, collapsed like two rolls of dough as he hurried back to his safe haven – the Director's office, where the colour portrait of the Great Helmsman hung waiting for him.

MOTHER OR MAO

At lunchtime, I saw that people had broken up into small knots in the canteen. They seemed to be discussing something very hush-hush. Mother and I were trying to decide which group to join when I exclaimed in alarm: someone had very nearly bumped right into my bowl of corn porridge.

'Oh excuse me, I wasn't . . . looking.' Maly, excusing herself awkwardly, turned her distracted face the other way.

Mother asked, concerned: 'What's the matter? Is there some way I can help?'

Aunt Maly shook her head and tried to walk away. But I had her by the left sleeve. She changed her mind, and sighed, 'Over there, in the corner. Let's go and sit down, and I'll tell you about the latest disaster.'

I felt flattered that Maly should want to confide a secret to me and ran after the two grown-ups. The gravy slopped over the rim of my bowl, causing Mother to snap, 'All the vitamins you so sorely need are in the sauce. Would you please just take it a little easier?'

When we were seated in our corner, Maly, looking around furtively, proceeded to tell us the entire story in one breath. 'Yesterday there was a denunciation meeting—'

I nodded wisely. I was as proud as a peahen that I already knew something the adults were only just hearing about.

'— concerning the old cook, Jou.'

'What? That good Uncle Jou? The one who makes such delicious fried aubergine? He's such a sweetheart – if he stepped on an earthworm by accident, he'd never forgive himself!' I exclaimed.

Mother gave me a dig in the ribs and Maly went on.

'When Jou was just a few months old, sometime in the Twenties, his father went to work on a steamship that went back and forth between China and America. In the Thirties, the civil war prevented him from returning to his wife and only son. He remained in the US, leaving Jou's mother to raise their son by herself. In 1948, just before the founding of the People's Republic, Jou's father sent his wife his life's savings, to pay for her passage to America, with the understanding that as soon as he got enough money together, he would send for Jou in turn. Of course you've guessed – it never happened.

'After 1949, when the borders were closed, Jou's father cursed himself for being such a numskull. He should have borrowed the money for his son's passage, but it was too late. They have continued to write to each other all these years. Until last week, that is. The camp authorities had an order to open every single piece of mail belonging to camp inmates, not only letters addressed to counter-revolutionaries, but to 'clean' persons too, including the canteen workers. And now Jou is in big trouble. Thursday of last week, the Director monitored a letter from Jou's mother. Actually, there was nothing suspicious in it, just the regular scoop. His mother wrote that her health was failing and that she missed Jou and his two children, her only grandchildren, terribly. But the very fact that Jou had been in contact with someone in the decadent West, in the heartland of Capitalism no less, was enough to brand Jou a spy and an enemy of the State. The Director commanded the canteen supervisor to make Jou swear that he would disown his mother, and never, to his dying day, write her another letter, or else . . .

'But that Jou is such a simple fellow! Bless his illiterate soul, the Cultural Revolution has simply passed him by. He is a cook. Before the Revolution he made meat and vegetable stir-fry, and now that the Revolution is in full swing, he makes vegetable and meat stir-fry. To him, the world has remained the same. That's why he thought it was a bad joke at first, when his boss ordered him to break off all contact with his mother. "Party Chief of the Kitchen Division," he pleaded, "we all have a heart, and that heart is made of flesh. Am I right? Don't you yourself feel love and gratitude in your heart for your mother? Or do you believe we've simply sprouted from some rock somewhere, like bamboo shoots?"

'His chief did his utmost to convince Jou of the gravity of the situation, but Jou only beat his breast, vowing he would rather die than refuse to acknowledge his mother. That's why the denunciation meeting was called, in the end . . .'

Maly paused. Her wrinkled eyelids were red, and she swallowed. 'Now I understand why I haven't received any letters from my parents in a year and a half. I am much guiltier than Jou. The camp authorities must have been reading my letters from Hong Kong for years, and burned them!'

Mother said quickly, 'Maly, stop having such negative thoughts. You can't be certain that they are holding back your mail, can you? Perhaps your family has been too busy to write . . .'

Sheepishly, I looked the other way. My mother was lying, and we all knew it.

AN UNINVITED QUADRUPED

I woke up from my nap and went outside. The cool face of the autumn sun fixed me with an indifferent stare. Yet the sunlight did still have enough heat in it, evidently, to paint the leaves of the maple tree a fiery red. Against the little clumps of white clouds drifting here and there in the clear blue sky, the leaves looked like leaping flames performing a war dance of regret for the departure of the joyously spirited summer.

Schah . . . ssschah. . . A breeze leaped up and invited the coppery leaves to get up off the ground. Away they twirled together, the wind and the leaves, dancing arm-in-arm. The breeze blew my sleepiness away. It gave me an instant urge to visit somewhere. I had finished my homework and my work at the mill didn't start for another two hours. I could go and have some fun, with a free conscience.

Where should I go? Not the canteen, because it was around this time that the kitchen staff was given its daily dose of political indoctrination. Not to Laifu the carpenter, because Mother would not allow me to talk to a young man all by myself. According to Mother, anything might happen – a fellow like that was quite capable of taking an axe and splitting my head open like a ripe watermelon – even though I couldn't picture that nice man doing such a thing. Still, I kept out of his way, just to be on the safe side.

Suddenly I had a wonderful idea: I would pay a visit to the pigsty. The swine-keeper usually couldn't afford to take any time off for brain-cleansing: the pigs thumbed their noses at orders from on high. They simply would not stand for it if their keeper failed to keep them supplied with fodder and water every hour, or if he didn't clean the excrement out of their stalls in a timely manner.

I could smell the pigsty from miles away. Soured pig manure, rotten leftovers from the canteen, mouldy hay and fermenting vegetables – it was a mixture rank enough to cancel out the fresh air of the fields, creating an island of nauseating smells. But the idea of fun, the prospect of finding some distraction from my chronic loneliness for a little while, made me immune to the stench.

Pyup-pyup-pyup. A grey-haired man was pouring a thick mass of vegetables and hay into the trough, muttering a string of endearments to the animals. What a bunch of greedy hogs! They couldn't even wait for the man to finish filling their trench. As soon as they heard the first *pyup!* they were already at it, never once bothering to lift their fat snouts, so that their necks and heads were soon coated with the grimy swill, which oozed down their napes back into the trough.

'Uncle Rui, are you busy?'

After exchanging the customary greeting, Rui said, 'Just a moment, when I'm done with this row of troughs, I have something terrific to show you.'

The monotony of life in the camp made my curiosity more highly inflammable than ever. 'Uncle, let me help you with the feeding, then we'll be finished sooner.'

I ran to the shed to fetch a small bucket. Frenetically I dipped it in the tub of pigswill. Then I hoisted up the brimming bucket and let the contents splash into one of the troughs.

'You've got to divide up the feed more evenly, child.'

'I will try, Uncle.'

Just look at him measuring out the pigswill like pernickety Pete, as if he's still in his laboratory weighing out chemicals . . . You could see that he used to be a professor.

Finally! It was half an hour later when, with beating heart, I accompanied Rui to his room. He led the way in, and a few seconds later showed me a basket, in which . . .

'Oh, it can't be *true*! A puppy! Oh, look at that fluffy fur around his neck. Hey, open your little eyes, do, please – Look, Uncle, he has pitch-black eyes, they're like two perfect little round marbles!'

I fondled the little dog's head, and an arrow of pain pierced my heart. I was so transported with rapture and surprise that it scared me.

I knew all too well that keeping pets was not permitted. I didn't quite understand why. I did know that I used to feel I was a traitor to the Father, Mother, Lover and Mistress All-Rolled-Into-One whenever I had to divide my love between a cat or a goldfish and the Quadruple-Oneness. For I had had it hammered into me from infancy that I must be one hundred per cent loyal to the Great Helmsman until my very last gasp.

I was afraid that a ghastly punishment was in store for Rui if he kept the puppy. 'But Uncle,' I asked, 'this isn't *allowed*, is it?'

'Oh, it's all right. This morning I showed the little dog to the Director. And you know what?' he said, nuzzling the silky fur of the animal's belly, 'It was the first time that I ever saw the Director smile! I immediately gave him a long list of uses the dog could be put to once he was grown – for example, herding the pigs when they are let out to forage in the harvested fields or nose around the garbage dump; or guarding the chickens against the weasels . . .

'But, child, it wasn't even necessary. The Director cut me short, saying, "I know what a big help a dog can be . . . As a matter of fact, at home, when I was a boy, we used to have three dogs . . . In the daytime the dog can help you with the pigs. In the evening I'd like him to come and sleep with me."' Rui grinned. 'I saw at once that the Director has a soft spot for dogs.'

I jumped in the air and yelled, 'Yaay! We're allowed to keep the puppy dog!'

The puppy, startled, looked around sharply. I would do anything, stand on my head if necessary, to make the animal happy.

'What's his name?'

'I only found him yesterday, he was under a tree by the road. I haven't thought of a name for him yet.'

'Ahuang,' I said, 'the dog with the golden fur.'

'Mmmm, I think that's a fine name.'

Today I didn't even notice the stench of the pigsty – now that Ahuang had stolen my heart. I was smuggling a whole supply of provisions for the puppy under my arms. My red woollen scarf, the one with the green checks, which was to be Ahuang's blanket; a piece of corn bread that I had furtively stuffed into my trouser pocket during last night's dinner, and a little wool pompom that used to dangle from my winter hat – I had secretly snipped it off this morning. After all, a baby dog needs something to play with, doesn't it?

Rui soaked the bread in a bowl of water and placed it before the dog. Sure enough, he gobbled it down noisily. In no time at all he had licked the bowl shiny clean with his pink tongue.

The swine-keeper-slash-biologist Professor Dr Rui shook his head: 'It would actually be better if he had some milk. By the looks of him, he is only three or four weeks old, and puppies that age need mother's milk.'

Where could I find some milk? In the six months that I had been here, I hadn't ever had a drop of milk – not even a whiff of it. Only the wardens and head guards were entitled to milk . . .

Got it! 'Uncle Rui, may I take Ahuang with me, in his basket, for half an hour?' I asked.

'No whole milk, understood? Dilute it with a little water, otherwise it will give Ahuang the runs.' Rui had understood at once what I was planning to do and was giving me instructions just in case.

I brought the puppy to the canteen. Aunt Liu, she was the one! For I knew that Aunt Liu was the cook whose job it was to prepare the special meals for the privileged higher-ups. First I softened Auntie up by showing her the cute little thing. As soon as I saw Liu's eyes begin to sparkle, I begged her for a cup of milk.

Liu immediately put on a poker face and said, in a dark and dangerous tone: 'And risk getting sentenced to forced labour just like your mother? That's what's in store for me if *they*,' and she indicated the ceiling with her head, 'found out that I'd given the precious life-sap, which is exclusively reserved for revolutionaries, to a four-footed animal.'

I sneaked a glance at the pan in which Liu heated up the milk and suggested, 'Hey, you know what? Instead of throwing out the water that's used to rinse out the pan, you can save it in a little bottle for Ahuang.'

'You are a crafty one, aren't you!' Liu tapped her middle finger against my forehead and let me have my way.

~

A few days later, Aunt Liu whispered an exciting piece of news into my ear: 'Yesterday morning I went to the Director's room at seven, as I always do, to bring him his bowl of warm milk. I set the bowl down on the table and left the room. When I'd gone only a few steps, I suddenly realised that I had forgotten the wicker cosy. I went back to the office and peeked in the window – I didn't do it on purpose, Buddha is my witness – but, Merciful Heavens, Lian, my child, what did I see? The Director was feeding Ahuang, from *his* bowl of milk! I've never seen our chief acting anywhere near so human.'

The news that the Director was sharing his precious food with a dog soon made the rounds of the camp. But strangely enough, nobody was jealous of Ahuang, though they'd have given their eyeteeth to trade places with the dog, even if for just one little sip of milk. A timid friendliness now lurked in the eyes of the detainees whenever they bumped into the Director. It was as if they harboured some hope that the dog would make him kindlier and less vicious.

Ahuang soon grew into a huge dog. When he ran, I couldn't catch up with him any more and when he barked, twigs fell from the trees. In the daytime he helped Rui watch the pigs, chickens and ducks; at night he curled up at the Director's feet. Being very nosy, he liked to sniff at every prisoner who passed. Then he'd wag his bushy tail and trot back to Rui or the Director.

Despite the fact that a dog's sense of smell is said to be a dozen times keener than a human's, Ahuang was the only inmate who did not seem to sniff any political tension. He just gambolled about happily, treating everyone as his equal. After having their feelings trampled on for so long, the prisoners found solace in the fact that there seemed to be one beast left on this planet that was intent on keeping humanity and affection alive.

THE ALMIGHTY PROMPTER

The sky was steel-grey more often than it was sky-blue, and the winter breeze swelled into a biting wind. The ground turned hard as a knuckle, and the prisoners underwent ever-lengthier thought-remodelling sessions.

It was General Assembly day. The canteen was bursting at the seams with detainees and camp personnel. The four camp cadres were seated on the podium. The skin on their faces was more tautly stretched than your bladder when you badly need to go. There was a rumour that there was going to be a very important announcement.

No one in our dormitory had been able to sleep a wink last night; we were too excited thinking about what the news might be. We were all secretly hoping that the Communist Party would set a number of prisoners free just before the Chinese New Year; there was much speculating about who the lucky ones might be . . .

Usually the assembly hall was like a bazaar, with vendors touting their wares at the top of their lungs, and potential customers haggling over the price as if their very lives depended on whether the thing cost a few fen more or a few fen less. But today you could have heard a pin drop. Seated next to Mother, I felt dizzy with the hope, the worry and the uncertainty that tore at every detainee's heart.

After an endless preliminary ritual – with ingredients such as the singing of 'Mao, the Sun that Never Sets', the shouting of the slogans 'Long Live Mao the Party Chairman' and 'Good Health to the Party Vice Chairman' (each repeated three times over), and the loud public confession of any bourgeois thoughts polluting the prisoners' minds that morning – we finally got to hear what it was all about.

There was no question of anyone being sent home. The Director told us that on the fifteenth of January, one week before the Chinese New Year, a team of inspectors from the Central Committee would be coming to visit the camp, and preparations were to be undertaken before the visit: 'It is our *rre-vo-lut-ion-ary* task to show the Inspector how thoroughly all you bourgeois intellectuals have reformed yourselves! And how much mental cleansing you have achieved so far!' He shouted out the words as if a hippopotamus was stepping on his foot, and lied through his teeth like the grandfather of all liars. Everyone was aware of the truth: all the Director was worried about was saving his own skin. Were the inspection team to discover the wretched conditions under which the detainees were expected to work and to survive here, or the inhumane treatment they received, he'd be a dead duck.

Early the next morning the prisoners were rounded up to clean the camp – first the dormitories, then the canteen and common rooms and, last but not least, the courtyard. The Inspector had to be convinced above all else that the prisoners' living conditions were hygienic.

'Hygiene . . . never even heard of it,' Maly muttered. 'In the four years that I've been locked up here, the camp has never once been cleaned. The Director is acting like a mule that sticks a leek up its nostril and pretends to be an elephant.'

She was right. Even I had never, in the six months of my stay, seen anybody scrub the dormitory floor. The convicts were totally drained when they returned from the forced labour in the fields. They didn't even have the energy left to wash their faces. Where would they find the strength to clean the dorm? Besides, the beds were pushed so close together that there was no room to squeeze a broom in between.

A month ago, I had wanted to surprise the others by drenching the floor with soapy water. But the water had taken a good three weeks to dry; since there were no windows, the sun and wind never penetrated here. At the end of the third week the mosquitoes had decided to use the puddles on the floor as a breeding ground for their eggs and larvae. I was on the receiving end of some pretty dirty looks. At her wits' end, Mother borrowed a pile of old newspapers from the Director and spread them over the floor. The newspapers absorbed the water in a few days, and Mother used very colourful language to caution me that I'd better leave the filthy dorm alone in the future, or else . . .

To expect any kind of occidental New Year's celebration was wishful thinking. Not only had the camp authorities revoked the prisoners' home leave: they also made them work on Sunday. So New Year's Day had been spent scrubbing, mopping and polishing.

The following day, the prisoners had to muck out the pigsty and the chicken coops. For the first time since the camp was built, a mat of plaited straw was laid down to cover the dung heap, to spare the inspectors from being exposed to the beastly stench. I just don't understand it, I thought, don't those bigwigs, of all people, know that stench to the nose is perfume to the proletarian soul? Besides, the pigsty was not on the planned inspection route. But apparently the Director wanted to play it safe.

Nor were the inmates left in peace at night. Every dormitory had to choose a leader, who was charged with organising speech rehearsals. A mimeo-graphed sheet of remarks composed and written by the administration was handed out to every inmate. It featured questions which the Inspector might be expected to ask, such as: 'Do you think forced labour has contributed, in your case, to giving you a brand new proletarian mindset? What does a normal day in the camp look like? Can you describe it in a few words?' Underneath each question was an answer sanctioned by the authorities.

The speech exercises entailed learning the questions, and, more impor-tant, the obligatory answers by heart, so that the inmates could rattle them off without a stutter if they were addressed by the Inspector.

For me, there was a delightful, if perverse, satisfaction in watching the adults getting drilled by their coach. The grown-ups seemed to have a par-ticularly hard time remembering the answers. And when they did manage it, they'd forget which answer belonged to which question. Or were they just pretending? When asked, 'What do you usually have for lunch?' they would answer: 'Revolutionary Party Official, thanks to our camp's brilliant leadership, we are undergoing a very effective ideological transformation here. I expect that I shall crawl out of my old bourgeois snakeskin in the near future, and change into a proletarian dragon forthwith.'

To the question, 'How is your revolutionary brainwashing going?' they replied: 'Chicken soup with giGANtic pieces of chicken in it, stir-fried bok choy with strips of MEAT and steamed WHEAT-flour bread.'

There were marks on certain words to show where the accent should fall, and the detainees were asked to stress those syllables emphatically. Every time someone gave the wrong answer, the dormitory would explode in laughter. I began to suspect that they were doing it on purpose. My suspicion was confirmed by the fact that the guffaws kept growing more raucous and sardonic. Some people even rubbed their own cheeks in consternation if they recited the right answer by mistake.

I licked my lips greedily as I tried to picture the fictitious menu. We had never had that kind of food in the canteen, barring the mill-workers' late-night suppers. I considered it a despicable sham, and realised the adults around me must be feeling the same way about it. They would close their eyes and drone the words on the page, sniggering occasionally when, coming to their senses, it suddenly hit them what nonsense they were spouting.

The entire exercise was a farce, but the fact that no one dared refuse to take part in the performance meant that it was more of a tragedy than a comedy. The climax was the Director's threat that if anyone dared to depart from the prescribed text and gave the Inspector the real story of what went on in the camp, he would be 'personally' responsible for seeing the inmate's sentence doubled.

A TRUE ANIMAL LOVER

Since the inspectors were to spend an entire day in the camp, they would get to see with their own eyes what sort of lunch and dinner the prisoners were served. This caused the Director great anxiety. He could force his fellow inmates to lie about the menu, but he could not stop the Inspector from seeing, let alone eating, the prisoners' food – or, more accurately put, their swill. The camp did receive an annual allowance from the State to buy food fit for humans, but he had spent most of it on fattening up the guards and himself; he had put nothing aside for a rainy day. For how could he have foreseen that those damned nosy parkers would come snooping around?

The camp had about eighty pigs, two hundred ducks and four hundred chickens, but these could only be slaughtered after the autumn harvest, otherwise the camp would run into a horrendous deficit. The Director and his cronies managed to scrape up a little money, just enough to procure forty pounds of the cheapest vegetables and two pounds of meat. But the kitchen staff rebelled when the Director insisted that they prepare a banquet – what with, they'd like to know? The vegetables might just about do: if you added enough water to make them swell up to twice their size, they might be made to look like something. But the meat? Even if they cut it into slivers no bigger than the tip of a needle, there would never be enough to feed two hundred and fifty people. The big day was tomorrow, and the Director was tearing his hair out.

'How much more did you say you needed?' he asked the canteen's head cook, exasperated.

'Mr Director, Sir, I really don't mean to cause any problems for you, but without twenty more pounds of meat or so, I cannot prepare the dishes you want. I am a cook and not a magician who can just shake a cow out of his sleeve.'

'Go back to the kitchen. I'll be there in a minute.' The Director's eyes were suddenly blazing with an inspiration. He rushed straight to the pigsty: 'Ahuang, come!'

His loyal buddy wagged his tail friskily as he gazed up at him. He blinked his velvety eyelids and radiated happy astonishment from every pore: the sky is still blue, it's not time for bed, so how come you are picking me up now?

A tender smile crept over the Director's features, but he coughed energetically to eliminate that dangerous sentiment from his breast. Rui, who was bent over a trough, looked up when he heard Ahuang barking so exuberantly.

The Director said, 'Tonight you will get to hear the camp directorate's official decision about Ahuang.' Then he called the dog to him and quickly left.

The sixty-seven-year-old Rui had been through a lot in his life, and there wasn't much that could hurt him deeply. But desolate tears were criss-crossing his weather-beaten face . . .

The Director first went to the office of the two assistant wardens; the three of them walked on together to the kitchen. 'Ahuang, my love, please jump on the scales,' the Director wheedled, as his young friend cocked his head quizzically. 'Hup-hup! Just stay still there a moment . . . Thirty pounds, my-oh-my, that breakfast milk of mine has certainly done him the world of good . . .' He was putting on a show of indifference, of callousness even, so that his fellow directors wouldn't laugh at him for being a softy who harboured affection for a dog. According to the Party, you were a true revolutionary only if you had it in you to sacrifice your own mother for a Communist objective. And right now that objective was: to make a favourable impression on the inspection team.

There was no need for explanations. The kitchen staff knew full well what this was leading up to. Uncle Dong, a broad-shouldered cook of about fifty, was chosen to execute the necessary preparations.

A VERY IMPORTANT VISITOR

We were roughly shaken from our sleep by a furious banging on the door. Aunt Qu, whose bunk was situated closest to the door, wrestled herself out of her warm blanket and sat up on the edge of her bed. She grumbled, 'What now? What's all the big stink about this time, in the middle of the night?'

It was Aunt Wen, the chief of the kitchen staff, who waltzed in and came straight to the point: 'New order from the Director's office: at lunchtime, make sure that the strips of meat in the dish Fried Bok Choy are clearly visible, on top of the vegetables. Save them for last – don't eat the meat until you have finished the cabbage.'

This announcement drew sleepy giggles. As if this too had been rehearsed, everyone assented in chorus: 'Okay, we'll make SURE that the Inspector can clearly SEE that we are served MEAT with our meal.' Disgusted, I turned my back on them. I tried to go back to sleep, to dream that I was flying – on my way to another country where I did not have to lie to survive.

The almighty loudspeakers squeaked, grated and crackled until everyone was wide awake. The irritating bellowing did not let up; it was nerve-wracking. The whining blare of bugles announced the reveille, a call to action:

> Onward, onward!
> Let us storm the headquarters
> of the Capitalist citadel!

After breakfast it was time for roll call. The prisoners were drawn up neatly in rows, as usual, in the courtyard. The Director arrived to take the muster in person.

'Number *One!*'

A greybeard stumbled forward and answered in a dull monotone, '*Dao*, present.'

The Director wrinkled his nose as he examined the human specimen before him – a mere wreck of a man who could hardly even stand up on his own two feet. He barked at him, 'Did you just roll out of bed, or what? Couldn't you have combed your hair? What do you think we give you people water for? For washing your ugly snout, of course! I fuck your grandfather!' Suddenly everybody began patting their hair flat, trying to comb it as neatly as they could with their fingers. 'And those glad-rags hanging off your body, Number One! They look like a baby's nappy! Did you decide to put on that tramp's clothing today on purpose, to advertise your contempt for the Dictatorship of the Proletariat?'

The gang of slave labourers turned pale. They all began fussing and pulling at their threadbare clothes. *Tchhh – tchh – tchh* . . . the sound of ripping fabric rippled up and down the rows.

This only increased the Director's irritation. He screamed, '*WHY* must you look like a herd of water buffalo that's just dragged itself out of the mud, *toDAY* of all days? You look like a bunch of decrepit deadbeats standing at death's door! What's the intention here – to humiliate me before the inspection team, by rubbing my nose in soot? Goddamn bastards born of unwed mothers! Back to your barracks! Go wash and dress yourselves properly, for once in ten generations! I give you half an hour to clean yourselves up. If after that I spot another filthy tramp like this one in my camp, he will spend a month as the pigs' houseguest!'

The prisoners pursed their lips indignantly. They always looked like this! Why was that a crime, all of a sudden? But nobody dared to ignore the Director's order. They spiffed themselves up as well as they could, the way they used to in years gone by, when they had not yet undergone the magical transformation that had made cow-devils and snake-demons of them all.

When they tried to leave their dormitories half an hour later, they found their way barred. They were not allowed outside: the Inspector had arrived and was touring the clean, orderly and politically correct prison camp. They were herded into a confined area like a flock of sheep. 'Don't talk so loud!' was the command. The guards were on their best behaviour today.

At eleven they were marched to the canteen. On the way there, the head guard yelled, 'I warn you: if any of you departs from the text by so much as a single word, he's in for it!'

I followed the slave labourers from a distance and entered the canteen after them. The walls were plastered with posters. In large characters it was written:

We bid a hearty welcome to the Revolutionary Inspection Team, which has come to bathe our prison camp in its bountiful aura! We bourgeois intellectuals are determined not to die before we are reborn as true proletarians. Should we accidentally pass away before that happens, then we shall make sure that we don't close our eyes as we breathe our last gasp.

A row of people in grey Mao-suits was seated on the podium. The women resembled scrappy fighting-cocks, whereas the men looked more like some old lecher's frustrated concubines. I scanned the line-up intently, but could not figure out which of them was the Inspector.

'Silence!' cried the Director.

One of the men on the podium climbed up on a chair, since he was too short to reach the microphone. He began to read from a bunch of papers:

'The east wind prevails over the west wind. The rivers all flow to the sea; all the peoples of the world are moving towards the Communist camp. He who causes the most heads to roll is the greatest hero; he who foments the greatest rebellion, is Mao's most loyal follower . . .'

After each sentence he scratched himself under the armpits, as if he were crawling with lice. Was *that* supposed to be the Inspector . . . ?

When the little man finally finished his oration, the meal was served. Everyone got a small bowl of rice, with a tiny quantity of stir-fried bok choy and a few strips of meat on top. Ordinarily I would have gone nuts just looking at it, but today it gave me a funny, unpleasant feeling. The bits of meat were dark red and lean, not the pinkish, fatty meat we were used to. I couldn't bring myself to take a bite, and looked around. Some people were gobbling it up as if it truly was a feast, but there were many others who could hardly swallow a bite.

The evening meal was distinguished by an unheard-off treat: rice porridge with mung beans and dates! The inmates lined up for seconds. Today they were allowed unlimited second helpings. The porridge was so thin that you could count the grains of rice and beans on the fingers of one hand. The only way to feel satisfied was to eat one bowl after another.

At around eight o'clock, almost two hours after the onset of the feast, the first casualties began to collapse on to the floor. They lay on their backs unable to move. The watery porridge had distended their bellies, blowing them up as round as an upside-down wok and as heavy as a mill stone. They just lay there moaning shamelessly. If they bawled too hard, their bellies quivered like a bowl of gelatin.

Fortunately the Inspector had already left by that time. The Director rounded up twenty young men and ordered them to fetch a dozen or so wheelbarrows from the shed. The gluttons were heaved on to the wagons, stomach and all, and then dumped in their dormitories. They looked like pregnant women being wheeled to the delivery room: the only difference was that their bellies bore nothing but water, with a grain of rice or two thrown in for good measure . . .

Still, nobody felt like laughing.

~

*I was sitting on Father's shoulders and was screaming with excitement. Because –
Grandfather Heaven and Grandmother Earth! – a goat, dressed in a yellow-gold
cape with red stripes, was dancing on a high-wire; a young lady was playing on
her erhoe, on two sheep-gut strings, and singing an ear-piercing song:*

Wusong, bare-fisted now,
Slays the tiger Jinqianbao

The excitement reached such a pitch that I almost wet myself.

'And now for Ahuang's high-wire act!' a man wearing a clown costume announced. Hey, what was the Director doing in the circus?

I followed the clown's pointing finger and saw, instead of a high-wire, a cross-beam over a gate, just like the one at the entrance to the camp. It was so wide that the sure-footed dog would easily be able to run over it, even with his eyes closed. What was so special about that? Or was Ahuang going to perform some other trick, something more difficult? I searched the audience's faces for some clarification. I sniffed the air – it smelled of gunpowder.

An animal trainer climbed up on top of the gate and cast a long rope over it. He jumped to the ground as nimbly as a monkey, and twisted the other end of the rope into a noose.

'Ahuang, slip your head into the noose!' cried Gao the Clown. The dog wouldn't listen and kept running in cricles. But Gao was a clever clown. He made his voice go all soft and crooned in a singsong tone, 'Ahuang, my sweet child. Come here, and we'll find some yummy bones for you to chew on.' Sure enough, within seconds the dog was panting expectantly at his feet. Noisily the clown instructed his assistant to hold the noose open in front of Ahuang's snout, and – whoops-a-daisy! Ahuang had neatly put his head through. The trainer ran back to the other end of the rope, pulled on it – rrrrrrrrrrrrrrrrrrrr – and now Ahuang was dangling from the top of the portal. The Acrobat with the Golden Fur was kicking his four legs wildly and jerking his head around.

I felt as if my throat were being cut. I wanted to scream, but I could not. I tried to breathe, but that too was nearly impossible. Shrieking with laughter, I bounced up and down like a pumped-up basketball: 'Oh, oh, look what a clever trick Ahuang is performing! Spinning around by a rope around his neck . . . ! A noose around his neck . . . !' I turned to the audience, slapping myself on the cheeks, the chest and the belly and screeching like a maniac: 'Ahuang is the best acrobat in the whole wide world! He has a killer technique! Long live A-hu-ang!!!'

Phut, phut . . . Behind my back, Ahuang was fighting for his life. I turned back towards him, laughing even more dementedly: 'Silly, don't struggle so, that only makes the noose tighter! Mr Clown, dear uncles and aunts, look – the rope is much too tight! He can't perform that way . . .' I flew, as if possessed, back and forth between the ring where the clown was standing and the dumbfounded audience. Suddenly it seemed as if I myself had become the main attraction, because everyone was looking at me. And Ahuang jerking his legs around up there all the while, with his eyes popping out of his head . . .

Looking up at my playmate, I saw that all of a sudden he didn't feel like being in the circus any more. He just gave up. He hung there motionless.

I began laughing again hysterically. 'Hey-y-y! Stop it, Ahuang, you're making us scared. Open your eyes . . .'

But Ahuang acted as if he didn't hear me. The audience applauded and laughed soundlessly. But no one lifted a finger to untie the acrobat from his perilous perch. I knelt down in the dirt and started kowtowing helplessly to everyone, over and over – donggg-dongggg-donggg. My head banged on the parched ground like a glass marble hitting a stone floor. The brown earth turned red with blood. I jumped up again, my arms flailing towards the ceiling. Weeping and laughing all at the same time, I called out to the animal trainer, 'Isn't it time to lower Ahuang now and give him his reward?'

But the show was over and the audience was moving towards the exits, chattering contentedly. Father grabbed me and began dragging me home. I sank my teeth into Father's hand and managed to wriggle out of his clutches.

I ran to Gao the Clown and looked him straight in the eye: 'What have you done with Ahuang?' The clown avoided my gaze, but I continued staring at him, my eyes following his like a magnet. Aauuuww! He'd given me a hard kick in the stomach! I fell and slid backwards on my bottom, leaving a skid mark a good two yards long . . .

I woke up screaming. With my hands stretched out I felt my way to Mother's bed, crying, 'Mama, where is Ahuang?'

'Ehnnnn . . .' There were sleepy grunts and groans from all sides. Mama pulled her blanket over my head and whispered, 'Shh, it was just a dream. Try to get some sleep. Nothing's the matter.'

'Really? I was so scared.'

I heard Mother sigh and slipped back between my own clammy covers. But I couldn't get to sleep again.

QIN'S ADVICE

Unexpectedly, Qin broached a subject that I had been studiously avoiding for some time: the Lily Theatre.

'Lian, when was the last time that you gave one of your history lectures?'

'Sorry, Sir, I . . .'

'You owe me neither an apology nor an explanation. Every time you speak in a negative way about China's past and her historical figures, you are left with a bad taste in your mouth, isn't it so?'

I nodded eagerly – how had he guessed?

'Child, I commend you. The gloomy picture our country evokes is clearly not to your liking, and you are looking for an escape hatch. I admire that. I myself am an old cynic, convinced that life has nothing more to offer. That is why it does me good to see that the younger generation yearns for a different outlook on life.'

I could never have predicted that the thing I had been dreading for months would take such a gratifying turn: instead of being criticised for giving up on my Lily Theatre lectures, here I was being *commended* for seeking another way of looking at the world!

'Lian, even though common sense tells me that I should try to see history in a more positive light, my mindset has hardened like my arteries: you can't teach an old dog new tricks.'

I nestled my head against his chest and slung my arms around his waist. We were both trembling – the very picture of powerlessness incarnate. In my quest for optimism and gladness, I could not turn to Mother for support. It was true, of course, that Qin was unable to give me that support as well, but the difference was that he wished that he could . . . I was discovering that even grown-ups did not have all the answers. How scary the world was, if you thought about it! Notwithstanding Qin's strong arms around me, I was shaking like an autumn leaf.

'Don't cry, please, or I shall feel even worse than I already do. I have been giving it a lot of thought lately: how can I help you further? Lian, my child, I am forced to admit it: I have no magic card up my sleeve. I am unable to give you a positive interpretation of the past or the present. I am giving up. I am letting you go.'

I pulled and tugged at his coat, howling so desperately that my lungs nearly burst, 'Uncle Qin, don't let me fall! What will I do without you?'

'Lian, little girl, letting go is not the same as letting you fall. An experienced doctor lets a patient go if he can't cure him, so that the sick one may find a more effective healer. Child, child, you are the sunshine of my old age and, oh, you don't know the half of it, how you brighten my life! I will never let you down. You have my word – the word of a prisoner who stared death in the face for ten long years.'

I stopped sobbing and looked at him dubiously. He really meant what he said! I grabbed his right hand and dragged him to a pile of flour sacks, on top of which we planted ourselves, side by side.

Qin said, 'A few days ago I was reminded of the well-known saying, "Knowledge is the sum of all aspects of the universe, and religion is the sum of all knowledge." Do you understand this sentence? It means that if rationally we don't know which way to turn any more, we can always resort to religion.'

'But religion is opium for the mind.'

'Who taught you that? Karl Marx said, "Religion is the opium *of the people.*" That is quite a different story.'

'I don't understand. What's the difference then?'

'Marx's wording is more subtle. It is non-judgemental. Literally, what he is saying is that religion is the "sigh of the oppressed creature", the "heart" sought by those living in a "heartless world". Religion is a must, in other words, for those who are in need. It is a very mild point of view.'

'Do you think he was right?'

'That, you will just have to figure out for yourself, Lian. My child, if I may be allowed to give you just one piece of advice, it is this: don't let anyone tell you what to think. Buddha has given you a brain: put it to work. And now for my proposal: I think you should tell your history stories to Cannibal from now on.'

'Cannibal? You mean the Lightbulb?'

'Yes, the Monk.'

'The Slobbering Worshipper of the Father, Mother, Lover and Mistress All-Rolled-Into-One?'

'Right, the Eternally Laughing One.'

'You can't be serious!'

'I used to think the same about him as you do now, but I'm not so sure these days . . . on the contrary, I suspect that if there is a way out of the labyrinth of your pessimism, it is to be found only with Cannibal's help. He can be your guide.'

I was silent. What could I say to him? That I had grave doubts about the sanity of his suggestion? Usually the things he said were much wiser than they seemed at first blush.

THE NAMES OF THE MONK

Walk up to Cannibal, just like that? It was such a weird idea that I needed time to get used to it. I mulled over what I remembered about the man and tried to put my finger on what kind of person he was. But it was an impossible task, because he was just like a *yaojing*. As soon as I had formed a picture of him in my mind, he would change into something else.

I wished I could discuss it with someone, somebody who would give me wise advice. I didn't have the nerve to turn to Qin for help. 'What?' he would ask me, 'haven't you been to see him yet?' *Then* what would I say? As for Mother, I could expect only moralising sermons from her, and that was the last thing I wanted.

Suddenly I knew what to do. I would go to my silent companion and loyal audience – the Lily Theatre.

⟡

From far away, sounds of spring came to greet me. Birds cheeped, grass-hoppers chirped, frogs croaked and legions of insects whose names I didn't even know sang in their sweetly piercing little voices a hymn of praise to the most fecund time of the year. A breeze tried to fondle my hair, but managed only to tousle it into stringy strands that whipped my face. Laughing at the wind mockingly, I tossed my head, showing him my destination: the lake.

'You know, spectators of the Lily Theatre, that Cannibal is a funny one. What did you say? Why doesn't he have a normal name like everyone else? Don't ask me, I wouldn't know. In any case, ever since I've been here, almost a year now, that is the name he's been known by. I was there when he received his other names, but more about that later. Everything in good time. First of all I will tell you how he got his nickname "Cannibal". Maly, my upstairs neighbour – you know, in the upper bunk bed – explained it to me.

'Three years ago, on the national holiday of the First of October – before Mother was sent here – the prisoners were served a banquet. According to Maly, it was a hundred times better than the meal we were served a few weeks ago, when the inspection team came to visit our camp. There were strips of meat as thick as your thumb. Maly was squatting in a corner and guzzling down the meat like a vacuum cleaner. As she regretfully licked her bowl clean, she saw that a large circle had formed around Cannibal. Only that wasn't his name yet, see? She went to look, her curiosity getting the better of her. *Ppfff!* She burst out laughing: big, strapping fellows and women with grown-up children were all standing around, their mouths hanging open, gaping at Cannibal's chopsticks. From time to time he would take a piece of meat out of his cabbage and deposit it into one of their outstretched bowls . . .

'The mood changed only once his bowl was empty and no more handouts could be expected. A number of the bystanders patted their stomachs, belched as was proper and then started baiting Cannibal in a teasing, even scornful tone, "Hey, why don't you eat the meat yourself? Are you afraid of tapeworm or something?"

'Cannibal put his utensils down on the ground and said, "Before the

Cultural Revolution I was a Buddhist. Alas, I am no longer permitted to practise my religion." He gazed at his public circumspectly. "That is to say, not openly. That is why I call myself a vegetarian these days."

'"A veggie-muncher," someone in the crowd sneered, by way of explanation. "But do you get enough protein and other essential nutrients to stay in shape?"

'"Look at a gorilla. It could pick you up and fling you right across the canteen like a ping-pong ball – and it eats nothing but bananas and other fruit."

'The onlookers had no comeback for that. Someone enquired, "Can you explain the theological doctrines behind the Buddhists' vegetarianism?"

'Cannibal's face lit up. "In the *Little Red Book* it says, Religions are childish misinterpretations of the phenomena of the universe. So, most esteemed audience, I ask that you please employ this revolutionary mental weapon to palliate what I am about to say. And that is: reincarnation. That is the answer. A living thing can assume different forms, in successive lives. In one life it is a person, in another life it can just as easily be a pig. That is why, if I were to eat this meat, I might be munching on my grandpa, if after his death he was reincarnated as a pig.'

'"*Woh-woh-woh, woh-woh-wah!*" The crowd doubled over with laughter. Their guffawing filled the entire canteen. Some of them were truly tickled by this notion; others were just laughing to cover up their own fear. Supposing he was right!

'But one man with a pale mug yelled: "Eat your grandpa? What a cannibalistic idea!" Whoa, that caused the mob to see it in quite a different light. They yelled, in chorus, "A cannibal, that's what you are!"

'And do you know how Cannibal got his second name, "Lightbulb?" Once every two months, the male prisoners are given leave to visit the barber in the nearby village. Every time that he goes there, Cannibal tells the barber, "Just shave my head."

'"Completely bald?"

'"Yes, bald as a lightbulb."

'He was given the nickname "Monk" last year, when he'd finally had enough of the guards' kicks and curses and petitioned the authorities to be allowed to return to the Qingyun Temple in the Wutai mountains. There he hoped to pay his respects to his old meditation teacher and to resume his life as a monk. He had been apprenticed to his master since the age of five; it was assumed at the time that he would succeed him. At the start of the Fifties, however, he became curious about the "Communist" State that Mao had founded; it was said to be a paradise on earth. He said goodbye to his master, left the mountains and trekked into the interior. Since he was one of the few people who still knew how to read Sanskrit, and thanks to his thorough grounding in Buddhism, he was offered a post at Teachers' University. The ruthless political upheavals of 1953 and after left him badly shaken, but he never gave a single thought to returning to the safe haven of Wutai some day . . . until last year.

'You can imagine what the Director's answer was: "Well, well, hadn't you better beg your mother to stuff you back into her belly, since life out here isn't to your liking any more? Opportunist! When there's more fun to be had in the secular world, you leave the temple, but as soon as it gets a little too hot for comfort here, you wish to return to the mountains. No way!" The Director relished licking the honey pot of his power; he liked to twist Cannibal like a helpless rabbit in his bear-claws, scratching and pinching him here and there, thus prolonging his own exquisite enjoyment of Cannibal's torment.

'"The Eternally Laughing One" is a more recent invention by the inmates. I haven't been able to discover when this name was first coined, but the fact is that Cannibal, in the past six months, has become increasingly prone to bursting into laughter, guffawing ever more heartily and uninhibitedly – like a baby that's being tickled and cuddled by its doting mother. Even the most exhausting work in the field, the most humiliating denunciation meeting, cannot extinguish Cannibal's good-natured cheeriness. He is the only one who wanders around the camp whistling, and I'm sure if he weren't seventy-two and a little unsteady on his feet, he'd be skipping. His attitude to his incarceration is unique. "Isn't it wonderful here?" he'll say. "We don't have to rack our brains to find an original topic of research or write an important treatise; we don't have to do any shopping, since we have our meals cooked for us three times a day. And where in Beijing would we find such marvellous fresh air? Here we live a healthy life, performing physical labour in the great outdoors. This is precisely what our ancient masters hailed centuries ago as the privilege of the immortals. Besides, try to put yourself into the shoes of Mao, the Greatest and Wisest Leader of the Universe. What else is He to do with a bunch of intellectual snobs like us, who know too much about ideals and understand sod-all about reality? I can understand why He has stuck us in a camp: to rub our noses in the cold hard facts. This is a land of peasants. We cannot expect a democratic system on the Western model to grow up here just like that."

'He shouldn't have said that. Even though there are a good many turncoats among us, nobody can countenance Mao's treatment of the intelligentsia. This last comment earned Cannibal his nastiest nickname of all: "Slobbering Worshipper of the Father, Mother, Lover and Mistress All-Rolled-Into-One."'

When I had finished speaking, nature's concert took over once more. An unbroken chain of sound wrapped itself around all living things and whispered sweet nothings into my ears – in the name of love, of life and of love of life. What was I making myself hot under the collar for, over ideology and all that silly business? Why couldn't I just enjoy *being*, simply for itself?

No, it wasn't that simple. I wanted to know the exact score, to sort it all out – therein lay the key to my happiness. I said quickly: 'Tell me, spectators of the Lily Theatre, what do you think of Cannibal? Is he half-baked, or is he a genius? Is he the one who can deliver me from my blues, or isn't he?'

THE GREEN SEA

Two months went by. I had not said another word to Qin about my history-talks or about Cannibal. Then one sunny day I returned to the lake. I went and stood on my familiar rock and said, 'Hello there, spectators of the Lily Theatre! It has been a long time since I visited you. Are you angry with me? Oh, please don't be, because I really did *want* to visit you, but I was in such a muddle! Those talks about China's history really rattled me, so a couple of months ago I decided to stop agonising about my fatherland's sad past and its depressing present. And, spectators of the Lily Theatre, you can see that even without my worrying about it, the earth keeps turning round.'

The all-embracing silence and the fresh air that permeated every pore of every living being, enfolded me as if there had never been a problem between us. The soft wind whispered in my ear, 'Hey, Lian! You're back. Finally! Welcome home!' There wasn't even a pinprick of reproach in his voice. I let myself relax totally, but at the same time all my five senses quickened . . .

Smell! Spring was in the air. Ribbons of fresh, resinous odour caressed my nose and made my heart race. Unfurling flowers exhaled their sweet, mesmerising breath, nearly sending me into a trance. Light-green buds poked their timid heads up here and there from the brown branches, while others were already boldly and irrepressibly flaunting bright-yellow blooms. Wild flowers were strewn over the grass like stars in the night sky. When a breeze darted past them, they batted their eyes saucily like coquettish beauties. The water-lily fronds in the pond sparkled, dazzling in the sun.

A pair of robins was busy building a nest in a silver birch. Elsewhere two blackbirds were beginning to warm up their vocal cords so that when they gave it full throat, their love song would sound even more seductive. The birds' warbling mingled with the murmuring of the brook that flowed along the pond to the wheat field; their song was the lovely duet 'Springtime Sonata'.

I followed the stream and reached the field – a deep-pile carpet of dark green. A gust of wind, and suddenly the carpet turned mint-green – the plants bowed low, revealing the bright lining beneath their skirts. I ran into the green sea and sank into its outstretched arms . . . My fears, my doubts and worries evaporated. The boundaries between me and my surroundings faded bit by bit. I was melting, didn't exist any more . . .

> *free as a barn swallow*
> *wide-open as the wheat field*
> *transparent as the pregnant spring air*
> *light as the dancing grasses*
> *gay as the smiling flower faces*

Feel! The wind was gentle at this season, velvety as Mother's caressing hand. My pores opened wide and a strong current of blood pulsed its way through my blood vessels and was pumped into all my extremities.

Look! Nature grows and blooms, heedless of people and their vicious, murderous ways. The universe is far above human folly; it goes its own way, year in and year out. Nothing and nobody, no matter how powerful and fearsome, can hold back the cycle of nature.

Listen! Hear the silent, yet clearly audible voice of nature. Was this the path I should take, then – was this the way out of my pessimism, the escape hatch I had been searching for?

Should I try viewing the harsh facts – such as forced labour, brainwashing and denunciation meetings – as nothing but hallucinations? Could the re-education camp, the pigswill I was served every day and the filthy, windowless, cockroach-infested dormitory be figments of my imagination? They were things that seemed awfully portentous, but here in the wide open, fragrant, colourful wheat field, they carried no more weight than a mosquito attempting to disturb a symphony.

I twirled around, looked up, let the orange sun pour light into my eyes, and cast my vote for nature.

I ran back to my dormitory, fumbled around in the straw on my bed and drew out the triangular shard of glass that was my mirror. I had found it four months ago, on my way to the public latrines. In order not to arouse any busybodies' suspicions, I kept it safely hidden beneath the straw. Every so often, when everyone was in the fields, I would take it out.

But the last time had been over a month ago. Today, I suddenly felt like looking at myself: I did not know why.

Was *that* slob there me? My left plait was sloppily braided, it sported a big bump in the middle. Strands of hair tangled down over my face like a floor-mop. 'I look like a neglected poodle,' I thought out loud.

But underneath the messy hair I could see my eyes dancing. Never had I seen such sparks of excitement twinkling in those irises. Where did they come from all of a sudden? I raised my hands to my head to comb the mop back with my fingers.

But wait a minute! What the . . . ? The white patches on my hands and arms were gone! There was no trace of them! Hastily I rolled up my trouser legs. Buddha Almighty! I stared at the smooth clear skin on my shins and was struck dumb.

I was quiet for a long time. Then I exploded. 'How can you expect me to believe . . . !' I roared at my astonished image in the mirror, as if I suspected the other Lian of playing tricks on me, 'How can my chronic, stubborn vitiligo have vanished into thin air, just like that?'

Ten minutes went by. But the blotches did not return. My skin still refused to show a single blemish. I just couldn't understand it. Think, I ordered myself, how did I come to be cured? I had drunk the root tea that Kim had provided me with for forty days at most, and that had been almost a year ago, before the Director had forbidden me to associate with Kim and her family lest I infect innocent peasants with my poisonous bourgeois ideas. Since then I had done nothing more about my skin condition. I didn't know why, but the favourite saying of my grandpa in Qingdao went spinning through my head:

> *When you have nothing left to wish for,*
> *You will be drenched in good fortune*

I continued the inspection. The grey trousers, originally a light blue, hung around my waist like a rag. My jacket glistened like a suit of black armour. The material was coated with a disgusting layer of dust and grease, which made it glint like metal under the room's fluorescent lights. How *could* I have let myself go like this?

I dragged a wooden chest out from beneath Mother's bed and rummaged in it for a clean outfit. Then I went outside. I didn't know why, exactly. To show off, I feared. But except for the kitchen staff and the swine-keepers, the only people left in the camp were the wardens. And even they were indoors. The courtyard was deserted. Still, I was conscious of my posture. Was my back straight when I walked, was I sucking in my stomach? Or did I look like poor Ahuang trotting along? I felt a thousand eyes on me, every one of them detecting a defect in my posture and deducting points for it.

I remembered my cousin Fengyi, the belle of her village, and tried to think how she walked. Like this: very slowly and gracefully. I tried imitating Fengyi as subtly as I could, but, Grandpa Heaven!, how could I be expected to move like that all the time? To reach the gate, which was only two hundred yards away, would take me at least an hour at this rate!

AWAKENING

After he had made the decision not to attend my lectures any more, Qin stayed away from the Lily Theatre. But the history lessons continued as before. One day he told me about the Second Agricultural Reform in the Fifties. It was during that campaign that the landlords had been made to renounce all their possessions, including their concubines.

I did not know what in Buddha's name prompted me to ask the professor the idiotic question, 'Is it true that the landlords' concubines were for the most part good-looking?'

He shook his head, gave a sigh, but couldn't help smiling in the end. 'Lian, you are getting to be a big girl.'

This time it was my turn to be nonplussed. What was he talking about?

Qin went on, 'You don't belong here. You are now at a stage when the only way for you to start knowing yourself is to be with young people your own age.'

I had, in fact, completely forgotten that I was a child. In the eleven months I had lived in the camp, I had adjusted to the adults' ways. I had long outgrown the need to play with my peers. The only one I missed was Kim. But I didn't even think of Kim very often. How was she doing? It was the first time in months the question had occurred to me . . .

During our home leave Mother asked me to run some errands. Dawdling on my way to the university store, I studied all the people I passed intently. The girls my age especially attracted my attention. One girl had a flat nose, another lips that were too thick, the next one had very shapely legs . . . Oh, no! I was overcome with self-consciousness. How could I take another step, when my own legs looked like the bamboo poles for holding up the mosquito net!

I wonder why I'm so interested in girls these days, I thought. Boys and adults left me cold. All the boys my age or older seemed to have that nasty stubble on their upper lip – sometimes even on their chins. They looked far from clean and their voices honked like rusty hacksaws. But most of all, and this was what was most repugnant about them, they stank. They gave off an indescribable odour, like . . . just like . . . That was it! Like rotten cauliflower. I avoided them like the plague.

Grown-ups, it was fair to say, did not smell of rotten cauliflower, but I did not find them attractive either. Their only topics of conversation were prosaic things, like denunciation meetings, the latest political developments, the work in the fields and, at a pinch, the cooking and the washing. They never blushed when they were paid a compliment, and hardly ever seemed to get depressed when criticised. They lectured me to 'act normal' when I got the giggles or when I was hopping up and down with enthusiasm. As if *they* had the exclusive rights to decide what was 'normal' . . .

TAKING THE BULL BY THE HORNS

Three months to the day after Qin had counselled me to seek out Cannibal, I finally decided to chance it, in case he could cure me of my blues.

I walked to the southernmost corner of the canteen where the lone figure of Cannibal was polishing off his lunch all by himself.

'So, Lian, you have come.'

There was something arresting in his voice – but what was it? I squatted beside him and began chattering away. With his knowing gaze, he seemed able to look right through me. Suddenly I understood that he had known for ages that I would come to him some day. His 'You have come' had not been meant as the standard greeting, but something more along the lines of 'Here you are at last!'

I tilted my head, studying him attentively, and wondered what prompted this grown-up man to behave so like a child. For surely only the very young and very naïve believed in premonitions, yet this man wasn't embarrassed about showing that he had known I was going to come . . . I let my small-talk peter out in the end, for I realised that Cannibal was waiting patiently for me to come out with what had really brought on this visit.

But before I could start, he jumped in with, 'I cannot judge if your stories are historically correct. My expertise does not lie in that direction. All I can do is comment on the *vision* you have of the historical facts which *you* accept as being true.'

I said quickly, 'That's all I'm asking for.'

'When do you wish to begin?'

'Uh . . .' Mother could not ask the Director for yet another teacher. If we failed to find an opportunity to meet in the daytime, then it was not going to happen. At night, after toiling in the fields, he'd be much too exhausted and would not have any time for me . . .

But he himself came up with a solution. 'Shall we make a date for Sunday afternoons, after denunciation meeting? That is to say, whenever we don't have home leave, and Aunt Xiulan and I cannot go home?'

'Oh, but don't you need that time for buying eggs and nuts on the black market?'

I immediately wished I hadn't blurted out that tactless remark: for of course Cannibal would never eat an egg, the embryo of a living thing, as he reverently called it.

He just looked at me, and got up to rinse his bowl. I called after him, 'At the lake, behind the barracks!'

A NEW PERSPECTIVE

I had come to know the Lily Theatre's loveliness mostly from my early-morning visits with Qin, when the morning mist drew a veil over the lake and I had to shout out my historical monologues in order to drown out the frogs. But this time, the mist had been chased away by the intense heat of the midday sun. Instead of the mystery and serenity of early morning, it was now the brilliant clarity and vitality of the scene that moved me.

My jaw dropped. The cobalt-blue hill in the distance had turned an emerald green. And not only that: the same hill now had a twin sister, except that this one was standing on its head. A spring breeze caused it to ripple, like laundered sheets fluttering in the wind. The mirror images had something mystical about them – which image was real and which was an illusion? The lake's looking-glass surface, in which I had once seen Qin's likeness, could make a reflection appear so absurdly real . . .

Rrshh-rrshh . . . A rustling of clothes broke the silence. When I looked round, I saw that Cannibal was choosing a place to sit down for himself. I checked the urge to help him, because he didn't look like he needed help. I thought of Qin: he would plunk himself down in the mud if he weren't led to a dry spot. But Cannibal calmly found a place that suited him, then crossed his legs in the lotus position and closed his eyes.

I stared at my new audience; I secretly doubted he would be able to follow my story in his meditative state. I brushed the thought aside, however, and began, trusting I did have his full attention. My talk was about the political manoeuverings that the Wisest Leader of the Universe had devised and carried out since 1949 in order to eliminate His opponents systematically, one by one. I also spoke of the dozens of lethal mass-movements that He had called to life, ostensibly to further the creation of a Communist Paradise, but in reality meant to secure His own throne.

I was just beginning to hit my stride when suddenly I was startled by Cannibal's voice . . .

'Lian, Lian!' Cannibal, was saying, shaking his head. 'How bitter you are about the Never-Setting Sun! I had better stay out of your way, I think, because your anger is like a time bomb that's about to go off – it could blow us sky-high any minute, Him and me both!'

'Well, do you approve of what He has done? His manipulation of the CPC rank and file, for instance, to make His own dreams of empire become a reality?'

'Do you know the saying, *A fly doesn't suck an egg that has no crack in it*? If the Communists had used their brains instead of blindly believing what He preached, then He would never have managed to hitch them to His bandwagon, or, in your words, to turn their revolutionary enthusiasm to His own private ends.'

I just stood there flabbergasted. But a huge bubble of anger was ballooning up inside me. What an idiotic thing to do, to condone what Mao had done with that rotten old saying!

Cannibal could read my thoughts. 'I don't condone it either, little girl, I just want to show you the connection between cause and effect. The problem lies not only with Him, but also with Him *and* His fanatical worshippers. In point of fact, He has done nothing more than to allow them to harvest the fruit of their own foolishness.'

This only caused the indignant balloon in my belly to swell larger. 'The people had hardly any education, they weren't capable of rationalising.

Don't you think it was unfair of the smarter ones to take advantage of the people's ignorance?'

'*C'est la vie*, child. Haven't you heard of Darwin's law – the survival of the fittest?'

I wasn't listening any more. Bitterly disappointed, I turned away from this cynical man. But he went on, unperturbed: 'That is the most common mistake people make: the great majority of our countrymen, including yourself, blame the Great Helmsman for their suffering under the Communist regime. But they cannot, and will not, understand that without their own collaboration, their subjugation would be impossible.'

'Collaboration? No one does that! We aren't nuts.'

'No, but we *are* stupid. For what do we do? Well, we look, first of all, at our neighbours. Are *they* opposing Him? No? Well, then why should *we* stick our necks out? It's a vicious cycle. The less people there are with enough guts to take a stand, the more dangerous it becomes for any single individual to offer resistance. And guess who is reaping the profits from all this? The Invincible Leader!'

The icy lump in my stomach seemed to be on fire; I was racked with a sharp pain. 'For Buddha's sake! Excuse me for swearing, but I'm so mad I'm going to explode! If I am to believe you, people like us can get kicked around like a bunch of stray mutts, yet we're not allowed to complain, because it's our own bloody fault!'

'But Lian, it is easy for us to change all that. Not by going after the scapegoat in word or in deed, but by becoming more aware of what we are doing, and accepting the consequences.'

'Are you calling Him our scapegoat?'

'Yes. He has actually done nothing wrong. All He did was to follow His heart: he wanted to implement His ideas about government and look after His own interests. Isn't that what every human being wants? I am convinced that any simple farmer endowed with His talents, guts and luck would have done the same thing. Nobody is a "saint", don't delude yourself. We are all mortal, we all have needs and desires. The point is that some day, we'll have to stop blaming Him for our misery. Then we can concentrate on bettering ourselves instead.'

'In what way?'

'By assuming the responsibility for our own happiness. That way, we'd no longer feel the need to worship our leader as a god, nor place our fate into his hands. Then, if things went badly for us, we would have only ourselves to blame, instead of pinning it on the god we had created.'

For a moment, I perked up at the thought of the future that Cannibal was painting. He was right: how you live your life is up to you. Yet the bad feeling in the pit of my stomach prevailed. Oh, Buddha, how could I *not* blame Him and the CPC for the misery everywhere? Just look, for instance, at the fresh corpses floating in Willow Lake behind the University every morning – the tortured bodies of professors and teachers who, in the end, opted for the release of death over a living hell. Just listen to the heart-rending weeping of children whose parents are being deported before their eyes, or the lamentation of spouses who are hardly granted any time to say goodbye before being sent to separate prison camps and who don't know, by Buddha, when or whether they'll ever see each other again. Just smell the sad stench of hospitals, where the maimed lie groaning . . .

I threw myself headlong on to the grass and began pummelling the earth with my fists. Floored by impotence and fury, I directed all my outrage at Cannibal. Grabbing his wrists and kicking him in the shins, I cried, 'It's so unfair! Uncle Cannibal, tell me how we can talk ourselves into *not* being livid at Party leaders who don't think twice about sacrificing a billion people in their own personal quest for power! You don't feel our pain, do you; you plead for *forgiveness* for the Party . . .'

He let me kick him and gazed at me, unruffled and calm, holding me by the arms so that I would not fall. Eventually I sank to the ground, spent.

'Lian, look at your uncle. Please look at me, even if it's only for one second. Do you really think that *I* have no reason to hate the regime? My only brother, a prominent brain surgeon, was clubbed to death three years ago; his corpse was left on the railway tracks to make it look like suicide. And all this just because he had once said that knowing the *Little Red Book* by heart wasn't enough if you wanted to remove a tumour from a patient's head! Do you know why I couldn't return to Mount Wutai last year to resume my life as a monk in the temple of Qingyun? The fact that the Director refused to give his permission was immaterial; don't you think I would have tried to escape otherwise? Listen to me – you are the only one I have ever told this to: a month after this I heard from one of my former brother monks that our Master, the highly venerated Qingyun, was burned to death by the Red Guards back in 1969. He was one hundred and sixty-three years young at the time. Having outlived one dynasty, two emperors and ten presidents of the Chinese Republic, he died at the hands of a bunch of snot-noses calling themselves Red Guards. His death made me an orphan – Master Qingyun was like a father to me. Can't you see how I hated our country's regime? Do you truly believe that I can't sympathise with how rotten you feel, a child who has been through so much misery by the tender age of thirteen?'

He felt the muscles in my arms relax and gazed at me tenderly: 'But, my little Lian, if I were to allow myself to be swept along by your despair as well as my own, then there would be only one thing left for us to do: to bawl, to wail endlessly, to weep until we don't know which end is up any more. And what good would it do? I *must* open your eyes, so that you may rise above these concerns, so that you may have a glimpse of the eternal sunlight hiding behind the black clouds. As an adult, I feel it is my obligation to you. *Now* do you understand what I'm getting at? Did you come looking for me in order to drag me down with you into your despair over the Cultural Revolution – or did you come looking for some insight that will release you from it? So – *now* do you still hate your uncle?'

I looked up at him, laughing through my tears, and flung myself into Cannibal's arms. Smoothing the tangle of my hair with his bony fingers, he said softly, 'Child, child, the day will come when you will be happy, without dread, without sorrow or torment, I assure you. Your uncle used to feel that way when he was studying to be a monk in the Temple of Qingyun. What a wonderful sensation it was . . . it was like being a wisp of cloud floating through the thin air, feeling one with the universe, one with both heart and soul . . .'

I didn't need to study to become a monk – not for now, at least. Here at Cannibal's side I was already in seventh heaven. Qin had been right. If anyone could cure me of my gloomy outlook and give me a brand-new lease on life, it was Cannibal.

A CHANGE OF CLIMATE

'Attention, attention! Today at half past eight there will be an emergency meeting for all detainees and staff. Location: the canteen. Everyone must attend. The shift work in the fields is suspended for today.' The loudspeakers repeated this announcement over and over until my subconscious was no longer able to weave it into my dreams.

An earthquake – again. Right above me, Professor Maly turned over in bed, causing the bunk bed to shake and creak. Strips of morning light crept cautiously through the ventilation holes into the dormitory, garlanding the room with silver ribbons. In the broken light, I saw Mother's groping fingers stirring in the bed next-door. With much mumbling and grumbling, Mother managed to dig up her watch from the nether reaches of her pillow. 'It's only five a.m.! What can possibly be so urgent that we have to be woken up at such a cock-a-doodle ungodly hour?'

'Hmmmm . . .' Mother's words drew a flood of sleepy and plaintive throat-sounds from her room-mates. Even though they were all annoyed at the loudspeakers that were interrupting their night's sleep – as a rule our sole reprieve from Party interference – nobody was genuinely angry. I gathered this from the way the 'hmmmmm's trailed off into lengthy, mellow endnotes. Over the past few months there had been a general feeling in the air that the Cultural Revolution was in for some kind of positive change. The ideological typhoon had been raging for seven long years and had pushed the stamina of an already starving and degraded populace to the limit. It would not be long before there was a mass uprising. The Wisest Leader of the Universe would not *be* the Wisest Leader of the Universe if He failed to bring his political blitzkrieg to a timely end. For all 'good' rulers in history have always known exactly how much privation, war, fear and suffering they can pile on their subjects without provoking them to rise up in revolt. Could today be the day we would hear the long-awaited news of a change in the offing? No one dared to express this furtive dream out loud, of course.

Just as we did every morning, we got out of bed, brushed our teeth over the stinking ditch in front of the dormitory, and rubbed our faces with our grubby grey towels, in total silence. At eight thirty we were neatly drawn up in rows on the canteen's wooden benches. The noise of chatting and yelling that usually marked political gatherings was notably absent today. People were holding their breath.

I was sitting next to Mother. Soon after my arrival in the camp, the Director had said that it couldn't do any harm for me to attend the meetings, even if I *was* a child. On the contrary: this way I would get a head start on the cultivation of my proletarian consciousness.

'Look, Mama, the portrait of the Vice-Chairman of the CPC is missing!' I whispered into Mother's ear, loudly enough for people sitting within fifteen feet to hear my words clearly. I was pointing at the podium. Mother raised her right hand and drew a half-circle in the air with it. Even before her open palm cracked down on my left cheek, I was already doubled over: I reckoned this blow might knock out at least two molars.

Pow! I fell facedown on the ground. In spite of the pain, I first brought my hands up to my jaw, because I fervently hoped some of my teeth had been punched out. Then I would get up with a mouth full of blood, and all the aunts and uncles would feel sorry for me and berate Mother. But alas, all I had was some abrasions on my forehead, cheeks and the bridge of my nose. Mother never hit hard enough to arouse indignation in others; that way, she could go on thrashing me without ever having to face the consequences.

Sure enough, the Vice-Chairman was in dire straits. According to the official document now being read out to us, the Party leadership had avoided a fatal crisis just in time. The Vice-Chairman, together with a few ministers and secretaries of state who were his alleged accomplices, had attempted to overthrow the government. When word of their plot leaked out, Mao had them arrested and launched an anti-revisionist campaign against them.

With a throbbing pain in my left cheek and question marks swimming inside my head, I frowned, my eyebrows bristling like a rolled-up porcupine. Was this good news, or was it bad news? Since I didn't dare ask Mother, I tried to work it out for myself. The fact that the Father, Mother, Lover and Mistress All-Rolled-Into-One had weeded out another nest of opponents didn't impress me in the least, for He had engineered that feat dozens of times. The question that did concern me, however, was: had this incident finally made the Leader come to His senses a little? Would it make Him realise that these never-ending political mass movements would eventually ruin the country?

As was to be expected, the carefully worded document admitted that the government was indeed concerned about the social unrest and economic recession that had been holding the nation hostage for eight years. However, according to Mao, it was all the fault of this gang of counter-revolutionaries and revisionists. Luckily, now that their devilish plot had been unmasked, the government could lead the people into rebuilding a nation of order and prosperity. But when the last clause of the document was read out, my heart took a leap. The Party held out that it was conceivable that some easing of the re-education policy, and a shortening of bourgeois-intellectuals' sentences, was foreseeable. There was hope, in other words, that Mother would soon be released and that Father, too, would return home some day, at long last.

CONFLICTING FEELINGS

I was sitting in the dorm doing my homework. Suddenly the door opened: Mother was back. It was three in the afternoon. 'Isn't there any work left to do in the rice paddy?' I asked, astonished.

Mother tried to wipe the mud stains from her face but succeeded only in smearing them together into a thick brown mask: 'There's always something to do, but I have to go and speak with the Director in his office.' After unrolling and smoothing down her trouser legs with deft strokes, she trotted off to see the Director.

'Shouldn't you wash your face first?' I called after her, flabbergasted that a woman as particular about hygiene as Mother should dare to see the camp's overseer with such a filthy mug.

Forty-five minutes later Mother returned, beaming. 'Lian, as of today I am a free woman! Tomorrow we are going home, for good!'

The ceiling was swirling around before my eyes – I felt as if I were floating. Tears poured down my face. Instead of joy, I felt only sadness – sadness over the injustice and despair that the two of us had had to endure over the past year and a half. I ran to Mother, clasped her tightly, then buried my head in her arms so that she would not see me cry.

Images and sensations from the past came flooding back. I saw Father waving to us from the moving train; I heard Mother weeping like a little baby, and wondered why she was so sad; I could taste the yellow dust-clouds thrown up by the trucks taking Mother and the other detainees away from the children they had to leave behind in the unwelcoming Accommodation Centre.

Mother stroked my head and said, 'Don't make so much noise, or the others will hear what lucky dogs we are. I am one of the first four detainees to be allowed to leave the camp. The other two hundred and forty-six must wait for their own release, and only Buddha knows how long that will take. You'll make them feel twice as bad by showing your feelings so openly.'

'But why are you being allowed to go home before the rest? Are they . . . are they . . . going to make you . . . fill more textbooks with lies?'

'Shhhh . . . ! You'd better watch that blasphemous tongue of yours! That's no way to speak about the Party! No, child, not this time, thank God. The new Vice-Chairman of the CPC has just outlined a new political course for our nation. He commands us, among other things, to begin teaching again. Uncle Yie – remember him, the tall, skinny man who gave you the crow? – used to be the Dean of Teachers' University. He has been asked to start enrolling new students for the coming year. Our university will be offering courses again for the first time in seven years! Professor Yie and I have been assigned to write a book, to be entitled *An Oral Modern History of China, 1911 to 1949*. I have just read the letter the Vice-Chairman sent to our faculty: the term "faithful to history" is to be the basic premise and touchstone of our assignment. So what do you think? Is our country finally headed in the right direction, or what?'

'But why is this project so important all of a sudden?'

'What a silly goose you are, Lian. By setting up this research project, the Party wishes to make sure that the experience, knowledge and insight of the generals and the highest party officials – those who have not yet been purged by the Cultural Revolution, that is – will be recorded in timely fashion. Soon there won't be anyone left alive who was around before the founding of the People's Republic.'

'So what time do we leave tomorrow?'

'Around eight o'clock. Uncle Yie and the two other gentlemen who have also been granted their freedom have chosen to return on the regular weekend-leave transport that departs on Saturday. Not I! I don't wish to stay here a minute longer. That is why I asked at the Administration Office if there was any other way of getting to Beijing. By a stroke of luck, there's a tractor-truck going to the capital tomorrow to pick up new equipment for the summer season. We have permission to leave on that.'

Boy, oh boy, what an effort it was to keep my face straight! I was practically out of my mind with excitement, but Mother had made me promise I wouldn't gloat, in case I made the ones we were leaving behind green with envy.

Mother tied a huge luggage-roll on to my back. Inside it we had stuffed my quilt, pillow, clothes, toiletries, washbasin and stacks of books. Thus weighed down, I could not stand up straight; all I could see was the muddy road beneath my feet. The load on Mother's back was even more impressive, and she was carrying two bulging bags besides, containing a thermos, a fly-swatter, a folding stool, enamel bowls and plates, shoes and rubber boots.

Mother and I were thankful to Buddha, however, for having our faces turned to the ground, because the prospect of saying goodbye to our former comrades weighed heavily on us. What would we say to them? That we were overjoyed to be escaping this living hell? That it would soon be their turn to be released? But who were we to predict such a thing? The Wisest Leader of the Universe was known to change his mind as regularly as day fades into night.

Suddenly my load felt lighter. I turned around gingerly. I saw two arms, then a pair of kind eyes. Professor Maly was lifting my roll up to take some of the weight off my back. Maly was silent, and I was terrified of blurting out something that might hurt her. Suddenly I heard other footsteps behind me; the ground shook and groaned. It was the detainees, come to wave us fortunate ones off. I felt an extraordinarily strong bond of fellowship with my former comrades, who were walking behind us in total silence. Tears mixed in with the mud at my feet; all I really wanted was to turn round and run right back into the familiar dorm.

Tooo, too, TOO! The tractor began to growl and I saw Mother flinging the luggage up on to the flatbed. Maly relieved me of my backroll and hoisted it, too, into the well. The driver, Tiangui, a young man whose usual assignment was chopping vegetables in the kitchen, climbed into the driver's seat and took hold of the controls. The vehicle lunged, and a deafening roar fanned out in all eight directions of the wind. Black smoke spewed from the exhaust pipe sticking up out of the tractor's bulbous nose. I stared at the wondrous contraption, fascinated.

Tiangui's shout interrupted my musings. 'Lian, climb up into the back, sit down and hold on tight to those bars. This tractor can really shake!'

At the same moment Maly grabbed me by the arms and said with tears in her eyes, 'My child, I congratulate you on your release. Do your best at school and make something beautiful of your life!'

Her words acted as a fuse that ignited over two hundred other voices: 'Yunxiang and Lian, congratulations! We wish you all the best!'

A drab mass of drained faces, matted hair and skinny arms was waving at us enthusiastically. There wasn't even a grain of envy; they were all overflowing with love and sincere good wishes. Up on the tractor's flatbed, Mother, who was generally disinclined to show her emotions, ripped the ragged scarf from her neck and started slapping it against her knees while uttering heart-rending screams – how shamelessly vulgar of her, I thought, just like a peasant wife that has to watch her only dairy cow die.

I dived back into the wall of people, blindly shaking the hands of uncles and aunts, and crying, 'We'll go home together! We'll all go home together!' I zig-zagged left and right, banging my head against the chest of whoever happened to be nearest, and just for a moment, I was convinced I was dying of sadness, helplessness and the conflicting emotions boiling over inside me.

Two strong hands grabbed hold of me and dragged me back towards the tractor. I knew it was Professor Qin: he had picked me up in the same way that he might hoist a flour sack in the mill . . . I let myself go limp in his arms, trying to make myself twice as heavy, so that Qin would have to work twice as hard to drag me along. Grandpa Heaven, was this to be our last contact ever? I wanted to stretch the moment out for ever . . .

'Listen to me, Lian, do you want to go home, or not?' Qin's voice was alarmingly gruff.

Strange, though, to my ears, his voice sounded sweeter than ever. Even if he screamed at me, I would still adore him.

'Uncle Qin! I don't *want* to go home! I want to be with you! Let's start all over again. From the beginning. This time . . . this time I won't be so negative any more about history, really, I promise! Uncle Qin, we'll . . .'

Qin's grip slackened and I almost sank to the ground. He quickly looked the other way, but I had seen his tears. I steadied myself, holding on to his trouser leg.

'Uncle Qin, what am I to do? Tell me what to do. I do want to be free, I want to go home, but I can't go without you.'

Qin knelt down in front of me, placing his hands on my shoulders. 'Child, child! I will always be with you, because you have built a little nest in my heart. You live in me, just as you'll always live in Uncle Cannibal . . .'

I looked around. Where *was* Cannibal?

'Don't worry. He'll show up. In his own good time. He cares for you even more than I do, because loving is something he is better at . . .'

'Lian, why don't you come sit next to me at the controls?' It was Tiangui, hoping to get me to compose myself by distracting me with this enticing offer. Through the bead curtain of my tears, I looked at the wondrous rumbling contraption and the two gear sticks wrapped in red plastic, and my curiosity won out over my sadness.

~

Five minutes later we were rattling over the twisty track towards the city. I had given up my comfortable seat beside Tiangui to Mother. I was sitting in the back. As we passed the last strip of tilled land that was still part of our camp, the figure of a man appeared out of nowhere. It made Tiangui jump, but he skilfully managed to keep the gear shifts under control so that the tractor did not swerve from the track. Somewhere in the back of my mind, I understood that this apparition had something to do with me. I squinted in order to see better into the distance. It was Cannibal.

He ran out of the green rice paddy, waving his emaciated seventy-year-old arms at me frantically. I wanted to wave back at him, but my own arms were suddenly made of lead. Fortunately, Mother asked Tiangui to stop for a moment. I wanted to jump from the tractor and throw myself into Cannibal's arms, but found myself unable to do anything but remain lying on the floor of the flatbed with jelly knees.

Cannibal leaned against the side of the tractor and gazed at me wordlessly. Memories of our sessions together at the Lily Theatre rose to the surface: how he had criticised me mercilessly, but had at the same time helped me haul myself out of the trap of my pessimism, showing me the way to a luminous horizon of hope. What would I do without his guidance, now that I was returning to a normal life? Would I manage to fit in?

Cannibal pulled his right sleeve up over his hand to dry my eyes and cheeks. 'My child, you are a big girl now, and big girls don't cry over every little thing.'

'You call this a "little thing"? Why, I can't take you to the Lily Theatre any more; we'll never have discussions about Chinese history again. Never!'

'Who says?'

I stopped sobbing abruptly and looked at him in surprise: 'Oh, but then are you going to be freed soon, as well?'

'That's not what I mean. Ah, little girl, there is nothing I want from life any more. People who have no desires cannot be disappointed.'

That is so typical of Cannibal, I thought. Philosophising all the time. Was it really necessary to start on such a heavy subject, at a time like this?

Realising I had misunderstood him, he hastened to add, 'I mean, I may very well be stuck here for a long time. But I can still listen to your history reports.'

My eyes shone. 'Of course! When you come back on weekend leave, naturally! Let's make a date for me to come and visit you!'

Tiangui was impatiently fiddling with the controls. The tractor grumbled and sulked and Mother gave me a poke in the back, 'We have to go now.'

Tightening his grip on the tractor's fender, Cannibal answered me, 'It's a date. Flat 307, Building 24. Remember my address. I'll see you in two days!'

Suddenly I felt the strength surge back into my legs. I got to my feet and an urge came over me to jump out of the flatbed. Cannibal had made me conscious of the funny nagging feeling in my stomach: I was already unreasonably homesick for the camp and I really didn't want to leave. I wanted to stay with Cannibal and 'learn to experience freedom under the yoke of detention', as he'd have put it ...

What possessed me to think that way! Balancing on the lurching tractor, looking back at the aged Cannibal who was energetically hobbling along, trying to keep up with us, I realised I did not have the right to *want* anything ... I was only an unresisting pebble, swept along in the Revolution's relentless tide.

'Uncle Cannibal! I'll never forget you! I'll come and see you every time you're home on leave!'

Huge clouds of dust eclipsed the figure running after us ...

NECTAR OF THE GODS

Little by little the fresh breeze dried my tears and restored my composure. The fields of vegetables and wheat claimed my attention, and the tanned backs of the farmers weeding them.

The road hardly deserved to be called a road: the tractor pitched wildly, like a rocking horse. At first it was sort of fun, but several hours of being jolted around like this was no picnic.

Three hours went by, and we had covered only half the distance. The springtime sun baked my face to a ball of fire, and my throat was burning, too. The same thing was bothering Tiangui, evidently: he suggested that we find someplace to have a drink.

There were no shops to speak of out here on the plains. Peasants received only a handful of yuan at the end of the year as their wages for the entire twelve months. Cafés were unknown here and all the teahouses had been shut down at the beginning of the Cultural Revolution.

Tiangui turned the engine off and left Mother and me to wait under an ancient willow tree. He ran to the nearest village, returning half an hour later out of breath but with some good news: 'I've found a shop, three miles further on, in Communism Is the Best Without A Doubt – a pretty big village. That's where we're going.' He climbed on board, looking rather pleased with himself.

We walked into the store, a pitch-dark little room of about six feet by twelve. In the dim light of a lightbulb thickly coated with flyspecks, we saw an ancient little man with a goatee. The goods on the shelves were of the same vintage as the shopkeeper. Thermos-cans, soap, toothpaste, rubber shoes and lanterns, all emblazoned with the brand name Workers, Farmers and Soldiers Are the Leaders of Our Nation, constituted four-fifths of what was on sale here. Everything was smothered in a thick layer of dust.

Mother looked around and asked without much conviction, 'Can we buy some bottles of soda pop here?'

The old man waved his right hand to swipe away the buzzing bluebottle that was depositing its droppings on his swollen purple nose. After pondering it over, he narrowed his wrinkled eyelids and enquired, 'Female comrade, what did you just say?'

Tiangui became impatient. 'Come on, Grandpa, do you have anything to drink?'

'Tea, you mean?'

'Well . . . sure, if you have nothing else. But wash the bowls with soap before you pour the tea.'

After we had polished off the entire pot of tea between us, Mother asked, 'What do we owe you?'

'Two fen . . .' the old man said apologetically. 'Look, normally it only costs one fen, but I washed the cups with washing powder and you know how expensive soap is . . .'

Mother placed a coin on the counter. As we walked back to the tractor, we heard the tremulous voice of the old man call after them, 'Thank you all! Thank you all! Buddha bless you! With those three extra fen I can finally buy the medicinal herbs the doctor prescribed for my grandson. The poor boy has been hobbling around with the trots for four months now: but, you see, the herbs are so horribly expensive!'

I noticed that Mother was blushing.

After another two hours of bumping along, the outskirts of Beijing were within sight. Here the roads, lined with stores, were for the most part asphalt; the passers-by were no longer wearing muddy, shabby and old-fashioned clothes; some women even had stylish hairdos. We were now not only thirsty, but hungry as well. Tiangui took us to a busy thoroughfare, where we entered a real store.

I was so used to grey, dusty and colourless goods that I had already clean forgotten everything about my last weekend leave, and was practically blinded by the riot of colour: the red apples, the yellow bananas, the glistening oranges, the white rolls and the silver sweet wrappers – it all seemed unreal to me. I grabbed Mother's hand excitedly and sputtered: 'Goodness gracious, Mother, look at all the *yummy* goodies!'

Mother dragged me over to the counter and said, 'Lian, do you want an orange or pineapple drink?'

I looked at her, dumbfounded. What kind of question was that? Mother might as well have asked a starving beggar if he preferred his carp in a black bean or a sweet-and-sour sauce.

I took my bottle of soda pop into a quiet corner and let the divine nectar seep down into my throat drop by drop. The sweet, delicious liquid caused my blood vessels to dilate. Slowly but surely I made room for this new ecstasy. My pleasant little life is starting all over again, sang my heart.

The soft drink had cost fifteen fen.

PART TWO

1973

∘⟋

When she turns around and smiles
the dahlia bursts from its bud
Where she passes, rustling,
the tall lilies shoot up

IT IS DARK IN THE TEMPLE

We arrived home at half past three. The trip had taken us over six hours, not counting rest stops. The driver had warned us before we set out that this type of tractor couldn't do more than fifteen miles an hour.

At night, back in my own bed at last, it felt as if I was still in Tiangui's vehicle. The whole bedroom rocked and my body rocked along in sync. The grumbling of the tractor's motor droned in my ears and I had to grip the bed frame tightly to stop myself from falling out. Finally, overwhelmed with exhaustion and confusion, I fell asleep.

Next morning Mother and I did a big spring cleaning in the flat. When everything was clean and tidy it was our turn, and we dunked ourselves in hot soapy water. Still wearing her bathrobe, Mother started combing the wardrobe for 'normal clothes' for me, since I had to walk around dressed as the daughter of 'clean' parents again. This meant finding clothing that was colourful, fairly fashionable, and made of a synthetic fabric like polyester; it wasn't supposed to have patches sewn on the elbows, the shoulders or the seat of the pants. But my clothes did not fit any more – I had grown so much in the past year and a half.

'Here is an old jacket of mine,' said Mother, 'you can wear that today. Tomorrow we'll go to the Mao Is the Compass of our Lives Shopping Centre to buy you some new clothes.'

I went and stood before the mirror. What I saw was a face scrubbed clean and shining with happiness. My cheeks were flushed and my eyes sparkled like dewdrops in the dawn's early light. My full lips looked as if they had been slicked with a burgundy lipstick. Was I really that girl there?

As soon as we returned from shopping the next day, I changed into my new jacket and trousers. Mother watched me disapprovingly. 'You can't even hold a fart in for one night, can you? Why don't you just wait until tomorrow, when you can wear your new clothes to school?'

I didn't even hear her. I just went on admiring myself, humming a song that tuned everything else out.

> The Proletariat East Wind
> crushes the Capitalist West Wind
> So – who is afraid of whom?

Bubbling with impatience and excitement, I walked out the door – and it was like entering a fairy kingdom. Spring was in the air. A pink sea of blooming Japanese cherry loomed up before me; tenderly translucent, blush-pink petals offered themselves to the fingers of the wind, as if to woo him. I whirled around and around, allowing myself to be drenched in the sun's gold and breathing in deep, as if taking my very first breath. A cocktail of floral essences gushed over me; my heart performed a somersault inside my chest. I wrapped my arms around myself, because I was afraid that I might be blown sky high, like a puff of pollen. And yet the earth still had so many other sensual pleasures in store for me . . .

Building 24, my mind prompted me. Oh yes, I was on my way to visit Cannibal! A shudder surged through me: I could not help thinking of Cannibal running after the tractor over the dusty country lane. Instead of being moved by the memory, I felt a wave of revulsion for . . . what for, exactly? I tossed my head and tried to concentrate on the close kinship I felt with this kind man, but was distracted by the riot of tantalising colours and by the beguiling smells of the adolescent spring. History, philosophy, wisdom . . . what was it all for? Wasn't it enough, simply, to embrace life as it was, to bask and melt in the warmth it had to offer? Why was it so urgent for me to visit Cannibal? So that I could learn to scrutinise things under a microscope, and then write a report on the nitty-gritty derivation of every little thing? I spotted a pile of bricks, and kicked it over, on purpose.

When I had climbed the stairs of Building 24 and Cannibal had opened the door for me, a powerful whiff of garlic temporarily disabled my sense of smell. Through the thin white downy hairs on Cannibal's head, I saw sunlight streaming resolutely in through the windows. His hair made me think of the withered reed stalks around the Lily Theatre – yes, *that's* what it looks like, I said to myself, while at the same time falling head over heels into the chasm of guilt: for how *could* I make fun of Cannibal's advancing years?

Without greeting me, Cannibal turned around and called, 'Xiulan, come here! You have three guesses: who *is* this young lady?'

The smell of garlic heralded the approach of Aunt Xiulan Ge. I took a step backward when I saw Xiulan rushing up. Aunt's fingers were stuck together with dough – like the webbed feet of a duck.

Aunt Xiulan nodded vigorously: 'Changshan! It really is as they say: Clothes make the man, but the saddle makes the horse. Just look at how different our Lian looks now that she isn't dressed in tattered camp clothes!'

Aha! So *that* was Cannibal's real name. Changshan – *Eternal Goodness*.

Xiulan had been a teacher of classical Greek philosophy before the

Cultural Revolution, and had been in the camp for two years. I had only met her a few times during my stay there.

'Lian, please go into the big room and go tell Uncle Changshan your history-stories. Yes, yes, I know all about your story-telling talents. I'm making noodles with huangjiang sauce. You'll eat with us later, won't you?'

I flushed. Cannibal had given away our secret. But at the same time, I was glad that he took me so seriously.

I waded through piles of haphazardly discarded shoes, a jumble of carrots, overturned brooms and woks strewn around the hallway, in the direction of the 'big room'. In contrast to my own home, where I was accustomed to an impeccably furnished sitting room, this space was used both as bedroom and living room. There was no sofa or easy chair to be seen – just a couple of wooden stools. Cannibal pointed to a double bed, and proceeded to climb up on it himself. Awkwardly, I went and sat next to him and – oops! – something sharp poked me in the buttocks. I jumped up and found a large bamboo back-scratcher. Cannibal apologised and hid the useful implement under one of the other pillows. He crossed his legs in the lotus position and shut his eyes – a sign that he was ready to listen to my lecture.

But I wasn't in the mood to hold forth. Frowning, I looked around the room in which I found myself. Over one of the stools hung Cannibal's dirty, threadbare coat. I suddenly realised how I abhorred the dirty rags my mother and I had shuffled around in for almost two years. Yet in some inexplicable way I felt more at home in this messy dwelling than in the squeaky-clean living room at home.

Cannibal must have been wondering why I had not yet started, because he opened his eyes. I avoided his gaze.

The silence remained unbroken. My lecture just didn't seem to want to get started.

After a while, Cannibal said, 'Buddha has clear eyes, my child.'

'What do you mean?'

'He perceived in good time that you were getting to be a real adolescent and that you needed to go back to a normal life, surrounded by young folk your own age. You have no idea how the world will open up for you . . . like the fantail of a peacock. Just try to enjoy it – drink it in, and take deep draughts. Come on, unburden yourself of your history tale, fork it over to your uncle, that way you can make room in your mind for all the new and beautiful things awaiting you on your life's journey.'

I blinked my eyes. Where did all that poetic mush come from, all of a sudden? I didn't know which way was up any more. I had been free for only a day and a half, and already he had managed to get me all mixed up with his talk of all that supposedly wonderful stuff awaiting me . . . What the hell was he driving at?

I asked for a glass of hot water. Another ploy to put off my talk. I tried to thread my thoughts like shells on a string. When I had been given what I had requested, I sat there silently, cupping the glass in my hands and blowing on the steaming water.

I pinched myself in the thigh, opened my little notebook and began my lecture. The enthusiasm that used to give my talks their special zing, however, had gone by the board. The passion to analyse and tie together historical facts just wasn't there. It had been superseded by a brand-new tyrant – a dreamer, to be sure, but none the less stubborn for that: the desire to be accepted by my new, or, to be precise, my old, environment; to be respected by my classmates, to be admired, even, and not least for my attractiveness. Captivating yet tormenting thoughts made it impossible to concentrate. I whacked my palm on my notebook, as if it was somehow responsible for my lack of concentration.

Cannibal opened his eyes and looked at me with his head tilted to the side: 'I know how it feels, Lian, when you're teetering on the threshold of a new, bewildering life. It feels the same when you draw out a lot before the statue of the Buddha: you want to read it right away, but it is too dark in the temple . . .'

It gave me the goosebumps. Cannibal had assessed my mixed-up feelings much too perceptively and all too clearly. Whereas it was the *mystery* of all this that intrigued me so. Uncle was like someone who cannot keep his mouth shut and gives away the thriller's outcome before you have the pleasure of finding it out for yourself. It made me seethe with anger.

I walked home through the streets, lost in thought. The sun's orange glow enveloped me and the satiny evening breeze, drenched with a perfume of spring, caressed me. But I did not notice. I felt cold inside, colder than the bitterest winter. And yet:

> Passion's little fawns
> caper in my breast
> They ferry me to the lake
> where, on the far shore, the mermaid,
> white silk rippling, waves me on
> I must *go there, I must go there* . . .

REUNION

After a brief talk between Mother and the Principal, I was allowed to go in.

It was as if time had stood still: it was recess, and Kim was sitting in the room all by herself. The contrast between the silence in the classroom and the hubbub in the hall, with students running in all directions helter-skelter, yelling and giggling, was as striking as ever.

Ting-tong-bong ting-tong-bong. Pushing chairs and tables out of my way and causing a number of them to topple over and crash to the ground, I charged up to Kim. I had often tried imagining what it would be like to see Kim again, but this was an immeasurably far cry from what I had expected. The excitement was overwhelming, and all I could do was stutter, 'Ki . . . Ki . . . Kim . . .'

Kim jumped up out of her chair, stared at me for a moment without blinking, then looked the other way. This standoffish reaction flummoxed me so much that I couldn't get any words out at all.

The other students began pushing their way back into the classroom. My former friends Feiwen, Qianyun and Liru crowded around me, scrutinising me from head to toe: 'Welcome home, Lian. Wow, if we'd met you on the street, we'd probably never even have had the nerve to talk to someone like you.'

I was about to ask what she meant by that, but then Meimei said snidely, 'Prison camp hasn't exactly done you any harm, has it!'

The envy in Meimei's tone was hard to miss, and it made me mad as a hornet. How *could* Meimei scoff at something like that! I wisely kept it to myself, however. Notwithstanding my newly won freedom, I wasn't in any position to show resentment over the persecution of intellectuals. That didn't stop me from hating Meimei's guts, however. I looked out of the window to avoid my classmates' stares of appraisal.

In the meantime Mr Wu, the maths teacher, had come in. I discovered, to my elation, that the topic he was reviewing was one I knew inside-out from my private tutorials in the camp; that left me an entire hour to fantasise freely about the fascinating new life stage I was about to enter, according to Cannibal . . .

At twelve o'clock I waited for my bosom friend at the school exit. As was her wont, Kim came out only when everyone else had gone. Ecstatic about being alone with her at last, I rushed up to her with open arms. I imagined myself the hero of a Russian novel, a young officer in the Tsar's army, as I had seen it depicted in book illustrations – an empty, cavernous ballroom lit by crystal chandeliers, with me flying towards the loved one I had missed so desperately . . .

Kim blushed and looked the other way, deliberately evading my rapturous gaze. I was aware of Kim's habit of putting on a cool front, but I couldn't bear Kim's indifference now that it was directed at *me*.

Kim walked up to me, pointed at her own head, then at my shoulders, and said, 'Look at us two! The giant and the dwarf!' I was flabbergasted. But Kim was right, she was now almost a head shorter than me. 'We can't hang around together any more. You've grown into a real young lady and I'm still the same old lump of unrisen dough.'

Hunching my shoulders to make my breasts less obvious, I tried to reassure Kim: 'I'm still the same Lian as I was last year, I swear. Here, in my heart.' I thumped on my ribcage with my fists.

Kim had to laugh. 'Oh, stop acting so melodramatic! Buddha, you sure haven't changed one stitch!'

That was enough to set my mind at ease. I turned to more important matters: 'How's the studying going? Are you keeping up with your lessons these days? How are your grades?'

'Pah!' Kim spat on the ground and glared at me viciously, tight-lipped.

I realised that my line of questioning had ruined the reunion for Kim. I attempted a swift about-face: 'I mean—'

'No need to explain!' Kim interrupted me, waving her right hand as if shooing away some stray mutt begging for a handout. It felt like a bucket of ice-cold water was being dumped on my head. 'I've got to go home. My mother is at the slaughterhouse rescuing bones from the garbage. I've got to make lunch for Jiening. She'll be waiting for me with an empty stomach.'

'What does she have a set of paws for? Can't she just start cooking it herself?'

Kim shrugged her shoulders. 'That's just the way it is at our house. Kim works like a dog and Jiening has a ball. She is the younger one, after all. Let's be fair.'

'Younger? There's only a year and a half's difference between you. A year and a half ago you were *also* doing her share of the work. And three, four, five, no, six years ago as well. Weren't you young yourself, back then?'

Kim took a deep breath. 'Just forget it . . .'

Realising that the Jiening problem was beside the point, I changed the subject back again: 'It doesn't matter if you are still lagging behind in school. I'm back now, aren't I? Let's do our studying together again, all right? I'll help you, the way I did before . . . Except that I don't know if I'll be up to scratch in every subject myself; but if everything turns out to be as easy as this morning's maths class, then we have nothing to worry about.'

The next day I was stumped for an answer when the history teacher, Mr Yan, asked me to name the 'ten military victories engineered by Mao between 1937 and 1949'. I stood there with my mouth open. What was he talking about? The 'correct answers' that my classmates droned off next were even more dumbfounding: six battles won by other military heroes were now all ascribed to the Great Helmsman! Apparently somebody had been busy mixing up facts in history's cooking pot. But that was what came of Qin's refusal to follow the prescribed textbook; now I was stewed.

Yet it wasn't the end of the world, either. All I needed was a couple of days cooped up in my room to learn the textbook by heart from cover to cover. That way I was sure to breeze through the history exam, which was really nothing but a memory test in disguise.

In the afternoon, Mrs Bai, the Grammar teacher, wrote on the blackboard:

> I'd much rather die of hunger
> in our own Proletarian State
> than, in a place like Britain,
> in Capitalist wealth luxuriate

Then she opened a book and calmly began reading. What was going on? Was no one doing any teaching these days?

Liru, who was sitting behind me, whispered, 'It's exercise time. Look at the blackboard!'

'I *have* looked at it.'

'All right then. Write a denunciation article using that motto as the title.'

'A *what*?'

'Don't you know what a denunciation article is? It's a kind of essay.'

'Lian Shui and Liru Xiao. If you wish to continue talking, I will ask you to continue your conversation in the hall,' Mrs Bai warned us.

I fell silent and looked around the classroom. Pens were busily scratching: some students had already scribbled half a page. I'd better hurry up, I told myself. I bit on my pen and stared at the nonsensical slogan on the blackboard.

After half an hour Mrs Bai got up and walked up and down the rows of desks, peering over the students' shoulders to read what they had penned on paper. When she got to the hairy Weimin – he had stubble of five or six bristles on his chin – she exclaimed, 'Well done!' A little later Guoxiang, a second-caste girl, received similar praise. Bai asked the class to listen to Weimin and Guoxiang's exemplary essays.

Buddha help us, was *that* what a denunciation article was supposed to sound like?! I bent over my notebook so that Bai wouldn't get it into her head to ask me to read my own essay out loud. Mercy! If this had been a writing test, I would have earned a big fat zero for it, no question about it. My heart sank into my shoes and I was totally unnerved, especially when I thought of Kim. I hated having to disappoint Kim, but I would have to tell her I would not be able to help her with her studies after all.

At lunchtime, Mother, noticing that I was depressed, asked, 'Aren't you having a good time at school?'

'Mama, I'm afraid I'll have to do the year over again.'

'How come?'

'I've fallen dreadfully behind. For example, I have no idea how to compose a denunciation article.'

'Is that so? Didn't Mrs What's-her-name, your Chinese grammar teacher in camp, teach you that?'

'No! Mrs Zhao gave me instruction in basic composition methods, but that's quite a different story.'

'How different can it be? Just look over your classmates' essays, and copy what they did. It couldn't be simpler. How can you possibly fail in such an elementary subject as Chinese grammar?'

I gobbled down my rice and retired to my room. Mother had a point: all I needed to do was parrot my classmates' essays and it should be in the bag. I tried to recall the gist of Weimin and Guoxiang's essays. It struck me that their compositions bore a striking resemblance to a slanging match between a couple of fishwives. There was nothing there that smacked of reasoning, argument or logical conclusion – it was nothing but a string of curses, slurs and threats.

Guoxiang's essay was the one I remembered most clearly:

'Live an affluent life in godforsaken Great Britain? I'd rather bite the bullet and if necessary die a hero's death in my impoverished but Socialist Paradise! Whoever has the bear's gall not to support my choice, is clearly a spy of the British imperialists. Traitors to our Fatherland – turtle-eggs, they are – belong in prison! I'll gladly give those class enemies their just deserts! I just hope that the children they'll have some day will be born missing an arsehole, so they'll suffocate in their own shit!

'Let's all shout together: Long live the Great Chairman Mao Zedong! Death to capitalists, revisionists and all enemies of our Communist State!'

I can write that kind of essay too, I assured myself. All I needed to do was picture myself accidentally caught between two scolding hell-cats, and make note of their verbal exchange.

～

Kim came to my house; I had been looking over her completed schoolwork. Her understanding of physics, maths and chemistry was better than could be expected: compared to a year and a half ago, she was lagging considerably less far behind. Exams were in six weeks, and I hoped that Kim would have made up enough work by then to scrape by, even in science and maths. As for the 'easy' courses – which was how history, Chinese grammar and political instruction were known (except that Kim always used to fail these as well) – this time I expected Kim to walk off with a seventy for them, or perhaps even eighty. There was nothing to it. All Kim had to do was to rattle off the pertinent textbooks by heart. Together we devised a timetable listing exactly which lessons were to be committed to memory.

A FAIRY-TALE EVENING

When Mother got home, Kim immediately got up and started sliding her open books and notebooks into her satchel.

I looked up at the clock, surprised. 'Hey, Mama, just as I thought – I was asking myself how come we weren't through with our studying yet, but you're home almost two hours earlier than usual . . . Kim, where are you going?' I ran after my friend, who was making for the front door, pleading, 'Mama, please tell Kim she doesn't have to worry about your being here, tell her to stay until we're done with our homework, please!'

'I'm sorry, Lian, but this time I'm afraid I have to disappoint you. It would be better if Kim went home now . . .' Ignoring my protests, she went on, 'We're going out tonight.'

Tyee-aaah . . . Kim was already out the door. 'See you tomorrow, Lian. Goodbye, Mrs Yang.'

Bursting with curiosity, I just nodded curtly at Kim and asked: 'Where are we going, Mama?' Mother hardly ever took me anywhere, we went out once a year at most.

But Mother had already disappeared into my bedroom. I found her standing in front of my wardrobe, the doors flung open. 'Answer me, please!' I begged her, bubbling with excitement.

'Where is that blouse I bought you last month?' Mother was turning the whole closet inside out, ignoring me.

'You mean the fancy one? In the top drawer, up there on the left. You put it there yourself, don't you remember? I'm not to wear it without your permission.'

'You may wear it today. I'm going to visit the daughter of the former Defence Minister, General Dong. I have to interview her.'

'For your book *An Oral History of the CPC*?'

'Good guess. You may come along. I'd just as soon not leave you alone at home at night. Besides, this daughter of Dong's has a daughter herself – she's about your age. So you'll have somebody to keep you company while I am occupied.'

'Yippee!' I immediately took off my old clothes and put on the pretty blouse. It was a lovely gold colour, with red discs and purple squares.

Mother combed my hair and braided it into two long, thick plaits. I twisted and twirled in front of the mirror and suddenly began giggling, at nothing in particular.

Mother went into the bathroom, where I observed her powdering her face until she was as white as a ghost. How pretty Mother looked now! No longer did she look like a peasant who's toiled away the years under a scorching sun. Under normal circumstances, Mother took out her powder box only at the Chinese New Year. The visit to Dong's daughter must be a pretty important affair.

'Are you hungry yet?'

I shook my head vehemently, patted my stomach and yodelled, practically, 'Not-a-t-all . . . !'

Mother's eyes crinkled when she saw me hamming it up, and she laughed, 'Okay, Okay, I know where *you* want to go . . .'

Taking this to mean a yes, I stopped my play-acting and started pulling at Mother's sleeve. 'Come on, let's *go*.'

Before Mother had been sent to the camp, when Father was still working in Beijing, we used to attend concerts in the city twice a year. On those nights, we didn't eat at home at six thirty as usual, but dined at around eight instead, as patrons of the posh Restaurant Moskou.

Our home was situated on the outskirts of the city, so it took us two hours to get into the centre, where Dong's daughter lived – the sprawling capital just seemed to go on for ever. After an hour's bus ride, we got out near the entrance to Restaurant Moskou. By this time it was seven o'clock. The fiery summer sun had taken cover behind mountains clad in black, having stripped off their blue-green mantles and laid them down in the slumbering vale, neatly folded in readiness for the morning.

The restaurant was set in the middle of a park. Street lamps with water-lily shades dispelled the night's menacing gloom. Downy moss transformed the path into a splendid mint-green runner that led Mother and me up to the milky-white buildings of the Restaurant Moskou. Drifts of baby's-breath planted along the road emitted whiffs of perfume that went straight to my head and blurred the boundaries between dream and reality.

As soon as we set foot inside Restaurant Moskou, I stole into the lobby like a thief. With my head tucked down low between my shoulders, I peered left and right, and up and down. I hardly dared breathe, out of fear of breaking the silence. The honking and roar of the traffic, the sweaty smell of the passers-by, all seemed to have been vacuumed right out of this building. Mmmm – a pleasant coolness enveloped me. The lobby had something of a desert oasis, it was a place too far elevated above everyday concerns to be considered real. There was a pillar more massive and towering than a thousand-year-old pine, embellished with – sure enough – handsomely carved pinecones. What a lot of work the artist had put into it!

In the cloakroom I had to hand over my coat to a young gentleman whose back was as straight as a spear. With a gallant smile, he hung the garment on a little hook. His gleaming, pomaded, slicked-back hair and his spotlessly white shirt, punctuated by a smart black bow tie, were sharply at odds with what he really was – just an ordinary *fuwuyan*. I clamped my tongue behind my teeth with some effort and managed to conceal my embarrassment over my meagre, shabby appearance.

No, we could not go into the dining room just yet, the tables were all occupied. What a performance! In an ordinary eatery, the next batch of guests hovered over you, watching as you chewed.

When we were finally seated, Mother ordered beet soup for me and cream of chicken for herself. As soon as the waiter was out of earshot, I tugged at Mother's sleeve: 'Can't we cancel our soup order? Either the one you ordered for me, or your own, I don't care which.'

'Why? Aren't you hungry?'

'Haven't you seen the prices? Two and a half kuai! They'll pluck you bald while you're still breathing, in this place!'

'Shhhh!' Mother raised her eyebrows and put her hand on my shoulder.

I composed myself and worked on appeasing my conscience. What was I making such a fuss for? Everyone here seemed to consider it perfectly normal to pay such a monstrous price for a dish of soggy vegetables. But my brain kept rattling like an abacus. Two and a half kuai. Kim's family could live for a week off that! Twenty pounds of cornmeal cost exactly two kuai and forty cents.

But when the delicious soup, redolent of fresh butter, was shoved under my nose in all its glory, I suddenly forgot all about my principles. It took me only a few seconds to guzzle it down. While Mother carefully sipped her soup at a seemly pace, I was already squirming with impatience. What glorious course was next?

A faint whiff of apricots reached my nostrils. Very carefully, I turned around, afraid of scaring off the odour if I made a sudden movement. To my disappointment, I couldn't smell it any more . . . or, yes, perhaps there it was! One moment a ribbon of the perfume would tickle my nasal passages; the next, as I strained to sniff more of it, it was gone without a trace. It was as if the scent were an impish, pretty little thing playing a game of tag with me. Little by little I inched towards the source of the heavenly fragrance. When I finally steeled myself to look up, I caught a glimpse of the stylishly dressed young lady who was wearing the elegant scent. I cast my eyes down again at once. But the enticing perfume reaching me from that neighbouring table had made me forget everything else for an instant. I prayed to Buddha that this moment might last an eternity.

FANRUI'S TRIUMPH

At eight thirty we got off the bus. We were in the centre's West End, the so-called Xidan District. Rows of ramshackle tenements and grey apartment buildings lined a street on whose sidewalk the nightlife of hundreds of families was in full swing.

Summers in Beijing are unbearable, as a rule. Seeing that most families lived in just one room, where the temperature, even at night, hovered around ninety degrees, they would seek some coolness and relief from crowding outside, in the open air. There were straw mats spread out on the ground everywhere for young children to crawl on and for old people to nap on. Young men were squatting beneath the street lamps playing chess or cards; young women were huddled in circles, on little benches, fanning themselves, chatting and trading gossip. Some families that were slightly better off owned transistor radios, which naturally had pride of place in the middle of the sidewalk, so that the entire community could enjoy the 'music' – the blare of screeched political slogans. The smell of tobacco, cheap tea and sweat all blended into one; the women's chattering, the children's laughter and the shrill revolutionary songs on the radio intermingled in a pandemonium of noise. Under the meagre light of the street lamps, it was just like one large family.

After a ten-minute walk, Mother and I arrived at a wider street lined with elegant, lofty poplars. It was unusually quiet there.

'Halt! Your papers!' Out of a dark cubicle came the dazzling flash of a bayonet, followed by the head of a soldier.

Mother hastily pulled out a letter of introduction, signed by the Vice-Chancellor of Teachers' University, from her coat pocket. A flashlight came on and a couple of minutes later a hand emerged from the guardhouse window as a voice boomed: 'Second building to your left, third floor.'

I peered into the darkness; only now did I realise that we were standing at the entrance of a residential compound hermetically sealed off from the outside world. Mother looked left and right. By the looks of her, she was impressed by the stately edifices. Soft amber light spilled out of the generously proportioned windows of the snow-white apartment buildings. Flowerbeds crammed with orchids and peonies basking in the shade of willows and birches gave the place the look of a fairy-tale landscape.

A short while later we were at the door of General Dong's daughter's apartment. We knocked.

'Come in!' a bell-like voice chimed from the other side of the door. The door opened and we stepped into a spacious hall. Heavens, this space was larger than my living room at home! A harsh fluorescent light dazzled my eyes.

'Good evening, Mrs Yang,' rang the bell-voice again, 'and this must be your little daughter.'

Mother said, 'Good evening, Miss Fanrui Dong. This is my daughter Lian Shui. Lian, this is Miss Fanrui, the daughter of Mrs Heyuan Dong and granddaughter of General Dong.'

Opening my eyes, I saw a girl a little older than myself standing before me. I was too shy to look her directly in the face. All I could see for now was Fanrui's silk blouse, which was embroidered with peach blossoms that bloomed especially where two round swellings pressed up against the gossamer fabric. A black belt accentuated Fanrui's slender waist and led the eye down to a tight lavender skirt.

A skirt! I hadn't seen a living soul wearing a skirt since I was six years old. Wasn't it awfully revisionist, to wear something like that?! Or did the Party bosses' families have such iron proletarian consciousnesses that there was no way they could be corrupted by this Western style of dress?

'Welcome, little Lian,' said the skirt-wearer.

Now I was forced to look Fanrui in the eye. She had a roguish, somewhat uptilted chin, sensual lips, and skin as smooth and shiny as porcelain. Her complexion was the colour of the moon – fair, with a pale yellow tone. The lively eyes danced around friskily; I wished they would stop moving for a moment so that I could read their expression, whatever that entailed – high spirits, or curiosity, or something else. I had once heard that babies are supposed to be able to feel the presence of their mother even with their eyes closed, through their skin. I realised that at age fourteen I must still have that ability, for even though I didn't have the guts to glance at Fanrui for more than a second, I had a sense that Fanrui was sizing me up.

The little princess had to be thinking that I looked rather comical. Mother had taken pains with my hair, which hung in two geometric plaits – but it was a hairdo that had been out of style for ages. The blouse I was wearing suddenly felt cheap; in Fanrui's eyes, the colours probably clashed. The blindest of the blind could see that my trouser legs had been let out twice. How I wished I could turn into a mosquito on the spot – so I could go and hide behind one of the picture frames hanging in the hall!

'Mama, visitors for you!' Fanrui called out.

'Welcome!' A slim lady of around forty, but dressed like a girl of twenty, walked up to us and led us into the salon.

As if I had not been tormented enough, Fanrui followed close behind. She went and sat next to me on the leather sofa and attempted to start a conversation with me. Fanrui gave every word a coy little twist; my answers, in contrast, sounded like the common bellowing of a peasant. Fanrui's back was as straight as an arrow; her upper body was like a tender bamboo shoot. She'd incline her head gracefully every so often, while I just lolled there like a giant prawn, hunched over, my chest hollow as a crater, my head hanging clumsily on top. One thing was for sure: Fanrui was only being nice to me in order to show up the difference between her own alluring good looks and my sadly deficient appearance.

Our mothers seemed not to notice the psychological warfare being waged by us and kept on talking. After about ten minutes, Fanrui stood up. She evidently considered it a waste of her time to spend another minute with a provincial little boor.

So there I sat, abandoned by my conqueror. I had fallen into a bottomless pit: the desire to be a raving beauty kept sucking me in deeper, while common sense dictated that I haul myself back up to face the more sober truth. I tried to distract myself by listening to the interview.

Heyuan's story about her father contained nothing new; like all the other talented colleagues of the Great Helmsman, General Dong, after making an important contribution to the establishment of the People's Republic of China, had ended up being hounded to death by Mao. What particularly struck me, however, was Heyuan's complaint about the mistreatment of her family at the hands of the Red Guards.

'Oh, sure,' she said. 'In 1968 those fanatic young snot-noses took my mother, brothers, sisters and myself prisoner. But thank goodness, in the winter of 1969 we succeeded in obtaining our release, through the good offices of the Minister of Domestic Affairs, who had been my father's secretary at one time. But that's as far as his helpfulness went. The ingratitude of that . . . flunky!

'Just look at it,' – brimming with disdain and self-pity, Heyuan waved around the luxurious sitting-room – 'see the kind of hovel we're forced to live in these days!' Her finely-drawn lips flattened like a pair of earthworms squashed by a bicycle, and her eyes spewed fire.

Buddha! These people – just two of them, mind – were living in a four room flat, while only a ten-minute walk away, a family of four generations, eight to ten people in all, had to make to do with a single room measuring twelve by twelve! And this one had the temerity to complain about her apartment!

I sucked in wisps of cool air through the gaps between my teeth; I had to restrain myself, for there was more.

Mother said, 'I read in the classified newspaper *News for Top Party Officials* that since 1969, the year you were released, you have been affiliated with the prestigious Research Institute for Nuclear Energy as a scientific associate.'

'Oh yeah,' yawned Heyuan, 'I do stop by there from time to time. But what's the point, really? My salary is delivered to me in person at the end of the month by the administration secretary. Mrs Yang, or may I call you by your first name, Yunxiang? I like you and I trust you. After all, you are the best friend of the wife of the Secretary of State for the Ministry of Culture and Propaganda, who is an old acquaintance of my mother's. That is why I consider you one of us. I must confess to you that I haven't got a clue what that research business is all about. It's true, I did study physics from 1951 to 1955 at the University of Beijing, but it was more along the lines of – as one of my former suitors would put it – "Heyuan is better at breaking men's hearts than at splitting atomic particles."' She giggled, feigning embarrassment. Her face showed hardly any wrinkles; you could see that she used to be quite a beauty. 'My exam results – I passed with flying colours – were a new-year's gift from the Vice-Chancellor, a tribute to my father, naturally. Anyway, in 1969 I needed a job. I chose this appointment because the best physicists in the land work there; consequently, the conditions and pay are much better there than anywhere else. Besides, it's so convenient – only three minutes' walk from home.'

Mother kept her mouth shut.

I gulped.

⌒

A famished camel is still larger than a fattened horse. I wasn't jealous of Heyuan and Fanrui because of their wealth and privileges. I would never want to switch places with them. Just think – what if my father, too, were to be tossed on to the scrap heap by the Wisest Leader of the Universe!

It was past eleven when we said goodbye to Heyuan. From Mother's body language, I could tell that she was extremely gratified. On the one hand, she disapproved of the Dongs' many entitlements; on the other hand, she was flattered that such a well-connected and highly-placed person as Heyuan should have spoken so openly with her – and that person the daughter of the former Minister of Defence to boot!

Heyuan went into the hall and called, 'Rui, Mrs Yang and Lian are going home! Come and say goodnight.'

No answer. After a lengthy hiatus, Fanrui came tiptoeing out of her room, a finger pressed to her lips. 'Shh, we're recording some accordion music . . . !'

I pricked up my ears. Sure enough, somebody was playing a lovely tune. Judging from the sweetness of the melody, it wasn't exactly a bloodthirsty revolutionary song. Quite the opposite – it was a romantic ballad, straight out of godforsaken Europe. Wasn't it forbidden to listen to such songs, let alone to record them? In this house you had to readjust your thinking and see everything back to front: the residents, being the offspring of a proletarian Party Leader, must therefore be immune to all outside bourgeois influences.

I had to think of Professor Maly, who was still imprisoned in the re-education camp. Maly had once told me that the Foreign Language faculty at Teachers' University had waited five years for a tape recorder for the English department – in vain. And here was a teenybopper playing around with a real-live tape recorder with her pals, just for fun!

But still, like Mother, despite my distaste for the Dongs' many privileges, I felt attracted by the glamour of this élitist set. Even though I knew I would never be accepted by Fanrui's crowd, I nevertheless nursed a smidgen of hope that, had I been ravishingly beautiful, Fanrui might have made a little place for me in her exclusive circle . . .

FEMININE SECRETS

Six days before the summer holiday, the exam results were announced. Kim had a sixty for physics, history and political education, a fifty for chemistry and maths and a forty for Chinese grammar . . . not as good an outcome as we had secretly been hoping for, but a groundbreaking one, nevertheless. It was certainly the first time Kim had ever had a passing grade in *any* subject, and to have earned it in physics, of all things . . . ! Kim chuckled mutely. Even at this jubilant moment, Kim was unable to let go and show her feelings for even a split second.

Later Kim allowed that she now harboured the hope that one day she might achieve passing grades in all disciplines, and to score higher than a sixty, even, in certain subjects. It wasn't difficult, then, for me to talk her into doing two hours' extra homework every day during the summer break. Kim also agreed to take up track training again, so that she might notch up even greater victories in the Autumn Games.

⌒

It was six thirty a.m., the second day of summer holiday. As we started our warm-up, I was uncharacteristically hesitant. The brand new sun had magically transformed the athletics field into a carpet of gold that played catch with the pearls of sweat dripping from dozens of joggers' faces and limbs. After we had stretched our calf-muscles, Kim took her position at the starting line. I shuffled along behind, reluctantly. Kim, puzzled, looked at me a little testily.

I couldn't put it off any longer. 'Would you mind very much if I didn't try to keep up with you?'

'I would.'

'Come on, it's only for a few days.'

'But why?'

I shrugged my shoulders: 'Because . . .'

'Fine. Then I'm not training either.'

'Ancestors alive! Do you *have* to do this to me?'

'You took the words right out of my mouth,' said Kim. She pivoted on her heels and walked away from the starting line, as if to go home.

'Okay, okay, I'll explain . . .' Following her, I steeled myself before divulging my secret. It gave me a yucky taste in the mouth, as if there was sand stuck between my teeth: 'I'm sick. Well, not really sick . . . I have the curse.' Now that it was finally off my chest, I could breathe again.

Kim turned towards me and scornfully looked me over from head to toe.

I hung my head, deeply embarrassed. The first day, I had hardly had the guts to show my face in public. I didn't dare dawdle, since I was convinced people were pointing at me behind my back and whispering to each other, 'There goes that slut Lian Shui. So young, yet she's already menstruating like . . . like a married woman!' To teenagers, the monthly cycle was a sign of depravity, the penalty in store for any promiscuous female who, having slept with a man, was branded with that bloody mark for her sins. It was easy to cling to this belief as long as you had not yet started menstruating. But as soon as you got the curse, you got all confused. Even though you knew in your heart that you were innocent, you couldn't shake off the idea that it was something dirty and lewd, as you had had it hammered into you ever since childhood. I imagined my news must come as a shock to Kim, since it had to be hard for her to understand how her friend, whom she'd always assumed to be a good girl, could have turned into such a tramp. She had to be pissed off, for in her eyes I was surely a traitor for plunging headfirst into the basest bourgeois pleasures of the flesh, leaving my friend behind. How could I make it clear to her that that was the furthest thing from the truth? I was beside myself. My face flamed with embarrassment and I stepped back to let Kim pass, like a conscientious leper.

Kim intently scratched at the earth with her feet, digging up a clump of grass, and said, after an unbearably drawn-out silence, 'I'm sorry. Actually I do understand that sort of thing, after all we do have chickens and pigs at home. Only – I just couldn't believe you were already that far. But there's nothing to worry about, Lian. If you have stomach cramps, you should drink boiled water with sugar, and rest a lot. That's what my mother always does.' She blushed.

Shyly, I went up to my friend. 'Thank you, Kim, thank you so much for accepting that I . . . I promise I'll work out with you again when I feel better.'

'Just be careful! Wait till it's over, otherwise you'll come down with something.' Kim went along with the old wife's tale that if a woman performed physical labour when she had her period, her ovaries and uterus would get infected. Young men found it quite titillating when a girl said she couldn't play sports that day, because it meant she had her period – a condition they considered feminine, charming and sexually arousing.

I watched with admiration as Kim chalked up one lap after the other, leaving the other joggers trailing in the dust one by one. Even though my friend seemed to have resigned herself to the way things were, I felt I'd suddenly become a stranger to Kim. Aside from the difference in our castes, which was already an almost insurmountable barrier, something new had now come between us.

A month earlier, a few days before my first menstrual period, we had been instructed to practise press-ups in gym class. During the exercise, the teacher had come up to me and told me that my form was all wrong – my back sagged and my abdominals weren't contracted the right way. He pulled me up by the waist to show me and said, 'This is the position your back should be in.' Even though I realised his criticism hadn't been meant harshly, my feelings were hurt. I got up and ran to the benches behind the sidelines in tears. The teacher, perplexed, stared at my receding back, gestured feebly and stammered, 'What . . . what on earth did I say to . . . to . . . upset her so?' Of course I hadn't the foggiest idea, by Buddha, but that only made me feel even more rotten. The rest of the class stopped their drill and glared at the poor man angrily as if he had just committed murder.

The day following my outburst in gym class, Qianyun, one of my first-caste classmates, came up to me and said, 'You must be getting your period soon. I'm sure, knowing you, that you wouldn't have flown off the handle that way otherwise!'

I was so grateful for the attention that I blurted out everything that was in my heart. Qianyun nodded sympathetically and put an arm around my shoulder. I melted with gratitude. Finally, here was somebody who understood me . . .

A PILLORIED LOVE LETTER

I began seeking out Qianyun, who in turn brought me into her own circle of friends. To my astonishment and gratification, I discovered that these girls all spoke frankly and freely about their physical and emotional problems – about the curse, their relationship with their parents, their fears and doubts, et cetera. I felt at home in their company. I was flattered by the attention I received from Qianyun's friends, even though the envious glances some of them would send me occasionally alarmed me.

Kim never let me know what she thought of me or whether she considered me pretty, no matter how I dolled myself up. She gazed at me with detachment, as if looking at a piece of furniture, with no emotion whatsoever, or so it seemed. Just one time, when we first got to know one another, Kim had broached the subject of 'beauty', in a roundabout way. She had said, 'On my sixth birthday I decided never to go around with girls who were pretty or smart.' I had asked her what she meant, but Kim had sent me a look that immediately made me clam up.

A few days later, Kim and I had just started on our homework when there was a knock at the door. I didn't need to open the door to find out who it was. Feiwen's high-pitched voice and Qianyun's relentless torrent of words gave them away: it was the clan of six first-casters.

Liru was the first to storm into the apartment, exclaiming, 'What? Still swotting? Oh Lian, Lian, you take these things much too seriously! Do you really think that the teachers bother to look at our homework?' The other girls rolled their eyes up to the ceiling and spread their palms, as if it to say: there's no point trying to convert this bookworm.

I immediately got the message – I was being unsociable. I said quickly, 'All right then, I'll just finish it tomorrow. Come on in!'

It wasn't customary to make dates. It was considered bad form, even, to suggest to a friend, 'How'd you like to come round to my place tomorrow night, around eight o'clock, for a cup of tea?' The invited guest would immediately get her nose out of joint and wonder, 'What's she driving at? Does that mean that I'm not welcome any *other* time?' If you didn't backpedal at once and butter her up, chances were that the offended one would have nothing more to do with you.

The friends made straight for my bedroom instead of the more spacious living room.

'Oh. Kim's here *agaaain!*' Meimei remarked irritably.

Kim jumped up as if she'd had an electric shock. Quick as lightning, her hands shaking, she dumped her pens, books and notebooks into her satchel, trying to make herself as inconspicuous as a porcupine that's being attacked by a wild boar. She flung her bag over her shoulder with one hand and pulled out the chair she'd been sitting on with the other, offering it to the mademoiselle who happened to be nearest: Liru. Liru waited until Kim shoved the seat right underneath her posterior, then settled herself down daintily. She didn't bat an eyelid, as if it was her God-given right to be waited on by a third-caster.

Kim slipped out of the room like an eel, and out the front door. Her 'Have a good time!' and 'See you . . .' were uttered at a termite's volume. Only I could hear her. But I had my hands full: I had to find a place to sit for every one of my guests and I didn't have the time to worry about Kim.

I boiled some water and poured it into six large mugs. Into these I sprinkled some tea leaves, which floated on top of the water at first before sinking slowly down to the bottom.

My guests sieved the tea through their teeth; now and then you'd hear noises like *pfooh* and *vhyeh*, as they spat the leaves stuck to their teeth back into the beaker.

Liru talked as if her nose was pinched shut with a clothes-peg – this was considered refined – 'I gave that *scandalous* letter to the teacher yesterday . . .' She squinted and swivelled her head towards the window, feigning outrage. The rest of the group sent her looks that bespoke admiration and a measure of envy.

Liru went on, 'I simply had to gag when I came across that letter in my desk drawer! Teacher told me this morning that she would pin the letter on the propaganda board.' Her forehead puckered as if she'd taken a bite out of a steamed bun and found that she'd swallowed a thoroughly cooked maggot right along with it, and she drew her head down into her neck. The others heard her out with rising horror – this was going a little *too* far. Liru, suddenly aware of their silent disapprobation, hurriedly brought her little drama to an end, and looked around aggrieved.

The letter she was talking about turned out to have come from Wudong, a classmate of ours. Wudong had long skinny arms and legs, like most boys his age. His complexion was as pale and smooth as silk; there was no hint of any stubble – in contrast to the other boys in the class. Thanks to his effeminate, or, rather, handsome, appearance, as well as his first-caste status, all the girls in the class had a secret crush on him. The contents of his letter didn't amount to very much: it was exactly the sort of jumble of foolishness and banality that you might expect – as my friends knew all too well. For Liru had lent each of them the *corpus delicti* for a couple of days, to give them a chance to read it over carefully, learn it by heart, and – such was Liru's secret hope – come to envy the recipient from deep down in their guts. Even though no one said this out loud – it was, after all, too embarrassing to come out with it and admit that you wouldn't mind being wooed this way yourself – everyone knew that it was a consummate honour to be singled out as the object of Wudong's affection.

I wasn't much in the mood for the conversation about Wudong. I did want to be considered popular, and compete with the others over who was the prettiest, but I had lost all interest in boys the day I discovered the first sign of womanhood in myself. Tomorrow the letter would be posted on the propaganda board. I could already hear the shrieks of malicious laughter, the teasing and the baiting Wudong would have to endure. The thought made me shudder – that this boy, having opened his heart to a girl probably for the first time in his life, should be stabbed in the back by her, and have his heart nailed to the pillory! Of course Mao did teach you from the time you were little to tell on your nearest and dearest in the name of the Revolution, but in this case, Liru had reported Wudong out of a selfish need to reap admiration and envy from the rest of the class. For, of course, the first-caste boys, as well as the entire body of second- and third-caste students, had not yet had the chance to read this highly coveted letter. After all, there was no way for Ru to approach the boys directly. Girls her age were supposed to act as if they couldn't stand the boys. And talking with second- and third-casters was below her dignity. So Ru needed the propaganda board to make the rest of the class – the ones she could not talk to in person – envy her.

THE DOOR IS OFF ITS HINGES

After my weekly bath, I snuggled into my bed and dozed off in delicious slow motion. The hot mid-summer *foehn* sneaked through the embroidered net curtain into my room and played with my wet locks. The sunbeams tickled my cheeks until I dissolved away in lazy, blissful contentment . . .

A hungry mosquito humming an unintelligible song into my ear woke me up. The insect was dancing a bizarre jig above my face. I pulled the sheet up over my head and tried to go back to sleep. But suddenly my entire body stiffened, and I sat bolt upright. I suddenly remembered I hadn't visited Cannibal in at least two months!

I grabbed a flowery kerchief from my dresser and tied it around my unkempt hair. I put on a wide pair of trousers and an old blouse, and hotfooted it to Building 24. What should I say when he asked me where I'd been all this time? I had clean forgotten our last appointment. Shamefaced, I pulled at my blouse, which seemed to have grown too short and too tight from one day to the next. I was sorry that I hadn't taken the time to put on one of my new shirts, which were much looser. Just look at it, I scolded myself, this one is as clingy as rice paper! I hunched over to prevent street punks from noticing the curves and contours of my upper body and cuss me out for it.

It was Aunt Xiulan who opened the door. This time there were no prefatory gales of garlic and her fingers weren't stuck together with dough like a web-footed duck. It was dead quiet in the flat.

166

'My little Lian! You certainly don't have the ki-current flowing your way; Uncle Changshan has just left. Where to? I couldn't tell you, not even if you flogged me to death! He is like smoke. He goes when he goes and he comes when he comes. Perhaps he's gone to the Willow Lake, behind the campus? That place is bristling with the spirits of his drowned colleagues. Wah! If I were you I wouldn't go looking for him. Just the very idea gives me the goosebumps. But there it is, he is getting more clammed-up and stubborn by the day. It must be his age. When a toothless old geezer decides to head West, not even ten horses can drag him East.'

Aunt Xiulan was not to be stopped: 'A book without coincidences isn't a good book. You know, under normal circumstances Uncle Changshan is just like a copper pagoda – even a fire can't smoke him out of the house. He just sits there cross-legged on the bed, over there in the big room. I could smash every piece of crockery that we own to smithereens and he still won't be persuaded to go shopping with me or visit someone. But today the door is off its hinges: I hadn't finished warming up the porridge for our breakfast when *ch-leeuuuu!* he was gone! And today of all days is the day you come to visit, to tell him your history stories! What do *you* make of it? As certain as the fact that my ancestors' family name was Ge, today the door is *completely* off its hinges!'

'Well then, I guess I'd better go. Will you give him my regards?'

'But Lian, dear! Don't you want to wait around a bit? He could be returning any moment now.' Aunt tugged a tuft of dusty grey hair over her face in order to conceal her doubt over her own assertion.

'No, Aunt. I have homework to do.'

'Please come and visit your uncle on our next weekend leave. You don't know the half of it – he worries about you so! It's *Lian this* and *Lian that* all day long!'

I couldn't get out of there fast enough. Even once I was outside, I could still hear Aunt shouting after me, 'You'll come, won't you? Will you come? You *will* come, right?'

I clenched my teeth. The urge to go back and fling myself into Aunt's arms and, once and for all, have a thorough heart-to-heart with her, had to be nipped in the bud. No matter how dearly I would like to talk about Cannibal with Aunt, I'd never have the nerve to look her in the eye. I felt like the burglar who's waving his booty under the nose of the person he has just robbed.

THE TIGER'S JAWS

That night, there was to be a showing of one of the 'Four Classics' – *Lenin and the October Revolution* – on the athletics field. I was about to go to bed, but the music coming from the open-air cinema stirred something inside me. I decided to go and watch the movie after all, without telling Mother.

I was standing at the edge of the field. I could see very little of the screen this way, but I had learned it was better never to stand right in the middle of the crowd; in the dark, I wouldn't be able to protect myself from the groping fingers of crude boys and dirty old men.

The cool evening breeze pressed my clothes close to my body and I breathed in deeply. The air smelled sweet, like the memory of a long hot summer's day. The heat refused to take its leave, and hung around obstinately.

Or – was it something else? I felt a scorching heat wave welling up behind me. It seared my skin and at the same time caused cold shivers to run up my spine. Instinctively I took a step forward, to escape the source of the heat. But just as I'd feared, the conflagration followed close behind. I stiffened. Now it wasn't only the heat; I could also smell that odour that always made me gag.

A small, shrill, tremulous scream fought its way into my throat, but got stuck halfway – I clamped my mouth shut on it, because acting unafraid seemed the wisest thing to do at that moment.

A croaky voice throbbed in my ear: 'My darling . . .' His burning breath scorched the downy hairs on my neck.

Whoooo-nnn . . . The screen went dark, blacker than blackest night. All the blood drained into my toes . . .

The panting behind me became more intense and suddenly I broke into a run. Oops! I hadn't seen the sand pile. I landed in the sand, face first. I could hear lumbering footsteps drawing near . . . I scrambled to my feet, which suddenly seemed to sprout wings. I dived inside the first building I came to and without thinking sprinted to the apartment of a colleague and good friend of my mother's.

Uncle Song gaped at me goggle-eyed. 'Does your Mother know you're out so late?'

I wanted to scream, There are *men* after me! But Uncle Song's paternal gaze stopped me from blurting it all out. Fathers aren't happy about daughters growing up, was what raced through my mind. I left him standing in the doorway, dashed back out of the building and listened intently: had I managed to lose those creeps?

Bwam! I had bumped into a man and a woman out for a stroll in the pleasant coolness of evening.

'Uncle and Aunt! Please help me!' I grabbed the woman's sleeve and sank to the ground.

'What's the matter? Aren't you Yian? Or is it Sian? Isn't our number-two daughter Yuejiao in your class at school?'

'There's a pack of crazed bullies after me! They want to kill me!'

'Come here!' Yuejiao's father sheltered my head under his armpit. 'Don't be afraid, little girl! What's your name again? Now, why should those half-grown thugs want to kill you? All they want to do is – *Aauwa!*'

I jerked my head around in surprise. Yuejiao's mother had stomped on her husband's foot on purpose. She said, 'Come, we'll take you home.'

'I don't want to go home! Please, don't tell Mother what happened . . . please!'

Yuejiao's father gave his wife a sign and Aunt whispered in my ears, 'We won't say anything to Mama, okay? Come, let's go.'

We halted below my apartment. Yuejiao's father went to fetch Mother. I grew more and more agitated.

'Shall I take you to the hospital, so you can be . . .' Mother's voice sounded like thunder and her eyes flashed lightning in the evening dusk. I didn't understand what Mother was talking about. I couldn't stop weeping and trembling.

'So! Are those ears of yours just a couple of pieces of rotten meat, or something?! How many times have I told you not to go to those shitty old movies!'

Yuejiao's father said, 'Madam Lecturer Yang! Don't yell at your child that way. She's already terrified enough . . . !' His wife stepped in front of me to prevent Mother from hitting me. That seemed to calm Mother down. She thanked Yuejiao's parents most civilly, in a manner befitting an intellectual, and promised them that she'd leave me alone. Shaking, I followed my mother upstairs.

Once inside, Mother began subjecting me to the third degree. Alternating blows with questions, she demanded to hear the minutest details, giving me a tongue lashing and a beating at the same time.

I wished those jerks had murdered me, then there'd have been no need to be abused and interrogated like a criminal. How naïve of me, to expect any sort of understanding or consolation from Mother!

'What the hell makes you traipse down there anyway, to that fucking cinema! It's like pulling teeth out of the tiger's jaws!'

I stopped crying. Now I was being accused of *asking* for it, for crying out loud! It was the last straw.

Or . . . perhaps that was it? Had it really all been my own fault . . . ? Could it be that *I* was the one provoking all that drooling and aggressive behaviour in the boys? Was I, basically, a whore? Why did those creeps bother only me, and not the other girls . . . ? My head spun, not from Mother's blows this time, but with doubt and self-hate. I pleaded to be allowed to go to bed.

'You? Sleep? Sure, and a monk can dream all he likes of sleeping with a wife! No way! You are going to write a self-criticism right *now*, at least two pages long! And you'll swear on the *Little Red Book* that you'll never, ever dare show your face at the movies again!'

My eyelids were locked in a deadly struggle to stay open and my head was reeling. I was a mass of molten ore one minute, an icy ocean the next. I bit on my pen and swore that I would never confide in Mother ever again.

It became quiet in the house. The light in Mother's room was turned off. Thinking I'd outsmart Mother, I slunk quickly into bed.

Mother whirled into the room like a furious tornado and ripped the sheet off my body: 'You sneaky little brat! Trying to pull the wool over Mother's eyes, are we? Well, here! Here's your reward – you asked for it!' She stormed over to the desk and tore the unfinished self-criticism in half, and then in half again. Smirking, she snapped at me, 'Now you can start all over again!' Mother was relentless. She stayed with me, wide awake, until the last character had been penned on paper.

At around three o'clock I was finally allowed to go to bed. I flopped between the covers, exhausted. I didn't dare lie on my side – my ears were painfully swollen. Finally I could cry my heart out. I fantasised that Mother had tortured me to death and that the neighbours came to gape at my poor body, all beaten to a pulp. It was wonderful to be dead.

∼

I couldn't see him, but I could hear his voice. Cannibal was seated on the opposite shore of the lake, under a dense jujube bush not yet in bloom. His words reverberated in the air. I couldn't understand what he was saying. The sound of his voice jigged up and down just like fireflies coruscating in the undergrowth. The leaves rustled, as if someone was hiding there.

A SIMPLE JIGSAW PUZZLE

The next morning I struggled out of bed with a crushing headache. I began counting the days until Uncle Cannibal's next weekend leave. I kept having to think of what Mother had insinuated. Had I provoked the assault? Was Mother right?

I bent over the washbasin and tried to make sense of my experiences, to see them in the light of Mother's accusations. I remembered the day someone had written on the blackboard, 'Meimei and Lian are a pair of worn-out shoes'. I'd dismissed it at the time as the rantings of a bunch of jerks who didn't know what they were talking about. Neither my good name nor my dignity had suffered so much as a scratch, at the time. But I felt quite differently about it now.

In the afternoon Mother asked me to buy some salt. On the stairs I met Meimei, who lived one floor below. Meimei grinned at me: 'Well! That was quite an honour, to get chased by those big boys, wasn't it! I saw you crying downstairs, last night. Why the crocodile tears? As if you weren't enjoying every minute of it. What a cheap little hypocrite you are!'

I froze as if hit by lightning. What the . . . ?! Did Meimei consider it an honour . . . ?

But Meimei's otherwise gentle features grew rigid with venom. 'Flies don't suck at an egg that isn't cracked. It's just that your bourgeois behaviour and looks can't help provoke decadent thoughts in any boy suffering from a weak political conscience. What – did you really think I wouldn't report you to the Youth League for your little slip-up?'

That was the straw that broke the camel's back. First I'd been chased by that lousy bastard, then I'd been grilled and blamed by Mother, and on top of it all I now ran the risk of being accused of a political crime! I'd have to kneel on the podium in the aeroplane position and have the bane of my bourgeois disposition squeezed out of my snake-head like venom . . .

I fell to my knees and begged for mercy: 'Meimei! We've been good neighbours for years. Don't report me, just this once, please?'

Meimei slapped my fingers from her trouser legs and, fuming, snorted through her comely nostrils, 'That depends how ready you are to undergo ideological rehabilitation . . .' But the bloodthirst that had flushed Meimei's peachy skin began ebbing away. An unusual sense of honesty had overtaken her. Bending her head towards me, she whispered, 'Just between you and me . . . Of course I realise that if you didn't look the way you looked, no pig would want to gnaw at you and no dog would want to sink his teeth into your shins . . . But just explain it to me, Lian – and if you try to pull the wool over my eyes, you'd better think twice – *how* come the boys tail after *you* like sticky glue, and not after me? Fuck your great-grandfather! Tell me, just where, exactly, do I fail to come up to snuff, compared to you?'

I just stood there flabbergasted: was Meimei joking? For Grandpa Heaven's sake, you can have them, please take them, all of them! They make me want to vomit! That's what I really wanted to say.

I scrambled to my feet and tried not to show how bizarre, how absurd it seemed to me. Keeping a straight face, I made a solemn kowtow to Meimei, thereby avoiding the risk of giving the wrong answer. I knew Meimei pretty well. The girl was quite capable of ratting on her classmate and neighbour with a smile, brightly denouncing her as a 'worshipper of Capitalism'. Throwing me into the abyss or sharing a joke, it was all the same to her. With Meimei, you could be sure of one thing: she had a talent for harnessing her personal feelings to political rationales. She excelled at expressing her hate, envy, spite and greed in a glorious, revolutionary manner, always letting someone else pay for it.

Now that I could be reasonably sure that I would not be reported, I got out of there as fast as I could. What a mess. Boys were harassing me with their obscenities, Mother was accusing me of asking for it, and Meimei was using political intimidation as a cover for her own jealousy. Who was left to come to my defence? Or was the bottom line that I was simply a slut who deserved to be kicked at and spat upon? I wished I were still in the camp, then I could run to Cannibal for consolation.

When I got home, I put away the salt in the kitchen cupboard and walked to Mother's room to tell her I was back. I pushed open the door and was presented with the sight of Uncle Song jerking up out of his chair like a cobra. Quick as a flash, Mother smoothed her blouse and yelled, 'What do you think your mitts are for?! Can't you knock?'

But Mother couldn't hide the pink clouds on her cheeks; and I noticed a similar display on Uncle Song's face as well. I couldn't help thinking of Qin and Pink Pig. Quickly I stepped back, closing the door behind me softly.

I pieced the jigsaw puzzle together in a trice. The forty-year-old bachelor Lecturer Song came round for a visit nearly every day. Every time he came, I was sent to bed early. If he was there in the daytime, I was sent out on an errand – for salt one time, some ginger the next, always in small quantities.

Father had been gone almost two years. I had once read in some medieval booklet:

A married woman is like a can with the lid popped loose:
She needs constant topping up with a fresh slug of juice

I didn't mind, really. At least Mother had some company this way. But her paroxysms of rage were another story. The more often Uncle Song popped round, I now realised, the more Mother turned into a powder-keg. She'd be sweet as honey to me one moment, and fly off the handle about the slightest thing the next. Feeling something that was almost relief, I rubbed my ears, which still burned with the afterglow of last night's thrashing.

ENTERTAINMENT FOR THE YOUNG PEOPLE

The merry band of six, having apparently developed a taste for it, had started dropping by my apartment more and more frequently. Every time I'd be sitting doing my homework with Kim, I would be wracked by the thought that the giggling gang might burst in any moment. There was little I could do about it. Making a date with them, so that at least they'd come at a time when Kim wasn't there, wasn't on the cards. It would have spoiled all the fun, and the whole point of the visit. But wasn't there some way I could make it clear to them that I really didn't welcome their visits?

I was constantly on edge. Every sound that could possibly herald the arrival of my friends made my hair stand on end. My palms were drenched and my intestines were all in a knot.

Kim acted as if she didn't have a clue. By Buddha, I hadn't the faintest idea what my best friend thought about this situation. I didn't have the guts to ask her, either.

Kim just kept working stolidly on, and every time I would cower, staring at the door pale as ghost, Kim would frown and mutter softly to herself, 'So – how did it go again, that formula?'

The *coup-de-grâce* came sooner than expected. At three thirty, there was a knock at the door. I was beside myself. I tried to catch Kim's eye, but was met with icy indifference. Was Kim jealous of the girls who interrupted our precious hours together, who took up so much of the time really reserved for Kim? Did she blame me for letting them get away with it, since it meant that Kim was obliged to leave as soon as they arrived – or didn't she care? Why didn't she just say something? Kim really knew how to drive me crazy!

I swore to myself that the moment I detected even the slightest hint that Kim might be unhappy about my contact with my other friends, I'd drop them like a hot potato. But Kim's empty, emotionless eyes betrayed nothing.

Hesitantly I opened the front door. The deluge of enthusiastic exclamations from my six classmates immediately swept away my disappointment over Kim's aloofness. Kim was already out the door. I didn't even bother saying goodbye. Like a parched leaf, I let my pores drink in the sap of friendship from girls of my own social class.

Feiwen stayed by the door. She said, 'We're not coming in.'

I was about to ask why not when Liru said, 'The Youth Activity Centre has been re-opened. We're all going. Want to come?'

I jumped a foot high for joy. 'Are you kidding?' I pitched my slippers into a corner as if they were frisbees and grabbed my sandals, which I put on in two shakes. Humming and singing, we ran to the Western-Europe-Is-a-Sinking-Ship-and-China-Is-the-Only-Island-of-Hope Building. That was where the Centre was housed, on the ground floor. I had never been there, for it had been shut since 1966. In the interim it had been pressed into service as a 'hotel' for cow-devils and snake-demons masquerading as teachers, professors or top functionaries. Students a few years ahead of me had been fortunate enough to enjoy the Centre's activities before the Cultural Revolution. They had been in their teens, whereas I was seven when the Cultural Revolution broke out. From their stories about the Centre, I gathered it was a mecca of sorts for teenagers. Here they could practise the arts of calligraphy, drawing and ballroom dancing, or play chess, ping-pong and badminton. There was also a small lending library with a selection of books aimed specifically at young people, where they could sit and read, borrow books, or participate in literary discussions – a particularly popular activity. And today I finally had the chance to behold the place with my own eyes!

When we entered the building, we were assaulted by the pungent smell of lime. The walls were a greyish white; they had just been painted, and in many spots the whitewash was not yet dry. The unfamiliar fluorescent lighting was galvanising, and we started sniffing around excitedly, like a bunch of nosy puppies. Even though it was the first time we'd ever set foot in the place, our minds were already furnished with a detailed map. We knew exactly where the library was situated, where we could find the ping-pong tables, and where we were likely to run into huge crowds of young people just hanging out. We walked around in a daze as if we had finally attained the wonderland we'd visited hundreds of times in our dreams.

The first room to our left was known as the House of Chess. It was packed in there, but so quiet you could have heard a pin drop. Every one of the twelve tables was occupied. Boys aged between ten and eighteen were peering earnestly at their chessboards as if their lives depended on it. Here was another reason why I didn't care much for boys. They got obsessed so quickly with whatever they were doing; whether it was their studies, or sports, or play, once they were immersed in some activity, they forgot about everything else, even their friends. And look, here was the living proof: the boys were so intent on their chess that they couldn't be bothered to look up from their game even for a second to pay homage to the newcomers. Yet whenever the seven of us walked down the street, we always attracted wolf-whistles from boys that were usually much better-looking than these ones here! No, these chess-players were nothing but a pack of silly asses endlessly plodding around and around their chess board barnyard.

We left the chess-players' heaven in a huff, and went to the big hall. In the eastern corner stood two ping-pong tables; at the western end was the library; in the northernmost sector was an exhibition of calligraphy, and at the other end, occupying the south, was a desk, behind which a woman in her early thirties was seated. Evidently the space also functioned as the Director's office.

There were long queues at the ping-pong tables: at least fifty boys and girls were awaiting their turn. Liru offered to queue for the rest of us, so that we could go and explore. We first sauntered over to the calligraphy exhibit. The black Chinese characters were set off starkly against the freshly whitewashed walls. There were a number of famous writing styles to be viewed, such as the Bamboo Lines, the Rippling Pond, and so on. These styles had been designed hundreds of years ago by artists intent on recreating and celebrating the beauty of nature. To a true connoisseur's eye, the very manner in which a character was drawn could evoke the most breathtaking landscape. For this reason it was particularly striking here that the calligraphic penmanship was not particularly in keeping with the subject matter. Thus the design Willows in the Spring Breeze had been employed to render the following slogan:

> Knock the two front teeth
> out of Professor Tianboa Jin's trap
> and then we'll see
> if he can still teach that crap—
> the bourgeois plays of Shakespeare!

In the reading corner, or rather the library, there wasn't a soul to be seen. Yawning bookcases displayed only a dozen or so volumes. From a distance the shelves looked like the mouth of a centenarian grinning from ear to ear: a black hole with just a few lonely teeth poking up here and there. The books that were there were ones I had had to commit to memory years ago: they were compulsory reading material if you wanted to pass the political education exam. The literary canon comprised *the Little Red Book*, the comic strip *Liu Wenxue*, the novel *The Cock Crows at Night*, and *The Diary of Lei Feng* – the only works that had survived the censor. All books pre-dating the Cultural Revolution had been burned by the Red Guards. Since that time, five new books had come out a year – if that.

Liu Wenxue was the tale of a nine-year-old boy. It took place during the Great Natural Disaster of 1960–1962. An old man – the nephew-once-removed of the sister of the third concubine of a former landlord – hadn't had a kernel of corn to eat for five days. Crazed with hunger, he crawled to a vegetable patch to steal a pepper that wasn't even ripe. He was caught in the act of gobbling down his plunder by a Young Red Guard named Liu. Liu nabbed the reactionary pepper-thief and wanted to haul him before the Party Chief of the Production Team. The old grandpa peed in his pants, because he knew what he was in for: five years' forced labour in a prison camp at the very least. He begged Liu to let him go, a request the boy naturally turned down – after all, the kid had been taught to skin all counter-revolutionaries alive. They got into a fight. The desperate senior citizen hit the stubborn little boy a bit too hard, with the result that the boy fell, hit the back of his head on a large rock, and died of his injuries on the spot.

The moral of the story was to emphasise how deep was Liu's hatred of the class enemy, how valiant his struggle. He followed Mao's words to the letter, until he literally dropped down dead. It was the way all children ought to behave, according to the CPC.

In May of 1961, Uncle Tianshou, the youngest brother of my father, had been subsisting on a diet of stinging nettles for two long weeks. Yet he was still ordered into the cornfield by his production team, as the rows were in dire need of weeding and there was hardly a farmer left on his feet. Uncle Tianshou was thirty-four years old and weighed five stone. He drifted over the dirt lane leading to the field like a flimsy sheet of paper. A spring breeze blew up, too feeble to tousle his bristly hair, yet stiff enough to cause him to lose his balance. He fell down, never to get up again.

I wasn't the least bit impressed with Liu Wenxue's heroic act. If the little brat had had just a speck of compassion, I thought to myself secretly, he wouldn't have put both his own and the old man's life on the line.

The Cock Crows at Night was a novel about a 'typical' pre-revolutionary landlord, a slave-driver of the worst sort. Every night at midnight he would crawl into the chicken coop and imitate a crowing rooster, so that his day labourers would think it was morning. That way he saw to it that they would spend a maximum of hours working in the fields.

The aim of this masterpiece was to remind present-day youth that they were living in paradise, compared to the hell their countrymen used to toil in before Mao's regime came into being.

The Diary of Lei Feng had been written by a soldier who loved Mao more than his own parents. (As luck would have it, the hero was an orphan by the age of two.) A paragon of altruism, he helped everyone he possibly could – he aspired to emulate Mao the way a sunflower emulates the sun.

It wasn't hard to see why this book corner had turned into an overlooked nook.

A DUBIOUS HONOUR

My friends shuffled around the hall in silence. No one wanted to be the first to admit her disappointment in this 'Mecca for young people'. Liru was still at the very tail-end of the line; it would take at least another hour before it was our turn to play ping-pong. How would we pass the time? To go home so soon would be a let-down. Even though there was nothing fun for us to do here, it was still the only place where you could hang out and socialise. In the lines at the ping-pong tables, boys and girls were chatting and checking each other out. Liru obviously felt in her element there, and didn't moan about the length of the wait.

As we stood there wondering what to do next, someone asked us, 'What year of secondary school are you in?'

We turned around and saw it was the woman who had been sitting behind the desk. Flattered that the Centre's Director should want to speak to us, we answered in unison, 'The third.'

'Are any of you interested in joining the Brigade?'

She might as well have asked us if we would like a replica of the Himalayas, cast in platinum.

The Brigade, short for Cultural Propaganda Brigade, was the latest incarnation of the song-and-dance troupe, a convention instituted in 1966. Every neighbourhood, school and work unit boasted such a company. Members were recruited from among the residents, student body or work force, respectively. The Brigade staged song-and-dance performances on festive occasions, or else by special decree of the Party. The idea was to hammer Mao's commands into the minds of the people in an enjoyable, compelling and effective manner. In 1967, for instance, the Great Helmsman had charged the populace with eliminating all Followers of the Capitalist Way. Two weeks later the audiences were treated to a show entitled *Good Riddance to Bad Rubbish*. Six girls with boyish haircuts, in military uniform complete with red armbands, stamped their feet on the boards. A man stood in their midst, waving a scarlet flag. They screamed, 'Death to the Revisionists!' – a song. Then a bespectacled old gentleman, dressed in rags, was dragged on to the stage; he was supposed to be the 'Capitalist Roader'. The six girls ran around him, brandishing their fists, spewing threats, kicking, beating and spitting on the poor man. The pace got more and more frenzied. The climax consisted of the man with the flag suddenly coming to a standstill and making a slashing movement with his right hand signifying, 'Off with his head'. At this signal, the young women flew at the poor old fellow like vultures, yanking his hair and banging his head on the floor. The old gentleman collapsed in a heap and was dragged four times around the stage like a sack of compost, to the strident accompaniment of revolutionary battle cries. The audience cheered hysterically, moved, inspired and all gung-ho to find some reactionaries of their own to smash to a pulp.

I had seen dozens of song-and-dance routines, but they were always the same. The only difference lay in the number of times the 'revisionist' was dragged around the stage and the order in which the different slogans were declaimed. Still, everyone loved going to these shows. There were always some pretty girls and good-looking boys to ogle at.

A tense silence prevailed among our group, since no one had the guts to ask which one of us in particular had caught the eye of the Youth Activity Centre Director.

'You, in the blue shirt, what's your name?' the woman asked.

Tyah! Meimei snorted through her nose. My heart flinched and my flesh jumped. The sound escaping from Meimei's nostrils betrayed how pissed off she was. I felt the dagger stares levelled at me; I was elated and terrified, all at the same time.

The woman asked me to write down my name and address and told me to be there every Wednesday and every Friday at three o'clock, after school, to rehearse a new dance.

I was thrilled. But I didn't forget my classmates. I scanned their faces. How serious was the jealousy situation? Could it possibly turn dangerous? Was there any way I could get back into their good graces? But to my relief, except for Meimei's sourpuss face I could find nothing too worrisome in my chums' expressions.

But of course – I should have known! It was perfectly normal for them not to mind my being selected for the Brigade. For my social standing was far below theirs. Liru's father was the chief of Military Hospital Number

706; Qianyun's father was a general who, until two years ago, had served in the Cabinet as Vice-Minister of Public Health; and Feiwen's mother was the daughter of the late General Zhao . . . My father, on the other hand, was only a doctor, and my mother a college lecturer. The difference in our standings was so great that, in their supreme self-confidence, my friends could not possibly begrudge me something like this.

A WORSHIPFUL DANCE

Two days later, at three fifteen, I joined five other girls and two boys in the Activity Centre's rehearsal studio. They were all the same age as me, but I didn't know them. Our brigade was drawn from the sprawling Wanzhuang District; we all attended different schools and were complete strangers to each other.

The 'new' dance was called *The Party Leads Us From One Victory To The Next*. I was the only beginner – the rest of the group had already been rehearsing together for a week and a half. Mrs Feng, the Centre's Director and the choreographer to boot, asked the company to perform the dance, to give me an idea of how it went. Basically, the dance differed only in one respect from all the other performances I had seen since I was seven: a new scene had been added which was nothing less than the exaltation of the Wisest Leader of the Universe.

Five girls stretched their arms towards the heavens and longingly cast their eyes upwards, to where a Never-Setting Sun was dangling. Next they swallowed their saliva emphatically five times, folding their arms across their chests with vehement passion. With their fingers interlaced, they rocked themselves, closing their eyes and gulping audibly another five times. The background music was somewhat less bloodcurdling than usual, it was almost romantic, even; the girls' lips parted with yearning. At that moment a boy jumped on to the boards, waving a red flag. His shouts drowned out the music: 'We will protect the Great Party Chairman by wringing all class enemies through the meat grinder!' This seemed to inject the girls with a new shot of belligerence, and their love for the Helmsman was commuted into pure bloodthirstiness. The girls' hands, soft and graceful only a moment ago, suddenly turned into executioners' claws as the five of them resumed their workaday revolutionary task: humiliating, abusing and murdering the actor playing the counter-revolutionary.

The first thing Mrs Feng taught me was how to use impassioned gestures

179

to act out my desire for the Wisest Leader. It had been comparatively easy to yell out, as loudly as I could, the classic slogan, 'Father, Mother, Lover and Mistress All-Rolled-Into-One, every cell in our bodies yearns for the Tender Raindrops of Your Love!' since I didn't have to pay too much attention to the meaning of the words I was mouthing. But now that I had to illustrate the phrase with arm gestures, the subtext suddenly became all too clear.

'Try to remember how kind the Great Party Leader is,' Mrs Feng suggested, 'as, for instance, when in 1949 He rescued our people from the Ocean of Sorrow.'

Partly out of fear of committing a political faux pas by expressing my love for Him ineptly, and partly out of a conceited desire to show the rest of the troupe how well I could dance, I tried my damnedest to imagine a Kindly Helmsman – without too much success. All sorts of irksome thoughts flitted through my mind. Willy-nilly, the things Qin and I had discussed in the flour mill or at the Lily Theatre came to mind ... I heard his voice thundering in my ears, fulminating against the masses, who according to him were only encouraging Mao's megalomania; Mao might be addicted to his own power, but then the common people were addicted to His power too ... For a few moments I allowed myself to slip back into reminiscences diametrically opposed to what I was supposed to be acting out here.

'Well, Lian Shui? We're waiting!' Mrs Feng broke into my thoughts.

I jumped, and forced myself to visualise a noble, benevolent Mao. It wasn't easy. All at once I remembered that I had often been told by colleagues of my mother's that I had such a pretty, winsome smile; I promptly pasted it on. Now Feng was nodding contentedly – my saccharine look apparently made up for my pathetic attempt at dancing. Next, Feng taught me to crane my neck up as high as possible and to open my eyes ardently as wide as they would go, before making a show of swallowing my spit, preferably with an audible gargle. 'This protestation of love for the Helmsman needs to be given an exceptionally artistic flavour,' she impressed upon me.

I did not have the nerve to ask what spit had to do with desiring the Helmsman. In the end I decided to just follow Feng's instructions blindly. I plugged away at it as best I could, trying to get the hang of it.

Now it was time to learn the steps. There was just no way that I could pull it off. I had always suffered from a horrible lack of co-ordination. Normally I was pretty good at covering up my deficiency, but under these circumstances there was, of course, no opportunity for that. If I had to pay attention to my arms, then there was no way I could get my legs to perform a different move at the same time. Liuhua, a strikingly graceful girl who was held in high regard by the rest of the group, crinkled her eyes and stifled a derisive chuckle.

After the scene in which we worshipped the Red Sun, we had to configure ourselves into a ship. One boy stood in the prow and pointed forward with one hand. This was the gesture of a Helmsman, signifying that He would lead the people towards a Glorious Communist Future. A lead dancer was to be chosen to walk behind this boy, swinging her hips beguilingly. She symbolised a populace of close to a billion people, drifting in His wake. For some unfathomable reason, Mrs Feng chose me for this starring role. This drew a gasp of protest from the rest of the group: they had all seen how clumsy my dancing was. I was having trouble enough as it was mastering the basic moves; now I would have to learn even more intricate steps as well. It was pretty clear that I wouldn't be able to handle it. There were several other girls in the troupe who were first-rate. Why wasn't the starring role awarded to one of *them*? By Buddha, I myself had no idea what had got into Feng.

Naturally, I would never admit that I did not deserve the honour. I knew I should feel as smug as a monkey at having my talent appreciated by the choreographer, and revel in the glory of being the principal dancer. I stuck my nose in the air and avoided the others as far as was possible. After all, popular girls were supposed to act like deaf-mutes. Only then were they worshipped for their inaccessibility, as marble monuments of pulchritude.

My need to be admired overcame my better judgement, and I became increasingly vain, shallow and insincere. All of Qin's teachings had flown right out of my head.

BETRAYAL

I didn't step out of the bathtub – I *bounded* out of it. Singing, I snatched my towel and dried myself in a few seconds. But once I had whirled to a halt in front of my wardrobe, my movements began winding down, as if in slow motion. My wavering eyes hesitated at each blouse, but my brain never gave my hands the go-ahead to take one out. Which blouse would Uncle Cannibal like best? The summer's breeze was dancing around me a little too friskily; suddenly I decided enough was enough, I had to cover up my nakedness, right away.

My choice, in the end, fell on a lilac blouse made of a fine synthetic material. But in the mirror, the corners of my mouth drooped despondently. No wonder people were gossiping about me. These breasts of mine were totally gross. The rest of my body was slim, frail even, but that only served to make those two big lumps of flesh even more prominent. My hips, too, were all wrong – their roundness made my waist appear dangerously waspish. Seething with envy, I thought of Feiwen: Just look at her, she just about zooms off into thin air, that one, on those long, straight, slim legs of hers! Hardly any meat on her hips, and a flat chest that looks so totally becoming. Why can't I just grow taller, lengthwise, instead of spreading sideways into this heavy, obscene woman? Tears welled up in my eyes when I thought of my favourite jacket, the one with the lace collar – the back had been completely ruined by black ink stains. Qianyun had told me that it was that pain in the ass Yougui who had emptied the contents of his fountain pen on it.

A week ago my bedroom window had been shattered. A large rock had come flying into the room, wrapped in a note that said, *Here is your just reward, you South Korean Spy!* Mother had called the police, and the first thing the officer asked was, 'Has your daughter slighted some boy or other, perhaps?' Whereupon Mother could think of nothing better to do than to assist him in his interrogation. I felt like such a criminal again! But what was it that I kept doing wrong?

In the light of all this aggravation, I was even more delighted that Cannibal's home leave was this weekend. I ran all the way to his apartment building and knocked on the door, almost exploding with impatience. First I heard some shuffling and stumbling inside. Then there he was, beaming in the doorway: 'I can't be-*lieve*-it! You haven't forgotten your Uncle!! Xiulan,' he cried in the direction of the kitchen, 'you were right! Lian has kept her word, she has come to see us.' He led me into the main room; his gait suddenly seemed sprightlier.

Aunt Xiulan followed us inside and placed a bowl of walnuts on the bed. 'Do you remember these? From the black market, near our camp. Haven't you missed them?'

I felt as if I had been stung in the heart by a bee: *of course* I missed the camp! Not only because of the treats you could obtain at the market: it was also the simplicity of the life itself that I missed. At least in the camp I hadn't had to twist myself into all sorts of contortions to escape any boys' clutches.

～

Cannibal sat down on the kang cross-legged and closed his eyes.

'Uncle, I haven't prepared a lecture.'

He opened his eyes.

'I'm sorry.'

'Why, there's no need to apologise. I'm sure you have your reasons.' He pushed the dish of nuts towards me and waited. 'Shall I crack one open for you? They're delicious.' Cannibal picked out a nice plump nut, held it up against the wooden headboard and – *ketch!* – smashed it flat with a little hammer. He separated the hull from the meat with meticulous care and presented it, almost perfectly intact, to me. I didn't feel like eating, but I accepted the offering out of politeness.

'Don't want it? Give it here, then.' Cannibal aimed the nut into the side of his mouth that still contained a few molars and – mmmm! – how he relished it!

'Uncle . . . am I a whore?'

Echechnn! Cannibal choked and – *kheh kheh* – coughed; his neck blew up to the girth of a hundred-year-old tree. I scooted over to him guiltily and slapped him between the shoulder blades, to help him cough up the piece of nut caught in his throat.

'Don't worry about me,' said Uncle when he had finished sputtering. 'There's nothing the matter with me; however, there *is* something the matter with you. *What* did you say? How in Buddha's name did you get it into your head to say something so preposterous?!'

'Then why are they always calling me all sorts of names?'

'Do they? What do they say, exactly?'

'Well, that I'm a landlord's concubine.'

'Didn't you learn about that, in history? How before the People's Republic, young people's marriages were always arranged for them? But if a man was rolling in dough, he could afford to pick out a concubine, preferably a pretty little thing.'

'Do you . . . you mean it's a . . . hidden compliment?'

'What do *you* think?'

'But then, why don't they just come out with it?'

'Child, have you forgotten what is written in the *Little Red Book*? To harbour any feelings for a sweetheart is to betray the Communist Party. No matter how great a trouble-maker he may be, no boy will stick his neck out and risk getting it caught in the noose of the Dictatorship of the People, by confessing he likes you.'

'They also call me a Spy from South Korea.'

'Just think about it. Where do the boys find their idols these days? The censored spy films, is where; and every one of the secret agents in those movies is extremely sexy, I must admit.'

'But why do they ruin my jackets and shirts with ink and smash my window?'

'*Why?* But I just explained it to you.'

'I don't believe you.'

'Is that so?'

'There are so many pretty girls at our school and they don't get attacked, only me, and . . . well, and maybe one or two others.'

Cannibal pulled a serious face. 'Now listen to me carefully. Do you understand the difference between pretty and sexy?' His words gave me goosebumps. I had the feeling I should stop up my ears. 'Or are you a boy yourself, perhaps? Do you know what kind of girl the boys like best?'

'Of course I do! Take Feiwen, for instance. She's the ultimate classic beauty, tall and stately.'

'Which Feiwen? Not Professor Peng's daughter? That lanky thing, as skinny as a rake?'

'How can you say that? According to all my girlfriends, a tall and slim figure is the most desirable attribute in a woman.'

Cannibal rolled his eyes upwards. 'Don't talk about things you don't understand!' My goosebumps turned to an icy crust, and I clenched my eyes shut. 'My little girl, you'd better get this through your thick skull: instead of hating yourself, you ought to . . .'

'Uncle, please don't say it.' He looked up, surprised. 'It makes me want to puke when boys show me they're interested. The last time you were home on a Sunday, some smutty creep told me, "You are my darling"! Isn't that sickening? And *mean?*' Cannibal said nothing. 'You'd have to be a foul-mouthed pig or a dirty old pervert to say that to a girl, wouldn't you? You, for instance, you'd never do something like that, not in a million years, would you?'

Uncle looked the other way. I suddenly felt panicked, as if a bottomless crevasse was yawning at my feet.

'Lian . . . I am truly sorry, but I have to admit it: I too am just a man, with the seven feelings and the six desires.'

Whooonn! My head felt as if it had been hewn in two. Not in my wildest dreams had I ever imagined that Cannibal – the one I had thought I could always count on, the only one I trusted in the whole world – that Cannibal too could have such base urges. And I had had such high hopes, that pure-hearted people did exist in this world, people untainted by this sleazy desire for female flesh! My priceless dream was shattered, my last remaining sanctuary razed to the ground. Even here in Cannibal's home I no longer felt safe, and that meant I wasn't safe anywhere. I felt like jumping up and storming out, but remembered how guilty I had felt after running out on Uncle so abruptly the last time. But what then? What should I do? I shrank away from him, assailed by an irrational revulsion for the air I was inhaling – for he was breathing the same air as I.

'Try putting yourself in their shoes. They don't know what to do about their feelings for you, that is why they are harassing you.'

I was so incensed my hair stood on end. What? Was he taking *their* side now? So – *I* was the guilty one, was I the trollop that made those poor, helpless boys come all unglued? I clenched my fists and forced myself not to scream. I had come here to complain about the boys' misconduct and, once again, it was *I* who ended up on trial. I was too sad to feel the sadness any more.

'Oh, child, it isn't *that* bad, is it? Come over here.' Cannibal put out his hand.

The older boys' smell, their panting and obscenities, rushed back to me and I realised with a start that Uncle belonged in their camp. Hate for the opposite sex gripped my heart and with a wave of my arm I swept the bowl of nuts on to the cement floor – *kwang-langlang!*

'What's the matter?' Aunt rushed into the room and saw the shattered dish on the floor and nuts rolling everywhere – under the bed, the table, benches and into shoes.

Blind with rage, I gave the broken plate another kick for good measure. Out of the corner of my eye I saw Cannibal gesturing to his wife to leave us . . .

'I am sorry, my child, it appears I have smashed the bowl of our friendship and trust to smithereens.' He avoided my eyes and – *heh . . . heh . . .* – couldn't stop sighing. I saw his eyes go red for a moment. But I didn't feel sorry for him – only for myself. *I* was the one who needed the sympathy, the whore whose lot it was to be kicked around and spat on by tens of thousands of people. Yet *I* was still supposed to show oodles of understanding for those who molested me, seeing that it was their God-given right to give in to their frigging seven feelings and six desires. All right then, this was war – war on the opposite sex. Starting with Uncle Cannibal – wait, not 'uncle' – no 'uncle this or uncle that' any more! *Tyelah!* I aimed one last kick at the shattered plate and said, as politely as I could, 'Oh, well, you know how it is, Cannibal. It's just that I . . . I have so much homework. I don't have the time to come and visit you any more, for the time being.'

'Xiulan!' Cannibal shouted. Aunt ran in to hear his confession. 'I deserve to be punished – I've gone and broken our beautiful dish.'

Aunt took a broom from the hall and said, 'On page 126 of the *Little Red Book* it is written: If you acknowledge your shortcomings, and are committed to changing them, then you are still a good revolutionary.'

Stooped over, with his head bent down, Cannibal inched his way down off the kang; he crawled under the bed and the table to pick up the nuts that had rolled into all eight directions of the wind. He slid a paper bag out from underneath the mattress, and dropped the nuts into it one by one.

A strange sensation seized me. I bit my lip, refusing to acknowledge what that feeling meant. I wanted just one thing: to say goodbye as politely as possible, and never see him again. And that's exactly what I did.

⌒

That night I saw the familiar lake again in a dream.

It was autumn, and gruesomely quiet. There were brown leaves and dead branches floating in the water, and as I glided over the lake in my canoe, beautiful, gleaming animals formed a circle around me. They were pleading and moaning. Just as I was reaching a hand out to them, I saw greedy jaws opening wide – the sharks.

The next morning there was a paper bag filled with nuts outside my door.

AN UNEXPECTED STORM

It was the middle of August. The fireball of the midday sun steamed the dense white clouds to a pink mist. Pedestrians barrelled home as if they had been swept up in the heat wave's centrifugal force.

I was sitting in my room, reading by the window. Everything was sticky. When I put my arms on the table, my sweaty elbows stuck to the tabletop that was covered in a film of condensation. Unless I shifted my weight every so often, my trousers, drenched in perspiration, would fuse to the chair. The stuffy air clung to my body like a suffocating feather quilt; I could not shake it off, no matter which way I twisted or turned.

At four o'clock a cyclone arose over the earth. It herded the clouds together, cloned them at record speed and poured buckets of black ink over them. The quilt suddenly became a band of steel wrapped tightly around my chest. *Whoo-woo, whoo-woo!* roared the whirlwind. With its giant's hands the twister shook the trees until they were yanked out of the ground, roots and all.

Dong, dong, dong. Something was banging on the window. I tried to look out, but could see nothing. The afternoon was like darkest night. *Tchin-tya, tchin-tya, tchin-tya!* Then the sound of breaking glass. By groping around blindly, I found the switch and clicked on the light. My desk was buried in broken glass, and in the window yawned a hole wide as a lion's jaws, allowing a gust of wind to enter and tear around the room. Shivering from head to toe, I stuck my hand out through the hole. Ice cubes the size of hen's eggs fell into my outstretched palms.

'Mama!'

When Mother entered my room, she quickly closed the door behind her, because of the fierce draft. 'Hailstones,' she explained.

Disconsolately I watched the crystal-clear, hard little balls dwindle in my hand before they returned to the atmosphere, leaving a minute puddle of water in my palm as the only proof of their existence. Back to the lion's jaws. Catching the hailstones in one hand, I used the other to stow the cute little balls in my trouser pockets. Gradually, as the wind gusts started tapering off, my haul began to grow more meagre. The roar of the storm, the cracking of falling trees and the hammering of hailstones on the windowpanes, roof tiles and asphalt halted. Silence proclaimed itself; it was as if mother nature were holding her breath, not wishing to disturb her alarmed children any further and wanting to rock them to sleep.

Jeeuuuu . . . Doors everywhere were flung open wide. Excited children's voices rang out in streets that had been deserted until just a moment ago. I looked outside, all agog. The inky sky had turned a transparent blue again, filled with drifting clouds like nimble white-frocked damsels daintily strolling, skipping and romping about.

When I looked down, I could see the damage the hailstorm had done in less than half an hour. A winter landscape in the middle of summer! Toppled trees lay everywhere; the occasional specimen left standing had been all but stripped naked. The few surviving leaves were studded with raindrops; they reflected the orange sunlight like so many little round mirrors. Only by looking at these remaining green leaves could you tell that it wasn't winter. The streets had disappeared under fallen trees and broken branches. Whooping, the children leaped over the littering obstacles. They poked around the tree stumps and under the leaves, stuffing their finds exultantly into sacks slung over their shoulders.

'What are they doing, Mama?' I asked.

'They are gathering the sparrows that were killed by the hail.'

'What for?'

'To eat them, of course.'

I grabbed a red shopping basket and raced outside. Some of my peers were accompanied by their parents, who were showing them the fastest way to find the little birds. My mother didn't feel like coming so I was on my own in my quest for dead sparrows.

I was hailed by the four daughters of the Teng family: 'So, Lian, you too!' I opened my eyes as wide as saucers: Tengshan, the oldest, was dragging a garbage bag that was already filled to the rim. 'How did you manage to find so many sparrows?' I asked, impressed. The sisters Teng gazed at my empty bag pityingly and said, 'You shouldn't just look in the bare spots, silly. Take a stick and use it to overturn the fallen branches. You'll find heaps of birds underneath.'

This useful tip came too late, unfortunately – it was soon dark: dinner time. The smell of fried sparrows came seeping out of kitchen windows. Now I was truly jealous of those lucky dogs who had managed to gather enough sparrows for a princely feast.

A SEED CARRIER WORTH HIS SALT

The decimation of the birds and the trees created a lucrative work opportunity for the third-casters. The university's maintenance department, unable to handle the heavy cleaning job by itself, hired unemployed mothers from the mud-hut quarter to tidy up the area. You could hear them at the crack of dawn, already hard at work clearing downed trees and fallen lamp-posts from the streets. When that was done, they began sweeping up the leaves and broken glass. The normal peace and quiet of the campus was shattered by the creaking and groaning of the trees. The racket was intensified by the women's ear-piercing chatter. From time to time you'd see one of them yank at a fellow blabbermouth's arms to shut her up, in order to hog the whole talk show for herself.

At three p.m. a party of five arrived at my flat to replace the glass and repaint the window mouldings. Within half an hour they had repaired the smashed panes and touched up the trim. I was seriously impressed by the speed at which they worked, as well as by the profusion of words they were able to rattle off at the same time. After they left, still jabbering, the apartment seemed, suddenly, as quiet as a graveyard. The smell of the wet paint gave me a slight headache. I decided to go outside for a breath of fresh air.

There was a sizeable orchard outside our building. A bounty of little green peaches and pears that must have been knocked out of the trees by the hail, lay rotting on the ground. They were too small to eat, but too large not to cause regret in the passers-by. Still, the leaves that had survived the storm glittered more ebulliently than ever. I sniffed in the garden's fragrant smells and felt right as rain once again. My sense of time and space, knocked out of kilter by the hailstones and my craving for sparrow meat over the past two days, was slowly but surely restored to me . . . Suddenly I realised it was already past four o'clock, and Kim wasn't here yet. Had Kim forgotten about our study date? An unpleasant premonition came over me and I tore off at full speed towards Kim's house.

The closer I got to the mud-hut quarter, the more clearly I could hear the din.

'Here comes the beam!'

'Watch out, the cement's on its way up!'

'Can I have some more nails?'

Everywhere, men and teenage boys were busy repairing their homes. At least half the dwellings had become virtually see-through: their roofs had collapsed and their windows had been battered in by the hailstorm. Even from far away you could see everything that was going on inside. Grandfathers and grandmothers were squatting on the three-legged remains of their kang, as toddlers nudged washbowls around the giant puddle that used to be the floor, squealing excitedly about how beautifully their boats were sailing. Housewives were wringing out bedding and hanging it from clotheslines that almost collapsed under the weight. I quickened my pace and prayed to Buddha that Kim's family's house might belong to the fortunate half that had not become open-air dwellings.

Bam! I had slipped and fallen into a treacherous mud puddle. The road was cratered with potholes that lay hidden beneath the pooling rainwater, making it hard to know where it was safe to step. Drenched to the skin, I ran the rest of the way to Kim's house.

When I got within sight of Kim's courtyard gate, I adjusted my stride – left, left, right, left – so that I would enter with my left foot: that was for good luck.

What a worthless superstition *that* turned out to be. The roof, the rice-paper windows and the door had all been utterly demolished by the hail. All that was left of the kang was its top; the mud-oven had dissolved. Unlike elsewhere, there was no sound of hammering; nothing stirred. The repair work that the other families were busily engaged in seemed to have gone by the wayside here. I peered around the nooks and crannies of this 'open house' until I finally caught sight of something moving. It was Kim's mother's backside: she was wielding a bamboo broom with all her might to sweep the water out of the room. This was as effective as trying to chop down a tree with a nail file, because as soon as the water level receded a little, more would come pouring in through the cracks in the walls. There was a sound, too: *tingtong, tingtong*. Could it be the sound of Kim's mother's tears falling into the rainwater? I was overcome with shame. What an utter egoist I was – praying for another hailstorm, so I could harvest more dead sparrows! Why hadn't it even *occurred* to me that not half a mile from the university, there were millions of people living in ramshackle huts, mud houses that didn't have a chance in hell of withstanding such an onslaught? The campus maintenance service made a big to-do over a lick of paint on the window-sills, but the mud-hut dwellers received not a speck of aid from the authorities, or from any agency whatsoever, to help them restore their most basic need of existence – a roof over their heads. While I was griping about the smell of a little wet paint, tens of thousands of third-caste families were in danger of drowning in the giant cesspool that was now their home.

A shuffling sound alerted Kim's mother that someone was standing there. Startled, she turned around and discovered me. Without a word, I took the broom out of her hands and started sweeping, to free up Kim's mother's hands for more important tasks.

Kim's mother drew a floating basin filled with bags of cornmeal from the water and waddled to the courtyard to prepare dinner. She improvised a makeshift stove by piling four red bricks on top of each other. Looking up at the twilit sky, she muttered, 'My poor child, you've been gone two hours in search of firewood, and you still aren't home yet. It must be pretty hard to find any kindling that's dry enough, today.'

Only now did it cross my mind that Kim was not home yet. Kim's mother gave me a gentle pat on the back and earnestly resumed her sobbing.

Seeing that there wasn't any firewood yet to cook with, Kim's mother resolved to tidy the house some more. She leaned over to pick up a mop, but the handle was so saturated with water that it snapped in two. She had to clutch the edge of the kang to keep her balance; her only clean blouse was instantly smeared with mud.

'A-yah, Old Grandpa Heaven, tell me, what did we do wrong, to deserve such a catastrophe? Couldn't You have dealt us, your ignorant yet law-abiding grandchildren, a lighter blow? As sure as I am a plucked hen that can't lay any more eggs, we have no clue what sin we have committed.'

Kim's father wasn't of the same mind, apparently. He had been sitting in a large tub floating in the middle of the room, smoking his long pipe. 'Hey, you shrivelled-up old bitch,' he warned her, irritated, 'quit your blubbering!'

Kim's mother, sending her husband a withering look, immediately stopped crying. 'All you know how to do is yell at your wife. If you were truly worth your salt as a seed-carrier, you would go over to your brother's, across the street. Why don't you? He has two strong sons and they could help us fix the roof and the walls.'

The father sprang from his tub like a bullfrog, charged towards his spouse, grabbed her by the grey hair and began ramming her head into the wall. 'You-expect-me-to-ask-for-help-from-that-selfish-conceited-snob-of-a-turtle-egg?!' The cadence of his invective harmonised most ingeniously with the battering of her head against the wall. 'You'll-see-me-help-you-out-of-your-misery-for-good-first!'

His normally gruff voice sounded shrill and off-key. He was cross-eyed with rage. Tufts of white hair flew in all directions and Kim's mother's face was turning blue. *Dong-dong-dong*. Her head made a dull sound in the half inundated house.

At this point I just lost it. I threw myself backwards, landing in the puddle. Beating at the water with my arms and legs, I splashed it all around – up, down, left, right. I *scrrrrreamed* blue murder. My shrieks flew up through the yawning roof and out to the east, west, north and south, ricocheting off the walls of the entire mud-house quarter.

Tcha-tcha-tcha-tcha. From all directions, footsteps could be heard squelching their way to the courtyard. In less than ten minutes at least sixty interested observers had poured in. Astonished as I was at seeing such a crowd, I stayed where I was, in the puddle – only because I didn't want anyone to see the green stripes of my underpants through my wet slacks. Kim's father, alarmed, let go of his wife; both were at a total loss as to how to deal with such an audience.

A quiet prelude was followed by a symphony of deafening tongue-wagging: 'Sure, sure, no wonder Kim's parents are quarrelling. They have no sons to help them fix the house.'

'What you say is true, Gangdar's mother. And they don't have the dough to hire any workmen.'

'Mother of Tiedar, *who* could pay for that much manpower? It's a curse, it is truly a curse, not to have sons!'

There was a din of comments and suggestions – the courtyard had turned into a street theatre.

Kim's father clearly felt ill-at-ease. He wanted to put an end to this spectacle. He attempted to paste a smile on his face and accomplished the sort of grimace you would make if you bit into a sour plum. Putting his hand over his heart, he apologised, 'Grandfathers and grandmothers, uncles and aunts, brothers and sisters, we are so sorry to have disturbed you . . .' His voice cracked, his eyes overflowed and he was stumped for anything further to say.

Catching sight of me, an excellent fib suddenly came to him: 'It was this girl here who started it. If she hadn't begun shrieking like a pig on the butcher's block, there would have been nothing the matter.' Reinvigorated, he rushed over to me, trying to haul me out of the puddle in an anything but friendly manner.

Now the chorus of onlookers let him have it: 'No, Father-of-Kim! You're wrong. That child there may be of a higher caste, but she has a heart of gold; she's like one of us.'

I found myself floating on cloud nine. Not only because of their kind words, but also because it had suddenly occurred to me what I could do to help Kim's family. Who cared if people saw my underpants! I jumped to my feet. Imitating Kim's father, I interlaced my fingers over my chest and begged the audience, 'Grandfathers and grandmothers, aunts and uncles, brothers and sisters, won't you please give Kim's parents a hand, just for *one* day, to help them fix their house?'

Kim's mother, who was usually proud of her own gumption in begging for help, stood nailed to the floor. She was so impressed by my nerve, and in such a tizzy herself, that she couldn't move a muscle.

'Mama?' A milky little voice broke the colossal silence: 'Can I help too? I can chop straw. For the mud for the roof, you know, the way Papa taught me.'

Suddenly the tongues loosened again. More and more people indicated a willingness to help. A man with a snowy beard was chosen to be the foreman. He stepped forward importantly and asked all around, 'Next Sunday, at the third cock's crow, we begin. Are you with me?'

'Ehn!' The audience grunted throatily to indicate it was agreed. The crowd dispersed, leaving only its footprints behind in the courtyard's mud.

Tchyaaaaa . . . The rickety gate opened and a mountain of firewood waddled into the yard. Underneath I could make out a skinny pair of legs that could belong to no one but Kim.

The mother ran up to her daughter elatedly, hoisted the mountain off Kim's back, and opened the floodgates, letting out a torrent of words: 'Guess what kind of blessing Buddha the Merciful has just granted us!' Skipping over the more unfortunate details just to be on the safe side, she began with the happy ending: 'Sunday the whole neighbourhood is going to come and help us fix our house!'

Kim shook her head; she couldn't believe her ears. Yellow and green sprigs of grass flew from her inky hair. Seeing the droll look of astonishment on Kim's face, her mother grew even more excited. She rattled on, 'If just *a single* word is a lie, may I change into a tailless old mare right here on the spot!' Kim, seeing me nodding my head in confirmation, was intrigued. 'Kim, eldest daughter of mine, today is Wednesday! How on earth can I get everything ready in only three days? The straw has to be purchased. You know how long the lines at the stores can be, especially now, since that damn hailstorm. Clay has to be dug out of the mountains in the Tongxian region. The beams from the old roof are still good, true, but they have to be repainted, otherwise they'll get riddled with woodworm. And what about snacks and drinks for all the neighbours that are coming to help us? Where will we get the money for all that? Aya, aya!' She waved her arms, covered her eyes with both hands and began moaning, partly out of worry and partly out of joy.

Kim's father knocked his pipe out against the stone slab that used to be the window-sill and said, 'Ma, I said you're a dumb bitch, and I'll say it again: you are and you will always be a cretinous animal! How'd you get so stewed up over nothing, all of a sudden? The straw's no problem, leave it to me. I'll ask for a day off tomorrow, after all, I've worked enough overtime. The clay and the beams: my department too. Kim can make roasted sweet corn. And you, you hopeless bellyacher, you can bake sweet potato slices. That's enough for eats. The only thing we can't afford is the liquor. Well, our neighbours will just have to understand how it is. And now, Mother-of-Kim, shut your trap and go cook us a nice big pot of corn porridge for our supper!'

'Ptyeh!' Kim's mother giggled like a teenager who has just had her first kiss from a boy. She practically danced over to the makeshift stove. She was mighty pleased that her husband had everything under control, and was giving his word that the repair work next Sunday would go off without a hitch. Instead of fuming at the man who had just beaten the shit out of her, she was proud of him – she knew that under his prickly skin there beat a kind heart.

⌒

At dinner that night Mother asked me if I felt all right – I looked so wiped out. I wasn't about to tell her about the events of the afternoon, and retired to my room early, at eight o'clock.

Once I was in bed, I felt as if my bones were crumbling into a thousand pieces, like the jimu-crane that's reduced to a jumble of blocks when a child carelessly jabs it with her elbow. But in spite of the exhaustion and physical pain, I was glowing inside. Going around with girls of my own caste – something I'd been doing a lot of lately – had clogged my ego with layer upon layer of vanity, hypocrisy and selfishness.

Kim's parents' fight, however, had made me come to my senses. No more shuttling back and forth between Kim and those two-faced, upper-caste twits any more. I much preferred staying on one side of the river only – the side the mud-house quarter was on.

A PICK-ME-UP FOR THE WORKERS

The midday sun baked the devastated landscape to a mellow brown. And everything damp – the swampy earth, the deluged plants, the soppy plumage of the birds, who had resumed their singing by now – everything was drying out splendidly.

Knowing that Kim had too much to do to keep our study date, I knocked off my homework early in the morning. There were plenty of chores at Kim's house that could use my helping hand.

Before setting out for the mud-house quarter, I opened the living-room cabinet and deliberated with myself – would it be a sin if I smuggled out some of my father's liquor, to give to Kim's family? The matter was quickly settled.

When I tried to hand Kim's mother the plastic bag containing five bottles of liquor, the mother spread her arms wide, palms up. As I had assumed she was reaching for the bottles, the bag very nearly crashed to the ground.

But Kim's mother was intoning a prayer of thanks instead: 'Merciful Buddha, such all-seeing eyes You have! You saw that we were feeling the pinch and couldn't afford to buy alcohol for the house-raising on Sunday. That's why You are now offering it to us as a gift, by way of my eldest daughter's friend!'

Kim ran up to me and rescued the bag from me in the nick of time, showing what she thought of her mother's histrionics with a shrug. Then she went back to her cleaning as if nothing had happened. Her mother had meanwhile climbed back up on her ladder. She was working on smoothing the top of the walls so that the roof could be bolted down on them more evenly in two days' time. Kim's father lay stretched out under a beam, whitewashing it with care, and Jiening was sitting pretty as a princess, installed on a tall stool and nibbling on the sugar-roasted corn kernels which her sister had knocked herself out to prepare for the helpful neighbours. Everything was exactly the way it was supposed to be.

THE NEWS SUMMARY

Tomorrow was the big day. Everything in Kim's house had been turned upside down. The bricks her father had bought lay in a pile in front of the door; you had to be a champion high-jumper to get into the room. A mountain of red clay had been dumped in the middle of the yard. The two hens that had replaced Whitey, but were able to lay only half as many eggs as their predecessor between them, saw to it that the entire courtyard was spattered with muck, provoking Kim's mother to address a Yangtze River of profanities to their feathered ancestors. Kim scampered up and down the walls, getting everything in shape for the following day. My job consisted of filling every vessel, pot or pan in sight with water, for mixing the cement and mud the next morning.

At eleven thirty I urgently needed to go to the bathroom. Kim's mother wiped her hands and started digging around in the debris in search of one of the pieces of wrapping or newspaper that Kim periodically brought home from the street. After uttering a multitude of imprecations along the lines of, 'Come on, roll out of your hole, you bloody son-of-a-bitch, or else I'll bash your stupid brains out,' her mother finally came up with a piece of stiff brown paper that had lain hidden under a pile of rags. She crumpled it into a ball, then smoothed it out again, tugging at it to the left and right until it was soft and creased as old leather. 'Here,' she said to me. 'Go easy with it.'

I found four middle-aged women already squatting over the holes in the latrine's wooden floor. My arrival triggered the off-switch on their motor-mouths. Their eagle eyes followed my every movement, from the moment I started unbuckling my belt until I squatted down, mortified.

Fortunately a chubby woman began confiding again: 'Now, where were we, then? Oh yeah, that kid, Erfu, as I said, he was hopping mad! Who wouldn't be! On top of everything else, he had given her two lengths of polyester! Enough for two shirts and a pair of slacks. Tell me, where do you ever find such a sugar daddy these days? That ungrateful hussy – what's her name again, Linwei, Weilin or Weiwei, some stuck-up name of the sort anyway – went ahead and gave Erfu the boot for a pale-skinned upper-caster . . .'

'Yes but is there any girl who wouldn't use her bed-pillow for a leg up the ladder? The problem is, not many girls are blessed with a "fortune" like Weilin's. Otherwise, just about anybody could hook a bigwig's son, and where would *that* leave us?' one of the others asserted.

'You call that sly-vixen mug and that slinky-snake waist of Weilin a "fortune"? I assure you, Mother-of-Yipin: no matter how sexy a lower-caste girl may be, she is and always will be a piece of dung under the shoes of those hoity-toity gents . . . !'

I shuddered. I got out of there as fast as I could. On my way back I kept thinking of Weilin, a girl I had never met.

BRAGGING RIGHTS

It was the first day of the 1973–1974 school year. I was seated at my desk in the classroom. It was already ten to eight. I kept looking at the door: where was Kim?

As usual, the girls had separated into two groups. The second- and third-caste clique stood yakking at the front of the classroom: it was a toss-up as to who could talk the loudest. Even from a distance, I could make out every word. Tieyan was saying, 'Listen, *your* homes suffered as much damage from the hailstones as' – pointing at her feet – 'my little toe, compared to the way *our* house was wrecked. Don't just stand there shaking your head no, like a drunken ape! You don't believe me? Just ask *her* – Yuehua, tell them! The huge date tree behind our mud house was torn up by the roots in the storm. It ploughed right through our kitchen. Every single thing was pulverised to sawdust when the roof caved in!'

In the silence that followed, Tieyan grinned triumphantly at her listeners: it was finally her turn to outshine her fellow caste members. The fact that it involved a major catastrophe for her family, wasn't the issue: it was still a tale to top all tales.

Compared to this group, the little first-caste club at the back of the classroom was relatively sedate. From where I was seated, I could observe the young ladies' elegant gesticulations, but I could not hear what they were saying.

If truth be told, it wasn't acceptable for a girl like me not to join in the conversation of either of the cliques, but I just did not have the slightest inclination to speak to any of them right now.

I didn't feel I belonged in either camp any more.

Dringgg! The bell, finally! Kim hurtled into the classroom and immediately made herself as small as possible. Her hair was sticking out all over the place, her wrinkled blouse was smeared with mud, her cheeks seemed even hollower than usual, and her eyes were popping out of their sockets with exhaustion.

At morning recess I rushed over to her. Kim said, with a sigh of relief: 'It's finished, finally! It's so great to sleep under a *roof* again!' She was hiding her hands behind her back, but I had already noticed there was black dirt under her long fingernails. It was obvious she had been too busy and too tired to take care of herself. I had been intending to propose starting our long-distance training again the next day, but now that I saw how bushed Kim was, I swallowed what I had been going to say.

But Kim seemed to read my thoughts. She smiled at me savvily and reassured me, 'I'll be waiting for you at six thirty tomorrow, at the running track.' Oh, how old she looked, with that sallow face of hers all puckered up into a smile! It gave me the goosebumps. What a gutsy friend I have! Dog-tired as she is, she's still thinking about getting in shape for the Autumn Games. If someone like that can't get ahead, who would?

TWO BOWLS OF BLOOD

A week later, as we were doing our homework, Kim was acting very strange. She kept glancing at me as if she wanted to tell me something, but then abruptly looked down at her notepad again without saying a word. I pretended not to notice and continued working.

Since Kim kept stopping to stare at me, it took her ages to finish her assignment.

In the end, I couldn't sit on my curiosity a moment longer.

'What's the matter?'

Kim looked away and bit on her pencil.

I had to repeat the question three times before I got to hear what was bugging my friend. Turning beet-red with embarrassment, Kim said, '. . . Weilin, that pretty girl, remember, Lian, you heard them talking about her, that time in the public latrine?' Kim blushed again – she wasn't comfortable talking about grown-up stuff, like boyfriends and that kind of crap. 'Yesterday afternoon,' she said, 'at around three o'clock, on my way to the Weasel Hills, I suddenly heard somebody banging on someone's door. It made my blood run cold: it sounded like the very devil himself, in a raging hurry to drag some poor dying soul back to hell with him! I took cover behind a wall and held my breath. I was bursting to find out what was going on. The door was opened from inside, and I heard an old woman's shaky voice go, "Aya! What an honour for us, to be paid a visit by the Young Grandpa Erfu!" Then I understood where I was: outside Weilin's house. From the mother's ingratiating and frightened tone, I gathered that a terrible calamity was looming over their home. "Yo-oung Grand-pa Er-fu," said the mother, straining her vocal cords and bellowing the name as if her life depended on it. Of course I understood at once what she was trying to do: it was her way of warning her daughters Weilin and Weilan about the looming disaster. "Can I get you some tea and a smoke?" The old woman scurried about like an ant in a red-hot wok, trying to cover up her panic with exaggerated cordiality. I could see everything through a hole in the wall.

'Is *that* Erfu? I asked myself – he was a skinny rake of a youth, not more than five feet tall. But his gall obviously weighed more than his entire carcass. He stomped around on his bowlegs with giant strides, hollering like the despicable loud-mouth he was: "Cut it out, you fossilised old bag – I've had enough of your arse-licking. Just tell me where that ungrateful fox-stinking cunt Weilin is!"

'The mother pleaded, "Young Grandpa, I know you are angry that my disobedient daughter has broken up with you, but hasn't she returned all your gifts and offered you her apologies? Can't you just forgive her, and leave her alone?"

'But before she'd finished, Erfu had kicked down the door to Weilin's bedroom. After the loud *bang!* came an avalanche of obscenities, featuring a complete rundown of both male and female genitalia, and I saw Weilin, in tears, being dragged out by Erfu – by the hair.

'Her little sister Weilan quietly slipped out of the house, to ask her aunt, who had two brawny grown-up sons, for help. Weilin's mother only has two bits of cheap goods herself, like my own ma. To give Weilin's cousins time to get there, the mother tried to stall for time by kneeling on the floor, keeping up an endless patter of supplication: "Erfu, think back on all the months that Weilin was so sweet to you, and show her some mercy . . ."

'The noise soon lured fifty or so spectators into the courtyard of Weilin's house. They were keen to see what kind of barbarous atrocity Erfu was up to now, and listened apprehensively, but also with some amusement, to Weilin's ma's entreaties. Nobody lifted a finger to help the poor mother and daughter. I had run in there too, meanwhile. The comments coming from the audience seemed designed to egg Erfu on: "What sort of a girl – I mean, a girl with normal skin on her face, not cowhide – would jilt her boyfriend just like that? How can that poor boy face life now? Dumped by such a frigging bitch! . . ."'

Kim looked down and stopped speaking.

'Well? What happened then?'

Kim's face flushed a liverish puce. She refused to go on. But I would not give up – with much pushing and pulling, I managed to drag the rest of the story out of Kim in the end.

Erfu cussed Weilin, kicked her in the belly and looked around defiantly. In the eyes of his audience, Erfu could make out alarm, confusion and even pity, and it gave him a rush. As the mother began firing off a new plea for mercy, hoping that Weilin's cousins would get there soon, Erfu began unfastening his trouser buckle and digging around in his fly. With much ado, he finally pulled out his itty-bitty little job, ordered Weilin to genuflect before him abjectly, slammed her head into his groin, and caterwauled like a vampire who's caught sight of some juicy blue neck veins. His audience kept quiet. Some of the women covered their children's eyes. Like an animal, Erfu prodded himself into the struggling Weilin, who seemed at that moment more dead than alive. Erfu panted and grinned. His mouth was all in a twist, as if he was both pissed-off and ecstatic at the same time.

'I was so mad I was about to explode,' Kim went on, 'but I didn't dare make a move. No one did anything, not even the venerable elders, nor the most powerful men. Who was I, then, to make a fuss? Suddenly, from outside, we could hear a string of obscenities too foul to repeat, and then Weilin's two cousins came storming in, empty-handed. Having been caught by surprise, they had not thought of picking up a cleaver or hammer as they ran out. Erfu hastily pulled up his pants, but his leaky earthworm, dribbling foam, was still hanging out of his fly. Weilin's cousins roared like lions when they saw their favourite girl-cousin lying there unconscious, naked from the waist down. Looking around for a weapon, they spotted two large commercial stoneware bowls which their aunt had brought out in order to offer Erfu some tea. They snatched up the bowls and hurled them point-blank into Erfu's face.

'"Wah!" The rapist uttered a scream of pain and collapsed to the ground like a puddle of diarrhoea. Weilin's cousins cupped their bowls to the hole in his skull to catch the bright red blood spurting out. Only when both bowls were filled to the rim did Erfu's head finally stop bleeding . . .'

'Was he dead?' I asked, aghast.

'Who? Erfu? Are you crazy? You don't kick the bucket from losing a mere two bowls of blood! He did have to go to the hospital though. He had to have twenty stitches in his head, his parents had to pay eighty kuai for it. That's four kuai per stitch! What do the surgeons use, gold thread or something? Eighty kuai is just about three months' salary for Erfu's father!'

My patience was being tried here: what difference did it make to me, where Erfu's parents would find the money? They had raised him to be a low-down dirty brute, and now they were paying for it. What *did* interest me was how Weilin was doing. I asked, 'But Kim, what happened to that pretty girl, I mean, that pretty, uh . . . woman?'

'Weilin? Oh, that one, she's got nothing left to lose, now. She can't go back to her pale-skinned first-caste boyfriend, can she! Who'd want her for a wife, now that she's lost her cherry, and a third-caster to boot?'

A lump rose into my throat. 'But *she* hasn't done anything wrong, has she? I mean, she was raped . . .'

Kim frowned, throwing me a hostile look. 'So? Do you think there's any point trying to talk sense into you rich folk?'

'Oh, so now it's *my* fault! I was only trying to stick up for Weilin!' But I knew I shouldn't blame Kim; as a matter of fact, Kim was right. People of my caste showed no mercy, neither among themselves – just look at how often they snitched on each other to the Party – nor in their relations with the lower classes. And why should they? I decided never to bring up the subject of Weilin, ever again.

◯━

For a long time, I wondered why Weilin didn't report Erfu to the authorities and why Erfu failed to file a complaint against Weilin's cousins. But apparently everyone felt that justice had been served, first by Erfu's harsh punishment of Weilin, and then by her cousins' score-settling with Erfu. It was felt that the case was closed: all parties had had their just deserts, so why get the police or the courts involved?

I found out that the neighbourhood was ruled by two street gangs, The Flying Tiger and The Wild Dragon. Absurd as it might appear, the residents were quite happy about the existence of these rival gangs: for at least each side saw to it that its own protégés weren't in any danger from the opposing mob, making for a delicately balanced stand-off. Actually, the mud-hut dwellers did have to admit they were being fleeced and terrorised by their own street gangs, and that they were scared to death of them – but that part was just a necessary evil. On one point the two sides were in total accord: if a first-caster did some injustice to a third-caster, then both factions lunged for the rich man's jugular. The mud-hut dwellers were known for their uncontrollable tempers and cold-blooded vendettas, and for the way they exacted hideous vengeance without ever leaving a trace.

COMPETITOR NUMBER 4027

After training for three years – albeit with a seventeen-month break in the middle – the time had finally come. The Autumn Games were tomorrow; excitement and impatience were ricocheting inside my heart as if it were a trampoline.

At three in the afternoon classes were finally over, thank Heaven. I waited impatiently for the students to leave the classroom. Then I rushed over to where Kim was sitting. My heart was pounding in my throat, I was so nervous I couldn't get the words out. It was a shame, because I was so anxious to share my excitement with Kim.

Kim remained seated on her chair, cool as a cucumber, as if it was a day like any other day. She said, 'I still don't understand that formula. Can you just help me a minute?' She reminded me of the dope in an earthquake whose house is shaking like a bowl of jelly yet who insists on turning off the lights before running out of the door. How could Kim possibly be puzzling over some silly maths equation at such a crucial time? For years we had been working up to this moment. All our hopes and dreams were riding on it. Tomorrow, when Kim captured first place, all the class bullies and snobs would have to bite off their own tongues and swallow them whole before they'd dare make fun of her, or bash her in the shins, ever again. I was longing to see it happen: to see the others finally being forced to consider Kim a success, or at the very least an integral member of the class, deserving of a place in the classroom pecking order.

On further reflection, I could understand Kim's nonchalant front. Hadn't I myself had to struggle, over the past few hours, to suppress and conceal my excitement about tomorrow? Both Kim and I were pretty clear-sighted about what we were up against. We had thrown down the gauntlet, challenging Kim's destiny and a social system which had decreed that Kim would belong to the lowest caste from birth, with all the humiliations and deprivations that that entailed.

'Sure,' I answered, 'I *will* explain that formula to you some time . . . after the race.'

Kim put her maths book down, as if I had just taken a load off her shoulders. She opened her satchel and drew out a neatly folded piece of paper that had the number 4027 written on it in red pencil. She held the strip of paper up to her chest and then behind her back. Her eyes danced with joy. It tickled me to detect a glimmer of vanity lurking there.

'Sew it on the *back* of your T-shirt,' I advised her, 'then everyone will see your number,' implying that Kim's opponents would never see anything of her but her backside. I meant it as a shot in the arm, and the corners of Kim's mouth did turn up, even if for just a fraction of a second. Then her face clouded over again with worry. She bit her lip and seemed to have trouble coming out with the question: 'Is it . . . is it permitted . . . to take part wearing just a plain old blouse, instead of a T-shirt?'

Grandpa Heaven, I had totally forgotten that Kim didn't own any sports clothes, and of course the first- and second-casters would be wearing T-shirts for sure. I could already picture the scene: tomorrow the smarty-pants would point at Kim and hoot with laughter: Look at that penniless piece of scum! Where did she get the hippopotamus-hide to dare to show up here without the proper gym clothing? Oh, maybe she's just lost her way. She must have ended up at the starting line by mistake. Yoohoo, Kim, get the fuck out of there!

But I shook my head to banish the thought and said, 'Sure, why not?' in a voice fierce enough to scare off a whole battalion of thugs. 'The whole point is what you *achieve*, not what you wear.'

CHAMPION WITHOUT THE GLORY

I got to the athletics field behind the school at six forty-five a.m. The field consisted of two parts: an oval 400-metre running track, and inside that, the football field, where the long jump, high jump and 'grenade' throw would be taking place. Close to the field was a towering cement podium that had been festooned with decorations for the occasion. Brightly coloured little flags and banners waltzed around its pillars. A row of tables and chairs had been set up on the dais for the sports teacher – the chairman of the day's event – and the school's two principals, plus four younger teachers who were acting as secretaries and score-keepers on this occasion.

Kim had signed up for the 'grenade' throw and the 1500-metres, I for the long jump and the 100-metre sprint. At seven o'clock, the sports instructor blew the whistle. The students were ordered to fall in by their class representatives; each class drew itself up into a four-columned configuration. After another whistle, these quadrangles marched up to the stands in orderly fashion. The sports teacher rearranged the classes on the track like metal chess pieces on a magnetic chessboard. Kim and I were in the same row. Today Kim's plaits were remarkably symmetrical; her eyes betrayed a furtive excitement and grim determination.

The shorter distances were run first. I ran the 100 metres in 16.9 seconds. Ten minutes later came the announcement that I had finished in sixth place. Kim ran up to me, primed for battle, socking her fists in the air. She was over the moon on hearing of my modest success. In the long jump, I made 3.35 metres. Since there were only ten participants in the event, this rather pathetic accomplishment earned me third place, no less.

Around three o'clock, I heard over the loudspeakers that the moment we had all been waiting for was at hand – the 1500-metres final was about to start! Students were pushing their way over to the track from all directions, creating a rampart dozens of layers deep at the start and finish lines. I saw no point making my way there, because from the back of the wall you couldn't see or hear a thing anyway. One or two athletic show-offs were able to secure a capital perch for themselves: they climbed halfway up the lamp-posts, and were the envy of the entire school. The rest contented themselves with a spot around the track somewhere, craning their necks and squinting their eyes to gawk at the eight finalists.

The races were the most popular event. Unlike the long-jumpers and high-jumpers, who competed in relative obscurity, the competitive runners attracted all the attention. The winner of a track race was a demi-god; the champion of the 1500-metres was an immortal.

Kim was one of the eight finalists, and she had the inside track. The seven other girls arched their backs and out of the corner of their left eyes they glared with disdain at this scrawny interloper who, in their opinion, would do better taking herself off home for a good meal, instead of fouling up this toughest and most prestigious of races. Just look at her, their conceited sneers implied, the slattern isn't even dressed properly; she's not even wearing a T-shirt.

Kim knew what they were thinking, and reinforced their opinion by not giving any sign of preparing herself for the starting shot. She just stood there stiffly, not moving a muscle, unlike the others, who were showing off like mad, doing all sorts of warm-up exercises.

'Jeééééyyyy!' Kim was the object of derisive catcalls and whistles from our classmates. 'I'd know that noise anywhere,' I muttered to myself. Except that this time their jeers held not just contempt, but also bafflement – their insides were all in a twist. It was the first time they had seen Kim competing in anything, and it made them feel uneasy. What if Kim should actually win? How could they ever stomach it if Kim the Loser emerged from this with something positive under her belt? Their prejudice was like a splinter in their tongues; removing it entailed tearing out some of the healthy flesh with it. And that wouldn't be much fun. They were dying to see how Kim would do, fervently hoping she would fail miserably, so that the splinter would be left alone.

In a most uncharacteristic move, for me – God only knows how I had the gall – I started barging aside every person standing in my way, and in no time at all I had managed to procure a prime spot for myself at the starting line. I was standing just a few feet away from Kim.

The noise was deafening; the students were all trying to hide their excitement and jitters by rat-tattling like submachine-guns. Yet I convinced myself I could hear Kim's heartbeat, steady and calm, as if she were in a trance. What was she thinking about? I so wished that Kim would look in my direction! *Kim, I'm so scared. How will we ever live it down if you . . . if we . . . if you don't make it?* In spite of my trepidation, I wanted Kim to have all that was mine to give . . . if only Kim would give me the chance, that is, if only she would glance my way for just a second . . . I was convinced a single look from me would be enough to show Kim the feeling I had inside – this impulse to fly to her side as a disembodied spirit, hover over her like an angel and whisper in her ear that I loved her and that, no matter how far apart we might be, she would always have a place in my heart . . .

But Kim would not have been Kim if she had not stubbornly refused to look at me. I knew my friend well enough for that.

At the very moment the man on the tall metal stool had begun shouting, 'On your marks! Ready . . .' Kim turned to face me head-on and with hungry eyes sucked in my gaze and all that it contained. In that instant, we both knew that nothing and nobody would ever come between us – no failure, no harassment, no catastrophe of any stripe. A crazy thought struck me: I felt like shouting – and I really meant it – Come on, let's go home! What do we care if you win or not! Let's leave well enough alone. There's nothing to be scared of any more!

'Set . . . go . . .'

Pang! The starting pistol made me jump. I saw Kim calmly hanging back as the other girls shot off like sprung arrows. Kim just stood there watching. But suddenly, as if waking from a hibernation, she began to run. She caught up with the others in no time at all.

Once they passed the 800-metre mark, most of the runners started tiring visibly. Their stride became laboured and they gasped for air. Kim, however, kept up her original pace, running as if she had never heard of fatigue.

I abandoned the starting line and started following Kim around the track. As I went, I could hear our classmates 'encouraging' Kim on: 'Hey, listen over here, Kim, you dried-up potato slice! Give up, c'mon, you know you can never do it; drop dead!' But it had absolutely no effect on Kim's speed. She was already on her fourth lap, while her fellow contestants were still sweating away on their third . . .

'Now we'll see that half-wit pack it in!' the classmates were yelling. But they didn't sound as cocky as they had before. Uncertainty had them by the throat, and that didn't happen very often when it came to something as routine as taunting Kim.

The sports teacher jumped off the platform and gaped in amazement at the stopwatch held by the timekeeper at the finish line. He ran towards Kim yelling, '4027, keep it up. You're pulverising the school record!' Kim acted as if she hadn't heard and continued running like an automaton, at full speed, towards the finish. The teacher snatched the stopwatch out of his colleague's hand and pointed his right hand like a radar-gun at the puny girl sprinting towards them.

Pale as a ghost, but determined as a kamikaze pilot, Kim shot over the finish line.

'Seven minutes fifteen seconds! Seven minutes fifteen seconds! Seven minutes fifteen seconds!' The teacher's eyes were glued to the stopwatch and he repeated the time like a mantra, as if he felt a need to corroborate and testify to this remarkable feat.

Over the past three years, I had often tried to picture how deliriously happy I would be when Kim became a champion. Now that it was so, I could hardly even stand up. I was tottering on my feet, and everything and everyone around me seemed to be floating off into space. My ears were clogged by a monotonous *whoooonnn*. It was only after my brain had managed to regain control over all of my body that I saw that Kim was standing next to me.

Strange, though: Kim's face was grim. She was staring straight ahead and biting her lips, which were drained of all colour.

I looked around. The throng at the finish line was staring at Kim open-mouthed. They could not believe their eyes. This scrawny, scruffy little ragamuffin had nabbed first place in the most important race of these Games? Was it a nightmare, was Buddha playing a dirty trick on them, or what? It had gone very quiet. The very air seemed frozen with disbelief.

Students who weren't in our class had begun wondering what the winner's name was, while Kim's classmates hung their heads like wet mops that have seen better days.

'Not too shabby, for such a slip of a girl . . . and then to go and break a school record too, to top it all! That girl has got some guts!' said a heavyset boy from the fourth year. His comment got the hubbub started again. The more the spectators raved over Kim's record time, the more incredulously did they shake their heads.

This gave our classmates an ingeniously devilish idea. They dilated their nostrils, sniggered snidely through clenched teeth and snarled at Kim,

'Winner of the 1500-metre – hey, what's the big deal here, anyway? It's no different, really, than an ass trotting round and round a millstone!'

'Hahaha!' roared the rest of the class.

'Aaaarh, what a scream! Fucking accurate analogy, I say! Still . . .' Yougui, the classmate whose face looked twice as fat as it really was because of the ugly pimples on his cheeks, wagged his stubby index finger in the air and granted, '. . . you have to give it to her, Kim is an *industrious* ass. Every miller should be so lucky, to have such a pack-animal!'

'Heeheehaha, heeheehaha!' It was the other members of the class, sounding for all the world like donkeys themselves. Not just any old donkey, mind, but an ass that's just come to the realisation that there's a gleaming set of castration-shears clamped to its balls.

The girls covered their mouths and giggled in a manner befitting their sex. They disapproved, naturally, of the boys' foul language, but the gist of it did find some resonance in their stuck-up hearts. They told each other, daintily, 'It's just as well that poor Kim is good for *something*. Just *think* how dreadful it would be – excuse my language, but there's no way to put this delicately – if that piss-poor guttersnipe was neither pretty nor intelligent *nor* strong . . .'

I had a hole in my heart; all my blood was pouring out of it. And with that blood, my exhilaration at Kim's success drained away as well, together with my high hopes and the will to go on dreaming. In the resulting vacuum, all that was left was hate for my vicious classmates – the kind of hatred that's so deep it puts down roots and so high that it reaches to the clouds. I did not dare look at Kim. If I was so torn up inside, what must it be like for Kim?

I had often seen medallists being showered with praise and admiration, but had never asked what for. How could I have been so blind? Could I come up with the name of a single famous champion who hailed from the lower castes? Quickly I ran all the heroes of the Autumn Games over the past three years through my mind, and cringed. They were all first-casters, every one.

Please, Kim, forgive me for leading you astray. I didn't get it before: there is no respect for those who are not considered qualified in the first place.

At last I summoned the courage to look at Kim. Hey, where had she gone? Why, of course! The grenade-throw! I rushed into the middle of the soccer field.

'Watch out!' I heard a man's warning shout behind me. Only then did I see where I was. I broke out in a cold sweat: I had entered the target area. Metal hand-grenades, as big as beer bottles, whizzed over my head. One hit the ground right in front of my big toe. I ran back to safety as fast as I could. Spying a teacher with a yardstick, I pounced on her, all but poking my nose into the woman's notebook: 'Has Kim Zhang been up yet?'

The teacher ran her finger down the list of names and said, 'Here: Zhang, K. She has thrown five times. Her best result is 15.8 metres.'

What? I had never managed more than ten metres. I asked quickly, 'Has anyone improved on Kim's score? Kim Zhang, I mean?'

The woman laughed, 'My girl, if we had even *one* other student who could throw that far, we'd have the entire district sewn up.'

Reassured, I started looking for Kim. I found my friend by the long-jump sandbox. There she sat, all alone and sad.

'Kim!' I waved my arms and shouted enthusiastically, 'You're in first place for the grenade throw as well!'

Kim glanced up but hung her head in gloom again on hearing what I had to say. Now all my fears were confirmed: neither of us would ever be happy about anything any more. Even winning the Olympics wouldn't change a thing.

The sports teacher came running up to us, his face glowing. 'Student Kim Zhang, congratulations on your success!' He stuck out his right hand, but she ignored it. The fellow must have interpreted her refusal as a manifestation of shyness – after all, it was virtually unheard of for a teacher to honour a student with a handshake. Undeterred, he jabbered on, 'You may come to my office tomorrow, around lunchtime. I have nominated you for a spot in the District Autumn Games. What size are you? A small, I'd guess, right? I'll have a uniform ready for you tomorrow. Will you come and pick it up? Then we can see about setting up a training schedule for you right away.'

What? Was Kim going to be a member of the school's prestigious gym team? Was she to wear the blue nylon uniform from now on, sporting the coveted white-lettered logo 'Middle School Number 54'? Compared to this, the honour of being chosen to be 'Student of the Three Virtues' was no more than the split-end of a hair from the neck of a grandfather chimpanzee!

But I was afraid. And my fear only deepened as the sports teacher stood there oblivious, whistling a cheerful march and tapping his foot in macho fashion, waiting for Kim's acknowledgement. Kim stuffed a hank of hair into her mouth and bit down hard on it, as if to hold back a volley of furious curses.

The teacher, who still had no clue, asked impatiently, 'Well, are you coming tomorrow, or not?'

As the straw that broke the dromedary's back, the loudspeakers began to blare, 'Results of the grenade-throw: first place, Kim Zhang, 15.8 metres, a new school record by 1.2 metres, no less! Second place . . .'

Now the teacher's enthusiasm knew no bounds; he was so delighted he wanted to slap Kim on the back. But Kim pulled the clump of hair out of her mouth, shrugged out of the teacher's reach, and began to run. Like a wounded lioness. If this had been the 100-metre sprint, she would have won the gold, for sure. But what was the point of that? What good was a gold medal, to her?

I conjured up my most saccharine smile to make up for Kim's rude behaviour and to put things right with the teacher – the same winsome smile that had stood me in good stead dozens of times when I had had to ward off an attack by second- or third-casters. But this only befuddled the gym teacher even more. First there was Kim, who had thrown the highly sought-after opportunity of participating in the District Autumn Games back in his face; and now here I was, usually so standoffish with my male teachers, flirting with him like mad all of a sudden, only Buddha knew why . . .

As soon as I saw that he wasn't angry with Kim any more, I ran off to a quiet spot under the willow-trees, far removed from everything, and from everyone.

At five o'clock the prizes were handed out. Since Kim failed to show up, I asked if I could accept in Kim's place. For the first prize in the grenade-throw, Kim was given a diary with an elegant red plastic cover. On it, embossed in gold, were the words, *The thoughts of Mao Zedong are an atomic bomb for the mind*. For winning the 1500-metres race, she was presented with a white enamel washbowl with two blue carp on the bottom, ringed with a more modern slogan: *With Mao, we are all like fish in water*.

At around half past five, I went to Kim's house. Her mother took the washbowl from me and rocked it in her arms as if it was her little baby boy. She owned only two other luxury items like it; they had been given to her by her favourite Uncle Qinyuan as a wedding present. She had had them repaired at least five times. Even the most brilliant soothsayer could never tell, from examining the sorry relics, what they had looked like originally. Kim's mother got even dizzier with excitement when I told her that Kim had won the washbowl in the Autumn Games. Wiping the dust off the sides of the bowl with her sleeve, she called, 'Kim, where are you? Why haven't you told me this yourself? Just wait till your father comes home. He'll be so proud!' Then she turned to me: 'Miss, I'd never even have *dreamed* that my daughter could earn so much dough, in such a short space of time! This kind of thing costs at least five kuai in the shops, you know. Think how many matchboxes I'd have to glue, to buy one of these! The calves grow stronger than the cows and the children outstrip their parents, my mother, may she rest in peace, always used to say. It's so true!'

I found Kim sitting by the stove, throwing twigs into the fire one by one. Now that she wasn't running, her face was red-hot, slick with pearls of sweat. I tried to catch her eye, but Kim kept turning the other way. Leaning against the stove, I pleaded, 'Kim, you've got to admit that what you achieved today *was* a great victory . . . !'

Kim looked up at me. Two pairs of empty eyes met, then melted into a puddle of futility, like snowflakes. I couldn't take it any more. If Kim went on refusing to say anything, I would never know how badly I had hurt her, or what I should do to make up for it. The simmering guilt inside me finally boiled away all my shyness and inhibitions, and I stammered, 'Kim? Do you blame me for . . . for pushing . . . pushing you into competing in the Autumn Games?'

Abruptly Kim jumped up from her stool, coming face to face with me. Her nostrils quivered and she burst into tears. It was only the second time that I had ever seen her cry. Clutching my shoulders, Kim keened shrilly: 'How can I be mad at you? Who else in the whole world cares as much for me as you do?'

I hugged Kim hard; it was too much. We wept together.

Kim's mother entered the kitchen carrying a sack of cornmeal. Seeing the two of us standing there crying, she was about to ask us why, when Kim told her bald-faced, 'Mama, the twigs I fetched from the Weasel Hills yesterday really ought to dry in the sun another day or two. Look at all the smoke they make!' She dried her eyes irritably and signalled to me to do the same. Her mother, who was still flying high on the prizes that Kim had won, fell for it.

Kim pointed at the setting sun. 'Shouldn't you be going home?'

'Er . . . yes, well . . . maybe I should . . .' I would actually have preferred to stay with Kim all evening.

'Go on, go home, or your mother will be worried. Expect me at three tomorrow, as usual. You promised to explain that maths formula, remember?'

YOUNG ASTRONOMERS

The summer breeze had whipped itself up into a real autumnal squall that was lashing the brittle leaves out of the trees. The hot, sweltering air grew light and airy and soared into the deep blue yonder; there it was transformed into silver clouds that sailed by in slow motion. Which was just an optical illusion, of course: up there, thousands of metres high in the stratosphere, the feathery clouds were, by all accounts, racing along at breakneck speed. But here below, I wasn't conscious of their astounding swiftness – what I perceived was only a slow-motion semblance of the real thing.

The orchard in front of my building announced the coming of autumn in its own fashion. The green branches were bowed almost to the ground under the weight of the fruit that they had tenderly nursed to ripeness during long months of pregnancy – red apples, golden pears and orange apricots.

Kim's long, hard struggle began to bear fruit as well. She was beginning to understand much more of the lessons at school; we finished our homework within an hour these days, whereas two years ago we had needed at least two hours. Seeing that there was nothing left to do by four thirty, it was natural for me to turn to my favourite hobby: reading.

But it wasn't as simple as all that. Since 1966, the libraries had been burned to the ground, their doors firmly nailed shut. All the Youth Activity Centre had to offer was three or four bundles of pamphlets. There were quite a few books at home, to be sure, but these were all to do with medicine and history, subjects which I was ignoring at this point.

Ever since I was very young, I had always loved astronomy. I read, or, to be accurate, I *looked* at every book on the subject that I could lay my hands on. Six years ago, when Meimei's father, my downstairs neighbour, was taken into custody by the Red Guards who ransacked his apartment, I found, in the building's rubbish bin stacks of popular-science magazines, including the excellent *Young Astronomers*. The Guards had taken the jewellery, the china and other valuables, but had simply dumped the specialist reading matter, which was of no use to them, into the bin. I had snagged some forty issues of the journal all told, and they had given me great pleasure over the past six years. I was never bored. This was in part because I was beginning to understand the gist of what I was reading, a little more each time, and in part because I knew I had no other choice.

I took the pile of *Young Astronomers* from the bookcase and asked Kim if she wanted to read them with me.

Since the Autumn Games, Kim's attitude had changed somewhat. She now valued learning more than she ever had before, and was receptive to new knowledge of any kind. But to sit and admire pictures of black-and-white blobs just for the heck of it, that was going a little too far for her.

'No,' she said, 'you go and pore over your stars and your satellites. I'll just get down one of those fat anatomy books of your father's, I think.'

If there was one kind of book that I would have liked to ban, banish and burn – and on this point alone I was in total agreement with the Red Guards – it would have been those dealing with anatomy, books jam-packed with pictures of the human body. I *hated* my own body, which just kept on growing and assuming ever more indecent shapes. I didn't even dare to look in the mirror any more, at that half-grown woman's figure bulging with . . . well, the whole works. Yuck! I dreamed of escaping from my body and living only in the spirit. No, I much preferred thinking about *celestial* bodies – at least those distracted me from thinking about my corporal one.

Of course I could not offer this as an argument against Kim's choice. But that did not mean I couldn't try to interest Kim in astronomy anyway. 'Look,' I said, pulling my most recent discovery out of my hat, 'the night sky changes all the time.'

Kim laughed as if she had just heard a good one.

Now I knew I had her. I insisted: 'You would think that the stars always remained in place, wouldn't you. Uh-uhn . . .' wagging my index finger, 'Wrong!' Pulling out twelve issues of *Young Astronomers*, I went on, 'Here are twelve photos of the night sky as it looked in 1963, from one month to the next. She how the stars keep shifting a little bit every month?'

Kim glanced at the magazines with sceptical amusement; but soon she began to study the pictures more closely. 'Well what do you know,' she remarked, 'the Milky Way is in a different position every time.' She grabbed a step-stool in order to get more issues down off the shelf. Intrigued by this phenomenon, Kim immediately wanted to look it up in the magazine to find a scientific explanation.

Don't say a thing, I warned myself. I wasn't about to tell Kim I had been trying to find such an explanation for years, with little luck. I was glad enough that Kim was beginning to show an interest in the subject.

The upshot was that Kim, when it was time for her to go home at half past five, asked if she could borrow a pile of *Young Astronomers*.

Putting on a stern demeanour, I said: 'Only if you finish them within two weeks and give them back.'

Kim eagerly agreed. Meanwhile I was laughing up my sleeve: she's walked right into my snare, with her big flat feet!

A week later Kim brought the journals back.

'Have you read them all?'

Kim tore a sheet out of her notebook covered with jottings. Not only had she read them all, but she had also pondered the most difficult problems, such as how to calculate the frequency and duration of an eclipse of the sun, how the craters on the moon are formed, and whether there might be life on Mars. She wanted to borrow more issues, but I decided the time had come to set certain conditions: from now on, we would have weekly 'astronomy conferences'.

The more we delved into what we had read, the clearer it became to us that we knew less than nothing, practically, about celestial phenomena. Since my hoard of magazines no longer satisfied our hunger, the search was on for astronomy books with a little more meat to them.

That wasn't easy either. Where to start? Since 1966, the publishing houses had printed only the *Little Red Book*, to the virtual exclusion of everything else. Since 1971 they had come out with perhaps five or six other works a year, but these had been gone over with a fine-tooth comb by the censor, so nobody was interested. Most of the bookstores had closed down, and the few that remained open were sparsely frequented.

Kim and I set out to look for one of these bookstores. The closest one was a little less than three miles from my apartment. New China, the store was called. But that didn't mean a thing: all bookstores had been given that name, just as most of the girls born after 1967 were called *Hong* – or 'red, revolutionary and progressive' – and the majority of boys was named *Weidong* – for 'defender of Mao Zedong'.

We tiptoed into the shop. As was to be expected, there wasn't a soul in sight. You could have heard a pin drop. Only that wasn't *quite* the right expression: you could have heard the shopkeeper's snoring without any interference. A man of around – judging from the ear-splitting chain-sawing of his snores – forty was passed out behind the counter, snoozing with great zeal, his head buried in his folded arms.

We found ourselves in a dilemma. If we were to snoop around his shop quietly, the man might accuse us of stealing when he woke up; if we coughed loudly to rouse him from his slumber, he'd probably get angry. Kim signalled to me that we should leave the store quietly. But she wasn't too smart about the way she followed her own advice – she kicked open the door, which was equipped with a self-closing spring mechanism.

Tyeeya! whined the yawning door, its hinges in dire need of lubrication. The bookseller shook himself all over like a dog that's landed in the ditch and, still pretty much in a fog, looked up with somnolent eyes. At the entrance he discovered, to his displeasure, the culprits who had disturbed his sorely needed rest.

But Kim stepped back into the shop, cool as a mint lozenge, and said, shaking her head in heartfelt sympathy, 'Autumn's only just begun, yet the wind is already wicked enough to blow the tiles off the roofs,' thereby shifting the blame for the squeaky door on to the wind . . .

The man, his eyes heavy with sleep, glared at us and grumbled irritably, 'What do you want?'

I was no slacker either. I offered him a sweet smile and answered, 'Revolutionary Comrade Old Uncle, we are looking for a book about astronomy.'

The honorary title I bestowed on him was to weasel into his good books, of course. After all, the shop worker was always king, and the customer always the slave. All stores were owned by the State; the shop workers drew a steady salary, irrespective of whether they sold even a single item a year or not. As a matter of fact, they couldn't stand the customers – all they ever did was come and disturb the storekeepers' well deserved rest.

The man twisted his lips into a purple knot. With this pout he pointed mutely to the east, where the books about the natural sciences were filed; he couldn't be bothered to show us where to look.

The only 'astronomy book' we found looked more like a comic book. It was entitled *Farmers are the best scientists: One hundred proverbs concerning weather predictions. With fifty illustrations.* Kim leafed through it and kept exclaiming, 'Look, here's another saying my mother often uses.'

I read along over her shoulder. In this position we came upon a colour plate sporting the caption: When the clouds look like fish scales, then we don't need to rotate the grain.

Kim explained, 'It means, clouds shaped like that show it's going to be a hot afternoon. If there's wheat lying in the courtyard on a day like that, the sun will bake it through and through. So it isn't necessary to turn it over every now and then.' She shed light on the other sayings the same way, one by one; she was thrilled to find a science book she had no trouble understanding.

After counting out seventy-five fen for it, we went home feeling very pleased with ourselves.

THEORY AND PRACTICE

After finishing our homework the next day, we ran outside with our new acquisition. We studied the book page by page, until we stumbled on an aerial photograph of weather conditions similar to our own. It wasn't easy to bring our search to a satisfactory conclusion, though. The act of flipping through the book was like stoking a fire: disagreements kept flaring up. I interpreted the photographs and captions much too literally, according to Kim. If the saying went, In the sky the little sheep are herded homeward, and here on earth the young trees are torn up by the roots, I would start comparing every cloud in the sky with the ones pictured on the page. If their bodies weren't exactly tubular, or if they were missing the pointy tail of a real sheep, then I would declare that the adage did not apply. It started getting on Kim's nerves. 'What an egghead you are! When have you ever seen clouds that looked *exactly* like sheep? This isn't a drawing lesson, Lian. The point is that sheep-shaped clouds can be an indication of strong winds. That's all. Does my mother measure the clouds meticulously, one by one, before warning us, "Children, you should dress warmly today, because the wind is going to go tearing through the sky like a hungry witch"?'

I kept my mouth shut and my thoughts to myself: are we, or aren't we, conducting a serious scientific investigation here? Kim's mother goes only by her own instincts. How would she know better than what it says in this strange book?

In order to put an end to the argument once and for all, we hoisted a handkerchief up into the air. I was hoping it would hang down limply, but the wretched thing puffed out, spreading its wings, and Kim gave a triumphant chuckle. This proved to be a turning point, and Kim began to edge ahead of me in the field of astro-science. Encouraged by her victory, Kim kept borrowing more and more magazines from me, devouring them at lightning speed.

After a while we reached the chapter *The Night Sky*. One of the photographs showed a pale moon with rings around it, the inner one a lavender colour and the outer one a bluish-grey. The caption announced, The girl in the moon is wearing two coats of the finest silk; the beggars' teeth will be chattering in the morning. We had to wait five days to behold that phenomenon – and even then, it was just a single pink ring around the moon that we saw.

The next day we had a row. Kim's teeth were chattering from the cold – I thought she was doing it on purpose, but Kim said it was because the moon had had a ring around it the night before. I maintained that the reason it was getting colder by the day was that winter was on its way. 'Besides,' I said condescendingly, 'the expression didn't mention just *one* ring. It's only when you can see *two* rings that that particular forecast counts.' Now it was Kim's turn to get really pissed off. Despite being painfully shy, she started lying in wait for Meimei's father in the stairwell of my apartment building, every evening around six o'clock. Under normal circumstances she would never have had the nerve to even *look* at the man, let alone accost him. He had been released from prison camp not long ago so that he might resume his research at the planetarium where he used to work. When all was said and done, the government didn't want to fall behind: China too wanted to send a satellite into space, to keep an eye on the Capitalist nations, so that, some day, the whole world might become united into one blood-red proletarian sea.

Kim waited over an hour for Meimei's father for three days in a row, before she finally managed to buttonhole him. It was almost seven p.m.

'Old Uncle,' she greeted him as politely as she could, 'here in this book it is written, "The girl in the moon wears two coats of the finest silk; the beggars' teeth will be chattering in the morning." If the moon has only *one* ring, does it count anyway?'

It took some switching of gears for the man of science to adjust to this extraordinary line of questioning. Used as he was to technical terms and standard research methods, he needed a little breathing room to get into the spirit of this kind of folk wisdom. He saw Kim's face turned up to him, grave and expectant, as if he were the oracle who had the final word on such matters, and had trouble suppressing a smile. Suddenly an idea occurred to him. He said, 'So, little girl, what you really want to know is whether a single ring around the moon can predict a chilly morning?' Kim blinked her eyes as if she were being asked if she wanted to go to heaven when she died. 'Then what you ought to do is draw up some statistics.' She batted her eyelids again, this time as if she had been asked whether she knew how to find the ladder leading to paradise. He could see that she hadn't really understood: 'What I mean is that for let's say a period of half a year, you might keep track of how many times a single ring around the moon presages cold weather. Then, by calculating how frequently this occurs, you'll be able to arrive at a valid conclusion.'

Kim's face brightened – she blinked her eyes once more, and ran up the stairs, having clean forgotten to thank her academic adviser.

Out of that first conversation between Kim and Meimei's father arose another delightful consequence for us: the scholar invited us to visit him in his study. Yippee! There we found books piled upon books, from the floor to the ceiling. This time, after being grilled by Kim with technical questions, Meimei's father's urge to grin quickly disappeared. Seeing our ravenous eyes, he offered to let us borrow some books, on the condition that we would truly read them. He stipulated that we could take two books at a time, and when we brought those back, we would have to show him our notes. He might as well have tried to punish a fish by letting it drown in the sea. Kim was on cloud nine.

We stopped bothering with weather forecasting, now that we could see the folk-sayings for what they were. Our fascination with stars in the sky returned as strong as ever. We found out that what was known about astronomy was being constantly revised by astrophysicists studying the firmament through their telescopes at night. Kim and I did not have a telescope, but it didn't matter. In *Young Astronomers* it said that even with the naked eye you could find out a lot about the stars.

Kim quoted, 'How do you think the people of the Renaissance, who were philosophers, artists, mathematicians, physicists and chemists all wrapped into one, arrived at their important astronomic discoveries?' Kim had a memory like a steel trap. She could usually recite any passage verbatim, without tripping up. 'Primarily by means of primitive, home-made tubes with pieces of glass stuck inside, hardly deserving the name scientific equipment, and, of course, with these things.' She pointed to her own eyes – eyes that were glittering with a famished craving for knowledge.

TWIN STARS

One night towards the end of October, our parents gave us permission to go star-gazing. We walked over to the campus athletics field and spread an old tablecloth out on the grass. It was nine p.m. There was nobody to be seen or heard within a radius of a mile except us. The only sound was the languid chirping of one or two crickets. The grass was still lukewarm, and in the glow of the night it glistened like the cascading black hair of a dreamy-eyed maiden. The trees around the field cast stately shadows. They neither moved nor rustled, like sentinels standing guard in front of a palace.

Above our heads the moon played a silent serenade to our stars. The pinpricks of light in the canopy of night were like clear, dulcet chimes made inaudible by the huge distance separating Heaven and Earth, but they managed to give an impression of a lilting piece of music just the same. Some of the stars were dark and nearly invisible one moment, dazzlingly bright again the next – it reminded me of the high and low notes of a piano sonata.

I had fallen under the spell of the stars. The last thing I felt like doing was investigating the night sky through the eyes of a 'young astronomer'. Feeling guilty, I looked at Kim, who had taken a book of colour plates of the constellations out of her bag. She held it upside down, turned it right side up, frowned, and put the book down again.

Thank heavens, I was thinking.

Kim smoothed the tablecloth on the grass, then stretched out on it. That was a good sign; it looked as if she too just wanted to make the most of the spectacle of the stars. I went and lay down beside her.

A chill stillness enfolded us. The hard earth felt spongy underneath us because of all the things that grew there. The seemingly motionless trees at the edge of the field kept a vigilant watch over us; the chirping of the crickets just served to underscore the stealth with which nature normally carries out her work; the fresh breeze felt like a warm caress to our faces; the dark sky with all its twinkling stars was like a crystal refracting the light . . .

Possessed by the blinding beauty of the night, my physical body lost its crushing grip on my spirit. My soul rose up and, looking down on my life from a dizzying height, took a rather dim view of it. 'Lian Shui . . .'

I was jolted from my trance by Kim nudging me. Leaning on my elbow, I turned towards my friend.

'Can you see the evening star, over there?' Kim pointed to one of the brightest stars and said, 'That one is you.'

My elbows wobbled as I sought Kim's eyes, astonished. What was that? How was it that Kim, who usually never even gave me a second look, let alone a compliment, was so generous, all of a sudden, with words of praise? About *me*?

The sheet had moved out from under me, probably because of the way Kim's words had made me start. Sprigs of grass were tickling at my bare neck and ankles. Letting out a groan, I rolled smoothly back up on to my elbows. My finger started walking towards Kim, stopped about four inches from her nose and then pointed up at the night sky: 'Do you see that brilliant point of light, next to the evening star? That's her twin sister; that is you.'

Kim squinted but she could not focus on the place I was indicating. Cupping her hands to her eyes like a pair of binoculars, she tried again. Then she turned towards me, wagging her forefinger as if to say: Don't you try pulling the wool over my eyes! I never read anything about *two* evening stars . . . Or is it just that I don't know enough about astronomy?

I felt sorry for Kim, whose nose was constantly buried in her books these days, more so than my own, but I didn't dare admit it was just a joke. I could just picture the way Kim's eyes would spit fire at me if she discovered that I had been pulling her leg the whole time.

I explained, 'It is logical that we cannot see the companion evening star. It is several million light-years younger than the current one, so its brand-new light may take thousands more light-years to reach our planet. But one thing's for sure: its light is definitely on its way here. And such light! I'm telling you, this star shines ten times as brightly as the moon – it is beauty incarnate. *That* is . . . you.'

SOME BAD NEWS

It started out as just an ordinary autumn day. I was sitting down to breakfast with Mother, gazing out of the window in silence. The sky was just like a gorgeously painted vase, in constantly shifting permutations. Lemon-yellow, claret-red and chestnut-brown leaves had been called up by the mild autumn wind to eddy around in an endless dance. I saw it, but I was in a strange mood – too strange to appreciate the sight. I shovelled my rice porridge into my mouth like a robot.

'Oh, Lian, before I forget,' said Mother between two bites, 'yesterday I ran into Aunt Ge.'

Ge? My chopsticks pointed in the air like a pair of wagging fingers. I could not place the name, at first.

'She told me,' Mother continued, 'that Uncle Changshan is in the hospital. He was admitted two weeks ago. Is it true you haven't been to see him in a long time? That's what Aunt Ge told me, at any rate.'

Tingtangtang . . . My chopsticks slipped out of my hands and fell clattering to the floor. Aunt Ge! Uncle Changshan! It was as if I were listening to some fable – those two names sounded so unreal, like something out of a distant past. I bent to pick up my sticks and took my time sitting up again. What was Mother saying? What had she said? Was Uncle ill? In hospital? Uncle Cannibal . . . ?

'Aunt said that Uncle Changshan was diagnosed with liver cancer two weeks ago. He was rushed to hospital. *Gai*, what can they do for him? It has already metastasised . . .'

I wasn't hearing so well what Mother was saying. I was picking at my sweater – I had an urge to rip it to pieces.

'. . . I promised Aunt that you'd go and visit him very soon . . .'

'I have exams. I *can't*. I don't have the *time* . . .'

'Nonsense! Uncle Changshan has always helped you, first in the camp, and since you've been back as well. And now that he is at death's door, are your exams suddenly so important that you don't have the time to go cheer him up? This is not the Lian I know!'

I had begun stretching my sweater out of shape breadthwise. I kept my mouth shut. I prayed to Buddha that Mother would forget her promise to Aunt. I felt like a traitor. Where was my conscience?

THE POET'S DAUGHTER

That evening, at nine o'clock, someone knocked at the door. It was Uncle Song. He rubbed his hands together and stammered bashfully, 'Would, would it be poss . . . possible by any chance if . . . if a guest of mine slept here for one night?'

Mother pulled the ball of yarn closer to her right thigh and answered, without looking up from her knitting, 'Since when have you felt the need to act so overly polite with me? You know it isn't necessary. Of course your guest can stay here.'

The man gave a sigh of relief and explained his quandary: 'You see, it's too risky to have a guest sleep over at my place, in the Building for Bachelors. You get my drift, don't you?'

Security brigades of individual work-units often carried out raids on rooming houses in the dead of night, to round up peasants illegally residing in the city. But they also had another agenda: they drooled at the thought that someone might be committing adultery, or that there could be some hanky-panky going on involving unmarried persons intent on earning the epithet of 'worn-out shoe'.

I remembered that once, when I was four years old, I had witnessed a scene involving my upstairs neighbour, a widower and teacher of mathematics, in the dead of night. He had been dragged out of bed by five sadistic thugs of the housing-search unit, and paraded stark naked before dozens of spectators screaming with laughter – his own neighbours. Even though it was the height of summer, he was shivering from his ears to his toes. That's how ashamed he was.

'A dog that doesn't know to keep his member at home where it belongs!'
'What a dishonour to heap upon his ancestors!'

The monsoon of curses and expletives coming from the spectators dragged him down even further, as if there was a millstone around his neck. I had thought to put in my own two fenworth: 'This grown-up mister doesn't even wear pyjamas at night. He sleeps naked, like an animal!' The bystanders had guffawed when they heard my comment. It was only a year ago that I found out the real reason why the neighbours had been so mean to him. When the security corps forced an entry into his flat, they happened to discover him in bed with his fiancée . . . ! Sex before marriage was of course no less a punishable offence than daring to disobey the Wisest Leader of the Universe.

Uncle Song continued, 'It's like this, see. The daughter of Wenyou Xiang came round this afternoon to drop off her father's latest volume. We got so involved in talking that we clear forgot the time and now she has missed the last bus home.'

Mother promptly let the half-finished sweater fall on to her knees and asked, her eyes as wide as wagon-wheels: 'Whose daughter did you say? Not the daughter of Wenyou Xiang, the one who wrote *The rock is tall and steep*?'

'Yes indeed. That's who she is.'

I pricked up my ears. Xiang was not only famous for his poetry, he had also held the post of Vice-Minister of Culture and Propaganda before the Cultural Revolution.

Mother, skipping the usual hoo-ha of 'of-course-she-is-most-welcome-in-our-abode,' simply asked, 'Would she like the sofa in the living room or would she prefer to sleep in Lian's room?'

'I'll bring her up here in a minute; you can ask her yourself.'

I slipped into my room and took out my fanciest blouse from the dresser.

A contagious laugh presaged the arrival of its owner. I rushed to the front door, where I found a tall, slim girl awaiting me. I was ecstatic.

'Aháh . . . Good evening, Madam, Miss. My name is Youxin. I have come to disturb you. Ha, ha . . .' Her giggles filled the house with dancing sunbeams.

'You are welcome in our home.' Mother shook hands with her and then asked where she would prefer to sleep, in the living room or in my room.

The girl turned her head towards me and looked me over from head to toe, eyebrows dancing and the corners of her mouth upturned: 'If the young lady doesn't mind, I would love to share a room with her.'

Mother placed a camp bed at the head of my bed, so that the two beds formed an L. Youxin pulled the undersheet taut and fluffed the pillow until it was light as a soufflé. It came as a pleasant surprise to Mother how helpful Youxin was. My mouth hung open, too: how could anybody make herself at home so quickly in a totally strange environment?

Youxin sat down on her impeccably made bed and jiggled her slender yet feminine legs. She was sizing me up with her eyes, as if she were an art teacher judging a student's painting, not quite certain about what to say by way of encouragement. I turned from her gaze as casually as I could – I felt I didn't quite come up to scratch. Sitting next to this nearly grown-up girl with such relaxed, elegant and self-confident airs, I was beset by a feeling of inferiority. Youxin's expression, on the other hand, was very friendly, and put me at ease.

'Come here,' said Youxin, 'that blouse isn't all that bad, basically.' It was the best one I owned! 'Only, you should leave the top button undone.' Solicitously but firmly, she pulled me closer, touching my collar with her soft, tickly fingertips and unbuttoning it. Now that she was up so close, the hyacinth fragrance of her hair drifted up my nose. I had gone rigid with shyness. A cool draft penetrated my blouse via the open collar, and down along my torso. I felt much more comfortable all of a sudden . . . I had never known it could feel this good, to wear my blouse open like this.

Youxin let go of my shoulders and said, 'You haven't told me your name yet.'

'Lian.'

'Ah, "Lian", *water lily*. A charming name.'

Was she saying that only to emphasise the contrast between my name and my looks?

'You must be in your first year of the secondary school.'

'My third,' I corrected her, proudly. I wanted so much to be considered an adult.

'Oh, you are fourteen, then?'

'Yes. But in eleven months I'll be fifteen.'

'So. You are three years younger than me. That isn't so terrible, you know. Your turn will come.'

Then Youxin quickly changed the subject: 'Last week Uncle San He came to visit us, the film director, *you* know. He told us that in spite of his advanced age, he has had a change of career: these days he is putting the pigs and the sheep through their paces, instead of actors. Prison camp has made him lose all his hair, but not an ounce of his sense of humour!'

Xin was talking about one of China's greatest celebrities as if he was the bicycle repairman from around the corner. My desolation turned to awe – awe for this girl who felt as comfortable among the élite as a water buffalo in the mud.

At ten o'clock Mother came in to turn out the light. Youxin and I began chatting softly. Now that it was dark and I did not have to look Xin in the eye, I felt bold enough to speak freely. I asked Xin about the latest fashions: which hairdo was 'in' these days, and what colours for blouses were popular.

But it was clear Xin wasn't interested in my subject matter; she kept returning to the subject of boys and girls.

'Two months ago, at the beginning of autumn, Mimi Yue and I were strolling down the shopping centre of the Chongwen District . . .'

'Mimi Yue? The daughter of Lizhi Yue, the writer?'

'Yes. Damn, now I've lost my train of thought. Oh yeah, so we were walking around there, window-shopping. Suddenly a group of boys in their early twenties popped up out of nowhere. They wanted to be introduced to Mimi. Oh, of course you don't know Mimi. A beauty, I assure you. She often gets asked to sit for billboard pictures, as a model.'

'How pretty exactly?'

'Well, you know, as soon as men see her, they want to kiss her. But let me finish my story, will you? It really happened, I swear. Of course Mimi wouldn't give those punks the time of day. After all, she can have her pick of any son of any Communist Party Central Committee member she likes. But of course she did sort of enjoy being pursued, I mean, who wouldn't? Let's be honest. But as fate would have it, a second gang showed up. They turned yellow and green with jealousy when they saw the other guys trying to chat up such a gorgeous chick. They spat on the ground and stamped their feet three-times-three on their phlegm, to show their contempt. Then, without further ado, they began pelting each other with bricks. Mimi hung around a little while to watch, but when it started getting tedious, we walked into a shoe store. A little while later we heard the ambulance. Ten boys had their heads cracked open and one had a broken ribcage. Hihi, haha! Guys can be such idiots, can't they?'

I didn't understand what was so funny. Eleven people seriously injured in a senseless fight, and that was supposed to be a hoot?

Youxin was clearly a little disconcerted. She added, 'Lian, you may be too young to understand. You don't know what it is like for a woman to be desired by men, especially if they risk their lives for you.'

That night I had the strangest dream: my father too had become a VIP. He took me to visit his old friends, whose names regularly appeared on the front page of the *People's Daily*. Everywhere I went, boys leered at me lecherously.

The following morning, the feeling that my dream had really been true stayed with me for a long time.

BRIEF BUT INTENSE

Mother had not even taken her coat off yet when she drew a letter out of her pocket and said, 'Aunt Xiucai, from Hunan Province, is arriving the day after tomorrow. She is coming to stay with us for two weeks.'

'Oh, that will be fun!'

'I don't know that it will be such fun for Aunt Xiucai, because she is suffering from a chronic infection of the uterus. She is coming to Beijing to visit a number of gynaecologists that have been recommended to her.'

'What a pity that Father isn't here, he could have introduced her to the top specialists in Beijing.'

'Do you remember your cousin Liqiang? He is coming too. Aunt writes that his school is involved in a Learning from the Workers internship this month. So he can easily miss a couple of weeks. You can imagine what a waste of time it is to fill lemonade bottles six days a week, eight hours a day.'

Well, well! Liqiang, the boy who was always such an ace at marbles and who cheated at cards!

Two days later, someone knocked at the door at eight in the morning. Mother hastily shoved some messy clutter under her quilt, combed her fingers through her hair and opened the door.

A greying woman scurried inside, grabbed my hand and said, 'My merciful Buddha, is this our little Lian? Last time I saw you, you were missing two front teeth.'

'Good morning, Aunt Yunxiang!' Both Mother and I jumped, on hearing a booming male voice.

I stood face to face with an oak of a fellow, at least two heads taller than I was. Even though he had shaved carefully, I could detect bluish stubble on his chin. His dark eyes were remarkably shiny and he was smiling gallantly, like a real gentleman.

After breakfast the aunt and nephew went to unpack their suitcases. They had been given my room; I was to sleep on the sofa in the living room.

Aunt was yawning, and Mother persuaded her to take a little nap; the train ride had worn her out.

Mother went to her study and began reading term papers. As was my wont, I spread my homework out on the dining table and began working on my sums. Liqiang took a book from the bookcase and went and sat down on the sofa to read.

'Don't *you* need to rest?' I asked, turning towards him. The boy's face radiated energy; my question obviously amused him. Flustered, I hid my head in my books.

It was as if he could read my thoughts. He picked up a chair and came and sat next to me. 'Oh, are you doing maths? That's my favourite subject at school.'

Usually it was I who explained everything to Kim, but now, with Liqiang next to me, suddenly even the simplest calculation was beyond my grasp. I just sat there biting on my pen nervously.

No matter how often he explained the equations to me, I just didn't get it. I could have throttled myself! I'd never imagined I could be such a moron. But Liqiang's patience was infinite. He seemed happy to explain the laws of algebra to me ten times over, all in the same courteous tone.

I was upset, yet I was also touched. Did he consider me a pain in the neck? Impossible, otherwise he wouldn't be so nice and forbearing. But why was he so respectful towards me? What had I done to deserve it? All I knew was that, if you believed the bourgeois novels, a man could swallow a lot of nonsense from a woman, if he liked her or was in love with her.

Buddha! Could it be that Liqiang liked me? I got a funny feeling in the pit of my stomach. I shut my eyes, hoping to drive that idiotic delusion out of my head. I really had to nip this thing in the bud – I decided I would start annoying Liqiang, as a way to squelch my stirring feelings for him. There. Suddenly my eyes were back in focus, and I had no trouble understanding the formulas any more. I pushed his hand off my maths books and began solving the problems myself, effortlessly.

'Leave me alone!' I waved him off every time he tried pointing out there might be an easier way to do the calculation – until I finally managed to piss him off altogether.

Without saying a word, he returned to the sofa, where he tried to concentrate on his book once more. He must have been wondering why I had suddenly come down on him so hard.

By the afternoon, after my nap, my resolve to ban Liqiang from my heart had weakened a little. I was looking for an opportunity to make it up to him, although I didn't know exactly how. We struck up a conversation. He told me he was a member of his school's basketball team. No wonder: he was tall, strong and athletically built. I wanted to learn to play basketball too. So we made a date to go to the athletics field together every morning.

The next morning, at six thirty, as I was combing my hair at the bathroom mirror, Liqiang came in to brush his teeth. A meaningful look was exchanged. It seemed to me that I knew exactly what that look meant, even though I couldn't have put it into words.

We got to the basketball court at six forty-five. Liqiang observed my handling of the ball with a critical frown, and after I had taken two shots, he told me to stop. According to Liqiang, I was holding my wrists all wrong and my timing was off as well. My nice cousin had suddenly turned into a strict, stand-offish gym teacher. That wasn't my idea of fun at all. To make it clear to him that he should be treating me as a cousin, not as a pupil, I did the exact opposite of what he told me to do. He scowled and shook his head. It made me feel good to be teaching *him* a lesson, for a change. Until he came up with an unfair counter-offensive: he began imitating me, aping my inept shuffle and faulty posture. I could have been standing in front of a mirror; that's how relentlessly accurate his portrayal of me was.

I couldn't very well blame him, because I knew I had got what I deserved. The only response I could think of was to yell, 'Stop it! You're acting like a clown! You're making a ridiculous ass of yourself!'

He stopped for a moment to look at me. Who, when you got right down to it, was the ass here? Mortified, I jumped as high as I could, trying to pull his arms down to his side, to stop him from parodying me. It didn't work, naturally. All he needed to do was stretch his hands a little higher, and they were completely out of my reach. I bounded higher, landing even harder on the ground. I whined and I pleaded, trying to grab hold of his arms, without any success.

I stood there trying to catch my breath, glaring at his sweating face with that awful mocking grin.

We walked home side by side in silence. Liqiang was approaching manhood. It took him less time to get over the quarrel, and he made an effort to cheer me up. Tossing the ball in the air, he jumped almost three feet high, wheeled around a full 360 degrees, then caught the spinning ball on one finger, like a seal in the circus catching a striped ball on his wet nozzle. Despite my confusion, I was delighted with his showing-off.

The next basketball practice found me more willing to learn something and Liqiang acting less aloof and bossy towards me. After a while, I succeeded in pitching eight out of ten throws into the basket. Liqiang was proud of me. He ran up to me, bowed and gave me an encouraging pat on the back.

I felt as if I had been plugged into an electric socket. My whole being tingled, from my earlobes down to my heels. It was the sort of throbbing that hurts and feels exhilarating at the same time. Now I started trying even harder, because I wanted another pat on the back. This time, however, I managed to score only four baskets out of ten. I looked down at my shoes, crestfallen. But Liqiang gave me another pat anyway – and again I didn't know what had hit me. After a while, he started reaching out and brushing my shoulder whether or not I had done well. The stars in his eyes and the colour in his cheeks told me that he too got a charge out of touching me.

I suddenly had the sense that Mother's stern eyes were on me. Her words droned through my head: Don't you ever get mixed up with boys, or there will be big trouble! I consoled myself with the rationalisation that we were only playing basketball, where surely an innocent pat on the back was par for the course.

Three days later the film *Lenin in 1917* was being shown for the thousandth time. That gave Liqiang and me an excuse to go out at night.

'Come back as soon as the film is over,' said Mother, sighing, 'I don't understand why the children keep wanting to see those same old rehashed films, over and over again. Perhaps they've just become addicted to seeing dark shadows on a white screen?'

Giggling, I stepped outside with Liqiang. The moonlight had painted the world of night silver; it draped the trees, the buildings and even the garbage pails lining the streets in a soft, dreamy effulgence. Liqiang was whistling the theme of the film, 'The struggle against the Japanese invaders'. But the way he was whistling it, it didn't sound militaristic at all – on the contrary, it sounded enchantingly romantic. It made me feel totally relaxed. All my worries and fears dropped from my shoulders. I felt myself getting lighter and lighter, emptying my mind of everything, little by little, the way an accomplished meditation master would . . . Carried away by the moment, I slapped Liqiang on his behind: I, who only a week ago was still walking around with a healthy loathing for boys and who had even convinced myself that their smell made me gag, was giving a man a friendly spank on his bum! I had expected my hand to bounce off his bottom, as it would have in Mother's case, but this felt as if I had hit a steel plate. Liqiang's buttocks were all muscle. My respect for him rose several notches. I wanted to press myself up against him. I was absolutely sure that Liqiang felt the same way.

⌒

It was very early in the morning, and Mother was already up and about.

Today was Sunday, and she was boiling water for the bath. Everyone was to have a turn: first Aunt Xiucai, then Mother, next me and finally Liqiang. At around twelve o'clock, when I stepped out of the bathroom in my bathrobe, I ran into Liqiang standing in the corridor, fixing a wall sconce. He greeted me, screwdriver in hand.

Then it happened. His eyes slid from my wet hair to my face, and down to my shoulders, which protruded from the robe that was a little too large on me; then down along my hips and finally to my bare feet.

My heart ran amok. My blood beat up against my ribcage, which suddenly felt much too tight. Liqiang's eyes scorched my skin, and every vessel in my body melted. I was petrified. From over three feet away, I was sure I could feel the shudders running up and down Liqiang's body.

He tried to catch my eye, but I knew that as soon as I gave in and looked at him, something ... quite irreversible would happen, for both of us. I bit my lip and forced myself to look over at the kitchen window. Ten, twenty seconds passed and still I heard his rapid, heavy breathing. It was not until almost a minute had gone by that I awoke from this wild, frightening dream. Only then did we dare look at each other. The flames in our eyes had been doused, leaving only the crimson ashes of our embarrassment.

I now realised how wonderful it was to fall in love, but also ... how terrifying. Who needed that! I began avoiding Liqiang, like a child who keeps away from the stove after he's been burned.

Following the incident outside the bathroom, Liqiang did not show up at breakfast. He had a splitting headache.

Three days later, Aunt made her son get dressed so that she could take him to the hospital for a brain scan. It had never happened before – her strapping boy suffering from such a headache for four days at a stretch, with neither a fever nor a cold to blame it on. From the living room I could overhear them arguing bitterly. Ten minutes later, Aunt shyly came into the room and asked, 'Lian, would you please help me with something? Would you just go to Liqiang? He would so much like a word with you.' She tugged at my arms: 'Please help your Aunt! Convince him it's necessary to go to the doctor. All right?'

Reluctantly, I opened the door to Liqiang's room. When I saw his pale, sunken cheeks, I felt revulsion, not pity.

'Your mother has asked me to convince you to go to the doctor. Well, are you going, or not?' I was shocked by my cool, curt tone.

Liqiang's eyes had been shining with hope when he saw me come in.

Now dark clouds dimmed them again. He closed his eyes and seemed utterly unmanned.

Now it was *my* turn to cry. Not because I felt sorry for him, but because I couldn't help being such a cold-hearted witch.

THE PHOTOGRAPHS

Aunt and nephew were packing their bags. I was in the hall, cleaning out some drawers. They were so full of junk that they were almost impossible to open, let alone push back in. I pulled out old newspapers, magazines, documents and ID passes and threw everything into the wastepaper basket.

From time to time, Liqiang would throw a shy but affectionate look in my direction. It was clear he didn't want his last day with me to go by just like that. He came over and stood next to me, then squatted down by the wastepaper basket and started rummaging around in it. I hadn't the slightest interest in knowing what he might be looking for. Suddenly his face broke into a smile, for the first time since a week ago last Sunday.

I looked down and saw him smoothing the creases out of an expired student card that I had thrown out.

'That's a lousy photo,' I snapped. 'Besides, if you want a picture of me, all you have to do is say so. I have lots.'

He wasn't used to being spoken to, let alone to being offered something, by me any more. He stared at me, unable to find his tongue.

I searched through the drawers and found a pile of photographs Mother had taken of me at my last birthday. I tossed the set at him and said, 'Pick some out yourself.'

Liqiang, spreading his hands like a fan, accepted the photographs reverently. He admired each one in turn lovingly, worshipfully, while weighing the merits of one over the other.

When I saw that he found them all so lovely that it was impossible to make a choice among them, my head began spinning with guilt; my feelings for this boy were indescribable. My knees buckled under me, and I collapsed on the floor beside him. I was weeping shamelessly; I wasn't worried about Aunt or Mother overhearing me. I was immoderately sorry that I had been so cruel to him over the past week. In my heart of hearts, I knew that I cared deeply for him too, but was too scared to accept his love. It was all so new and so strange.

I looked at Liqiang, hoping he would forgive me. He was smiling through his tears. I placed my hand in his. He almost crushed my bones with his grip. It did not make any difference to me.

I didn't know how long we had been sitting there like that, but all at once we were jolted out of our daze by Aunt's shouts.

'Hey, future forefather of ours, aren't you packed yet? We're going to miss the train!'

I hastily stuffed the pictures – all of them – into his breast pocket. He bowed down low, as if to make it easier for me, and gazed deeply into my eyes.

LEARNING FROM THE PEASANTS

At the end of November, Mrs Meng, the English teacher as well as our homeroom teacher, walked into class without any books in her arms. This was interpreted as a good sign. We girls, trying not to show our excitement, began whispering among ourselves, while the boys stuck their fingers in their mouths, wolf-whistling to create a festive atmosphere.

Mrs Meng only needed to clear her throat twice, dryly, and you could have heard a pin drop.

'In three days' time, on Friday 29th November, all third years will begin a one-month internship in the Commune of the Five Red Stars'.

'Hurray!' the class cheered wildly. A month of no school, a month of spending the whole day in the fresh, free, open air! Well, of course we realised that we might have to work pretty hard out there, but as for the rest of it, the internship promised to be a real holiday.

When the class had calmed down somewhat, Mrs Meng went on: 'Chairman Mao says, *Learn from the peasants*. His words express that truth of truths: one may find the most splendid traits of the proletariat among the peasants. Ever industrious, they are prepared to suffer hardships without a word of complaint. Moreover, they never, ever lack faith in the wisdom of the Great Helmsman's leadership, and they follow Him with total revolutionary obedience. That is why Mao sings their praises: *The peasant class has the most highly developed political consciousness of all*. Once you go into the countryside, you will notice the wretched conditions in which the peasant classes cultivate our primary subsistence crop, wheat. Observe their positive attitude towards hard work and a life of poverty. From them you will learn the spirit of revolutionary self-sacrifice; only then will you truly be able to understand why Mao has called upon the peasant class to be the guiding light of our nation.'

It was clear why the Helmsman was promoting the people who were stuck at the bottom of the social ladder to its highest rung. He was using the peasants to put the intelligentsia in its place, literally and figuratively – to put down all intellectuals and educated officials, anyone capable of critical thought. I could see right through Mao's 'Learn-from-the-peasants' call: in light of the shortage of farming machinery, the peasants could use quite a bit of help during the harvest season. By creating the student internship Learn from the Peasants, the government solved the manpower problem, since the students worked for nothing.

After Mrs Meng had laid out the ideological aspects of the apprenticeship, she came to its more practical consequences: when it was over, we would be graded on how hard we had worked. This mark would count towards the Student-of-the-Three-Virtues selection in December. It flashed through my mind that neither Kim nor I had considered the fact that willingness to perform hard physical labour was one of the criteria. I shook my head to unsnag the springs in there, thinking: What a golden opportunity for us, and it's falling right into Kim's lap! Here was another chance, second only to the Autumn Games, to show my classmates that Kim could be a success. If there was anyone who had no compunctions about working hard, it was Kim. By helping out in the vegetable garden at home, she had become expert at ploughing, sowing, digging and mowing; she hiked into the hills daily to find firewood, carrying home bundles that weighed more than she weighed herself.

Finally Mrs Meng came round to what we all considered the most vital piece of information: the sleeping arrangements and housing assignments. Since most villages did not have hotels, youth hostels or dormitories, we would be divided into groups of four to six, each group to be lodged in the home of a different peasant family. You hoped you would not get assigned to a group containing your arch enemy, of course. I felt I couldn't bear it if I had to sleep in the same room as Meimei. On the other hand, I would jump for joy if I ended up in the same group as Kim. I realised, of course, that my wish was as crazy as a chicken that dreams of soaring into the sky like a swallow, since, notwithstanding the sermon about Learning from the peasants, Mrs Meng would never go so far as to allow students from different castes to share the same lodgings.

Indeed, when Mrs Meng read out the list of group members and their assigned addresses, I noted that students from different castes were kept strictly separate – the way it ought to be, the way it had always been and, perhaps, the way it would always be. My group included Qianyun, Feiwen and Liru, first-caste girls every one.

At eight o'clock on the allotted day the class was all present and correct, waiting at the school entrance for the conveyance that was to take us to the Commune of the Five Red Stars. A yellow dust cloud, rimmed in black, was drawing closer, and we could hear honking in the distance, alloyed by the clatter of steel.

'There it is!' cried Mrs Meng. 'Form two lines; boys go first.'

The tractor flung up huge sprays of sand and belched pitch-black exhaust fumes. The contraption came to a halt right in front of us with a creaking groan and a few impressive final convulsions. An athletic young man, with bristly hair sticking up out of his battered straw hat, jumped out of the cab to release the iron catch-chain of the tailgate. I suddenly saw why Mrs Meng was ordering the boys to get in first: there was no ladder, no rope, nothing to hold on to for you to heave yourself into the wagon bed that hovered six feet off the ground.

The boys tossed their bags into the truck-bed and leaped up against the sides – whup! – like leopards. They grabbed the side rails – their biceps bulging like cannon balls – and, building up speed, shinned up into the loading bed. Now they could afford to pay attention to the girls waiting down below. Their swaggering expressions left no doubt as to the implication: grab hold of our powerful hands, and we'll hoist you up.

My legs were shaking. I saw a couple of girls dangling in the air like limp sacks of garbage – they could not muster the strength to make it to the top in one heave. The boys were forced to hold on with all their might as the thrashing cargo helplessly pleaded to be let go. It was a ludicrous sight. I was dithering – I didn't know what to do. But Mrs Meng was getting impatient: 'Are the rest of you coming, or not?'

I started, and looked around. Only three girls remained who had not been hoisted up yet: Meimei, Kim and me. Meimei was wiggling her ass coquettishly, waiting patiently for her prince – the tall, slender Wudong with the delicate feminine complexion – to haul her up.

And Kim? There was no one, of course, who would extend a helping hand to her. Mrs Meng was still screeching at them. Kim bit her lip and flung her bag into the wagon – *tonng!* Next she walked to one of the rear wheels, planted a foot on it and wedged her way up inch by inch.

As I was marvelling at this athletic feat, I heard a warm male voice: 'Lian, here's my hand. Trust me. I'll pull you up.' It was Wudong. His black eyes suddenly looked brown – from the tenderness with which he spoke to me, I was reminded of Liqiang . . .

'*Tyeee!*' Meimei didn't even take the trouble of hiding her disappointment and envy.

Before I realised what was happening, I had been hoisted up. I was standing nose to nose with Wudong and made myself ascribe his heavy breathing solely to the physical exertion of pulling me up.

In the end it was Shunzi who helped Meimei climb in, which did not go down particularly well with her. Even though he was both class representative and secretary of the third-years' Communist Youth League, he was and would always be a second-caster. To be given a helping hand by him was clearly below her dignity. She stood a chance with any number of first-caste boys who had their eye on her, but she had ruined it by setting her sights on Wudong – Wudong, whose arsehole was where his eyes should have been: he hadn't even noticed her.

At two in the afternoon, our conveyance finally drew to a halt with one last shudder. We found ourselves in a quadrangle, in the midst of a golden sea of corncobs spread out to dry. Behind the square was a block of mud huts. Other than that, there was nothing but the rustling unharvested corn as far as the eye could see.

Kwalá! The chain was released once more and Kim and the boys bounced down like footballs. Wudong held on to the side of the wagon with his left hand, while with his right he beckoned me to jump down, an encouraging smile on his face. I felt Meimei's eyes drilling into my back like scorching laser beams. I took a step sideways – perhaps Wudong would notice Meimei and help her instead. Ever since my encounter with Liqiang, I didn't feel any need for a boy's attentions.

Wudong looked at me in surprise as Meimei shoved her delicate fingers into his hand. He helped her down, his eyes never veering from my face. Once again I realised how intensely beautiful, but at the same time how excruciatingly painful the feelings between a boy and a girl can be. The whole business was distressing, for Wudong as well as for Meimei. I myself felt nothing. My only concern was for Kim. I wanted to help Kim – out of love, and maybe out of just a touch of narcissism, too.

Mrs Meng asked for a middle-aged man to be fetched from one of the mud huts. He was the head of the production team to which my class was assigned. He sauntered up to us grinning from earlobe to earlobe. There was an uncanny resemblance between his teeth and the commune's primary crop: his teeth were coated in a thick layer of plaque the colour of corn kernels.

We drew ourselves up neatly before him in long rows, in anticipation of

232

his proletarian sermon. But the man wasn't quite ready yet. He pressed his thumb against the right side of his nose and – *phiee*! – a stream of beige mush shot out of his left nostril. Using his index finger, he did the same thing on the other side, resulting in similar pickings. Upon accomplishing this, he cleared his throat and spat on the ground. Shifting his weight from foot to foot until he was satisfied that he had discovered his centre of gravity, he finally spoke: 'Kids, it's been raining pitchforks for three days without a break. See those cornstalks over there? They're plastered with green mould. Hai, what a shame!'

I rolled my eyes in astonishment: shouldn't he be addressing us as 'revolutionary comrades', as was required? Shouldn't he be saying things like 'the red wind from the East quells the black wind from the West'? Shouldn't he be telling us we should cleanse our bourgeois brains, and that peasant sweat makes the best soap? This man must have the gall of a lion, to speak so candidly about the real point of our internship!

Slapping his palms against his thighs, he was shaking his head: 'And such thick, hefty cornstalks they were, too. If they weren't so rotten we could have used them for firewood! Oh well, no use crying over spilled porridge . . . But lucky for us, way over there, we got the stalks covered with mats in the nick of time. Boys and girls, help us bring them in as quickly as possible, into the big barn. Then at least we'll have something to burn in the cold winter months. Thanks in advance! Okay, I'm done. You can go to the canteen now. Your food is already out on the tables for you. And I reckon they've prepared something really special for you, you can count on it!'

'Hurrah!' we shouted with relief. We all jumped up, headed for the canteen, when Mrs Meng admonished us, 'Remember the iron rules of the Revolution!'

Oh, no! There was still a sermon from our teacher to endure. Another of those endless disquisitions over what kind of proletarian thoughts we ought to cherish and how to transform ourselves into blood-red offspring of the Father, Mother, Lover and Mistress All-Rolled-Into-One. I submitted to the lecture with my eyes and ears plugged up, hopping from one leg to the other.

Finally, time for the payoff: chowing down! That is, the 'something special' the team leader had described turned out to consist of one steamed wheat-flour bun per person. According to Kim, ordinary farmers ate wheat only on feast days. On top of that we were given two hunks of cornmeal bread each, plus two slices of pickled radish. Funny, normally I would hardly have been able to get such a thing down, but today it tasted better than *bapaos* stuffed with shrimp.

After the feast, we took off in search of our host families. Mrs Meng, bags in hand, walked up to me. Oh, Buddha, our teacher must be a mind-reader! She probably knew how much I detested her hypocritical lectures. I shrank, expecting a reprimand.

But my fears were groundless. Mrs Meng said, in an almost human tone, 'Uh . . . did I tell you? I am bunking with you girls!'

I squealed and called out to Liru, Qianyun and Feiwen. Heavy bedrolls notwithstanding, we went skipping on our way. We felt honoured that the teacher had chosen our group to sleep with, even if her sanctimoniousness sometimes bugged the hell out of us.

The relentless rain had soaked the dirt road to the village; with every step, our shoes stuck in the mud. I realised what a luxury it was to walk in the city on asphalt paving. If the girl ahead of me didn't watch out, she'd spatter my trousers and even my jacket with mud. It could be just plain earth, but it could also be excrement – children's poop, or cow pats. Here in the countryside, any place was considered an ideal spot for doing your business. My stomach churned. But I mustn't throw up, otherwise I'd get labelled a bourgeois cunt by the others and then I could kiss good marks for this internship goodbye.

By the time we got to the village proper, even the dirt paths had disappeared, but as my eagerness to see my new lodgings returned, I began to feel much better. As we went along we saw groups of our classmates enter their host families' yards one by one.

I looked at the huts and asked myself how in Buddha's name it could be that these had not utterly dissolved in the recent heavy rainstorms. Constructed of earth, the huts had had their four corners rounded off by wind and weather erosion, and appeared dangerously rickety. Rice paper that had yellowed and turned brittle with age was stuck into the windows. Each house consisted of two tiny rooms. I guessed that the bed must occupy at least three-quarters of the living space. To get in you had to fight your way through flocks of chickens, ducks, pigs and sheep, all cackling, quacking, snorting and bleating at the strange-smelling visitors who had the gall to disturb their peace. I saw how some of my classmates, upon knocking at the gate, were dragged inside by the wife and her brood, welcomed with a rough but touchingly enthusiastic hospitality. Compared to these country-dwellers, city folk were just a bunch of cold fish. The longing for a similarly heart-warming reception impelled me to quicken my pace. I too couldn't wait to meet my hostess.

Tyeeah . . . We pushed open the courtyard gate . . . Let the chorus of protest from the roaming livestock begin! Hello, this house was built of brick! I might as well have been back in the city. Compared with the huts we had just seen, this was a mansion, a castle. It was a house with at least three rooms – and what rooms! They all had high ceilings and real glass window-panes. Most eye-catching of all was the pump in the middle of the courtyard. That meant that, unlike our classmates, we would not have to traipse half a mile to the well for every little thing.

'Good afternoon! Anyone home?' We knocked. There was no answer. Disappointed, I followed the others inside.

In the outer room, a table and four chairs were pushed against one wall. Over the table hung a portrait of the Father, Mother, Lover and Mistress All-Rolled-Into-One. On either side of the photograph, somewhat paradoxically, were displayed scrolls devoutly inscribed with this year's New Year's resolution:

> Buddha bless us
> by filling our pigsty
> with many little ones
> and our wife's belly
> with just as many sons

Next to the verses hung a print honouring the new year. It was the picture of a huge red carp – symbol of abundance. On the back of the fish sat a chuckling little boy, dressed in the characteristic toddler's get-up: short trousers with a wide-open fly. His little pink willie – symbol of heavenly good fortune – was dangling over the carp's jaws. Juicy peaches – symbols of health and long life – lay scattered around the fish and the boy.

On the table, right beneath Mao's picture, there was a bowl of cookies and fresh fruit – an altar of sorts, dedicated to the Great Helmsman. In the past, only the family's ancestors used to deserve this kind of veneration – a practice denounced by the Wisest Leader of the Universe as 'feudal and counter-revolutionary'.

There were also two beds, one double and the other single, both made of wood – quite an extravagance in the countryside: even in the city the peasants, for the most part, slept on slabs of stone.

The walls behind the beds were hung with pictures cut out of colour magazines. This too was a luxury – most peasant families papered their walls with old newspapers. The pictures featured bright-eyed actresses posing in revolutionary peasant or workers' garb. Their faces shone with a proletarian fighting spirit and their outstretched arms were invariably levelled at some pale-faced, bourgeois-leaning professor, or perhaps a spy from Hong Kong. But if you looked more closely, you could detect, behind the belligerence, a sexy pout as well, which didn't quite seem to fit this kind of Communist propaganda; two nourishing breasts were always shown bulging beneath the masculine clothing, while out of the corners of the eyes slipped a sidelong come-hither look. No wonder the peasants loved those pin-ups . . .

Flanking this room on either side were two smaller rooms. One was just large enough to accommodate a kang, which held a wooden trunk – the dowry chest. The bridegroom's parents filled this chest with clothes for their future daughter-in-law, so that she would have enough to wear for the next few decades. The other room was full of junk, a place where shovels, rusted plough blades and other old farming equipment were stored.

I looked out of a window and noticed, in a quiet corner of the courtyard, a couple of flowerbeds. Red, yellow, purple and white chrysanthemums turned their lively faces towards the sun. It began to dawn on me why Mrs Meng had wanted to stay here. In this environment, the relative affluence and refined tastes of this particular peasant family towered head and shoulders above the rest. What was Mrs Meng to do? Should she stop lecturing us about 'learning from the peasants'? If she did, she would be replaced in two shakes by colleagues who were less averse to lying. Should she have chosen the poorest host family, and slept in a hovel for thirty days? Mrs Meng was only human, after all. And who, no matter how impressively they might natter on about Communist Consciousness and stuff like that, did not prefer the comfortable life?

At around six p.m. we heard the scraping of a shovel being dragged over the ground and the creaking of the courtyard gate. Mrs Meng got up at once.

'Mama, they're here!' cried a cheerful little voice; we saw a robust woman marching towards us. Without breaking her stride she detached a four-year-old who was clinging to her trouser legs and hissed urgently, 'Go fetch your brother. He's digging Grandma's vegetable plot. Tell him he has to make a fire in the stove, to boil water for our guests.' The woman's face overflowed with cordiality; she nodded at each of us warmly. In rural areas, people didn't shake hands when they greeted each other – a nod of the head would do.

'I just don't know where to hide my cow-leather-hide face, I'm sure! I'm so sorry to have left you waiting in this disgusting mess. But – what can you do? A woman who has to earn all the ration-points for the entire family, and two useless children besides, good for nothing but getting underfoot . . .'

Liru picked up a dust cloth, wanting to help her by wiping down the table. But the lady of the house said, 'No, Miss, such dirty work is not for the likes of you.'

Mrs Meng came to Liru's aid: 'But that's the whole point of our coming here!'

The farmer's wife turned, looked Liru, Qianyun, Feiwen and me over from head to toe and shook her head. 'I don't understand why the team leader brings in these porcelain dolls. To every animal its own nest. Young ladies ought to be out for a stroll in the city and leave it to peasant children to wallow in the mud like water buffalo. That's the way life is, am I right? If you hoist the bottom to the top you're committing a sin against tradition – it's a sin against nature.'

I held my breath: in the city, any pronouncement like this would be regarded as radically counter-revolutionary. But our teacher had some experience with this kind of thing; she knew that peasants seldom ran the risk of being criticised, no matter what came out of their mouths. Unlike the intellectuals, they hadn't the foggiest notion that their opinion could influence the politics of the nation . . .

'Ma'am, it wasn't your team leader who made the decision to send the students to the countryside,' she tried to explain.

The farmer's wife blinked, because to her, the team leader was the highest leader that existed, the one who wrote the law, carried it out and watched over it jealously.

'It is the CPC . . . I mean, the Communist Party of China, that has called the apprenticeship Learning from the Peasants into being. Besides, as long as we are on the subject of tradition: what good would it do to let young ladies from the city keep their fine, delicate doll's complexion, when the children of the countryside have tanned and weathered faces? Mao says: *The darker the skin, the more revolutionary is the heart.*'

These last words wiped the confusion from the farmer's wife's face. She roared with laughter: 'Hahaha! Hey, that's hilarious! The stuff those fancy gents come up with never makes sense to simple souls like us, but one thing's for sure: no villager *wants* to have dark skin.' All at once she clammed up. We saw her blush to the very roots of her hair. Only now did it occur to me that our hostess's face was far less tanned than that of most country folk. Her skin was conspicuously pale and smooth.

Kwatyah! The woven corn-stalk gate to the courtyard flew open and a boy hurtled up to our hostess like a miniature typhoon. He pressed his face into her coat, hugging her round the waist and yelling, 'Mama, Grandma said that I ploughed like a real man today!' Spreading his arms wide, he went on, 'I finished a stretch of earth *this* big in less than an hour! She's going to give me a new shovel at Spring Festival!'

The farmer's wife pushed his head out of her coat: 'Tiedar! Don't wipe your snot on my clothes! Well, it was about time we had a *man* around the house.' She proudly stroked his head and said, 'Hurry up and wash your filthy little mug. After that you can say hello to our guests.'

Tiedar peered past his mother into the main room, rubbing his dirty face

237

against her coat again: 'No, Mama, first I have to use the privy.' He dived into a straw hut in a corner of the yard.

Psss! I couldn't keep a straight face any more: what a well-brought-up young man! Was there any other peasant boy his age who would use that expression, 'I have to use the privy'?

'Gouzi!' The loud bellow issuing from the straw hut made me jump. And again, *'Gouzi!'*

Whoop! A huge mutt leaped out of nowhere and dashed to the place where Tiedar was emptying his bowels.

I heard the little boy talking to him, 'Good boy . . . no, not just here . . . over there! You haven't licked that spot yet, okay . . . good dog, yeah . . .'

I closed my eyes, uncertain of what to do next: vomit or laugh? Was toilet paper *that* expensive, then?

At nine o'clock we began preparing ourselves for bed. Undressing was the most embarrassing part. Five pairs of eyes followed every movement I made: from the unbuttoning of my shirt to the removal of my jacket and trousers. Not that it was only me they were staring at: they were busy studying every inch of each other's bodies as if it was communal property. As an only child, I wasn't used to being stared at by my peers, especially not while practically naked. Professor Maly had told me once that there was an English word, *privacy*, that could not be translated into Chinese. You were supposed to be an open book for each other, mentally and physically. Mentally in the sense that you were supposed to know each other's deepest thoughts and most intimate feelings; that was why under the leadership of the CPC people took part in twice-weekly thought-sharing sessions. In addition, at political meetings held three afternoons a week, you were expected to expose your innermost feelings to the critical scrutiny of others, while being taught by the Party how to think in the correct proletarian way. In the physical sense, it meant a total absence of privacy; it was considered one's birthright to check out someone else's body, evaluate it and make remarks about it. In the public toilets there were no walls between the squatting holes; the public baths consisted of cavernous spaces where the patrons could monitor whether someone had a potbelly from miles away.

THE ADVANTAGE OF PALE SKIN

At eight o'clock prompt, we girls were lined up fifteen feet apart at the edge of a corn field east of the village. Each of us was assigned a fifteen-foot strip along which we had to bundle up the cornstalks and drag them over to the dirt path skirting the field. The boys then loaded them on to a wheelbarrow and wheeled them to a big barn a mile off. We had to gather and arrange the stalks, which were scattered higgledy-piggledy over the field, tie them up with a piece of string and drag the sheaf over ground that was pretty well impassable, with stubble sticking up everywhere. The cornstalks had been carelessly cut, not close enough to the ground.

The wind lashed my face with an iron whip. Sweat was pouring down my back in buckets and my jacket collar was soaked with a ring of sweat. I had grown totally unused to hard labour; I thought my back would break in two. After a while I lost all sensation in my body. Still I refused to straighten up for even a moment's rest. The air hummed with an almost tangible tension – a silent competition was in full swing. The one who finished her strip first would win top marks in the day's evaluation. At the end of the month, the results were to be tallied up, to determine the final grade for our internship. With a pang of nostalgia I thought of the camp, and working in the mill with Qin. That too had been hard work, but then I had had Qin for company, as well as his diverting, thought-provoking history lessons. On top of that there was the compensation of the extra meal, with real meat. What kind of incentive was a silly old grade, compared to that?

I straightened up, and suddenly broke into a cold sweat: I was lagging severely behind. The others were busy at work yards ahead of me. Kim was somewhere behind me, true – but that was because she had already started on her second swath.

It wasn't fair. I really had done my best. I could not believe I was such an incredible klutz – but the facts spoke for themselves. Still, now that I had fallen so far behind, there was no great harm in wasting another minute to catch my breath. If it's cracked anyway, you might as well smash a stone jug to pieces.

Surveying the scene, I noticed that my classmates would look over at Kim from time to time with novel and unprecedented respect. Kim was the fastest worker by far. It more than made up for my shocked discovery of my own pathetic performance. Hadn't I predicted it, three days ago? I knew that Kim would excel at this internship.

239

Just as I was looking Kim's way, she straightened up. Sauntering nonchalantly over to me, Kim silently began – *crrts*, *crrts* – to help me harvest my strip. I – that is to say, we as a team – caught up with the others in no time. I saw eyes narrowed with envy everywhere I looked.

We were anxious to finish our allotments as quickly as possible; help from a friend was as welcome as raindrops to parched lips. But in this silent contest, who was prepared to lose precious time by going to bat for someone else? Aside from Kim, there was no one willing to stick her neck out.

It wasn't only the students who considered Kim's gesture heroic: the real-life peasants felt the same. If a young man lent a young girl a hand with her share of the farm work, it was considered a sublime declaration of love. Was that the way they would characterise this city-child's good deed?

At suppertime we got to hear Kim's praises sung over the loudspeakers. These had been written by the Secretary of Propaganda of our class, Wanquan. My cornbread tasted much better, all of a sudden. Never before had such extravagant praise been showered on anyone in listening range of an entire production brigade community! *Surely* this meant the start of a more tolerable life for Kim, and the demise of her sorry reputation!

❧

That afternoon, I found out why our hostess was financially so much better-off than her neighbours. Eight years earlier, she had been reputed to be the most beautiful girl in all the six villages of this mountain-region. She was unusually light-skinned for a peasant, her lips were red as cherries and her eyes sparkled like a crystal stream. The country bumpkins swarmed around her like bees around a honey pot. The winner was a peasant who worked in construction in a neighbouring town and was actually paid in hard cash. It was primarily the latter consideration, naturally, that had clinched the deal and ended the furious beauty-chase by all the other suitors baying at her heels. Most peasants were paid their 'salary' just once a year, in December. This consisted of any corn and vegetables remaining after the yearly production quota had been handed over to the State, supplemented by a handful of change. The cash they got was chicken feed, considering it was all they had to buy the basic necessities such as salt, matches, toothpaste and, at a pinch, even some fabric for clothes.

Ten days after the wedding, her husband had returned to the city to work. Every month he sent fifteen kuai to his prized new bride – a fortune really, enough to make even a deaf-mute burst into song. On this income the family could afford to have a large house built, and the wife could furnish it with a dab of city taste. This explained why the woman had blushed so deeply the previous evening, when she had said peasants preferred light skin, too.

The next morning, Mrs Meng entered the room with a stack of letters in her hand. There was a letter from Mother: *Father is coming home!* It gave me a shock. I should have been glad, of course, but all I felt was confusion.

At the end of the second work day, Kim's name was again broadcast over the village radio as being the most outstanding intern. The sky seemed wider and bluer to me, the work in the fields lighter, now that Kim had risen so high in her classmates' estimation.

∽

Not a day went by that Kim wasn't singled out for plaudits over the village loudspeakers. In the canteen, she was no longer shoved aside when it was her turn to be served; the girls did not stick their noses in the air when they walked past her any more; and although it did take quite a bit of self-restraint, the boys were even able to keep their legs in check whenever their kicking reflexes were activated at the sight of Kim.

After supper and before the nightly political meeting, we had half an hour of free time. I would never forget how relaxed and happy Kim had been strolling with me along the corn fields, where she would show me the most efficient way of tying up the stalks. Kim's spine was as erect as a bamboo shoot with self-respect and pride when I contrived an excuse to have her explain the farming techniques to me all over again.

THE STONE-GIRL

It was the beginning of the third week of our apprenticeship. Most of the girls in my class had already begun menstruating: this put them out of commission for at least four days of the month, days when they were unable to work hard or to earn points for their efforts, whereas Kim heedlessly went on chalking up stellar performances day after day. No wonder, then, that their jealousy swelled up like a bee-stung tongue. In the canteen, I began to overhear talk like: 'Yes, well, our "model intern" has a pretty easy time of it, doesn't she? *She* doesn't have to think of her body, because her body is no different from a boy's!' At first I just laughed it off, because getting your period wasn't exactly a picnic: Kim, just be thankful you don't have to deal with that problem yet! But the special consideration Mrs Meng accorded girls who were having their periods did confer a certain cachet. For instance, they did not have to show up in the fields until ten in the morning, and were allowed to totter home at four. In the evening, if they wrote Mrs Meng a note saying they had the cramps, they were excused from the nightly political meeting. They had only to whine and the teacher would give them permission to fetch a bowl of warm water from the canteen's central kettle to wash with, while the rest of us did not have the right to even a drop of lukewarm water if we were dying to soak our icy feet. This encouraged some of the girls to make a big deal of getting their period. It was these same girls who drummed Kim out of their circle and booted her back to the lowly rank she had enjoyed before the internship.

It was, and was to remain, a covert war of nerves, to be sure: the boys, normally the *agents provocateurs*, sadly could not be recruited for pestering duty under this particular set of circumstances. It was essential to keep the menstrual business a secret. It would create a scandal if the boys were to find out that a girl was turning into a woman. Puberty, like anything else having to do with sex, was taboo. The male contingent of our class was therefore still pulling its punches with Kim; the broadcast station was still hailing Kim's work performance every day with panegyric bulletins; nor did Mrs Meng ever pass up an occasion to drop Kim's name at the daily political meetings, speaking of her in the most glowing terms.

During our walks together in the fields, Kim's chattering was starting to peter out into longer and longer pauses, however. One evening, Kim stopped short in the middle of a muddy lane and asked point-blank, 'What's a "stone-girl"?' My heart sank, because that was the term for young girls with an hormonal abnormality preventing the onset of menstruation. I knew this only because before I got my first period, I had screwed up the courage to read up about it on the quiet, in Father's medical texts. I did not have the heart to tell Kim how keenly I felt for her. Kim was sixteen already, two years older than most of the girls in our class, but she was one of the only ones who had not yet begun menstruating. I knew why that was. Kim was simply too skinny. Her diet was inadequate; she didn't take in enough vitamins or protein. But she was definitely not a stone-girl. I had seen photographs of patients who had that condition: those poor girls were as hairy as monkeys or European men. You certainly couldn't say that about Kim.

All the way back to the village, I said nothing. Kim, picking up on my mood, kicked at clods of earth with her feet, and said, forcing a laugh,

'Even Jiening's overtaken me. Soon everybody will start thinking *I'm* the little sister. She got the curse last summer. It sure shocked the pants off my mother. But you should see her little breasts, a real woman! She gets away with doing even less work around the house now, because when it's that time of the month she *mu-u-sn't do-o hea-eavy wor-rk.*' It was priceless: by stringing out the words like that, she had captured her mother's rural dialect down to a T.

'Pfffch!' I couldn't help it – I had to join in Kim's laughter.

~

It was raining cats and dogs. All of us, our hostess included, couldn't go into the fields; we had to stay home. To start the day, under Mrs Meng's leadership, we held a political meeting, at which each in turn – except for the teacher, of course – was expected to spit out her bourgeois thoughts. Qianyun, for example, confessed that her hair felt sticky and stinky – we hadn't had a bath in nearly a month. She immediately went on to censure herself, saying it was revisionist and capitalistic thinking to let dirtiness bother her. For had Mao not said that filth of the body means cleanliness of the soul? She announced, 'I must learn from the peasants. They only wash themselves in the summer, when the water in the river isn't too cold. Who do I think I am – longing for a shower after only twenty-three days?' Having made a clean breast of it, she sat down again. Qianyun was a sly fox. By taking herself to task, no one could throw back in her face that all it would take to remove the substance of her counter-revolutionary complaint – the black smudges on her legs and shoulders – was a bowl of cold water.

In the spirit of self-preservation, we made quick work of similar revisionist sentiments in ourselves, such as our longing for a few strips of meat and some fresh vegetables in our diet. For three weeks our only sustenance had been bread and pickles. We said in unison, 'We are truly mortified by our desire for that kind of indulgence. The peasants make do with the same frugal fare all year long, yet they are the ones tilling the land for the basic necessities of life. No wonder the Wisest Leader in the Universe says of them: "Farmers are just like cows: they eat grass, but produce delicious milk." How could anyone in the whole wide world ever come up with a more magnificent eulogy for the peasant classes?'

Unfortunately, our hostess, who was sitting at the table darning her children's socks, interpreted our heroic proletarian self-reproach as a critique of her own housekeeping. Shyly putting in her own two fenworth, she asked, 'Could I just say something here? I really am terribly sorry that I haven't boiled any bath water for you. See, as a simple farmer's wife, I clean

243

forgot that people from the city have to wash themselves every fortnight or so! We villagers don't give a fig about being clean . . . Besides, the work in the fields makes us so dog-tired that when we get home we can think of only one thing . . . sleep. Where would we find the energy to collect firewood in the hills and heat water for a bath?'

The colour drained from Mrs Meng's face. She wanted to explain to our hostess that that wasn't what we had meant at all, but the woman continued implacably: 'Tomorrow I'll keep my son home from school. What's the point of those lessons anyway? Teachers with diplomas don't want to stay at a village school, and the schoolmasters who do want to teach here are only a hair less illiterate than we are. Tomorrow I'll send my little boy into the mountains to fetch the firewood, if it isn't raining, that is. Then in the evening, after I get off working in the fields, I can heat up some water, so you can finally have a good wash.' She rubbed her large hands together, crimson with embarrassment.

I wished I could go hide in a dark corner and cry. The chasm between the peasant folk and city folk was too much – I couldn't bear it, especially if the peasants started excusing themselves, on top of everything else! They were going to split my head in two like a watermelon, spilling out all the revolutionary slogans stored inside:

> Learn from the peasants,
> they are the leaders of China
> The darker the skin
> the more revolutionary the heart
> Dirt on the body
> means cleanliness of the soul
> Farmers are like cows:
> they eat grass, but produce delicious milk

The daily contradictions I was confronted with here in the countryside, the obvious schism between His propaganda and the naked truth, combined with my sympathy for the peasant class, made me so furious I didn't know which way was up any more. What had Qin told me again? How would Cannibal have reacted to this? Silently I prayed, 'Buddha, please show me the way!'

The other girls, meanwhile, taking their cue from Mrs Meng, had been trying their damnedest to persuade our hostess that we never meant to say anything negative about her. It had been meant as self-criticism; not as a critique of *her*. They finally did manage to get that into her head. Only with that load off her conscience could Mrs Meng end the political meeting, and we all joined our landlady at the table for a chat.

Liru posed the question that had been on the tip of everyone's tongue for nearly a month: 'How often does your husband come home?'

The landlady pulled her little daughter close: 'The father of my children usually visits us once a year, at the Chinese New Year, you know how it is. But if he's lucky, that's to say, if there aren't too many building projects and the money-pouch he's got hanging from his trouser belt is nice and heavy, then he'll sometimes come home for a week in the summer. That's a treat for the little ones, it is! You see, I don't know how to swim and when their father isn't here, the children always have to beg their uncle to take them to the river. It's so pathetic to see them wheedle and whine.'

Feiwen didn't beat about the bush: 'Don't you mind seeing your husband so rarely?'

'Just ask around, in the village. If you find even a *single* soul who doesn't envy our family from the bottom of his guts, you'll see my head rolling down the lane like a cauliflower! If the father of my children had remained a farmer, then we'd never have been able to afford such an elegant house.' She drew a half-circle with her head, indicating the hallmarks of affluence in the furnishings, and proudly stroked the head of her four-year-old daughter, who was wearing a jacket sewn of expensive polyester.

I had been under the impression that the husband and wife were not living together because they had been separated by the Cultural Revolution, as my own father and mother had been. I was discovering that there were people who *chose* not to be together. It was clear that the financial advantages of working in the city were so irresistible to a peasant family that this couple were prepared to spend the best years of their lives apart.

AN ELDER BROTHER FOR KIM

We were on our way home. The tractor, with its usual prodigious dust and noise, stood chugging in the middle of the village square, and again Mrs Meng ordered the boys to climb into the back first. This time, I grabbed the first hand that came my way, and let myself be pulled up. However, once I was up on the wagon, the hand that had helped me up would not let go. I looked up at its owner and the blood curdled in my veins – Wudong was standing there staring at me with his beautiful eyes brimming with tenderness. My 'rock-solid' refusal to believe in miracles experienced an earthquake.

Once I managed to evade the radiation zone of Wudong's keyed-up ardour, I elatedly began looking around for Kim, model intern and star of the loudspeaker news bulletins over the past month. The boys were probably fighting over who would get to haul her up.

But no.

Kim was standing down below all by herself. Swallowing her pride, she threw a timid glance at the row of boys' faces above her. She didn't dare look them straight in the eye, but she was still furtively hoping that one of her classmates – even if it was only *one* – would extend a helping hand. A painful doubt began to criss-cross Kim's stolid face, and it wasn't difficult for me to read her thoughts: Is it possible that all those words of praise, extolling me to high heaven for thirty days straight over the village loudspeakers, have done absolutely nothing to jack me up even the tiniest bit from the bottom of the heap?

I wished that I were endowed with the strong arms of a boy. Then *I* could have pulled Kim up. But alas, I was sure that if I attempted it, we would both end up in the mud.

Tootootoo! The driver was getting impatient.

'Quick! Get in!' Mrs Meng told Kim, then ran to the front of the vehicle and climbed in next to the driver.

Kim, jolted from her stupor, shouted to the driver to just hold on a little longer – she would have to scramble up on to one of the back wheels, as she had done on the way out, and haul herself into the cargo area that way. The driver stared at the scrawny girl in surprise, stumped as to why she was the only one who had not been given a leg up. Hopping down from his perch behind the wheel, he said in a loud voice, 'Here, girl, allow your elder brother to help you!' Grabbing her by the waist, he was about to toss her up. 'Wait!' she screamed, her spindly legs kicking agitatedly in mid-air, 'I haven't thrown my bags in the back yet!' Picking up her bags, the fellow swung her back and forth, luggage and all. His eyes twinkled cheerfully – apparently the weight of the girl with her rucksack and bags felt like nothing to him. Oof! She was up on top in the blink of an eye.

The class in the wagon had been watching this scene dumbfounded. How should they rationalise this turn of events: was it an honour for Kim to be helped up by the driver himself, or was it, on the contrary, yet further proof of her pathetically inferior status?

I didn't give a hoot about what the others might make of it, but I was left reeling, as if the sky had landed on my head. This scene had made one thing very clear: the high marks Kim had earned for this internship, all the kudos she had earned from our supervisors for her accomplishments, meant nothing to our classmates. Kim was, and would always be, the irredeemable third-caster who was to be snubbed, humiliated and picked on by everybody else.

Kim knew it too, of course. Self-consciously, she avoided the front of the wagon, tacitly assumed to be 'reserved' for first-casters. Only a handful of second-casters were allowed up front. The lucky few had managed this critical step up the social ladder either by showing a positive political attitude, or by having the good fortune of being to Mrs Meng's taste.

The third-caster Wanquan had even been made Secretary of Propaganda for the class, a promotion he had earned, in part, by being a tall, broad-shouldered youth – an attribute that didn't leave Mrs Meng totally indifferent. Mrs Meng was known to be a little man-hungry. Her husband, a bridge designer, had been banished two years earlier to a village in the southern-most corner of the land. In those parts the mosquitoes were so fierce they'd pick you up, toss you in the air a few times, and then leave you love bites that would spawn rampant malaria in your bloodstream. I could not blame her for putting Wanquan on an equal footing with the first-casters. Everyone rowed with the oars they had. Wanquan's oars were his manliness.

Kim's cheeks had gone all red, and I knew why. It was the first time a young man had ever paid attention to her, and it obviously didn't leave her cold. She had attracted somebody's notice, even if he *was* only a peasant. The future wasn't completely black . . .

PART THREE

1974

Even a candle
bears a fiery heart
and weeps red pearls
ere the parting embrace

Du Mu, Ninth Century AD

A STRANGER IN THE HOUSE

It was nearly that time again – in two days, the Chinese New Year would be rung in with cannonades of fireworks. According to the lunar calendar, it was the twenty-eighth day of the twelfth month of the year 2,876 – or something like that, anyway. I wasn't sure exactly, because more than a decade before my birth, the CPC had banned the lunar calendar, spurning it as an undesirable leftover of the feudal system under the emperors. Which meant that almost all the traditions and customs that had been tied to this calendar for centuries were banished in one fell swoop. Only the celebration of the Chinese New Year was still allowed. Chinese New Year was also known as the Spring Festival because it ushered in the birth and blossoming of the new year; it signified the expiration of last year's bad luck and the hailing of next year's good fortune; it meant the reconciliation of old enemies and the forging of new friendships. It was also a time to look back on the preceding year; the spirits of the ancestors were invited to pass judgement on their descendants' accomplishments. It went without saying that the living tried very hard to jolly their ancestors into a favourable mood, so that in the coming year they would continue to protect them and give them guidance. That was why the ancestors were buttered up with freshly-baked sweet rolls that were put out for them on the family altar. Even though it was February, the coldest month of the year, with bitterly freezing temperatures and a biting wind, the doors were kept open, so that the spirits could waltz in and out at any time. I remembered that my grandma in Qingdao had told me that the spirits couldn't open the door for themselves – their hands no longer had the strength.

Old debts had to be paid off now, because everyone wanted to start off the new year with a clean slate. No wonder that, before the founding of the People's Republic of China – when hogging private property was not yet against the law – tenants who had failed to pay their rent would flee to the mountains, so that their creditors couldn't catch them.

It was also a time for bathing. Second- and third-casters, who didn't have bathing or showering facilities at home, flocked to the public baths in droves. They forked out over fifteen fen for the privilege, enough to buy over two pounds of cornmeal; it was an expensive business, this bathing racket, and they could only afford it twice a year at most. Outside the gates of the public baths snaked endless queues of people who just *had* to take a shower in the week leading up to the New Year. There was no question of doing it any earlier or later, when the baths were much less crowded, because then you wouldn't be spotless for the holidays.

Housewives stayed up until the early hours sewing new clothes for the entire family; young and old had to be neat as a pin. Good food was also part of it, for sure; from the crack of dawn until the dead of night you could hear pigs and cows bellowing their last – it was to all intents and purposes the only time of year when the villagers had meat on their plates. Neither expense nor effort was spared: nothing was too extravagant. Sweets were taken out of the locked cupboard and displayed on the table; fruit appeared, not just on the altar, but in fruit bowls intended for mortal consumers as well.

Not a single cross word was tolerated during this time. Only good wishes and pleasantries were permitted. If only for that godsend alone, the Chinese New Year was a concept even the youngest children could grasp; they recognised it as the time when there was a rare abundance of food and when, for once, the adults' faces seemed happy and at peace.

Father had come home a month and a half earlier, when I had been away on my Commune of the Five Red Stars internship. When I first spotted him sitting in the living room, I almost cried out, 'Thief!'

It was weird: for all those years, I had been longing for his return. But now that he was home, I wasn't too thrilled about it. In the first place, I didn't feel at ease having a man around the house. I was used to living with Mother and now suddenly here was this wildly alien male grown-up hanging around. No traipsing out of the bathroom without any clothes on any more; I had to lock the door when I used the toilet; I couldn't toss my underwear into a corner of the sofa if I felt like it. When Father stroked me over the head, it set my teeth on edge. And, worst of all: I wasn't the centre of attention any more. Whenever Father brought home a special treat, like new clothes, or pastries, he divided everything fairly between Mother and myself. Before, everything had always been for me.

What bothered me the most were the constant misunderstandings. Last night, for instance, Father had pushed a newspaper clipping into my hand and said, 'You'll probably be interested in this news item.'

It was about an eleven-year-old student who was so good at maths that he was ready to go to university. What did Father mean? That I was a nitwit compared to that snot-nosed punk? That I should be working harder? I threw the clipping down on the table in a huff and snapped, 'What a pity *you* don't have a smart son like that one!'

He looked at me, startled and bewildered.

Mother observed our silent war with distress in her eyes, but when she tried to intervene, I acted as if there was no need. 'Nothing's the matter. Really. I love Papa and he loves me. Who said we have to *show* it all the time?'

Father had returned to Beijing for good. In accordance with Mao's directive number 28, the most important public institutions, of which Father's hospital was one, were to be repatriated to the capital. Father was part of an advance contingent of fifty workers who were supposed to make everything ready for the return of the rest of the staff. In theory, this was great news – the family was reunited.

It wasn't long before I realised that the privileges I had always enjoyed in the past as a first-caster and member of a doctor's family were about to start tumbling into my lap once more.

⌒

Father took out two tickets for the New Year's Gala and put them down on the table. The gala was held in the capital's ritziest building, which was therefore the ritziest building in the entire country – the Palace of the People, in Tiananmen Square. Before the Cultural Revolution we had been presented with tickets to the gala every year. It was always the same people who were invited – pot-bellied party bosses, stern-looking army brass, swank government bigwigs, all accompanied by their plump wives and spoiled kids. The entertainment that was offered was always the same. I wasn't exactly dying to go.

But Mother was over the moon: this perk showed that her husband had been totally reinstated and that the CPC no longer considered her family a bunch of counter-revolutionary and bourgeois-minded cow-devils and snake-demons: if you were politically suspect, you weren't welcome there.

Father said, 'It's just as well I got only two tickets, because I wouldn't know what to do with the third. You go, and take Lian. I don't feel like seeing so many people at once.' He was still suffering from culture shock, now that he had been thrown back into Beijing after years in the sparsely populated desert. His ears hurt from the noise in the streets and he got dizzy whenever he found himself wedged between walls of people.

Mother raised her eyebrows. 'Are you kidding? Me? Go to that high-faluting gala? Go and have fun with those big wheels who sent me to re-education camp and let my child waste away in a youth camp? As far as I'm concerned, those two-faced party hacks who impose Marxism on others while leading the most decadently bourgeois lives they can dream up for themselves can just go and celebrate the New Year in one of their own reform camps!'

'Come now,' Father tried to mollify her, 'can't you forget about camp and let bygones be bygones? Let's just turn over a new page and forget old grudges. It *is* the New Year, after all.'

'Me? Bear grudges? Of course not! But that doesn't mean I have to go over there and add insult to injury, does it? Let's just give the tickets back. Lian can hardly go by herself—'

'Are you crazy? This is a token of recognition from my work unit. If I turn down these tickets, they won't ever offer me anything special again.'

'But who can we give them to, then? Only government officials at Level G or above qualify for this kind of invitation. My colleagues aren't even at Level D. Where am I going to find suitable candidates?'

Suddenly I had an idea. Without beating about the bush, I said: 'You don't have to worry about it. I'll take Kim, that way I won't be going alone.'

Mother looked at her husband with bated breath, because she could see what was coming. Father frowned. 'Who is this Kim? It isn't that guttersnipe you used to do homework with, is it?'

Mother rushed to my defence: 'Watch your tongue. You're talking about Lian's best friend.'

Father, noticing my rising indignation, started back-pedalling, 'Lian, it's not that I forbid you to go around with third-casters. After all, you are fourteen years old. But people will start noticing who you hang out with, and in the long run . . .'

His spouse had to laugh: 'Come now! Surely you don't mean that as our daughter gets closer to a marriageable age, it will devalue her to appear in the company of people who are below her station? Lian is only fourteen! She's not an adult yet, surely. Let her do what she wants!'

Mother was tackling the situation with kid gloves; she was waiting to make sure that I wouldn't go into a fit over Father's scornful attitude towards Kim. Only then did she say carefully, 'Actually, Papa does have a point. Only first-casters are invited to the gala. How can Kim possibly go?'

'Don't you remember that Qianyun once took her country nephew to the gala? He wasn't even from a peasant-labourer's family like Kim, he came from one hundred per cent peasant-farmer stock! And yet did anyone bat an eyelid?'

They could not find much to argue with that. Mother said, 'Okay, okay, but make sure Kim always stays close. And if people ask who she is, just tell them she's your sister.'

That got up Father's nose. 'Well, well, how nice for Lian, to have a sister like that one.'

The stay in the desert seemed to have made Father more class-conscious than ever. He must really have had his nose rubbed in the many ways counter-revolutionary intellectuals had been vilified and the proletarians glorified in their place. Now that the revolutionary class system was being quietly repudiated and replaced by the age-old caste system, he had some serious catching up to do: he had to despise others the way he had been despised himself when he had been a bourgeois-leaning snake-demon. Oddly enough, on Mother it had had the reverse effect: she now nursed an implacable distaste for class and caste differences.

I told Kim the news on the day before Chinese New Year. At first she didn't understand what I was talking about, but when it finally did penetrate, she didn't dare even consider it. She was sure that she could never be involved in anything as grand as that. I pulled out all the stops to convince her, but Kim was scared out of her wits at the thought of all those revellers making fun of her.

'But no one will know who you are,' I said, 'there are thousands of guests; who will bother to look twice at a girl called Kim?'

Finally a long-stifled smile rose to Kim's lips. She laughed soundlessly, just as she had a year ago, when she had spotted, on her report card, the first passing grades she had ever had.

A SEAT ON THE BUS

At six o'clock on the dot, we were at the bus stop of the special bus service provided by Father's hospital. The sun and the wind were leaving orange smears in the steel-blue sky. The streaks were startling – if a painter were to try to copy them, no one would ever believe him, for who'd have thought clouds could take on such magical shapes and hues? With Kim beside me, looking forward to the gala that was to be *the* highpoint of Kim's life, waiting for the special bus that was to drive us straight to the palace, I was in seventh heaven.

I couldn't help ruminating about what the experience of taking a bus was normally like. Elbowing your way on to a municipal bus was like battling another drowning soul for a piece of driftwood in the Pacific Ocean; it could be a life-or-death struggle, literally, and required a cut-throat ruthlessness.

My musings were cut short by Kim, who grabbed me by the elbow and dragged me out of my place in line. Pointing at the approaching bus, Kim yelled, 'Quick, or we'll never get on!' Her voice sounded shrill and off-key with excitement, drawing all eyes on us.

I looked around; we were the only ones standing out in the road in front of the bus stop. Feeling the stares of the waiting passengers drilling into my back, I tugged at Kim's arm to get her to return to our original place in the queue. But that was a mistake. First of all, Kim was many times stronger than me – to budge her, you'd need the muscle to uproot a hundred-year-old oak with your bare hands. Second, once Kim was set on something, not even a bulldozer could nudge her to change her mind. I whispered into her ear, 'Listen to me, Kim! This isn't a regular bus. Look at all the people politely waiting their turn. Nobody needs to worry about not getting on. That's why they call it "Special Service" . . .'

Kim let go of my arm, somewhat abashed. But she wasn't about to throw in the towel: 'All right, but it's still better to be the first ones on the bus. That way we're sure to get a seat, see?'

I had to keep myself from laughing: 'But there are enough seats to go around.'

'Really?' Kim looked at the snaking queue sceptically, not entirely trusting my calculations. 'For *this* many passengers?'

I pointed triumphantly at two other buses that had rolled up behind the first. Now it was Kim's turn to be speechless. But I immediately felt contrite. All Kim had ever known was the regular public bus, which as a rule transported at least twice the maximum number of passengers allowed by law.

As soon as Kim had chosen her seat, she tried sticking her fingers out of the window. Next she stood up and sat down again twice in a row to test the leather seat, which was as bouncy as a haystack. When she was done with that, she shut her eyes and began humming an improvised, indistinct little tune.

I was happy for Kim, but I was also stumped; I hardly knew which way was up any more. It was only a month and a half since our thirty-day internship, in which we were supposed to have had it drummed into us that peasants were the true leaders of the nation; and now here was one of the daughters of that same leadership class being given a glimpse of her worthless inferiors – meaning the highest caste, of course – living high on the hog.

'Look, stars!' Kim had opened her eyes again and was pointing at the tall buildings and wide avenues that were festively lit with neon lights. I looked up: the sky was clouded over. But I understood what Kim meant. There were no street lamps in the mud-house quarter. The only lights one saw there at night were the stars in the sky. Here the boulevards themselves glittered like the firmament. Kim, on her cushioned seat, swung her spindly legs from side to side like a contented baby that has just been put to the breast.

UNCOMMON PLEASURES

At the entrance to the Palace of the People we had to walk through a metal detector that would start squealing with menacing bleeps every so often. When it did so, the people were asked to empty their pockets and open their handbags; in most cases, out would come a big bunch of keys that had triggered the alarm. Kim sidled through the scanner on tiptoe; the alarm co-operated and kept quiet. Her face lit up – if she had had her way, she would have gone back through another time. Her relief at not being fingered was boundless, considering that at school she was always picked on, no matter where she was going or how careful she was to avoid attracting attention. She smirked diabolically at me, like a devil who just happens to have got away with murder this time. I could not bring myself to smile; it embarrassed me to see how something as simple as that could send Kim over the moon. Eyes downcast, I marched inside, leaving Kim standing there all by herself, still obviously tickled to death by her 'close call'. Kim hurried in after me.

Out of the great hall's loudspeakers came a song that had been banned for ages:

> *Butterflies love flowers*
> *Flowers like nothing better*
> *than to be touched by butterflies*

Ever since the beginning of the Cultural Revolution, playing this kind of music had carried a mandatory six-month jail sentence!

Just ahead of me, I spotted a slim pair of legs encased in gleaming stockings. When I looked a little higher, I was thrown: the owner of these underpinnings was wearing a traditional Shanghai-style dress that accentuated her well-rounded buttocks, slender back and sensual arms. Kim gave my hand an urgent tug. I tried to silence her with a look that spoke volumes. It said, Here, in this palace for the Party élite, what is bourgeois is admirable, and what's proletarian is deplorable. You are just going to have to pretend tonight that Heaven and Earth have traded places.

Colourful balloons and garlands girded the marble pillars; the chandeliers' crystal pendants cast an evocative lacework of light over the shiny floors; love-songs drifted through the perfumed air; the gallant gestures of the gentlemen and the ladies' seductive smiles put the finishing touches to the romantic mood. Within a few seconds Kim and I had surrendered our ideological resistance. What we had been taught about Capitalist decadence was diametrically opposed to what we saw here with our own eyes. Lightly we tripped to the ballrooms, where all sorts of amusements awaited us.

The first game Kim chose to play was Dry-Angler. Displayed on a table were dozens of toy animals, each with a little hook screwed into its head. The object was to fish for them by means of a thin pole – the fishing rod. There was a long line, and Kim had already had two turns. But she wouldn't budge. By hook or by crook she was going to win a prize.

'*Ki-i-im*, there are another eight rooms in this building, with dozens of games set up in each one of them. If you keep hanging around here, you'll never get to see even a fourth of the entire palace by the time we have to go home. Is that what you want?'

Kim looked at me incredulously. She evidently still couldn't grasp the idea that she had been plunged into an infinite sea of pleasure. Grumbling, she reluctantly followed me to the next game – this turned out to be Tug-of-War. Kim's eyes immediately lit up, glittering: she spat into both hands, for good luck and a good grip. As was to be expected, her side won. The prize was a bilious-green bath towel for every victorious player. Kim played the game over and over again until she had won a towel for every member of her family. The referee slapped Kim heartily on the back. If it were up to him, this little girl would never call it quits. They had become great chums. Kim beamed every time he counselled a new player in a stage whisper, 'If you choose this girl's side, you can decide right now what colour towel you'd like to have!' She had become the centre of attention.

Finally she skipped over to me with four towels under her arm, her eyes glassy with bliss. I immediately led her to a room called *Wine of the Poets*. Here stood tables laden with pastries, savoury snacks and drinks. I wanted to surprise Kim; the abundance of treats on offer would blow her mind. But at first, Kim stubbornly refused to go in: 'Come on, Lian, let's just play some more games. I already ate.'

'But it's after ten. You've been in four tugs-of-war and three other games. Don't you feel like having a little snack?'

Kim looked at the tables and glared angrily at me. It was like asking a famished wolf if he might like a little lamb. Only now did I notice Kim fumbling in her pockets.

'Oh, so *that's* it! Don't worry, everything's free here.'

The higher up the social ladder one was, it seemed, the less one had to pay. Even though the Party big shots did not, on the face of it, earn very much more than the common people – did the Helmsman not trumpet the concept of equality and fairness for all – they did enjoy all sorts of fringe benefits as a substitute for hard cash. They received vouchers for meat, clothes, bicycles and watches, so that they would not have to purchase those goods on the black market; they were driven around in cars belonging to their work units and didn't have to pay a fen for the privilege; and they were invited to dinners and parties where they had ample opportunity to stuff their faces.

In the queue for the bar, Kim was ahead of me. Her eyes were popping out of her head: those triangular wedges – she had never seen *cake* before, let alone tasted any – the rainbow of drinks, the extravagant titbits . . . she devoured them all with her eyes, lost in a delightful dream.

Suddenly she heard a deep voice booming: 'Mademoiselle, please, after you.'

Kim looked around to find the person to whom the dapper young gentleman standing there was talking. There didn't seem to be any mademoiselle fitting the description. She shrugged her shoulders – she must have misheard.

'Please, mademoiselle, you first. You must be thirsty.'

Kim shook her head incredulously when she realised this charming young gentleman was addressing *her*. She stared at him without blinking.

I was embarrassed for her; I whispered, 'Say thank you and take a glass of lemonade, hurry up!'

The statue that was Kim was rooted so deep in the ground that it obviously could not be budged, but the young man went on smiling at her politely. He sent her a look that meant, If you *don't* want to go first, that's also fine with me. I was only offering.

Trying to be as nonchalant as possible about it, I slipped out of the line, dragging Kim along with me. Kim followed me like a robot. I didn't dare look back. The young gentleman must think we were a pair of weirdos.

When we reached a quiet corner, Kim rolled her eyes – she was melting with rapture. 'Did you hear that, Lian Shui, he called me "mademoiselle"!'

I was worried that Kim might think he fancied her. That would mean a rude awakening for Kim, because at this sort of event, the young men tended to treat everyone with exaggerated courtesy. But no, Kim was beaming like a toddler who has just learned to ride a tricycle, while gazing, starry-eyed, at her own Sunday-best clothes. Did she really look like a first-caster? Was there no way the people here could tell she was the classroom punching bag? She twirled around, her arms spread out like an angel stretching its wings before returning to Heaven. She looked back at the palace entry hallway and up at the ceiling, where the crystal chandeliers had stencilled the most intricate designs. Here, inside the four walls of this magical edifice, Kim felt herself safe. She didn't have to be afraid of being recognised by anybody; here she wasn't the schoolroom laughing-stock; here she was no longer the daughter of an impoverished peasant; here people assumed that everyone belonged to the élite and treated each other accordingly; here Kim was automatically accepted by everyone else. There was no question of Kim's having any fantasies about that handsome young man's amorous intentions: she had no illusions on that score.

So there we were, in the Palace of the People in Tiananmen Square, surrounded by luxury, the 'wealth of the proletariat' or whatever you were supposed to call it. We gazed into each other's eyes, and our giggles wrapped us in a wreath of giddy zest and delight.

We went skipping from room to room, no longer in search of any particular game, but simply enjoying it all at random. We basked in the unaccustomed atmosphere of freedom and levity. From time to time, in my elated state, it would suddenly strike me how Kim's wizened old-man's face was scored with laughter-lines. Some day, when Kim had enough to eat, she would surely start looking more filled-out; I was certain of it. I twirled around and let this conviction sink deep into my heart, my head, my entire being. Right now, in this fairy-tale palace, everything was possible and everything seemed simple to achieve.

THE POWER OF TABOO

As planned, Kim spent the night at my house. My parents would not allow Kim to walk home by herself in the middle of the night. We padded into the flat on tiptoe, but Father heard us; he had stayed up specially to wait for us. He entered my room in his striped pyjamas and whispered, 'Had fun? Played hard? You're probably all sweaty, right? Mama has heated up water for the shower and the bathroom radiator is on. Be careful and try not to make any noise. She is asleep.'

I closed the door behind Father's back and said to Kim, 'You go take a shower. I didn't sweat as much as you tonight, but I *am* very tired. I'll just brush my teeth here at the sink and then get straight into bed.'

Kim rubbed her hands over her sticky face and stood there dithering. On the one hand she'd love to take a good hot shower, but on the other hand she didn't trust it. There must be a snake in the grass somewhere – the fact that you could bathe at home was, in her eyes, pretty incredible in itself, enough to give you the chills. And then to be left to her fate all alone in that swanky, cavernous bathroom – who knew what sort of spine-tingling horror awaited her in there? She said, 'If you don't come, I'm not taking a shower either.'

My tiredness turned to irritation on the spot: 'Kim, I know you hardly ever get the chance to bathe . . . Oh, I'm sorry, I didn't mean to offend you, I didn't mean it that way, you know that, don't you? Still, here's your chance, finally, to take a shower, and you're prepared to just let it scoot away!'

But mule-headed Kim was getting ready to crawl into bed. At my wits' end, I copped my last plea: 'There's only one shower head and it's very cramped in the stall . . .'

Kim hurled her blanket on to the bed and glared at me as if to say: If you don't want to come, then just say so; don't give me any lame excuses. Suddenly I saw where Kim's indignation was coming from. In the public baths, it was the most natural thing in the world to share a single shower-head with as many as four others. You didn't have the luxury of being too prudish to parade nude before hordes of people. My drowsiness evaporated like magic. I would get such a kick out of seeing Kim take a shower in a private bathroom. So I said, 'Okay, I'm coming with you.'

The radiator must have been on for an hour at least, because a blast of hot air met us as we entered the bathroom. Kim pushed the only stool over to me, so I could sit while undressing. Kim herself remained standing; she tore her clothes off in a flash, hanging them on a hook behind the door. Then she checked out the shower, wondering if she could turn it on herself, and, if so, how. In the end she looked back at me, impatient for me to be done . . .

Acute embarrassment turned up the heat another notch. My face and my entire body were aflame. Funny, this was even worse than the time Liqiang had stared at me on that unforgettable Sunday morning; yet Kim was just a girl. How could that be? With my hands clutched across my chest – I was still wearing my undershirt – I hastened to turn on the shower for Kim.

Shaaaa! Water jets have no eyes. I wasn't undressed yet – and they drenched me from top to toe. The thin underwear clung to my skin, mercilessly emphasising each little curve and detail of my body.

'Ha-ha! Look at you! You look like a chicken that's hopped into the soup pot by accident! I was just going to warn you to take off your clothes before turning on the tap . . .'

Suddenly Kim's words froze on her lips. Her eyes slithered along the ins and outs of my body . . .

For a few endless seconds Kim stood there immobile, staring boldly at me. I felt my body parts rising and falling; I was only too conscious of my own shape. Quite independent of the inner world of my thoughts in which I had been wallowing all my life, it was becoming increasingly clear that this outer 'fleshy frame' of mine had a mind all *its* own. Without my needing to say, or think, or do anything, that frame, now ripe and womanly, could send its own message to others, and send them into a tailspin . . .

Shhhaaaah . . . The sound of the water-jets jolted us back to reality. Kim plunged right in. I had to peel the sopping-wet clothes off my body first and then there I was, bare before the one to whom I had lost my heart. Should I bend over, as if soaping myself, or just stand tall? I could not decide whether I should be ashamed of my body, or, on the contrary, proud of it. It was Kim's reaction that was the clincher. From the faltering little air that Kim was humming, I could see that my friend, too, had come unglued. One moment she would peek greedily at me as if she wanted to gobble me up, skin, hair and all; the next she'd look all nonchalant, as if to say: What are you *thinking* of . . . ? I'm only taking a shower here, that's all. Hurry up, otherwise it'll be even later before we get to bed.

I found myself sneaking furtive looks at my friend's body too. Kim's ribcage looked like a washboard; her joints were the fattest part of her body; her skin was just like a length of yellow kitchen paper: rough, creased and remarkably absorbent. Water-drops from the shower beaded the surface of my skin, whereas Kim's body sucked up the water like a sponge. The urge to wrap my rounded arms around Kim's skinny form was almost irresistible. I had to take a couple of deep breaths to stop myself from giving in to the impulse. Maternal instinct? Or was it something else . . . ?

Quietly we shut the bedroom door. Spontaneously, without a word, as if we had already given this audacious move long and hard thought before-hand, we pushed the two single beds together to create one big bed.

When I went to lie down in bed, I was as wound up as a piano wire. Kim lay down next to me, equally tense and stiff. We stayed like that for a long, impenetrable silence. I could not think straight. In vain I tried to concentrate, to try to figure out what Kim was feeling or thinking at that moment. After what seemed an eternity, Kim turned towards me and placed her hand softly on my stomach. I held my breath and didn't dare move a muscle. I was trying to figure out what Kim was after. But then Kim was probably wondering the same thing about me.

It got to the point where I had held myself rigid for so long that Kim's courage flushed itself down the drain. Finally she gave me a reproachful jab in the ribs. It wasn't a real rebuke, of course – it was, rather, a show of affection. No . . . it was more than that. Kim was curbing her desire to caress me, because she felt guilty about it. For her desire was clearly taboo.

Kim broke the painful silence. 'Come on, tell me something ...' She turned on to her right side and looked deep into my eyes, 'about your life in prison camp. I've never asked you about it.'

I was startled. 'What is there to say? It's a closed book. A lovely book, true, but it's all over and done with. I am back now. I belong in the city, to this life of freedom, with people my own age.'

'What did you say? What did you mean, lovely? Wasn't it like being in prison?'

'That wasn't the only thing. Or maybe just not for me. I had the best teachers there, in every subject, they were all professors and college instructors. I was spoiled rotten there. Professor Qin was the best history teacher you could ever wish for, and I was spoiled rotten by Aunt Maly, my English teacher, and by Uncle Cannibal ...'

'Cannibal? What kind of name is that?'

'That was his nickname. But he was the sweetest man in the whole wide world.'

'You were lucky.'

'You can say that again. Well, of course there were some bad things that happened there as well. After all, it wasn't exactly an amusement park or anything.'

'What sort of things?'

'They ... they weren't nice to people, sometimes they were very mean, and to the animals too.'

'But isn't that normal, wherever you go?' Kim rolled her eyes up to the ceiling. 'Where would you find people being *kind* to each other?'

'Still, it was different from at school, even in the way they treat you, for instance.'

'What do you mean?'

'Well, all the punks in our class do is kick you in the bum, that's all. In the camp the guards were much meaner, they messed with people in a real grown-up way. There was a doctor of psychology, a very nice man, and they called him "the Pink Pig", just because he was a little pudgy. And then, in full view of hundreds of prisoners, they made him dance on bags of fertiliser to break up the lumps. The guards howled with laughter, like a pack of hyenas.'

Kim remained quiet as a mouse. I could hear her swallowing, that was all. It was very chilly in the room.

I paused. I looked the other way and said, 'Let's go to sleep. I'll tell you more another time. Do you mind?'

Kim poked her head underneath my folded arms and nestled herself against my shoulder. Suddenly I was no longer afraid.

~

A flood of morning light penetrated the net curtains, which were fluttering softly in the wind. It was only now that I realised that I had forgotten to close the heavy drapes last night. Sunbeams the colour of peaches, smocked and tatted by the embroidered netting, painted the room with a flourish of floral designs – quite a change from the neat, angular lines I was used to.

Next to me someone else was waking up. Kim propped herself up on her elbow to look at me. I felt her gaze, but pretended to be asleep. I had a pretty good idea of what Kim was seeing: in the morning my cheeks were always tinged pink with sleep. My lips were probably red, my face soft and perhaps even ... tender ... Now why was I thinking that?

Kim's warm breath came nearer. I was so hoping that Kim's face would touch mine! My face was on fire. But just as it was about to happen, the fear that had retired for the night came back with a vengeance. It clutched me by the throat with such vigour that I almost suffocated. My eyes flew open. The dream was shattered. *A blind little giraffe with a broken neck was staring at her.*

Kim lay down again; we began to talk. About school and the looming exams. We were two ordinary chums again, as if nothing had gone on between us.

Kim said, 'Weren't you going to tell me about prison camp?'

I wasn't about to be let off the hook. And I suddenly knew exactly which story I had to tell Kim, no matter how hard it might be for me.

'A couple of days before Spring Festival,' I began, 'it was decided we'd all go to the village of Taohua Zhen, where there was a big new-year's market. It was six miles away, and we had to get up very early ...' I shivered. I could still feel the rutted, frozen lane beneath my feet. '... After a mile or so our feet started to ache, but that didn't spoil our excitement in the least. The prospect of shopping for the big holiday, and of a four-day furlough, kept us going.' I waved my hands overhead, as if to ward off the snowflakes drifting down from the slate-blue sky. I stuck my fingers into my ears. 'We can already hear the firecrackers, so it shouldn't be far now ...'

I had completely forgotten where I was. I could see the events of that day before me as clear as glass. My eyes glazed over ...

SKINNY BUT TENDER

'Just stay close to me,' Mother had warned me, 'the place is swarming with strangers.'

The deafening shouts of the hawkers extolling their wares and buyers haggling over the price, the exploding firecrackers, the bright yellow clothing of the peasants' wives and their children, the garish new year's prints, all cheered up the barren winter landscape. There was too much to look at and listen to; I could have used more eyes and ears in my head.

Eeya-eeeya! I dragged Mother over to see the donkey.

'Just a minute, my love. Mother first has to buy some eggs. Then we'll go look at the livestock together. Agreed?'

'De-li-ca-tes-sen for the new year's feast: frrresh monkey meat!' a heavy-set vendor was bawling from a street corner.

'Mama, hear that? That rotten bastard is selling monkey meat!'

'Shh! Come on, let's go to the livestock.'

Wow, what a crowd had gathered around the monkey vendor! It was like a circus. I crouched down low, so that I could work my way to the front by slipping beneath the grown-ups' arms. There were four cages, with two monkeys in each one.

'Freshly caught in the mountains! My brother knows exactly where to find the monkey families hiding out in their hollow trees! So – how about this for a treat to ring in the new year? What could be better than a delicious plate of red-roasted monkey filet?' The salesman was drooling at the mouth. His eyes trailed over the crowd, trying to ferret out any potential customers.

'How much?' asked an elderly woman with a straw basket on her arm.

'Special deal for you: three yuan a pound!'

'Hey, mister, just go wash your kids' nappies! You might as well pack up and go home; there isn't a dog at this market that's prepared to pay through the nose like that for your shoddy goods. Look at those pitiful bags of bones! There's twice as much gristle there as there's meat, there is. Three yuan a pound! You must be dreaming! Did you think it was juicy human flesh you were selling, or something?'

'Come now, eldest sister, don't you go around badmouthing my wares! The monkeys may seem a little skimpy to you, but their meat is as soft as butter. They're really just babies, you know. My brother waited until their mother left the tree to find food; then he ransacked the nest. Still, it is almost the New Year, after all, and seeing that I wouldn't mind going home a little earlier, two yuan a pound, then.'

'One.'

'One and a half.'

'It's a deal.'

He picked up a kettle of boiling water from a small stove behind him and asked, 'Which one do you want?'

'The plumpest one, there.' The woman pointed to a scared-looking monkey in one of the cages.

'Done in a jiffy.' The vendor poured the boiling water over the little brown monkey, which immediately uttered a torrent of heart-rending cries: 'Tyeeah-tyeeah!' A cloud of steam rose up from it as the scalding water dripped down its fur. Its face contorted and its little arms and legs convulsed with spasms of pain. The screeching was unbearable to listen to. 'Eeey-eeee!' was the sound that came out of its pinched throat. Finally, frantically, it began tearing out the hair on its body, crying and screaming for help all the while. Tears rolled down its already depilated chest. As it plucked the rest of its body clean at a furious rate, a hairless, pink little body was revealed. Within a few minutes it was stripped naked from top to toe, a groaning, weeping little red monkey.

That was exactly what the monkey-vendor had had in mind – to save himself the trouble of skinning the little thing himself.

When it realised that tearing out its fur hadn't done a thing to relieve the pain, the baby monkey began to tear at its own skin. Now the vendor sprang to life, because a shredded ape was a worthless ape. He opened the cage, laid the screaming monkey on the cutting board and chopped it – ktch, ktch – into three pieces. Then he wrapped the little corpse in an old newspaper.

'Four pounds, that's six yuan. Enjoy your meal, eldest sister.'

'Who'd like to share a monkey with me? I and my Ought-To-Be-Lynched-With-A-Thousand-Stab-Wounds will never be able to finish a whole one of these between the two of us,' a young man was asking the bystanders.

'I will,' an old man answered him.

The monkey that had shared a cage with the previous victim banged its head into the bars, wept and pleaded for mercy. It covered its eyes with its tender little fingers, as if that would save it from having to witness its own wretched fate.

The blood rose to my head; my skull felt as if it were about to explode with fury. I flew at the vendor, kicked over his kettle of boiling water and milled my arms around like a lunatic. I had no idea where I got the nerve, but I was screaming, 'Police! Police! Arrest this assassin! Over here! Uncles and aunts, don't you see what a murderer he is? Help me please, we have got to arrest him! Butcher me if you must, if you absolutely can't get through the New Year without pigging out on monkey meat!'

Stinging tears turned everything into a blur and suddenly everything went numb . . .

*   *   *

266

Kim wrapped her arms around me and wept along in sympathy. We warmed each other with our bodies; nothing could come between us ever again.

~

After breakfast Kim wanted to go straight home; she claimed there was much to do at home, on this second day of the new year.

I walked her out in silence. At the campus gate Kim took my hands in hers and said, 'This was the best day of my life.' And she laughed mutely. As did I.

AN UNUSUAL REUNION

When I returned home, I found the living room full of people. Mother was pacing around like a wall-eyed beetle and the others were smoking or wringing their hands. I had a hard time understanding what was going on at first. I was still under the spell of the glamour and glitz of the gala festivities of the night before, and frowned on seeing this grubby, raggedy crew.

My disconcertion didn't last more than a second, however. I shouted, 'Uncle Qin! Aunt Maly! Uncle Director Gao! Uncle Fu! What a surprise! What a gift from Buddha this is, to see you all again!'

At this, the entire company turned towards me. They smiled – but only fleetingly. Too fleetingly, strangely fleetingly. I grabbed Qin around the waist and rubbed my face against his jacket. The smell brought back the memory of the dusty lanes, the endless fields of crops and the steel-blue sky over the camp.

Qin pushed my head away and said, 'Aren't you going to greet your other uncles and aunts?'

Reluctantly I disentangled myself from the familiar warmth of the leathery old historian and offered myself, arms open wide, to Aunt Maly.

Maly took my face in her rough, parched hands. 'It does me a power of good to see that the younger generation is spared the ordeal of the camp.'

I beheld Maly's kind eyes, her sallow but delicate features; Aunt Maly gazed at me with a look filled with nostalgia and caressed my cheeks as if they were the leaves of a water lily. Both of us were speechless for a moment.

When I saw Director Gao, I didn't know what to do. He had been so kind to me, and then, how could he have . . . ? Poor Ahuang . . . All eyes were on me. I greeted him politely but diffidently, and turned to Fu as soon as I decently could. Uncle Fu was the only one who was sitting down. He was seated like a secretary, pen poised. I gave him an awkward hug and turned round – what was going on, anyway? What were they all doing here? What was Fu writing?

As if my arrival hadn't caused any interruption, Professor Qin started speaking again. He dictated: 'The faithful servant of the Communist Party, our revolutionary comrade-in-arms Changshan Luo . . .' He looked questioningly at the camp Director. 'Is it permitted to call a prisoner "revolutionary"? I certainly hope so, because . . . because this may be the last time that we can honour this exceptionally worthy man . . .' *Chooo!* He blew his nose and looked the other way.

My knees buckled under me. I looked from one sad face to the other. What the hell was this? I wanted to scream, He isn't dead, is he? Uncle Cannibal hasn't passed away, has he? I shook my head, then tossed it back and looked up at the ceiling. I started to pray . . . No, Uncle, please! Not before we've said goodbye!

I flung myself at Qin and demanded, 'He's still alive, isn't he? He is still conscious, he can still talk, right? I *know* he can.'

Qin pulled me to my feet and gently patted me on the back. 'Shush, calm down. What did you think we'd be writing this letter for, if Uncle Cannibal wasn't able to read it? In a little while we're all going to go and visit him together, and then we'll read it to him, to let him know that we—'

Maly interrupted, 'Fine . . . but let's just hope he'll still be able to hear us.'

'I'm going. All right, Mama?' I grabbed my winter coat from the coat rack and yanked open the front door.

'Wait! We haven't finished the letter yet!' Mother ran after me.

'Yunxiang, let her go. What's the point of her staying with us? Cannibal is waiting for her.' Qin's voice suddenly sounded startlingly clear.

But Mother ignored Qin's advice and ripped off my overcoat.

I went wild. I tugged at my coat. When I saw that I could not pull it out of Mother's hands, I tore outside without it.

WHITE LUCK

I ran all the way to Hospital Number 14 and tried to find the corner ward on the second floor. It was as if I had come this way at least ten times before – in a dream, perhaps? In any case, I knew exactly where to find Cannibal.

Outside his room I came to a halt. The penetrating smell of disinfectant seeped through the cracks in the wooden door. The stench was so intense that it numbed all thought and feeling percolating in my head. Only one thought remained intact: how I could ever confront Cannibal's death, or his imminent death.

I knocked at the door and Aunt Xiulan's pale face appeared. 'Ha!' – a shrill cry broke from her throat. But then she quickly pinched her lips shut between her thumb and forefinger. A flush of excitement sprang to her cheeks; turning around, she flapped her hands behind her back – a signal to me to follow her.

I walked behind Aunt Xiulan to a white bed at the window, where dazzling sunbeams were stealing their way into the room. I had to squint not to be blinded by the light. The pronounced smell of ether must be having a cathartic effect on me – the closer I got to the bed, the calmer I grew.

'Shan! Look who has come!' Aunt shouted into Cannibal's ear.

In the bed lay a head, just a head, at least that's what it looked like. The contour of the rest of his body was difficult to make out, even through the pitifully thin sheet. Uncle had become a husk of a man! That's what he reminded me of: a peach whose flesh has rotted away until only the brown core was left. I had to stop myself from groaning. Oh no! My beloved father, teacher of enlightenment and dearest man on Earth, is nothing but a wraith! I sidled to the head of the bed.

Cannibal struggled to open his eyes when Aunt called out to him a second time. At first his glance was hazy, but gradually the mist was pushed aside like a curtain, until his clear pupils were visible. But soon his eyes glazed over again . . .

Under the covers something stirred. Aunt immediately understood and lifted the corner of the bedsheet: there was his right hand.

'Little Lian, don't you see, Uncle Changshan recognises you and wants to shake your hand?' Pressing her mouth up close to his ear, she said, 'That's all right, Shan. Lian understands that you want to greet her.' She dabbed at his eyes to dry them and turned to me: 'See how his ribcage is pumping up and down. He is gathering up all his breath and his strength in order to talk to you . . . You have no idea how often he's been *daonian*-ing about you . . .'

That was when I finally burst into tears. I pressed my face to the place where his hand lay trembling under the sheet. I could feel the iciness of his limbs right through the linen. I kissed the sheet, in the hope that my warmth would somehow flow over into his arteries.

A nurse tiptoed into the room and asked Aunt to step outside.

'Ehn, ehn . . .' I heard a weak echo of the voice I knew so well rebuking me, '. . . At New Year, no one is allowed to cry.' I looked up at him and saw a faint but beatific smile on his wasted face. I got up at once and put my lips to his ear: 'Uncle, do you still hate me?'

'Phooey, phooey!' he panted and nestled his face next to mine. 'My sunshine, my dear little Lian, where . . . where'd you get that idea? I have never hated you . . . only myself . . . My meditation master in the Temple of Qingyun told me . . . that the main purpose of my life's voyage is . . . to overcome the seven feelings . . . and the six desires . . . So you see, I have . . . I have not succeeded. Little Lian, my little star, you are too . . . too . . .' He was gasping for air.

My knees were knocking together. 'Uncle, don't talk so much – it's tiring you much too much!'

Cannibal, blinking his eyes rapidly, went on, 'Can you . . . will you, from now on, remember only the good things your uncle has done for you . . . and forgive him the rest? My Lian-naaah . . . I want to depart with a light heart—'

'*Of course* I forgive you! But, Uncle, tell me what I am supposed to forgive you for, and why? You are the best, the kindest person I have ever known. No, don't go, Uncle, please don't die.'

He rolled his head from left to right to conjure up the broadest smile he could: 'Lian, my sunshine, do you know what day it is, today? It is the New Year. Today I am reborn. In Nirvana I will see you whenever I want to. I'll never miss you again . . .'

For an instant I thought that he was referring to the fact that I had neglected to visit him for so long. I kowtowed before him: 'Uncle, won't you forgive my heartlessness?'

A tear as big as a grape rolled out of his eye. He said, 'Lian, your heart is purer than the morning dew on the lip of a flower . . . and more delicate than the stamen of the azalea. How can you talk about heartlessness?'

I flung my arms around his neck and kissed his feverish lips.

'*Hyemmm*,' he sighed. His eyes glistened.

When I got to my feet again, I sensed Aunt's presence behind me. Xiulan stroked my head and said, 'Now your Uncle can go to meet his ancestors with a heart that is at peace. Changshan, all my life I have blamed myself for not being able to give you even a single child. But at least you have our dear little Lian, who is like a daughter to us, standing by your deathbed today. Buddha is merciful . . .' She was crying unashamedly.

'Xiulan . . . The White Luck . . . don't you remember? Isn't that what they call dying? Smile, please, both of you. I . . . I want to engrave your happy faces into my mind . . .'

Aunt and I, our arms around each other, smiled at him through our tears. And strangely enough, I did feel truly happy. But it was apparently time to go. Aunt had to send me out: 'The nurse has given me his medications. I have to take care of Uncle.'

SILENT WITNESSES

The frosty-blue sky coldly kept its distance. The pallid sunlight could not win out over the icy wind. Uncle Cannibal had been dead a week, after sinking away, gently surrendering, quite simply, to the corrosion of his body. My teeth were chattering as I left home. It was only seven o'clock, too early yet for school. But I couldn't stand staying in bed a minute longer and had told Mother that I was going to review my English vocabulary outside, in the orchard.

The naked brown branches stood out razor-sharp against the pallid sky. They made me think of the fingers of a skeleton crawling out of a grave. I shuddered. Where on earth did that crazy notion suddenly come from? I kicked at a broken twig studded with prisms of glittering frost. The twig cracked beneath my feet, and suddenly I froze. I knew all too well what that vision meant. The nagging feeling bottled up inside my belly, that had been bothering me for days, but that I had been refusing to give in to, was about to erupt in the still, chill atmosphere. Last night I hadn't slept a wink – I kept seeing Uncle Cannibal's portrait, framed with a black ribbon, before me.

I flung myself on to the stiff, unyielding ground and all the sadness that had remained buried for days bubbled up to the surface, tied up in anger and questions. Why had fate taken away my Uncle Cannibal so soon, too soon, much too soon? Blowing puffs of warm breath into hands nearly numb with cold, I asked a naked peach tree, 'Why is Buddha the Merciful doing this to me?'

No answer.

I insisted, 'What's the point of being born, only to die again some day, forsaking the ones we love?' I was crying softly.

Nothing.

I turned to look at a pear tree a little further on, hoping this one would not remain mute like the other one: 'Uncle said, Death is the White Luck. But didn't he know that every little thing inside me, and in Aunt Xiulan, too, would crack into a hundred pieces, when he left us? Then why did he say it?'

This tree, too, kept its own counsel in every language known to man. But suddenly it didn't matter any more. I scrambled to my feet and heard myself say, 'Could it be that death is a blessing for the one who dies, even if it's a curse for those who are left behind? Could it be that Uncle Changshan has truly gone to a place that's sheer bliss, as he said he would?' Giving the trees a break, I lifted my eyes up at the dense white sky. 'Well? Is someone going to give me answer, yes or no? Uncle Cannibal, at least, always listened to me.'

Uncle Cannibal was gone for good, and all I had now was the silence of the trees.

AN UNPRECEDENTED DEVELOPMENT

It was only a quarter to eight, fifteen minutes before the beginning of class, but the classroom was already packed and noisy. We were at our assigned places, each seated according to our rank and caste. As we chattered away, our minds were on just one thing – our exam results. In the final year of the middle school, grades were of paramount importance in determining if a student would move up to the next level.

It was now five to eight.

Three minutes to.

I looked at the door impatiently: Kim still wasn't here. Did she not realise how important this day was for her, for me, for both of us? For years we had been preparing for this moment. And now that the day had finally arrived when we would see what fruit had come of our labours, it looked as if Kim wasn't going to come!

Nervously I looked out of the window. Aha! Now I knew why Kim wasn't here yet: it was raining as if Buddha had forgotten to turn off the tap. On days like this, Kim always dawdled, not setting out for school until the very last moment, risking being late for class, in the hope that the rain would stop just in time. Then she'd streak to school like a rocket. The one and only umbrella owned by the Zhang family was, naturally, the exclusive property of her sister Jiening. Not that Kim was afraid of getting wet – far from it. A little rain was nothing to her, tough and hard-nosed as she was. But the thing was, when she got to school, our classmates could never resist the opportunity of jeering at her: 'Look at that water-rat! Kim doesn't *need* a raincoat or an umbrella. She is *used* to swimming in the sewage ditch! Hahahaha!'

The cheapest umbrella cost almost two and a half kuai. Kim's mother would have to fold and paste thousands of matchboxes to get that much money together, which would take days – if she could convince the matchbox factory to provide her with that much work, that is. With that kind of money, you could buy at least twenty pounds of cornmeal, enough to feed a family of four for a whole week. Rather than squandering such a prodigious sum, Kim was more than willing to subject herself to some extra mockery and derision from her classmates. There wasn't a Chinaman's chance that she would ever dream of asking her parents to buy another umbrella. But once or twice, when it had just been misting lightly, she had come to school with a tight-lipped smile on her face, secretly all puffed up about arriving with an umbrella. On those occasions she would saunter slowly into the classroom, as gracefully as she knew how. Until one day Tieyan, a bitchy girl from the second caste, discovered Kim's secret and immediately spread the word. Then of course we never heard the end of it.

Tiezhu, a second-caste boy, had started hollering, 'There *she* is again! That whore that would like to see a temple of chastity built in her name, no doubt! Look outside! Why on earth would anyone need an umbrella in such a light drizzle?'

No one spoke for a few seconds. But then the entire class, in a collective flash of inspiration, simultaneously arrived at the conclusion that of course, it was because Kim's sister wouldn't bother with an umbrella on this kind of overcast day that Kim was finally allowed to borrow it. It was a well-known secret that in the Zhang family, Jiening was queen and Kim the slave.

Tiezhu beamed to see his piece of news hit the jackpot. Now came the real fun – ad-libbing on the theme.

'Whenever Kim shows up with an umbrella, we'll know for sure it's *not* raining!'

The laughter, that had been a titter for openers, swelled into a drawn-out, enthusiastic roar.

Two minutes to eight.

Thirty seconds to eight.

Five seconds to.

It was as if Kim had stepped on the button of the school bell. At eight o'clock on the dot she stormed into the room. Her head had shrunk to half its normal size: the hair that usually stuck out in all directions clung to her skull like a film of shiny asphalt. She scuttled to her seat all hunched over, then lowered herself into it, stiff as a board.

Mrs Meng opened her folder; the whole class was sweating bullets.

'Ping Chen: mathematics sixty, physics seventy, chemistry fifty-five . . .'

The class held its breath. Ping himself had stopped breathing altogether, for the time being. It was a twofold ordeal for him: first the nail-biting wait for his exam results, and then dealing with his classmates' reaction to them. Luckily Ping occupied the safe middle ground, meriting neither envy nor contempt . . .

'Yougui Fang: maths thirty, physics thirty, chemistry thirty, biology thirty, Chinese grammar thirty . . .'

Now, you might expect the class, who never missed a trick, to burst into a storm of malicious and scornful laughter at this. But no, this time it was our turn to hold our breath. We glanced skittishly at Yougui with fawning, arse-licking smiles on our faces. And we were well advised to do so too, since even though Yougui didn't understand a thing in class, he commanded immense respect: it wasn't beyond him to crack your head open, break your legs or flog the living daylights out of you until your skin puffed up to three times its size. It was an open secret that he always carried a whip with him; the teachers turned a blind eye to it. Nor was there any use trying to reason with Yougui, since he would turn violent as soon as he found himself at a loss for words – something that happened all too frequently.

A leaden silence hung over the classroom.

Hurriedly Mrs Meng began reading out the test results of the next student, to distract our attention. Yougui grinned at everyone triumphantly and started rolling up his whip tauntingly, with swaggering deliberateness. Then he sat down again with a stagy flourish, his legs spread wide. You could still hear him cursing under his breath.

'Kim Zhang . . . maths ninety, physics one hundred, chemistry ninety, biology eighty, Chinese grammar ninety . . .'

My heart skipped a beat. Kim had done it! After years of trying, Kim had finally achieved what we'd been striving for. And her grades weren't simply good – they were stunning! Up until now, no one had ever scored a perfect hundred in any subject, let alone one as difficult as physics! I eyed my friend with unconcealed pride.

Kim had learned at an early age always to keep a poker face. She gazed at Mrs Meng impassively. Fine, she had heard her marks; wasn't it about time to move on to the next student's grades?

But, of course, the teacher could not let this achievement go unacknowledged. The girl who had always been considered the poorest student in the class had passed – and with such flying grades, too! She straightened her glasses on the bridge of her nose and fumbled for words. Casting a quick glance over the classroom, she concluded that for the time being there was no sense in trying to restore order. The students were all talking heatedly to their neighbours to the left and to the right – they weren't even trying to keep their voices down. Astonishment was written all over their faces: How can Kim, our poor little scapegoat, suddenly have come up with such brilliant scores?! Was everyone going nuts, or what? The whole world had been turned upside down.

'Silence! Silence!' Mrs Meng's shouts were as effective as the buzzing of a mosquito.

Kim's normally harsh features seemed mellowed and softened; from time to time she would look around, not without obvious satisfaction, at her classmates. But Mrs Meng wasn't a teacher for nothing; she had thought of something good. 'Kim Zhang, stand up and tell us how you managed to improve your scores.'

Suddenly the class was like a badly-tuned radio that is switched off abruptly by an irritated listener: it was so quiet you could hear a tuft of hair drop.

I could have died. Never in my wildest dreams had I dared hope that Kim would ever be asked to share the secrets of her success with the rest of the class.

Twenty seconds went by. Kim still had not responded to Mrs Meng's invitation. But nobody considered that too surprising. Everyone, Kim included, was flabbergasted. Kim couldn't believe her ears: she – out of all the third-casters, the filthiest, most pathetic specimen – was being granted the honour of addressing the class as its most exemplary student! The others just sat there rubbing their eyes in disbelief – this was unheard of.

The teacher repeated her request, and now Kim *had* to believe it. She pushed her writing table forward a bit, to give herself the room to stand up, and, leaning heavily on the desktop, raised herself up inch by inch. The sturdy, athletic young girl seemed to have turned into a feeble, creaky old crone. She hung her head; shyness tied her tongue in knots.

Mrs Meng came to her rescue: 'Don't be scared. Try to relax. Just tell us, as simply as you can, how you went about studying the material, how you managed to catch up so remarkably, after lagging so far behind.'

Kim looked at the teacher and finally opened her mouth. 'At first I thought it was hopeless, that I'd never get the hang of it, but as soon as I began to understand even the first word of the stuff in the textbooks, my negative attitude started crumbling bit by bit . . .'

The rest of her words were drowned out by the swelling crescendo in the classroom. Everyone was chattering again. This time the faces of her fellow students were dripping with evil sneers. I was brought down to earth with a bang. What sort of gibberish were they spouting now?

'Heehee, listen to the monkey-bum saying "my-negative-attitude-started-crumbling-bit-by-bit" . . .'

I studied my friend in dismay, trying to figure out what the jackasses were on about now. Since Kim's desk was in the first row of seats, she had her back to most of the class. Sewn on to the seat of her blue pants were circular brown patches three layers thick. These clashed vilely with the blue background and did indeed suggest the pink buttocks of a gibbon. Her two braids were plastered to her back; the downpour had soaked them through and through, and they were still dripping on to her coat. Two dark stripes stood out starkly against her drab jacket.

Pyah! Pyah! Yougui started snapping his whip and yelled out, 'The dingbat is lucky today! She's found a golden clog in the trash! Look, she's in pig heaven! More pig than heaven, I'd say! That piece of dreck is so dumb she's clearly forgotten her last name!' His words hit a bull's-eye; the class jeered loudly, calling Kim every name under the sun.

Kim clammed up, but she was still in the dark as to what the classmates were jeering at. When she turned around quizzically, her fellow-students started hee-hawing even harder. The roar became deafening. People like Yougui especially, whose own marks were lousy, were in hysterics, whipped into a frenzy by envy and shame. Some of the boys started pounding rhythmically on the desks.

Mrs Meng was wringing her hands; in this pandemonium she found herself momentarily at a loss. It was only by reading her lips that I could make out she was saying something along the lines of 'Silence'. She waved at Kim to sit down.

Kim sat down . . .

Bang! . . . on the stony floor.

Someone sitting behind her had taken advantage of the uproar to pull the chair out from under her.

A deathly hush fell over the class.

KIM'S CHOICE

It wasn't raining, but by a minute after eight the next morning, Kim had still failed to show up. Was she in such pain from her fall that she could not make it to school?

The periods crawled by slowly, as if on turtle feet. It felt as if time had stopped, just to bug me.

As soon as the school bell rang announcing lunchtime, I ran out of the building, straight to the mud-house quarter.

*   *   *

At Kim's house they were busy as beavers. Piles of matchboxes towered from the floor; Kim and her mother were having a competition to see who could fold and paste the fastest.

I breathed a sigh of relief. I scolded Kim, 'You gave me a scare this morning. I thought you might be writhing in pain, and had to stay in bed.'

Kim, shifting her weight a little, patted her left hip: 'I'm not all mended yet, but I'm well enough for this kind of work.' Calmly continuing with her folding and gluing, she didn't seem to think she owed me any further explanation as to why she had played truant that morning.

Kim's mother broke the silence. 'Miss Shui, you are from an educated family, and you know more about this sort of thing. Do you agree that it might be better for Kim not to go to school, so she can help me with bringing in the dough? That's what Kim thinks. What kind of prospects are there for a third-caster anyway, no matter how amazing her report card may be? I think she's right, but then, who am I to say? I'm just a simple soul, all I know is, the more boxes I finish, the more fen I have in my pocket . . .'

'Mama, stop putting yourself down like that!' Kim snapped. She slammed the paste brush back into the jar.

Kim's mother sent her eldest daughter a look of indignation and said defensively, 'Child, this very morning you asked my opinion about stopping school. Now that your best friend is here, can't I ask her what *she* thinks?'

Kim had leaped to her feet on the kang where she had just been sitting calmly folding boxes. Like a she-tiger prepared to tear to pieces any foe that so much as sticks a claw out towards her brood, she snarled at me: 'If you're even *thinking* of giving me a sermon about the importance of attending school and the magnificent prospects awaiting any student who excels, just keep your nauseating thoughts to yourself. You'd better leave me alone – don't you dare say a word to me about school right now! School just makes me want to puke. From now on, I'll go to school only when I feel like it, for a change of pace, when I get sick and tired of this kind of work. But don't expect me to work up a sweat trying to follow the lessons.'

Neither the débâcle of the Autumn Games victories, nor the fiasco of the internship aftermath, nor even the fallout from Kim's stellar exam results, had persuaded me that she was fighting an impossible uphill battle. But now that Kim was finally laying down her sword and putting me on notice that she never wanted to be reminded of our struggle again, I lost heart. I could not summon the will to protest.

My silence made Kim's mother uneasy. She climbed down from the bed and went to heat up water for tea.

'Please don't go to any trouble, ma'am. I couldn't swallow a drop.' I threw Kim a pleading look, but Kim continued folding imperturbably, acting as if I didn't exist.

I flew into a rage. I jumped on to the bed, squatting down next to Kim, glared at her and declared melodramatically, *'Cow-ard!'*

Kim was shocked. She wasn't used to this kind of behaviour from me. She stuttered, 'Say that . . . just say that again!'

'I said you're a coward. Did you hear me this time? I think you haven't got a drop of gall – just giving up like that, at the very first setback that comes along!'

'Okay, that's enough.' Kim scooted further down the bed, avoiding all eye contact with me.

I tried another tack: 'Apart from rain and hail, the sky doesn't give anything away for free. We have to work for everything we get, and the road to success is strewn with stumbling blocks, it can't be helped . . .'

'But this road you are talking about, it's a dead end.'

'How so?'

'Don't you *see* why everything always backfires on me, no matter how incredibly well I do?'

I shuddered thoroughly, and braced myself. I prayed silently to Buddha that Kim would not be able to put into words what I had recognised all along, but was still refusing to acknowledge.

Kim arched her eyebrows like an ancient monk who has beheld Nirvana, and joked, 'That's Life, dear Lian Shui. I wasn't worth a fen when I was born, and I'll never be worth a kuai. Third-casters are despised and scorned, that's just the way it is. First-casters are the only ones that have the birthright to win praise, respect and admiration.'

I racked my brains: I was determined to come up with a round of counter-arguments to fire back at Kim. 'Well then, then what about Wanquan?' I demanded. 'Isn't he a third-caster too? And doesn't he make a swell Secretary of Propaganda?'

'Wanquan? He's pulled himself up by his boot straps by means of his looks. For a third-caster, you have to admit he's abnormally good-looking. Broad shoulders, a square face, well-muscled arms and legs. He has a much better build than most of the skin-over-bones specimens in our caste. That's the only reason Mrs Meng let him have that post. Haven't you noticed the kind of marks he usually gets for Chinese grammar? Never over a sixty. Do you think he got the job because of his propaganda-writing abilities? Sure, and I'll teach your grandmother to suck eggs.

'Why do you think I'm spending all my time making matchboxes? To earn some money. I may not be much to look at, but at least I can do something about the way I dress. Just look at Tieyan. She's got a face the shape of a pumpkin and the complexion of an aubergine, but her clothes are polyester. It makes all the difference. Does *she* ever get teased? Well then! If I fold matchboxes twelve hours a day for just one month, I'll make enough to buy myself a new jacket. Then it won't matter whether I get a thirty or a hundred.'

'This is pure lunacy!' I was standing on the bed, yelling. 'If you really want to play at being a doll dressed up in a pretty frock that's got nothing between the ears but stuffing, that's up to you of course, but don't expect to get any respect in return! Would *you* have a high opinion of yourself, just for wearing an expensive jacket?'

Kim sent me a bitter look. 'Has it ever made any difference what sort of opinion I have of myself? From the very first day of primary school, I've had to watch my back every minute of the day, never knowing where the next insult or attack might be coming from. Well, I've finally had enough. I am not going to let my classmates harass me any longer. Nice clothes will shut them up; they won't be able to call me an ugly troll any more. What's so wrong with that?'

Her look cut through me like a knife. I was stricken with shame. Who was I to criticise Kim's hankering after fancy clothes? How could I be so sure that Kim was doing the wrong thing? Pinning one's hopes on nice clothes might not be the most sensible thing to do, but what else was there?

I decided to change tactics again. 'Aren't you afraid that the teacher will give you hell if you skip school?'

'Mrs Meng? You must be out of your mind! Meng would like nothing better than to see me stay away from school altogether. At least she'll have an easier time controlling the class, seeing that it's my presence that seems to spark off total bedlam.'

'You shouldn't speak so disrespectfully about our teacher.'

'Oh, no? Why, is she a saint or something? A sanctimonious hypocrite, isn't that what you mean? Don't you remember how, during our internship, she chose the most comfortable farmhouse to stay in, while foaming at the mouth about the necessity of enduring hardships if we wanted to achieve an exalted political conscience? Claptrap!' Kim went on, 'So tell me, then, why is it Qianyun who gets crowned Student of the Three Virtues every year by her? I'm sorry, but Qianyun never achieves higher than a seventy in any of her subjects; during her internship she was out sick half the time; and every kind of sport is apparently too much exertion for the poor little doll. What are her three virtues, then? I'll tell you what they are: her status as a first-caster, her father's important post at the Ministry of Public Health, her moon-face that everyone seems to find so exquisite, and, last but not least, her fashionable clothes. See that? She even has *more* than three virtues!'

I felt rotten. I peeked at Kim, who was once again totally immersed in the art of folding boxes. I didn't dare say anything; I did not know what to do. Kim's eyebrows were puckered, her lips were drawn in a tight line and clouds of irritation overcast her face. I resigned myself to wait for Kim to open her mouth again.

Once outside, I started counting the paving stones as I walked along, repeating over and over again It's true that Kim wasn't worth a fen when she was born and will never be worth a kuai ... it is true ... it *isn't* true ... it is true ... it *isn't* true ... The answer was to be found in whether the number of cobblestones came out odd or even. But whenever it came out positive, I did not believe it; and when it was negative, I would start counting all over again, hoping for a more favourable result this time. The stairs of my apartment building were pressed into similar service ... and even the number of bites it took to finish my meal at lunchtime.

THE PRINCESS ON THE KANG

The next day Kim failed to show up at school again. And sure enough, no one batted an eyelid. Her absence allowed the teachers to conduct their lessons in peace, without the constant interruption of rowdy outbursts from the class.

I was worried. Was Kim really serious about this? What did she want? To make a living from matchbox-gluing from now on?

At three p.m. I hurried to the mud-house quarter again. It was quiet in Kim's house. I called out her name a few times, but got no reply. I looked for some sign of life in the darkened room.

After quite a while I heard the rustling of clothes, and then a bell-like voice: 'She's gone to the industrial site.'

I tried to locate the voice and discovered Jiening sitting in the far corner of the kang. Couldn't she have said something before, instead of letting me fumble around in the dark? Jiening's voice always rubbed me the wrong way; it was a seductive purr, much too affected and contrived for a girl of fourteen in my opinion. Where had she learned to put on such airs? How had this odd duck ended up in this nest? The worst thing was that the other three family members worshipped her. Jiening, with her pale complexion, her pretty face and curvaceous little figure, was the household's crowning glory. The three others were always marvelling how it could be that Jiening showed so little sign of malnourishment and poverty. If for no other reason, that was why they went all-out to give her the upper-caste treatment. She didn't have to do any heavy work; she was the one who received the most nutritious food and the most expensive clothes they could scrape together. The comely Jiening was enthroned on the highest echelon of the lowest caste. She was a princess among paupers.

'Doesn't your sister's hip hurt any more, then? How far is it, to the industrial site? Isn't it at least two, three miles from here?' I asked Jiening worriedly.

'Oh, she won't have any trouble limping over there.' Jiening must have liquid ice in her veins.

'What's she doing over there?'

'What do you *think* she's doing? She's collecting scrap iron and copper, of course. What other reason would there be, to walk so far?' It was apparently beyond this young lady to talk normally – the words shot out of her throat like lethal bullets.

'Let me get this clear – she's trying to earn money by reselling scrap metal?'

By way of a reply, Miss Goody-Two-Shoes rolled her almond eyes up into her head, showing the whites. She apparently considered it a waste of breath to answer somebody as moronic as me. But then she leaned forward again and said, in a tone of mystery, 'Tell me something, Lian, now that I have you alone, tell me honestly, why do you insist on making such a fuss over Kim?' Jiening's sloe-eyes glittered as if she were peeking through the keyhole of a new couple's honeymoon suite.

It made me want to puke. I turned my back on Jiening and walked out of the room without wasting my spit on a reply for that venomous snake.

But Jiening wouldn't let me off the hook. Raising her voice, she called after me, 'If I were you, I would drop my sister. Now's your chance, now that she herself doesn't want to have anything more to do with you. Go back to your own upper-crust set, to the precious young ladies and gallant young gents with their blue-blood noses in the air. Go ahead, relish the perks that are yours by birth, why don't you, and behave the way the rest of your ilk behaves.'

I didn't know what to do: go back inside and give Jiening a box on the ears, or get myself out of there, to be out of hearing range of Jiening's poisonous words as rapidly as possible? Dragging my feet, I shuffled out of the hut while Jiening continued her sermon.

'That's how it is in life, Lian. Everyone has her own predestiny. It is written in Kim's fate that she must suffer misery upon misery. Even you cannot change that. Give it up, admit that it's so, learn to live with it.'

That really got my dander up. I stormed back into the room and screeched, 'Shut up, you evil witch!'

'See? I've touched a nerve. If you hadn't sowed all those ridiculous ideas in Kim's brain, about the glorious future awaiting those who excel, would she be so crushingly disappointed now? Don't you think I know what the two of you were up to, day in and day out?'

I hated the little viper. I turned around and spat out through clenched teeth: 'Save your fatalistic theories for yourself! *You* go ahead and resign yourself to the destiny of the third caste, if that's what you want. I'm not about to ditch Kim. She and I refuse to accept this dead-end lot of hers, together we'll fight it to the bitter end.'

'*Ptshh!*' The dolled-up she-devil burst into giggles.

I didn't get it at first. But, 'Who says *I* have resigned myself to the destiny of the lowest caste?' said Jiening. 'Look over here.' She slipped down off her throne and pulled out a brick from under the kang. Feeling around carefully, she eased out a thick stack of creased papers. She handed the stack over to me.

I couldn't believe my eyes. Surely no one received *this* many love letters! The handwriting belonged to a great number of different students at our school. Some were known to me – they were in my year. There were others I knew by reputation – they were renowned or notorious for some reason or other. What was striking was how many first-caste boys there were among them. Were their female counterparts not attractive enough for them, then? I gave Jiening another good look, and it wasn't hard to come up with the answer. She had something exotic about her, something the well-fed mademoiselles didn't possess – an almost unhealthy fragility, capable of wrenching a powerful surge of fond tenderness from a boy. Perversely, every now and then a wild, provocative flame would flare up in Jiening's eyes, a display that would make any well-brought-up first-caste girl blush, but that gave all the boys the hots for her.

There were other categories of secret admirers, too, including local street-gang leaders, the élite of the second and third castes. The letters were written in a variety of styles, depending on the language skills of the paramour, but their contents all boiled down to the same thing, pretty much:

Jiening, Jiening, my walking sugar cane!
Who wouldn't bite into you, if he weren't insane?
  Who wouldn't get down on his knees
  To suck you, like honey from bees?
Your luscious body, so sweet when it's licked,
Is what everyone's dreaming of, in the district!
  Come into my arms, please do
  I'll give you a warm cuddle or two
Come, Jiening, or I'll die on the spot!
Come, Princess, or in hell I will rot!

Jiening snatched the pile out of my hands and gloated, 'Just check around, ask your first-caste friends. Tell me, who else receives this many love letters, in heaven's name? Content myself with my lot? Me? You misunderstood me just now. What I meant was, you've got to accept your station in life, however lowly it may be. But that doesn't mean you shouldn't develop your strong points. The thing I have going for me is a lovely package, and I'm making the most of it to get somewhere. And these –' she fanned the sheets of paper in her hand, stirring up a cold gust of air '– these are the rungs of my ladder. The only problem is, I don't know what type of boy I should take advantage of. The ordinary second- and third-casters don't count, of course. What can you buy with their love? Both the first-casters and the gang leaders have some appeal, but even they have their disadvantages.' She cocked her head coquettishly and sank into a brown study.

I couldn't believe my ears. Only fourteen, and already so cold and calculating . . .

Jiening was talking more to herself now than to me: 'If I go with the rich guys, they'll give me status and expensive presents, but you can't trust them as far as you can swing a cat. In their eyes I'm nothing but a juicy hunk of flesh. As soon as they've had their fill, they'll dump me. The hotshot hoods have terrible reputations and they're always in and out of prison . . . On the other hand, they *are* third-casters like me, so they are more likely to stay faithful . . . Besides, they're so much more generous than those rich papa's boys: if your money comes from burglary and theft, it's easy come, easy go, which isn't the case if you're paid a salary, no matter how high it might be . . .'

I couldn't think straight any more. I was listening to Jiening's deliberations open-mouthed.

'What sort of boyfriend do *you* think I should go for?' Jiening paused for an answer, but none was forthcoming. 'Lian, are you asleep? Did you hear what I said?' Her shrill voice roused me from my daze. How thick-skinned did this ninny have to be, to even think that I might want to give her advice?

Tyeee . . . The door opened slowly and Kim's mother shuffled in, carrying a mountain of fresh sheets of matchbox cardboard. Jiening tugged at my sleeve and whispered, 'Just *one* word about my secret admirers and I'll see to it that you are never welcome here ever again.' At the same time, she slipped the letters under her backside and pasted her usual mask of indifference back on. She sat upright on the bed like a wooden doll, and stared straight ahead expressionlessly.

I made a beeline for the industrial site. The spring sun seemed ruddier and brighter now, compared to a few weeks ago. It was already four thirty, but the light was still brilliant. The trees lining the street had draped themselves in a minty green haze. The chirping of the crickets proved hard to ignore. I tried not to do any thinking.

After a forty-five-minute walk, I could hear the droning of trucks, a sign that I had reached the Red Flag Agricultural Machinery Factory. Behind it was a huge industrial site, with a landfill at its far eastern corner. The trucks made daily trips there to dump industrial waste, including a fair amount of rusted metal. This is what the mud-hut children were after; they could trade the scraps for a fen a pound at the junkyard dealerships.

All you had to do to find your way to the dump was to follow the trucks. But the main gate of the factory site was guarded by a little hut with an old man in it whose job it was to keep an eye on things. I gave it a wide berth and found an opening in the barbed wire. I pressed my hair flat to my head, tucked in my clothes and crawled through the barbed wire. *Tchh . . . tchh . . .* Too late: two long rips appeared in the sleeves of my jacket. The hole was much too small for me. Most of the iron-and-copper gleaners were skinny little third-caste kids between five and ten years old. I dusted off my knees and elbows and ran over to the landfill.

Whammmm! An orange truck dumped its entire load on to the refuse heap. Quick as a flash, a grey mass of scruffy kids dressed in rags rushed in. *Ching-cha-kalaka.* Using metal rods, they poked around in the rubbish to find the scraps they were looking for. Only the ringing and clanging broke the silence. From time to time you could hear a triumphant squeal, when someone had stumbled upon an unusually large piece of iron, and once in a while a fight would break out:

'Hey! That was in *my* spot! It's mine!'

'Give it back! It was right here, in *my* section!'

But this type of altercation never went on for very long; nobody was too anxious to waste precious time.

I looked for Kim, but couldn't see her anywhere. Hadn't Jiening told me this was where she had gone? Could she have gone home already? No way – this was the time of day when most of the trucks arrived to dump their loads. Kim would never miss such a golden opportunity of her own free will. And besides, if she had gone back, we'd have been sure to meet somewhere along the way. I walked over the tract of land and asked a group of children, 'Have you seen Kim?'

A little scoundrel of around eight with a rust-coloured stain around his mouth shot back, 'Kim who?'

'Kim Zhang, the girl who lives in the fourth mud-hut quarter block.'

'Oh, *that* big moron. She's scratching around over there, clawing through our leftovers.' With a wide, cheeky grin, he pointed to a mound of rubbish at the foot of a mountain of fill, half-flattened by previous search parties. There was Kim, bent over, digging through the rubble.

I was surprised at what the little fellow had said. Kim was rarely stereotyped as 'big'. But of course in the eyes of these little kids, my friend was a giantess. Then why didn't she make the most of it? Here finally was her chance to use her height advantage and her superior strength to stand up for herself. But no. Kim was a genius at turning every favourable situation into a liability. It was obvious that the children had organised themselves into a united front against Kim, and had managed to put her in her place.

I hurried over to Kim and began helping her hunt for iron. Kim threw me a scornful look that said: What are *you* doing here? Keeping me from my work, as usual?

Couldn't Kim see that I was the only soul in the world who showed her any understanding, who offered her friendship and love, and was always *there* for her? Actually, I had found myself conjecturing of late whether it was I who was playing the victim here. How else to explain why I kept running after Kim, only to be rebuffed time and time again? Was it the pain of rejection that I was after?

Kim and I stowed the pieces of metal we were silently fishing out of the rubbish into Kim's duffel bag, still barely half-full compared to the little kids' loot-sacks, which were about ready to burst. Little by little, Kim started letting down her guard. Together we made a good team: Kim raked through the rubble while I picked out the salvageable pieces of metal. We worked until we could hardly see what we were doing; the sun had gone into hiding behind the mountains and, judging by the gloom, it was already dinnertime.

Kim went first through the hole in the barbed wire and then extended a helping hand to me. I passed the heavy bag through to her, trying to hold it carefully in the exact centre of the opening, so that it wouldn't tear, and then crawled through myself, this time without wrecking my clothes. When I was back on my feet, I was chuffed; I was getting a little more expert at this barbed-wire business.

On the way home Kim's tongue loosened up somewhat: 'Tomorrow morning I'm going to go to the junk dealer's around the corner from us. This bag weighs at least twenty pounds – I'll get twenty fen for it. That's easy money. I only had to work three hours for it. Three hours of pasting matchboxes pays ten fen at most. From now on I'm going to the dump every afternoon.' But a shadow promptly fell over her joy. It was the prospect of being confronted every afternoon by a bunch of snot-noses who refused to let her have access to the 'fresh' refuse.

I sympathised: 'They're holy little terrors, those ones, like the seedlings of some poisonous weed. They may be young, but they're already throwing their weight around like full-grown hoodlums, the way they're terrorising you!'

Kim said, 'Oh, I can understand why those kids want to chase me off the dump. Scavenging is one of the only ways they have to make some cash. Teenagers have another method: they usually "earn" their money by reselling fruit and vegetables.'

I had heard of this particular 'line of business'. Posses of horse-drawn wagons streamed into the city from the countryside every day, transporting produce grown in the people's communes to the greengrocers of Beijing. Mud-hut-quarter teenagers would hide in the bushes along the road and jump into the wagons as they passed by. Then they would yank open the tailgate, sending cabbages, turnips and aubergines rolling down into the streets. *Whoop!* The children would scramble after them and within the blink of an eye all the vegetables had vanished without a trace. Finally they would climb back up inside the wagon to close the tailgate again. They had enough sense never to empty a wagon completely. They usually limited each haul to one-tenth of the load: that was more than enough, for otherwise the wagons might take a different route, in which case there would be nothing left to steal, and that wasn't the intention, of course. Even though the drivers were well aware of what was going on behind their backs, they never intervened. They were counting on the fact that the young rascals would leave most of the merchandise alone; a ten-per-cent loss was just part of the cost of doing business.

'Isn't it against the law, those vegetable raids or thefts, whatever you want to call it?'

Kim nodded. 'That's why I refuse to have anything to do with it.'

I suggested, 'Shall I come and help you every afternoon? Between the two of us, we can make twice as much.'

Kim let the sack fall to the ground. 'Great, then I can just go back to school as usual.'

Was she joking? I could hardly believe my ears. Wishes do come true when you least expect it. Was it written in the stars, then, that the two of us belonged together? That nothing could ever wrench us apart?

HUANGSHUAI MOVEMENT

The next morning, Kim was seated at her school desk at the impeccably punctual hour of five minutes to eight. I winked at her. Just let somebody, anything, try to take the wind out of our sails!

The chemistry teacher, Mrs Yang, walked in and started handing back the test that the students had completed over a week ago. Today she was scheduled to go over the most common errors, by way of revising the material we had been learning all semester. We held our breath, because this kind of session was always an exercise in mortification. We were about to have our noses rubbed into our stupidity over and over again: the formula that Mrs Yang had explained to us at least ten times, and had warned us about just as often, had *still* been wrongly applied in the test. The teacher wrote out the formula on the blackboard for the eleventh time, as patiently and as clearly as ever, no doubt just to make us feel even worse about making such silly and inexcusable mistakes.

But today something strange was going on. Mrs Yang was behaving in an unusually benign manner – a little timid, even. Her usual resolute demeanour, befitting her extensive knowledge of her subject, was blunted by a nervous dithering that wasn't like her at all. The weirdest thing was that in going over our mistakes, she kept up a sort of 'yes-but' patter.

'Well, yes of course,' she offered timidly, 'these particular rules don't really apply in the case of this formula, but, oh well—' she wrung a sour smile on to her face '—if you insist on adapting them that way here, that's fine with me too.'

What was that? Were we suddenly allowed to mess with the rules any way we felt like? I didn't recognise our teacher, who was usually so strict.

The class had a keen nose for this sort of thing. Hesitantly at first, a few students at the back of the room began to 'megaphone' loudly to the ones seated in the front, and the first paper areoplanes were launched. We remained cautious, however. Mrs Yang could chew us out at any time with, 'What *is* this – are you trying to raise hell, or what?'

But the scolding was not forthcoming. I looked at the teacher in astonishment. Mrs Yang was standing in front of her misbehaving class, her hands spread out helplessly; uncertainty was written all over her face.

Why didn't she *do* something . . . ?

The next class was biology. Mr Zeng asked Shunzi, the class representative, to hand out the stack of notebooks containing our corrected homework. Normally Mr Zeng did this himself, making use of the opportunity to compliment those who had done well, as a way of encouraging the rest to try harder. When I had my notebook pushed into my hands, I jumped for joy, because the teacher had written just *one* comment on it, expressed as a single character: *Brilliant!* It was unheard of to receive that sort of praise. But how strange, two of the answers were marked with a red X. Then what made me deserve that 'brilliant'?

There were cheers all around me; our classmates were showing off their assignments left and right. We had all received the exact same eulogy for our work.

During the ten o'clock break, we saw some of the teachers shuffling through the hallways with their heads bowed like wilted bok choy after a frost. After our break Mrs Meng came scuttling into the classroom and sent us home. This was icing on the cake.

'*What* did you say, Mrs Meng? No more school today? *Really?!* Nor tomorrow, nor Saturday? We're free! We're free!' A groundswell of hurrahs made the wall-maps shake like leaves, but Mrs Meng's face was grey with anxiety . . .

We hastily stuffed our textbooks into our satchels and rushed out of the building. Kim and I looked at each other: we didn't know what to think now. Buddha worked in mysterious ways. When Kim lost interest in studying, her conscience nagged her to go back to school; when she got to school, she was sent home. She narrowed her eyes – her face wrinkling up like a wizened old man's – and said, 'You mark my words, the CPC is starting to monkey around with our education again. If that's the case, I'd rather stay home and fold matchboxes.'

When I walked through the school gates again four days later, the whole building had disappeared from view. It was all wrapped up in paper, from top to bottom. Huge red characters screamed loud slogans from the fluttering walls.

The frail spring breeze fondled the fire-spewing paper and caused it to ripple in places. Around the midriff of the whispering edifice hung a slogan written in characters as big as a cow:

Follow the example of our revolutionary fellow student Huangshuai and purge the educators of feudal, bourgeois and revisionist elements!

I ran up to the building and began reading the broadsheets, which were entirely composed of denunciation tracts. Certain teachers were singled out by name.

One of the articles boasted the following 'headline':

Gong Wei, shut your mouth, it reeks of your arsehole!

The first paragraph read as follows:

Stop sullying our proletarian pulpit with all your bullshit about that Capitalist, Isaac Newton. Did you think that we, Chinese working men and women, wouldn't have discovered the existence of gravity for ourselves, without any help from that foreign devil?! Just stick out your chicken neck with that measly earthworm on top, and 'fess up to your true objectives in disseminating Newton's theories. We know what you're up to: you wish to influence us members of the younger generation into becoming toadies of the Capitalist West, so that, once we're grown up, we'll overthrow the Communist Party of our homeland! Gong Wei, hurry up and confess your counter-revolutionary motives, or we'll make bloody well sure that you do!

I skipped a part and read the last line:

Class brothers and sisters, let us shout: Death to the revisionists! Declare war on the reactionary teachers! Set the bourgeois world of the educators on fire! Victory to the Communists!

I took in a gulp of cold wind. Mr Gong Wei, nicknamed Einstein, was one of the stars of the faculty. His classes were said to be immensely interesting and entertaining, and just about every student who took his course could not help falling in love both with his subject, physics, and with him.

I read a few more compositions, but they were all of a piece: the finest teachers in the school were made out to be the 'gravediggers of Communism'. I wondered why Mrs Yang wasn't named anywhere; she was, after all, famous for her teaching skills, too. I tried to codify the indicted teachers . . . and sure enough, only the upper-grade faculty had been targeted. Come to think of it, it struck me as odd last Thursday that the older students had remained meekly seated in their classrooms when the rest of us had been dismissed. What that meant was that the seniors must have been indoctrinated in the new movement at some earlier date.

In the days leading up to each new political campaign, the CPC would send out a flurry of documents and pamphlets to different groups.

Cabinet members would receive memos marked with three little red crosses at the top. These contained top-secret information, for instance the real reason the Helmsman wished to see a certain minister liquidated – generally because the person in question had dared to cast some pall of doubt over the eternal truths of the Wisest Leader of the Universe. This would push the Never-Setting Sun into setting a new political movement rolling: first, to neutralise the influence of the wayward minister by dismissing local supporters from their government posts; and second, to create the impression that He had kicked this minister out of the cabinet for ideological imperatives, and not, say, purely as an exercise in flexing His mighty muscle.

Politburo members were given a document marked with two crosses. In this one, the true reason for the campaign was shrouded in a smokescreen of soft-sell about the parting of ways between the Great Helmsman and the 'revisionist' minister, though His anger at the politician in question did manage to slip through here and there.

Government officials of ranks one to eight got a dispatch marked with a single cross, in which they were informed of the general 'nature' of the movement in high-flying political jargon. These circulars were studded with directives on how to steer the populace for the duration of the campaign.

Civil servants of the ninth to the twelfth rank received letters without any crosses on them. Perhaps, these did not differ substantively from the propaganda that was published in the CPC's mouthpiece – the *People's Daily*. Workers, peasants and students had extracts of these letters read out to them. Under no circumstances was the original recipient permitted to leave them lying around, because they must not fall into the wrong hands

– the hands of the common people. Evidently it did contain some sensitive material after all. I occasionally heard things I would never have known otherwise, from my mother, who was a recipient of the circulars without the crosses. During the course of the last campaign, when Confucius was hauled out of his grave and not a bone in his body left intact, Mother had said at breakfast, 'According to the cadre document, the Minister for Trade and Development has tried making a case for allowing State-owned businesses some measure of autonomy. Therefore the Never-Setting Sun has declared him to be a "follower of the Capitalist way".' But when this same proclamation was read to us at school, our headmaster skipped that kind of detail. The struggles between the Wisest Leader and His political partners were none of the general public's business; knowing about these might set the common people thinking – and an independently-thinking proletariat was hardly conducive to a smooth state of affairs! Steering a fine line between disseminating information and withholding it, the Helmsman prescribed just the right dose of facts for each of the social strata: not an ounce less and not a lick more.

The schoolbell rang, and I bolted to the classroom. Kim was already dutifully seated at her desk. Mrs Meng pulled at a rope hanging from the wall, which switched on the public address system originating from the Director's office. At first the loudspeakers, after months of disuse, crackled like dead branches in the wind. The song that was being broadcast, 'The Communist Revolution Knows No Mercy', sounded as if it was being sawed into tiny pieces with a hacksaw.

After the battle anthem, the deputy headmaster, Mr Chen, coughed into the mike and delivered the following peroration: 'Red brothers- and sisters-in-arms, our country's educational system has fallen under the spell of the evil bourgeoisie. Students are forced to bury themselves deeper and deeper in books. They slog their way through the exams and are chained to their grades. *What'* – Chen's vocal cords were stretched so tight they nearly snapped; his hysterical shrillness nearly made us jump out of our skins – *'whateeever* happened to the teachers' political awareness? Isn't it their job to teach the younger generation to be the next defenders of the wisdom of Mao's rule? What is the point of clogging children's brains with Capitalist knowledge like algebra and Mendeleyev's Periodic Table? How many pages of the *Little Red Book* do the kids still know by heart these days? How often are they given a lesson on the Wondrous History of the CPC? Can they even tell the difference between Communists and Revisionists? Isn't it high time to ask ourselves some serious questions about the direction proletarian Chinese education has been taking?'

Smiles appeared on some of the students' faces. This sounded good. It looked as if we were about to enter a golden era. If they understood it correctly, there would be no more cramming, and there was more than a distinct possibility that all exams would be cancelled.

But Chen had not finished ranting: 'Two weeks ago, a student with an exemplary revolutionary spirit, a twelve-year-old girl named Huangshuai, wrote an open letter to the Politburo, in which she exposed these sinister developments in the educational system. Once again, the Great Helmsman has proved what a peerless statesman He is: He caught on right away that the bourgeois sympathisers have been as busy as bees undermining his Communist regime by pumping our schoolchildren full of putrid Capitalist knowledge! He has therefore launched a campaign to cleanse the academic world of Revisionist and Capitalist elements. As a sign of appreciation for the student who showed the proletarian initiative to draw attention to this dangerous trend in education, the Great Helmsman has named the campaign after her: the Huangshuai Movement.'

Next, the Deputy Director gave us some examples of how we should turn against our teachers:

'Has the English teacher asked you to learn the verb conjugations by heart? That is a reactionary act on his part, since students ought to be putting their memory to better use in remembering revolutionary slogans, not in learning the lingo of hairy foreign devils.

'Could the teacher be trying to manipulate you into becoming aspiring spies for the Capitalist West? Use your proletarian vigilance to figure out what Revisionist objective this type of educator has in mind!

'Has the Chinese grammar instructor given you an assignment to write an essay about friendship? Wrong, wrong, wrong! Your creative talents should be entirely devoted to proclaiming your loathing for the foes of the Helmsman and His Revolution, which can never be extolled enough, and the relentless war on capitalism.'

In conclusion, he said that every class should split into four groups after the broadcast, and put their heads together to weigh the teachers' misdeeds. Every group had to finish a denunciation article of a thousand words before lunchtime. The article would be transcribed that very afternoon on to a broadsheet as big as a door, to be hung in some spot assigned to them by the school authorities . . .

'Plaster the buildings, the trees, the lamp-posts, and everything that will hold a sheet of paper, with militant handbills! Set the school on revolutionary fire! Blow the teachers' bourgeois brains into smoke! Long live Mao! Long live the CPC! Follow Huangshuai's example! Carry out the ideals of the Huangshuai Movement until the bitter end! Death to the Capitalist educational system!'

You could clearly hear the fusillade of Chen's spit splattering the microphone; he was screeching like a pig on the verge of having its throat cut. Where was this all coming from? How could he be inciting such hate for educators, when he was an educator himself, after all?

I knew Chen to be a boring and clumsily incompetent teacher. How it had come about that this man, so obviously born with two left hands, had been assigned to teach handicrafts, had always been a puzzle to me. And now just listen to him haranguing us as the 'inspirational' guru of the movement! What had happened to Director Dong?

After Chen, a woman took the microphone. I recognised her voice immediately: she taught biology to the first years. I didn't know her real name – everyone called her 'Back-at-my-old-university'. As a graduate of some sort of night school, she was one of the few teachers who did not have a university education under her belt. In the chaos at the beginning of the Cultural Revolution she had seized the chance of obtaining an appointment at this school. Her colleagues had never raised any objection, nor did they look down their noses at her; she might not be one of the smartest, but she was obviously giving it her best, notwithstanding the spurious inferiority complex she'd adopted. According to the students, however, not a class went by without her saying, 'Back at my old university . . .' The fact that she had promoted her night school to a university in itself did not bother anyone, but the belittling tone she used towards her pupils as well as the scorn with which she criticised her colleagues, drove the schoolchildren's hackles up.

It was this woman who was now saying, 'Thank you for your speech, Comrade Chen, Chairman of the brand new Red Headquarters of the Huangshuai Movement . . .' What? Had Chen taken advantage of the situation to take over from Director Dong, then? '. . . As Deputy Chairwoman, I should first like to applaud the Huangshuai Movement . . .'

No wonder she applauds it, I thought, if it weren't for this campaign she'd never have crawled her way to the top of the school administration. Chen, the butter-fingered crafts instructor, and this biology teacher who was so incompetent that she had had to fight convulsively for a foothold every step of the way – it was black sheep like these who welcomed the political movement with open arms and were making use of the chaos to climb upwards like helicopters on vertical take-off.

'Second, I would like to issue a warning to Revisionist teachers like Yang, Wei, Tian and their cronies: hang your dog-heads and confess to your reactionary crimes, or the blind bullets of the Revolution will have no mercy.'

Tchhtchh . . . I could just about *hear* my teeth gnashing. If Back-at-my-old-university had her way, she would skin the finest of the teachers alive and barbecue them on a spit. For all those years, she had been living in the shadow of her colleagues, in her own perception at any rate; finally she saw her way clear to extract her revenge. And she had a valid excuse, too: she was only taking active part in the Huangshuai Movement . . . !

And what to think of Chen? Wasn't this a man who, every day of his life, had been hoping for the day when he could tear his betters off their high horses? It was riff-raff like these who would see to it that the campaign brought the best of the teaching staff to its knees; the school would soon be in ruins. As far as this sort of thing went, the Wisest Leader in the Universe was truly a genius. No matter what kind of movement He came up with, He always managed to drum up more than enough fanatical support for it all over the country. It was no surprise, then, that one of His dictums was, *Where there are people, there are quarrels.* And quarrels turned people against each other.

After Back-at-my-old-university had finished spitting out her gall at her learned colleagues, she calmed down considerably. Now she switched to her real order of business: the practical announcements, such as where the students should go to collect paper and paste for their wall posters, which class was assigned to deck out which particular wall, and the minimum number of characters a wall poster should carry. Once she was done with that, suddenly remembering she was now permitted to berate her colleagues with impunity and no provisos, she launched into another hysterical tirade:

'Class representatives, call on your classmates to drag your teacher down off the rostrum. Organise denunciation meetings and riddle the teachers with verbal machine-gun fire. Never stop criticising them until they admit that they did, indeed, try to teach you to be collaborators with the imperialist West!'

All eyes involuntarily swivelled to Mrs Meng, who cringed and shambled down off the podium.

Shunzi jumped to his feet and ordered the teacher. 'Go back to your office and wait there until we summon you to a denunciation meeting. In the meantime you can write a self-criticism.' He spoke insolently, as if he had been on a first-name basis with her for ever.

Mrs Meng, dazed and cowed, just nodded and left the classroom, shuffling her feet. Wanquan and other student ringleaders jumped up to help Shunzi divide the class into four groups.

It was not easy coming up with a satisfactory list of teachers' wrongdoings. We knew damn well that the educators had done only what they had had to do, in order to teach. The chemistry teacher, for example, had made us learn by heart the atomic make-up of the most common elements, such as oxygen and carbon. Without such rudiments, we would never get anywhere in this subject. Yet we were being ordered to set down page after page of 'reactionary crimes' committed by our instructors, before lunchtime. To make matters worse, Wangquan, Yougui, Shunzi and some of the other smart-Alecks kept trying to scare the pants off us with comments like, 'If you do a half-cocked job of listing the teachers' wrongdoings, that means you're breathing through the same nostrils as they are.' We couldn't risk having that sort of indictment thrown at us, since then we too would end up in the dock. It was better to throw all your scruples to the wind and simply lie through your teeth.

Seeing that I usually received high marks for my writing skills, I was chosen, or rather coerced, to be the official scribe for my group. I was made to sit down surrounded by a group of my classmates, and all began brainstorming intently. Each tried to outdo the others in thinking up the most bizarre offences that could possibly be laid at our teachers' feet. I kept writing it all down . . .

'Lian, write this,' said Xiuli. 'Hey Fatso Tomato-nose, why do you cram our heads full of those stupid atomic structures? Are you by any chance trying to distract us from the most fundamental thing – the heightening of our political awareness and the struggle against class enemies? Follower of the Capitalist way, don't think we haven't got your number: we know that you are using chemistry class as a diversionary tactic, so that we'll have no energy left for the Proletarian Revolution. It wouldn't surprise us if you were a secret agent of some imperialistic Western nation or other! Come on, confess your crimes, or else!'

'No-o-o!' Kejian had to go one better, 'you're much too easy on him, if all you say is "or else!" It should say, ". . . or we'll hack you into little pieces and feed you to the fishes".' He grinned triumphantly at Xiuli. Xiuli looked chagrined: why hadn't *she* thought of that?

'Take *this* down!' I practically jumped out of my skin. From behind me, a furious girl's voice was raving, 'The to-all-intents-and-purposes widow Mrs Meng . . . or, no, forget that "Mrs". Take it again from the top: Bitch in heat that can't stop drooling about your old man all day and all night, the one who's locked up – rightly so, I'd say – in the Yunnan prison camp! Did you poop your proletarian awareness down the toilet like diarrhoea or something? Where is your respect for the working class, how'd you get the *nerve* to correct the English pronunciation of a genuine Red working-man's daughter like me? Try it just one more time, and I'll rip your lips to shreds like a ragged dish towel!'

There was a dead hush. My hand was shaking like an old woman's. Weren't we going just a little too far? That was the question written on everyone's face, even if no one dared say it out loud. It was bad enough that Mrs Meng had not been allowed to see her husband for three years. Every kid in the class knew that at the time her husband was exiled, Mrs Meng had been carrying a heavy belly. Their little son, born four months later, had never seen his father. Whenever any of the students played with the little urchin, we'd ask him, for fun, 'Where is Papa?' The boy would then point at a wooden chest his father had once sent them, filled with bananas. 'Papa!' he'd say. And ten times out of ten, his mother's eyes would fill with tears . . . For that bitch Tieyan to make fun of the suffering of Mrs Meng's little family was more than most of us could take. Still, the thought of the slogan 'The Communist Revolution Knows No Mercy' made us keep our qualms to ourselves.

I shut down my brain and went on dutifully recording, even though from time to time, when I read over what I had written, I would cringe with shame. We had once been taught by the Chinese grammar teacher the difference between inferential and deductive reasoning, but this resembled neither. It wasn't much better than any old slanging match you could hear at the fish market. How had we got ourselves into this mess?

A SHEEP'S HEAD

By five minutes to three, my group had succeeded in fulfilling its quota, thank heaven: two expanses of wall poster, each as tall and as wide as a door, completely bescribbled with articles itemising and critiquing at least ten misdeeds committed by our teachers. But Wanquan was not particularly impressed with this achievement – he began yelling at us, 'Incompetent fuck-ups! I'm giving you another ten minutes. If you don't manage to cover another two sheets pronto, I'll denounce you to the Red District Chairman as saboteurs of the Huangshuai Movement!'

All the colour drained from the face of Yuehua, one of the girls in the group, and she began to sob, 'Revolutionary Class Representative Shunzi Ding, it's not that we aren't willing, but – Buddha's eyes are all-seeing – there's no way we'll be able to fill another two sheets with denunciations, in so little time. Take pity on us, and don't tell on us!'

It was clear that she was merely putting into words what most of us feared – Yuehua was not the only one who had gone white as a ghost.

Of course this wasn't lost on Shunzi, either. With a malevolent grin on his face he said, as cool as you please: 'That, comrades, is up to you.'

We all tried as best as we could to keep a lid on our anger. But you could hear our brains whirring: *Shunzi, you bastard son of an unwed mother, pee on the ground, and now look down. Do you see that reflection of a hairless dog? Exactly. That is you! You're wagging a tail you no longer have. And now that you've been given the chance, you just want to sink your rabid teeth into whoever is nearest, don't you?*

But, of course, nobody had the nerve to say it out loud.

Shunzi looked over his audience, which was obviously speechless with fear, and added triumphantly, 'The old reactionary order has been over-turned. Now *we* will be the ones to teach the teachers a lesson. If you don't co-operate and refuse to take them to task, how will we ever make it clear to those sleazeballs who's the boss around here?'

Shunzi decided it was probably time to stop showing off his clout. 'And make it quick! Or I'll be in deep shit.'

Aha, an admission! Now it was the rest of the class's turn to smirk. Shunzi must be worried that the new headmaster would haul him over the coals because his class hadn't made enough of an effort. Why didn't he just say so? We could see for ourselves that he was in a tight spot. But then he shouldn't have come out with that bullshit about 'the old reactionary order'!

At a quarter past three we had managed to put the prescribed number of words on paper, with some help from the other groups after they had finished theirs. We didn't have a choice: no one was too keen to hear an announcement over the loudspeakers the next day that he or she had been indicted as a 'stooge of the revisionist teachers', which was the threat Back-at-my-old-university had waved under our noses that morning.

Now it was time to hang the wall poster. A few boys went to the maintenance department to borrow a ladder from the janitors; I was sent to fetch a pail of paste and a brush.

⌒

It was quiet in the deserted corridors – most of the teachers were nervously writing their self-criticism articles. I walked on tiptoes; I didn't want to disturb anyone.

Suddenly I heard a woman sobbing. I pricked up my ears and looked around wide-eyed. It was a very unusual thing to hear a teacher crying. I halted at a door with the sign MATHEMATICS, YEAR 1.

Cautiously I bent down to look through the keyhole. There, directly across from me, sat Mrs Xu, wiping away tears. I was startled. I had always liked this particular young teacher.

Mrs Xu was saying,' . . . my class's wall poster? I have never tried to do anything but teach. How can they mouth off about me like that? What, in Heaven's name, have I done wrong?'

I turned my head slightly, to see who she was talking to. I could just catch a glimpse of a shoulder and a lock of hair . . . Oh, but that was Mrs Feng! Mrs Feng was a senior colleague of Xu's; she also taught maths to the first years. She put a hand on Xu's shoulder. I overheard her say, 'The only thing you did wrong was to choose this profession. Since 1949, the Wisest Leader in the Universe has launched campaigns against the "thinking elements" – that means us – every few years. Once you've managed to survive a whole parade of political purges like these, you can't help growing an elephant hide like mine. Do you see *me* crying over these childish insults? Why should I? Those children are as innocent and pure as the first winter snow. Without the prodding of the CPC it would never even occur to them to cut their teachers down to size. If you want to bemoan something, bemoan the fact that this leader is taking advantage of the students' ignorance and childish fervour to give himself a leg-up in his own power struggles way up there . . .'

Suddenly Feng stopped short. Guardedly she scrutinised her colleague's face. Fear and worry darted from her eyes. I, too, was shaking. I was just as aware as Mrs Feng was of how dangerous it was to speak the truth – to no matter whom – especially if the truth had anything to do with the policies of the Father, Mother, Lover and Mistress All-Rolled-Into-One.

The next morning there were throngs of students swarming outside the school buildings. We were pointing at the texts and commenting on them loudly. Most of us dismissed the rival classes' denunciation efforts as rubbish and praised our own masterpieces to the skies. There was one point, however, on which everyone unanimously agreed: the one who had written the most scurrillous and vicious text was singled out by one and all as the greatest revolutionary.

Here and there a few teachers could be seen reading their own indictments with their heads bowed. This they did as fast as they could, terrified that they might be beaten to a pulp on the spot. The older teachers knew this was not an irrational fear; during the last campaign, their former colleagues Mr An and Mrs Lin had each lost, respectively, all but half an arm and an eye in student-orchestrated clobbering bouts.

Everyone knew why the educators still risked coming here anyway. They wanted to know the exact tenor of the calumnies they had 'harvested', so that they would know which way the wind blew, and know which tack to take in their self-criticism essays in order to excoriate themselves most effectively. In doing so, they hoped to convince the Red Headquarters that they were ready and willing to take every reprimand to heart.

Kim wasn't there again, for a change. Still, what was the point, right now? Even picking your nose for food was a more fruitful occupation than going to school. Compared to this, pasting matchboxes didn't seem like such a bad idea.

The denunciation-article writing was already going a lot more smoothly – we were beginning to get the hang of it. Our scruples having evaporated, we didn't shilly-shally, cooking up one reactionary crime after another for whichever member of the faculty happened to be in the hot seat. Still, all the fun had gone out of it once we knew for sure that our verbal mauling would go unpunished – and was encouraged, even, by the Party. What we needed was a new challenge.

'Lian, take this down!' Meimei ordered. 'Mr Jiang is a *fiiiiilthy bourgeooois*.' She sounded like a caterwauling feline.

'*Wwwow!*' Four of the boys responded with energetic bellows.

Though I couldn't stand Meimei's whining, I didn't dare stop writing – it was imperative that I be seen actively participating in the campaign.

'Last month he had a go at the chapter The Reproductive Function in Humans. Why, I ask you – *why-yai-yai-yai-yaiii*?' That was what the come-hither yodel, couched in revolutionary language, sounded like coming from Meimei.

Tch-tch! The four boys clicked their tongues; they were drooling for more. I had the sneaking suspicion that some kind of mating ritual was going on here, but I dismissed my misgivings, my face on fire. One thing was for sure: I wanted to have nothing whatever to do with it.

Meimei was not to be stopped: 'It's pretty obvious why Jiang made us study that particular chapter: he wanted to spoil our virgin proletarian souls with that decadent, low-down bourgeois subject matter!'

'Ah-mmmm, that sounds *goo-oo-ood!*' the boys groaned.

My hands were shaking. I didn't dare look up – everyone around me was tittering. Apparently they all found it pretty funny. I went on writing it all down painstakingly, while the laughter just kept growing rowdier and coarser. I was still in the dark – I had to reread what I had written twice before I finally realised that they had been pulling my leg all along. Obviously, everyone *else* had understood that what Meimei had been dictating to me wasn't really material for a denunciation article at all; it was just an excuse to flirt with those boys. And I had been idiotic enough to write everything down word for word!

I stood up, flung my pen to the ground and snarled at them, 'I've

had it! Find someone else for the job. You are turning it into a circus.'

The rest of my group immediately stopped giggling; they looked at me
with eyes as alarmed as traffic signals.

'What do you mean? Just tell me *one* word that I just said that went against
the grain of the Huangshuai Movement!' Meimei, who had been acting like
such a hot little number only a moment ago, had suddenly turned into a
'revolutionary dragon'.

Meimei was right, of course. If I tried to report her, I would not have a
leg to stand on. Meimei, taking advantage of my hesitation, began bawling
me out: 'Go ahead, tell your revolutionary classmates: what did you mean,
exactly, with that "I've had it"? Are you by any chance trying to torpedo the
Huangshuai Movement, which was called into being by the Father, Mother,
Lover and Mistress All-Rolled-Into-One?'

That was enough to make the whole class go quiet. I cringed.

Meimei's intimidation had spoiled my entire day. I had no recourse but
to hide my distaste for this kind of showing-off. My only consolation
was the thought that when the craziness here was done, I could go see
Kim again. I was going to accompany Kim to the factory site to collect
scrap iron.

GREAT-GRANDMOTHER KIM ZHANG

When I showed up at Kim's door at half past three, she went directly to
the eastern end of the courtyard to retrieve the two hand rakes that we were
going to use to grub up the metal out of the refuse dump. Then she ran to
the kitchen to fetch the duffel sack.

On our way to the industrial terrain, Kim told me excitedly that she had
made one yuan and fifty fen in less than five days of selling scrap metal.
'This morning I went to the shopping centre The Black Claw of Capitalism
Will Never Eclipse the Red Sun.' She quickly caught herself, 'Actually, I
only happened to be passing by on my way to the matchbox factory. I
saw that in the shop To Defend Communism We'll Climb Mountains
of Daggers and Throw Ourselves Into Oceans Of Fire, the department
store that has the best prices, jackets cost fifteen kuai each, on average.
I've come up with one-fifty in five days. That means that in less than
two months I'll be able to buy one of those cool polyester jackets. What
do you think of that? I'd always thought that for me, clothes like that

300

were as likely as a trip to the moon, but it seems it really isn't *that* far-fetched!'

We had arrived at the gap in the barbed wire. Kim said, 'Remember the last time, how you ripped your clothes? Here, let me hold the wire. This time you won't get a scratch, trust me.'

Crits-crits, the rusty wires rasped, gritting their teeth to make room for me; I squeezed through the hole, put my foot down on the other side, and . . . whoops! The earth beneath my foot had given way, and I tumbled into a pit reeking of earth and mould. Grabbing around wildly for something to hold on to, I snared a handful of barbed wire.

'Let go!' cried Kim.

I let myself fall.

When I came to after what felt like a profound sleep, the first thing I saw was Kim's reddened eyes. I contrived a smile and said, as casually as I could, that I wasn't in any pain.

Kim balled up her fists. 'If I ever get my hands on those pests . . . I'll make sure they get theirs!'

Even before she had finished uttering those words, a cluster of heads came into view behind the mountain of landfill. They had been hiding there to watch Kim fall into their trap. Grinning broadly, they yelled out in unison sing-song, 'Who won't listen, must feel the pain! Sorry about your pretty girlfriend. It was really *your* legs we meant to break.'

Kim abruptly pulled her arms out from under my armpits. An unfamiliar, savage blaze was spewing from her eyes. She leaped to her feet, shook the kinks out of her clothes and stormed towards the troublemakers. Before the little terrors knew what was happening, Kim had already nabbed three of them and bonked their heads together. *Dong-dong-dong* echoed the skulls and *Tyeee Tyeee!* squealed the brats, like rats getting their throats slit.

Before the rest of the punks had a chance to take to their heels, Kim had kicked each of them in the knees. Some of them staggered about with their hands on their heads, others were kneeling, screeching, in the mud.

Kim stuck out both of her elbows in a pointy V and spat into both palms. 'If any one of you ever has the gall to raise even a finger against my friend Lian again, or against me – "Granny" to you, if you please – you can reckon on a pounding that'll give you a triple-decker of a lump!' A sadistic grin spread over her features; the thirst for blood almost made her go blue in the face. She began to hum a battle anthem, stamping her right foot on the ground to the beat:

> *Fight, fight, fight!*
> *For the Great Proletarian*
> *Cultural Revolu-tion!*
> *Fight, fight, fight!*
> *Until the class enemy*
> *is cru-ushed*
> *under the hoo-ooves*
> *of our Red,*
> *Red Comrades!*

Aching over every inch of my body, I started limping towards Kim. Halfway there I had to sit down; walking was too painful. I stared at my friend. Was Kim now going to turn into a bully herself?

Kim was still gloating over the pitiful spectacle her victims presented. Some of them were rolling on the ground in agony. Planting her left foot on somebody's back, she barked, 'Repeat after me!

> *'Great-grandmother Kim Zhang,*
> *we worship thee, oh Undying Conqueror*
> *and we shall never again contest*
> *Thy Overwhelming Superiority'*

The little boy started making anxious but respectful kowtows to Kim, repeating after her:

> *'Great . . . Great-grandmother K-kim Zhang,*
> *we worship you, Conqueror;*
> *and we'll never contest*
> *your superiority . . .'*

Kim roared with laughter, 'That wasn't it exactly, but I'll let it go . . .'

The ceremony was over. She swaggered across the littered battlefield to where I was sitting. As soon as she caught sight of me, however, the devilish grin vanished from her face. Sinking to her knees at my side, she said in a voice trembling with concern, 'Get on my back. I'm taking you to the hospital . . .' Bursting into tears, she went on, 'Lian, my very dearest friend in the whole world, it won't hurt very long, you'll get better soon, I promise!'

After hoisting me on to her back, Kim hurried through the streets with determined strides. Being carried by Kim was fine with me. I was consciously making the most of this trip, stamping every second of it into my memory.

I realised it was the first and probably the last time that we would ever cling to each other so tightly.

Once we arrived at the hospital, Kim lowered me on to the leather bed in Casualty as delicately as if she were dealing with a soap bubble. Then, wiping her sweaty face on her sleeve, she went to call a doctor.

I had to answer a long list of questions. Then I had X-rays taken. Over half an hour later the same doctor returned with the announcement, 'A fractured left upper arm and contusions to both legs.'

The physician asked the nurse to set my arm in plaster. But first she had to minister to my right hand. The attendant pressed a piece of cotton wool drenched with iodine into the small but deep cut in my palm. I cringed with pain. The nurse tried distracting me by talking to me: 'Well, little girl, what sort of mischief have you been up to, to get yourself such a nasty cut?'

Up until that point Kim and I had cautiously kept our mouths shut about falling into the pit at the industrial site. After all, it wouldn't do for a first-caste girl to be found hanging around that sort of neighbourhood, even less so for her to go nosing around a landfill. But the pain caused me to forget my resolve to keep mum. I blurted out: 'You wouldn't be wondering, if you'd seen those long, rusty spikes in the wire around the factory site.'

The nurse suddenly forgot everything else. She said, '*What* did you say? What was it that gave you that cut?'

I would have preferred to take it back, but the nurse whirled over to my attending physician like a tornado and whispered something in his ear.

The doctor looked at his watch. 'She got here about forty minutes ago.' He rushed up to me and asked me, 'How long ago was it, that you hurt your hand on that rusty metal?'

What was all the panic about? Leaning on the bed with my right elbow, I said, 'Oh, maybe an hour and a half to two hours ago. Why?'

'Get me a tetanus vaccine! Stat!' the doctor ordered. He stuck a thermometer under my armpit and bombarded me with questions that I couldn't see as having anything to do with arm fractures or contusions.

Kim grabbed my hand and clutched it tight.

The gravity of the situation sank in for real when the doctor asked his last question.

'Would you please give me the names of your parents, their work units and a telephone number where they may be reached? We must advise them at once.'

Suddenly I felt seriously ill.

'But – of course, why didn't I figure it out before.' His face brightened. 'Your name is – let me check my notes here – Lian Shui. Your father must be the head of our cardiology department, Dr Shui.'

Father worked on the fourth floor of the building we were in; he was immediately summoned downstairs. He read my thermometer, felt my forehead and asked the same questions. Finally he said to his colleague, 'In my opinion there's no great need to worry, but we can't rule out tetanus at this stage.' He smiled appreciatively at my doctor. 'Thank you for figuring out how she got this cut. You know how impossible it is at times to extract the truth from a child's mouth.'

The doctor blushed, the nurse beamed; the doctor became a little less taciturn. 'It is just unfortunate that we found it out so late. As a matter of course, a patient should receive the vaccine within sixty minutes of sustaining the injury. So we are an hour late. Let's just hope her body has the wherewithal to fight off the infection.'

Now Father noticed I was covered in black soot, brown rust smudges and red bloodstains and tried to keep a lid on his temper. 'Where the hell have you been hanging out? *Now* look what sort of scrape you've gone and got yourself into! Are you at all interested in staying alive? Just wait until your mother gets a load of this!'

Kim rushed to my rescue: 'It wasn't her fault, Sir. It was because of me.'

It was only then that Father saw who was sitting beside me. He glared at her. He wasn't an intellectual for nothing, however – he had learned to become adept at packaging his malicious thoughts in the glossy wrapping paper of hypocrisy. 'If I were you, my *little* girl' – he spat out that 'little' in such a way that no one could miss the way he felt about Kim – 'I would run along. This is no place for the likes of you.' After a pregnant pause, he corrected himself, 'I mean, no place for *healthy* children like you.'

I felt Kim's hand stiffen and grow as cold as ice in mine. Not even at the factory site, when I had tried to walk, had I felt such a stab of pain as this. Never would I forgive Father. Never! Pretending the pain in my arm was getting worse, I began groaning fearfully, just to worry Father.

AN OPEN SECRET

The next three days, I did not have to go to school. I had a note from the doctor excusing me from classes. It was a heaven-sent reprieve, for I had been wondering how I'd be able to stand another minute of school as long as the Huangshuai Movement was in full swing. So my accident could not have come at a better time. Let the others compose denunciation diatribes; I would stay at home and read.

The doctor had told me that starting the following week, I would have to come to the hospital every afternoon for 'wax therapy' sessions, which entailed having a plastic compress filled with piping-hot paraffin pressed on to my bruises. This was supposed to stimulate circulation and speed up the healing process. Whether it did or not, it meant that I would have to absent myself from school every afternoon for medical reasons.

Father had asked for some time off to stay at home with me, something that was hardly ever permitted if you held an important job like his. If forty-eight hours after the initial injury there were still no symptoms of infection, the danger was as good as over. Until then, Father would watch me like a hawk.

Apart from a nagging ache in my arm and legs whenever I moved, I felt pretty good. But I could not concentrate on my book; I couldn't refrain from hoping that Kim would pay me a visit. I kept going over in my mind the way Kim had gone after those kids at the landfill. I had never seen my friend behave like that. I only knew Kim as someone who took our classmates' abuse on the chin, her head hanging low, until her torturers grew tired of it themselves . . .

At around eleven a.m. Father received a phone call from his department. He had to come in at once for an emergency. Weiren Su, the commander-in-chief of one of the armed forces' most important divisions, had to have open-heart surgery. It would be a colossal political blunder if anyone but the department's top surgeon were to wield the scalpel in this operation. There wasn't a hair on Father's head that would *think* of ignoring the summons.

I considered the phone call a boon from Buddha. I had been getting all worked up about it: what would I do about Father, if Kim showed up?

⌒

The young physician sent by Father's unit to take over the vigil greeted me shyly and pulled the chair by my bed as far away as possible, as if I had some contagious disease. That was ridiculous, of course, because, being a medical man, he must have known that that wasn't the way you caught blood poisoning. Whatever the reason, he was acting as if I were a crocodile that was after *his* blood.

Happily, there was a knock at the door. As soon as I saw Kim standing by my bed, I forgot everything else. 'Doctor,' I asked the man, 'would you mind giving me some time alone with my friend?'

The physician got up, rolling up his journal into a tight tube. At the door, polite but embarrassed, he asked me to put the thermometer in my mouth in forty-five minutes.

But what had happened? Kim had a black eye, her lips were swollen and she had a purple welt on her cheek.

Kim rubbed both her hands over her face, as if she could wipe it all away. 'It isn't what you think,' she said, 'it wasn't the little bastards getting back at me.' A self-satisfied smirk stole over her face. 'They wouldn't dare.' The patent pleasure she took in mulling over her 'heroic feat' made my flesh crawl. 'I have Jiening to thank for this.' Pointing at her eye, she explained, 'The little slut! Do you know what my parents discovered, hidden amongst her things? A stack of love letters *this* thick!' She held her thumb and index finger as wide apart as possible, as if gauging the heft of a Chinese dictionary. 'But what was worse was that I had to hear it from the boys next door this morning! I also had to have them tell me that Jiening hasn't turned any of those letter-writers down, she's been making eyes at all of them! She seems to have an honest-to-goodness harem going there! It's been all over the neighbourhood as well as the school. It's been an open secret for a while – only my parents and I were in the dark! Did *you* know?'

I nodded.

The whites of Kim's eyes went purple with rage. 'Why didn't you *tell* me?'

'Because, when she showed me the letters, she threatened me – if I betrayed her, she'd see to it I'd never be allowed in your house again.'

Now Kim turned seriously venomous: 'And you let her get away with blackmailing you? That's just it! You are a coward! And Jiening is a low-down scuzzy sneak! My very own sister, born of my blood! We would never have found out, if one of her beaux hadn't stormed into our home last night . . . carrying a cleaver! Want to know who it was? The Flying Tiger gang leader, Erfu. The very same skunk who turned the *last* girl who jilted him into a half-digested egg-roll with a hundred neighbours watching! He kicked open the door, slammed his knife down on the edge of the kang and yelled, "I've had it, Jiening. What do you need those other guys for? Those skinny, pale-faced, spoiled first-caste brats! I've written you at least ten letters and sent you a hundred gifts and favours! Who d'you think you're dealing with? Fuck your grandfather! How'd you get it into that pretty skull of yours to jerk me around like this?"

'*Tchang!* He whacked the side of the kang so hard with the knife that the blade stuck there, on its edge.

'That made Jiening jump, and she said hastily, "Grandpa Erfu, I am yours."

'I couldn't believe my ears! Jiening was speaking in a honeyed tone dripping with tooth decay, she sounded like an emperor's concubine in the old films. Was that my little sister? With a mollified grin, Erfu asked

Jiening to go for a little stroll around the block. At eleven at night! My parents didn't dare say no – the knife was still quivering in the kang. I wasn't scared, though, and proposed going with them. Jiening decided that was an excellent idea. It was pure blackmail: unless her older sister came too, wild horses couldn't drag her out the door. You should have seen Erfu's face! As if he'd been spreading shit on his bread instead of peanut butter by mistake! But there was nothing he could do about it. Once we were outside, I discreetly hung back a few paces. Then, this morning when I went to drop off Mother's matchboxes at the factory, I ran into Erfu. He was lying in wait for me in order to rearrange my face a little, as you can see.'

'But you'd think, wouldn't you, that he'd want to butter you up instead, seeing that you're the sister of his sweetheart?'

'Do you think that if you're top dog of the most powerful street gang in town like Erfu, you need to do any buttering up to anyone? A knuckle sandwich, sure, when it comes to those he's a soft touch, he isn't stingy in that department, you can count on it. He had to teach me a lesson because I'd ruined his romantic tête-à-tête.'

I didn't know what to think. First those little bastards at the factory, and now this! Kim had made herself another enemy. And what an enemy. This one was more than capable of wringing the neck of anyone standing in his way, without batting so much as an eyelash. But I said, 'Still, there must be someone who can bring him to justice! We'll report him to the police!'

'Are you out of your mind? And don't do that thing with your eyebrows, Lian. Frowning doesn't suit you. Look at what I've brought you!' Elatedly, Kim emptied the contents of her trouser pocket on to my night table: a handful of fruit-flavoured sweets in wax-paper twists, as opposed to the celluloid the more expensive toffees came wrapped in. It was the most extravagant gift she could come up with; never in this life on earth would Kim ever think of forking out so much money for a treat for herself. 'Go on, taste one, to see if it's good.'

I chose a sweet and popped it in my mouth.

Kim gazed at me with a mixture of pride and smothered envy. My throat suddenly pinched shut. What an idiot I was! Kim had probably hardly ever tasted one of these.

'Ouw-ah!' I pretended the candy gave me a toothache. 'See that? My father was right. I shouldn't eat sweets.'

Kim hung her head; she was crestfallen. Her present wasn't a great success. But as I tucked the candies one by one back into Kim's pocket, Kim began to grin from ear to ear – who would have thought she would ever have such a mouth-watering treat all to herself! At my insistence, she carefully stuck one in her mouth. The lines in her face melted like snow before the sun.

Her whole being lit up with delight. I could have flung my arms around her, so happy was I at this sight. And perhaps this was the very reason that I felt so attracted to Kim: Kim could be so happy with every little crumb I threw her way. It made me feel alive.

Still swooning over the dissolving miracle in her mouth, Kim said, 'That showdown at the factory site has taught me a lesson: I'm never going to get down on my knees again to grub for money. If only I'd realised sooner how way below my dignity it was to fight over scraps with some snot-nose punks, I wouldn't have landed myself in so much trouble . . . and I wouldn't have landed *you* in it, either. Gluing matchboxes may be a tortuous way to make a few fen, but at least I don't get kicked around by anyone that way. So it's matchboxes for me, even if it takes all day and all night!'

I could already picture it: Kim as robotic pasting machine, gluing cardboard for the rest of her life. I asked, 'Is there really no other way to make money?'

'Sure. Hijacking farm trucks, *you* know. But I'd never want to get involved in any crooked business.'

I had to stifle the urge to say to her: Why should you give a rat's arse about moral and social principles? The laws were created by the high and mighty with the sole aim of protecting their own interests . . .

THE RED HORSE

After three days, Father could confirm with relief that I showed no symptoms of blood poisoning. The 'wax therapy' I underwent every afternoon only took half an hour; which left me plenty of time for other pursuits. But reading was difficult; the thing I sought in a book, the intersection of my own thoughts and feelings with the writer's, kept slipping out of my grasp, as if the author were playing a game of cat-and-mouse with me. I longed for some new kind of human interaction, but how to find it, I wasn't sure. My voracious hunger for fiction and romance could no longer be stilled with what was to be found in books. I began to write. I wrote little pieces in which nothing took place, in which everything happened inside the mind and the heart. I described the languishing looks of love, I compared the eyes, the hands and the lips of the heroine with the sun, the moon, roses, et cetera. Clichés plucked straight out of juvenile romances was the way Father and Mother would have characterised them. But I didn't give a fig whether my metaphors were romantic, old-fashioned or utterly unoriginal.

Previously, in the camp, the lake behind the barracks had been my sounding board. Qin had listened to me, Cannibal had listened to me, and both had told me what they thought, each in his own way. Even the frogs and the crickets had patiently heard me out. Where could I turn now? Who was left to listen to me? Kim's visits were becoming fewer and farther between; every minute of the day, apparently, was needed to fold matchboxes. Morosely I looked out of the window; my gaze fell on the campus orchard. I snatched my notebook from the bed and a minute later I was standing outside.

The downy, delicate celadon leaves had grown into viridian whoppers the size of your palm; combined, they provided every tree with its own giant parasol. Nature had it figured out just right: when it was cold, the bare branches allowed the sun to filter through unimpeded; now that it was hot, the trees were protected from the scorching sun by their own leaves. I began describing out loud my current preoccupations, and I felt very wise.

Later, I read the stories I had written to the trees. Once again, I imagined myself before an audience that hung on my every word. The rustling of the leaves was the applause interrupting my literary reading. What the leaves really thought of my yarns I wasn't sure, and I didn't really care to know, either. What mattered was that I felt considerably less lonely.

～

There was one thing that did not take the slightest bit of notice of the laws of nature, and that was the Huangshuai Movement. There seemed to be no end to the mass hysteria. The school was and remained a place of torture for the teachers, who had turned into zombies under the constant lashes of criticism and complaint. And as if that weren't enough, the past month had seen a new madness take hold of the academic world: the Zhang Tieshen, or Blank Exam Paper Movement.

When the university entrance exams were held, Zhang Tiesheng, a young peasant, had handed in a blank sheet of paper in protest against the 'bourgeois education system' which 'crammed the students full of Revisionist rubbish which the professors tried to pass off as knowledge'. The henchmen of the Wisest Leader of the Universe jumped at the chance this incident provided to give the institutes of higher learning a taste of purgatory. The Great Helmsman had not been at all content with the notion that only the high-school faculties would be purged of Capitalist elements. Instigating the Zhang Tiesheng Movement was the logical next step, for the universities, too, were in need of an ideological spring cleaning.

You could tell from the dark circles around Mother's eyes that she was going through hell. Like my school, the university building where Mother worked had been transformed into a paper house. The walls, the doors, even the windows were plastered over with denunciation articles. Mother's name was prominently featured in several places, emblazoned with a red cross, a token that she too had been condemned as guilty. I was not allowed to visit Mother's office any more. Mother was afraid, of course, that I would see the wall posters subjecting her to a verbal lynching. But that restriction wasn't enough to keep me from finding out the truth, for occasionally the denunciation meetings scapegoating Mother were simply held at home.

Two weeks earlier, when a student had pushed Mother off the rostrum, she had torn the cartilage in her right knee. Mother was not able to go to work the next day. When I came home at lunchtime, I found a mob of students crowded around Mother's bed, frothing at the mouth, shaking their fists and cursing her.

Appalled, I ran out of the house, down the stairs and out the front door, to the orchard. The silence that hovered between the trees seemed a world apart from the class struggle going on upstairs in my apartment. It inspired me with a deep awe. The branches that only a few weeks ago had flaunted fragrant flowers were now dotted with shiny nodules that, diminutive as they were, had already begun to assume the shape of peaches and pears. So too, I realised, were my own deeds bearing fruit. And with that, I suddenly understood: it was clear that Buddha wanted to show me what it felt like for a teacher to be so savaged by her students. If I had not actively participated in writing those cruel articles excoriating Mrs Meng, then Mother's students might not have been as abusive to her either . . .

Over the past three months, Kim had shown up at school once a week at most. Kim and I used school as our meeting place. Usually Kim would have some news to tell me, for instance the time that the match factory had given her a rush order and she had had to deliver five thousand boxes in three days. She had earned a whole extra fen for every ten boxes – a windfall! She giggled that as far as she was concerned, the factory could be caught short more often. I couldn't wait to hear what news Kim had come to share with me today.

During recess we retired to a deserted corner of the hall, where Kim told me, 'Today I'm taking a break from matchbox-gluing, because Mother says . . . I should take it easy.' There was something soft and bashful in Kim's words – it was something I wasn't used to. Kim blushed, and explained, 'Last night I started riding the red horse . . .'

'What?' I caught Kim by the arms, spun her around and whooped, much too loudly – my exclamation reverberated up and down the halls. If Kim hadn't smothered my mouth with her hand in time, I would have shouted it from the rooftops: You too, Kim – finally! I ended up whispering it in her ear instead. And Kim glowed with pride.

I stopped pirouetting to stare at Kim. Sure enough, the little knobs beneath her blouse had developed into pointy hillocks and her hips now jutted out from her narrow waist. How could I have failed to notice that Kim's face was no longer as sunken and gaunt as before? It was a little more filled out, and a rosy flush tinged the pale yellow of her cheeks. What had been a tangle of lustreless hair was now carefully brushed, and shone in the summer sunshine.

I felt uncomfortable studying my bosom-friend as if she were a stranger, but I had to admit that even when seen through the critical eye of some hard-to-please outsider, Kim could hardly be called skinny or ugly. The shabby, pathetic figure she used to cut had vanished: in its place was the very picture of a blossoming young woman.

NEVER SHOW YOUR FACE AGAIN

Kim was at school again. But this time she had nothing to report at recess. There were times when she did not even seem to hear what I was saying – she kept staring vacantly into the distance.

Kim had begun showing up more frequently at school, traipsing slowly and gracefully through the classroom. She was careful to steer clear of the class bullies, but if they managed to kick her in the shins anyway, she let the tears flow freely where in the old days she would have remained stubbornly dry-eyed. Curiously enough, her unusual reaction induced her tormentors to leave her alone.

One day Kim whispered in my ear, 'Once I deliver my boxes to the match factory this afternoon, I'll have a total of fifteen kuai, clear!'

I had to think for a moment. 'Four months ago you told me you needed a month or so to get your hands on such a sum – Why only now?'

Kim sighed. 'Jiening needed new summer clothes. Anyway, tomorrow's the big day. I've seen a blouse, it's the very latest style, it's really different-looking. I'm going to go and buy it as soon as I've made my delivery.'

I was happy for her. 'Oh Kim, I'm dying to see how it looks on you! I bet it's beautiful.' Kim's feminine curves and gentle features clashed lamentably with the tattered rags clinging to her body. I so longed to be able to admire a decently dressed Kim!

I arrived at school ten minutes early, on purpose. I didn't want to miss Kim's historic entrance.

Despite the fact that Kim hardly needed to be afraid of a beating from her classmates any more, she still took the same precautions as always, out of habit: only when the school bell rang would she set foot inside the classroom. But perhaps there was another reason for it this morning as well: she wanted to show off the fruit of her labours – what four months of collecting scrap metal and gluing mountains of matchboxes had achieved.

When I finally spotted Kim approaching the open door, I had a bit of a shock. Kim was wearing her new blouse, and it had orange and red stripes. Both nice cheerful colours, but . . . both at once? It was a little too much of a good thing. And why did the blouse glitter so harshly? As Kim walked in, her head held high, I could hear the fabric rustling. With scarcely concealed pride, Kim lowered herself graciously into her chair. *Scratch-scratch*. There was that grating sound again.

Over the loudspeakers rattled one of the sermons meant to inflame us with our daily dose of revolutionary fervour. It was still a matter of the most pressing importance to vilify the teachers. But it had been two and a half months since anyone paid any attention. Some just calmly went on with their conversations, others would make eyes at each other effusively. But today an ominous silence prevailed. Everyone stared unblinkingly at Kim's deafeningly loud blouse.

Yougui, who sat two rows behind her, stood up, ostensibly on his way to the bathroom. In passing, he touched Kim's mysterious blouse 'by accident'. He stopped for a moment and turned around, rubbing the fabric between his fingers. A devilish smile lit up his face. Then, drowning out Back-at-my-old-university's hysterical tirade on the intercom, he practically bellowed, 'It's a nylon raincoat! Look! Kim thought it was a classy blouse, and now she's gone and spent her money on *this* get-up here! Or did you *steal* it, Kim?'

Kim did not move a muscle. Stoically she endured the insults being hurled at her head without shedding a single tear, just as she had always done, over the years. I feared the worst. This time Kim would lock up her heart and throw away the key. The devils had discovered her Achilles' heel. I was the only one in the whole class who knew what sort of hell Kim had put herself through to make her dream come true.

During recess I rushed up to Kim to console her, but Kim pushed me away with the strength of a mad bull, then took to her heels.

That afternoon, when school was out, I slunk with lead in my shoes to the mud-hut quarter. I was pretty sure that Kim, in her misery, would not be able to tolerate my presence.

Kim wasn't at home, it turned out. But then where *was* she? This time, Jiening was nowhere to be found either. She was probably hanging out with her gangster boyfriend. Kim's mother, too, was out. Having bequeathed the matchbox job to Kim, her mother had been taking all sorts of temporary jobs over the last few months, such as street-sweeping, emptying public toilet cesspits, and laying sewer pipe.

⌒

Three weeks went by. One morning at recess, I noticed my classmates gossiping. It was Qianyun who broke the news to me: 'Kim has been made a member of the central committee of Erfu's gang!' What now?! I almost hit the roof. Qianyun told me everything she knew, in gory detail.

Two weeks earlier, Kim had introduced herself to a branch of the street gang that specialised in the hijacking of produce trucks; this sideline was actually the gang's main source of income. Kim had reportedly said she needed money for another blouse. The looters had almost bust a gut laughing at her foolishly modest wish. Look here! They pulled up their sleeves – their arms were jam-packed to the elbows with brand-name watches. And all Kim wanted was a shirt! But all right, what did she have to offer *them*? Now it was Kim's turn to grin. What did the champion of the 1500-metres race have to offer them? Or the undefeated grenade-thrower, for that matter?

The next day Kim leaped like a leopard into a wagon loaded with sweet peppers; before the others could blink an eye, she had the tailgate open. She beat the tallest of the gang members to it, the one that had muscles like steel balls. What normally happened was that this fellow would use his hands and feet to shovel the vegetables out of the truck bed, a chore that was slow, noisy, and almost sure to elicit protests from the driver. Not only that: the fragile wares were bound to get damaged. Kim's method, however, was to plunge her hands into the mountain of peppers and draw a straight line down the middle. *Whoop!* Before the swiftest pickpocket realised what was happening, Kim had deftly set the rows of peppers rolling down by the dozen. This feat was carried out so adroitly that the plump vegetables made a soft landing and rolled to a stop unharmed.

Kim's clever schemes and inventiveness made her stand out head and shoulders above the rest. She kept thinking up new ways the gang could make a quick buck. For instance, she suggested sending a boy to the factory site as a lookout, so that they would know when a load of steel plates was deposited next to the landfill. When that happened, the lookout would alert his comrades, in the middle of the night if necessary, to come and collect the goods. The story they had concocted in case they got caught was that they thought the factory had dumped the metal there as refuse. Who could blame them for that? For it was an unwritten law that anything lying around in the open at the industrial site was there for the taking. While of course it should have been obvious to anyone that if the factory was forced to store its raw materials next to the landfill, it was only because the warehouse was full. No one with a splinter of common sense or decency would think of taking advantage of an emergency to rip off the factory. But if people like Kim took it into their heads to do so, there was no legal stipulation stopping them. In any case, Kim was soon voted in as a key member of the gang's central committee.

With a mixture of awe and disgust, Qianyun wrapped up her account. 'To tell you the truth, I'd never have expected it of that pathetic little loser. So you see: poverty and misery are the parents of crime. Lian, I sometimes see you talking to her. If I were you, I would avoid her like the plague from now on.'

I heard out the story, sick at the thought of how selfishly inconsiderate I had been. I hadn't given Kim's humiliation over the gaffe with the blouse a second thought. And now it was too late. Had Kim finally taken the road she had shunned all those years, the one she had always avoided with such iron self-control? Could Kim, who had heretofore always clung to the straight and narrow, suddenly have taken the plunge into a morass of thieving and piracy? Or were my friends just pulling my leg?

The one thing that did not surprise me was that Kim had made it so far in the organisation in so short a time. It should have been obvious that Kim would have a knack for this sort of work, both physically and intellectually.

How could I have let it get to this point? If I had managed to find Kim in time, and talked to her, would she have taken this leap? Or was it just unfounded gossip?

As soon as school was out, hardly conscious of what I was doing, I trudged the route I had taken so many times. As Kim's house came into view, I realised I wasn't looking forward to seeing Kim again. Of course I was curious to see how Kim had changed, but I was scared – scared of a confrontation, scared of loss of face, terrified of rejection. I was overcome with shame. Was that the way to feel about my dearest friend?

Stepping inside, I almost choked to death. The heavy smoke plugging up Kim's house took my breath away. I didn't dare open my eyes because if I did the stinging cigarette fumes would make them water. Or rather, if I did, my eyes might take in what was going on in here.

A rough male voice made me jump: 'Hey, look at what a luscious piece of bimbette-ass Auntie Kim has gone and hooked for herself!'

'You must be out of your mind!' Kim coughed like a novice and clumsily flicked the ash from her cigarette.

I was shaking, yet I was watching my friend like a hawk. Since when had she started smoking? Kim opened her mouth as wide as if she was having her tonsils examined by a doctor, and yelled, 'Are you kidding? Me, lift a finger to hook *that* one? She is a louse in my bushy tail, I can't seem to get rid of her! No matter how I fart, shit or piss! It takes some doing, though, to get a first-caste cunt to grow so attached to you. Liannikins, come over here. Let my comrades-in-arms inspect your cuddly little kitten-face!'

Slavishly, I shuffled into the room, solely to get a better look at Kim. It wasn't only the smoke and the darkness that prevented me from seeing clearly.

I saw something glinting, little flashes of gold, that appeared only whenever one of those fellows spoke. It was only later that I realised it must have been their gold teeth.

I stumbled over to where Kim was sitting. A look of agitation stole over Kim's face, but she quickly recovered, and the mask came down again. She grabbed my hands to introduce me to the man who sat slouched against her: 'Go ahead, feel the skin on this first-caste baggage, as soft as a peeled egg.'

For a moment, I thought it was a subterfuge, an excuse for Kim to have some surreptitious physical contact with me, but apparently Kim really did just want to show off the 'goods', nothing more. I yanked myself free and ran out of the room. A great lummox of a fellow who was keeping watch at the door blocked the exit with his extended arm. Spitting out the cigarette dangling crookedly from his lips, he seized me and kicked me in the knees. Groaning, I fell to the floor.

'Who gave you permission to hit her? You seedless worm! How dare you attack a defenceless girl!' Kim's voice was shaking a little. I immediately forgot my despair. 'Lian Shui, tuck your tail between your legs and get the hell out of our lair! Don't ever show your face in here again! It's for your own good!'

Don't - ever - show - your - face - again - don't - ever - show - your - face - again - don't-ever . . . The words reeled through my head. I felt as cold as ice.

WORD OF MOUTH

Another morning, and Kim was back in her seat in class, as usual. The past few weeks had been a strain on me; I had been doing a lot of thinking. I didn't have the guts to go up and talk to Kim any more. And Kim didn't even deign to glance my way. Why Kim bothered to come to school at all, as she did just about every day, was a mystery. In the first place, there was no learning going on here, because we were still in the throes of revolutionary convulsions; in the second place, it seemed to me that Kim might make much better use of her time if she went out and 'earned' some more money. There was a time when I might have interpreted Kim's conscientiousness as her way of proving her good intentions: Look at me, at least *I'm* behaving like a perfect student, even if you all insist on looking down on me. But these days, there was no reason for her to give a damn about what her classmates thought of her.

Kim had undergone a true metamorphosis. She wore a new blouse every other day. And not just any old blouse, but a blouse of the finest synthetic silk and in the very latest style to boot. You could smell her a mile away, reeking of some brand-name face cream. She must also be getting more vegetables and meat to eat these days – her face looked rosier, lighter of hue, and more filled out.

But that wasn't why our classmates treated her with such respect; if that had been all, they wouldn't have bothered humbling themselves before her. Even the most intrepid among the boys who, at one time, would never have shied from putting Kim through hell, weren't so cocky now, always managing a slimy smile when they saw her. You could see them jiggling up and down like sycophantic grasshoppers whenever they could not avoid being in her company. They treated Kim as if she were a dangerous circus lioness being put through her paces for the very first time.

The memory of our last meeting, or, rather, our last confrontation, strangled every urge I had to start a conversation with Kim. And that was obviously just as well, because whenever I glanced in Kim's direction, I immediately felt an icy blast of indifference. And even if Kim were to give me a chance, what could I say to her? That it wasn't a very smart thing to do, to go against the law just to make a buck? That would be like trying to convince a carnivore that it is inhumane to eat meat. There was no guarantee that Kim wouldn't get pissed off and fly at my throat. For wasn't violence second nature to her now?

Yet I still couldn't help glancing Kim's way every so often. Was *this* my dearest friend? Was this what *used to be* my dearest friend? Why did cold shivers still run up my spine every time Kim turned her head in my direction?

A few days later new information came to my attention. I kept my ears open for the latest. Erfu's organisation had a new lease on life thanks to Kim's audacity and creativity. New goals were mapped out, new courses charted. They were starting a drive to provide protection for any third-caster who was a victim of vilification and ill-treatment by upper-casters. This they hoped to achieve by boosting solidarity among caste members. In the past, Erfu had sometimes tried to settle the score when one of his mates had been kicked around by rich folks' kids, but it had always been a hit-or-miss, spur-of-the-moment affair. Thanks to Kim's knack for organisation, the business was now handled in a more co-ordinated fashion. The third-casters were gaining fresh self-confidence. One day, I even overheard one of them threaten, 'If you lay a finger on me just one more time, I'll tell my caste-brothers. And then you'll be eating shit!'

The gossip – which was just about the only channel that you could count on for any sort of reliable news – was devoted to one subject only these days: the most recent exploits of Kim's mob.

The first- and second-casters weren't too happy, naturally, to see the lowest of the low create such a powerful alliance among themselves, but they weren't seriously worried yet. They were confident that the law was on their side; the police could always be counted on in case of a threat to the general peace. Still, they kept a close eye on what the gang was up to. Almost everyone agreed that those upper-casters who were now being taught a lesson by the mob more than deserved it: they shouldn't have been foolish enough to pick on the low-lifes in the first place. Nor did their dimwit brethren deserve any sympathy. Hadn't they all been taught from the earliest age not to mingle with the lower castes? Everyone could see that the gang violence was an exceptional opportunity to draw the line, once and for all, between the higher and lower castes.

Another reason the first-casters didn't fret too much about the mob was that its brutality was, nine times out of ten, turned on itself. The hoodlums were more prone to beating up their own than members of another caste. But that phenomenon was no surprise to anyone who bothered to take a good look around. I had long observed that in a family where the parents abused the children, the older siblings were bound to bully the younger, and the youngest chewed out the family pet. If there were no dogs or cats at home, you could bet your life that somewhere under the youngest child's pillow or mattress, you would come upon a doll with its guts ripped open and its face scratched to bits.

~

New rumours, and juicy ones too! The beauteous Jiening had dumped Erfu! My hair stood on end when I heard it. I knew what Erfu was capable of. Weilin, now Jiening . . .

It must have been written in the stars, that Erfu's second true-love should *also* leave him for some pale-skinned rich man's son. Such a disgrace, such an insult and humiliation for the commander of the most powerful street gang of them all! But he was forced to swallow his defeat like a knocked-out tooth this time. For the father of Jiening's new boyfriend was a general. When she broke the news to Erfu that she was leaving him, her new swain was standing right outside the door, flanked by his papa's bodyguards, complete with loaded revolvers at the hip. When Jiening was done with her speech, her boyfriend felt the need to step inside Erfu's room for form's sake and warn him he had better not take it into his head to take revenge in whatever way, shape or form – or his father would immediately see to it that his gang was washed up for ever. The warning did not fall on deaf ears: no little woman, no matter how tasty a piece of tenderloin she might be, was worth risking the organisation for.

~

Then I heard that Erfu was in love with Kim. Erfu? The guy who had never had eyes for anything but classic beauties and doll-like little princesses? Kim? That girl could outrun the most strapping fellow, lift a hundred-pound bag of vegetables off the floor as if it were a box of matches, smoke like the chimney stack on a power plant and curse to make a corpse grow cold. How could a gang leader with such pernickety tastes fall for a girl like Kim?

And he wasn't just a little bit smitten either, if the rumours were to be believed. For Kim, who had heretofore never aroused any emotions in a boy other than repulsion or an itch to molest her, it was an honour to be sure, to be desired by such an important man as Erfu!

It was really too crazy for words. It seemed Kim was threatening to resign from the gang's central committee if Erfu wouldn't stop 'bugging her' with his cloying attentions, ridiculous histrionics, declarations of passion and love and bucketfuls of expensive gifts.

THE TOAD AND THE SWAN

One morning there was a crowd of at least a hundred students huddled around a placard posted on the wall. That was strange, because the writing of wall posters had long become a mere formality. Nobody took the trouble to read that nonsense any more. Most of them were just carbon copies of the ones posted the day before, solely to fill the daily quotas and placate the school cadres. Why all the interest in that rubbish all of a sudden? It was a mystery to me. Was a new teacher being accused of wandering down the Capitalist road? But no, surely that didn't qualify as *news* as such.

Moreover, it was as good as impossible. In the four months that the Huangshuai hysteria had been dragging on, almost every teacher had had a turn at martyrdom. Headmaster Chen and Deputy Headmistress Back-at-my-old-university were the only ones who had managed to escape. Or else could it be that some clever opportunist had finally managed to outdo Chen in radical-red correctness, and had toppled Chen from his throne on the pretext of safeguarding the purity of the proletarian movement? But even that would hardly be earth-shattering news. Someone was always ousting somebody else, and the excuse was always the same: he was truer to his Party than the others.

But – of course! It wasn't a denunciation article that the students were gaping at, at all. I should have known – it was a love letter, pasted right over a disintegrating piece of political slander.

I wormed my way through to the front. There I found myself surrounded by giggling girls. I got a kick out of the boys' howls of laughter. What an impassioned piece of writing! I had to admit – it was a literary masterpiece. Quite a refreshing change from the delirious, drooling platitudes your run-of-the-mill lovesick fool usually trotted out. This writer knew how to express his emotions in a clear, logical, even sober manner. At the same time, he knew how to let his overpowering passions rumble like mountains in an earthquake before imploding in irresistible ecstasy . . . Truly, this was poetry.

But the more first-rate the letter, the greater the bystanders' mirth. People were pointing at certain characters, parroting this or that phrase, and testing out words for possible double meanings. What a field day they were having!

What flights of inspiration the author had managed to set off, with his amorous pyrotechnics!

I was grinning right along with the others, unmindful of how despicable it was of the recipient to make the letter public to the entire school, thereby nailing her secret admirer's innermost feelings to the cross. Actually, I wasn't laughing at the author, far from it: I was terrified I might someday give in to similar desires. Lately, whenever I found myself daydreaming about love, I was seized with wild heart palpitations. I had no idea, in Buddha's name, what to do about it. Whenever it happened, I would hastily sweep my emotions under the carpet and pretend to be the same old Lian Shui as before, the one who had absolutely no patience for love and considered the longing for intimacy a sign of weakness and spiritual decay. In this respect I surely was not the only one; otherwise my fellow students wouldn't be putting on such a display of excessive hilarity over the love letter.

My disgust with the addressee deepened as I considered where it had been hung. The wall poster was, in Chen's words, 'the guillotine of the counter-revolutionary, the Revisionist and the bourgeois-leaning scum'. By posting the letter here, the recipient had pinned her secret admirer to the very wall where the teachers were hung out to dry and used for revolutionary target practice – a clever move!

All in all, however, I was not too unhappy about this incident, at least it injected a little spice into the bland school diet. The whole Huangshuai business had grown as dull as dishwater.

But wait a minute – the handwriting was familiar. My eyes whipped to the bottom of the letter, and the laugh on my face died away: *Signed, Kim Zhang*. The envelope was pinned underneath. *Addressee: Wudong*.

Wudong, Buddha's gift to women. Even the stunning Miss Meimei hadn't stood a chance with him. Wudong. Kim. What could have possessed Kim to spill her most intimate feelings to *him*? She had spurned the golden chance of a gang leader's infatuated devotion because of Wudong?

I could have kicked myself for having had a laugh at the expense of this 'besotted letter from a brushed-off lover'. How could I have been so mean, to jeer at the writer? I'd been tossing rotten eggs up into the air and now they were pelting down on my head. I stank to high heaven. But how could I have guessed that the correspondent was none other than Kim? I'd have Wudong's scalp, and gladly! What was his heart made of – granite or something? How could he bring himself to kick around the heart of a lovesick girl like a football? How happy I was, in retrospect, that I had never responded to his advances! Or, on the contrary, should I have led him on, so that now I'd be in a position to pickle his feelings in brine?! But okay, there wasn't much sense in indulging in this sort of mental gymnastics

320

right now; what was done, was done. Kim had worn her heart on her sleeve, and it had turned her into an utter fool.

Where *was* Kim, anyway? I ran to the classroom. There she sat, all by herself, oblivious of the sword dangling over her head. Apparently she was the only one left out of the loop. Her eyes swarmed with question marks – the bell had gone, so where *was* everyone? I didn't have the nerve to look her in the eye. I prayed to Buddha that He would spare me from having to watch Kim go to pieces once she discovered the despicable trick that had been played on her.

When the classmates finally trickled in one by one, you could read the quandary in their faces. On the one hand, the skin on their bellies was bursting with glee and scorn for poor demented Kim – the horny toad that dreams of tasting the flesh of a snowy swan! On the other hand, they were terrified of her reaction, now that she was this tough-as-nails gangster's moll, whose fists didn't have any blinkers on.

It did not take long, however, for Kim to work out what was going on. From our classmates' sniggering and whispering, she gathered, slowly but surely, what the story was. Halfway through 'Director' Chen's revolutionary sermon, Kim stood up, pushed her desk over and started lashing out with her feet left and right, kicking at desks and chairs, whether there were students seated in them or not. With a great creaking, the tables crashed to the floor, crushing the legs of classmates and wiping the grins right off their faces. With their hearts in their mouths, they followed the temper tantrum of this goaded lioness; they feared the worst, seeing Kim tearing her way to the back of the room where Wudong was seated, shaking in his boots. They all jumped out of their seats when Kim came anywhere near them; some even shoved their desks obsequiously into her hands, to make it easier for her to vent her anger.

Wudong was cowering in a corner, protected by walls on two sides. He had folded himself as small as possible, to shield himself from Kim's blows. Spewing obscenities, she stormed up to him, halting right in front of his nose.

She looked at him.

The iron in her fists melted.

Her curses died on her lips.

The classroom became very quiet.

Kim's hot tears streamed down her fashionable blouse on to the cold, cold floor.

Finally it dawned on me: so *that* was why Kim had been coming to school every day – despite the fact that the 'lessons' were strictly for the birds! *That* was why she never wore the same blouse twice, why she had been lathering expensive creams on her face . . . that was why she was always staring blankly into space! Kim's heart had flown to Wudong and her romantic fantasies had smothered her common sense.

Wudong peeked at his victim and finally screwed up the nerve to break the silence. 'Kim . . . Kim, I really wasn't going to post your letter on the wall at first, *they* insisted . . .'

'Shut up!'

Kim raised her fist and punched, instead of Wudong's head, the wall next to his ears. It left a bloody print on the cement. A heartrending groan escaped her lips.

Her dream was shattered – by a despicable, singularly chicken-hearted Prince Charming, at that. If only he had kept his trap shut! Then Kim would have been spared this final disenchantment. To have her love rejected, that was something she could have seen coming – she knew better than anyone that she was the *horny toad*, and he the *white swan*. She might even, in the long run, have come to terms with his cruelty in making her letter public – the stony heart of her beloved prince serving to render the tragedy of her Great Love all the more poignant. But his cowardly behaviour wrecked everything. Was this the boy she had admired so? Who would ever have suspected that under Wudong's lovely skin there lurked such a mean-spirited, spineless jellyfish?

Kim wiped her bloody fist on her snow-white shirt and stumbled out of the room, sobbing without making a sound.

⌒

As soon as school was out, I ran home to the campus and dived into the orchard – an oasis of peace and ripening. The buds had grown into life-size pears and peaches everywhere. How long had it been since I had been here? Too long. I sighed with contentment and gratefully sniffed in the sweet scents. But the more I felt this place could offer me the peace that I sought, the more I was tormented by memories of recent events. Kim's ill-considered purchase of the garish raincoat masquerading as a lovely blouse; the solace she had found in the criminal underworld; and worst of all, her mad crush on that wimp Wudong . . .

I leaned against a pear tree. I felt how the tree was alive, felt the impatient stirrings of the fruit that was bowing down the boughs, felt the way the weight of my own body caused them to quiver. I asked the sea of green: 'Do you, by any chance, understand how appearances can be so deceptive? Wudong, that most desirable of Prince Charmings, today showed himself to be no better than a cow-pie lacquered over in pretty shades. Why couldn't

Kim have noticed it before? Did she *have* to throw herself at him, heart and soul? Though to be honest, I have to admit I was as shocked as she was this morning. Who would have thought that such a good-looking boy could be walking around with such rotten-to-the-core insides?'

The silence felt like a slap in the face. Although I should have known better, I had seriously expected the trees to give me some kind of answer. But the only reply was the all-pervasive fragrance of fruit and grass. I half-closed my eyes and in my imagination the scents became the arms of Cannibal, which lifted me up to carry me with him to Nirvana. I spread my arms and got ready to fly.

LABYRINTH OF LOVE

It was months before I saw Kim again.

The stories making the rounds reported that ever since the day of Wudong's betrayal, Kim could be seen – in public! – walking arm-in-arm with Erfu, something that was generally considered morally corrupt. You either shuddered at that sort of carrying-on, or you rooted for it, depending on whether you were a slavish disciple of the Helmsman or followed your own heart. Over her parents' objections, Kim moved in with Erfu. But no one could figure out why she kneed him in the groin every time he called her 'sweetheart'.

Kim's prominence in the gang was growing by the day, and even Erfu had to think thrice before shunning the plan of action she came up with. If his subordinates came forward with a new proposal, he'd say, 'I'll give it some thought.' What he really meant, of course, was, 'My girlfriend Kim will give it some thought.' But despite Kim's outstanding abilities as head of the organisation, and the deep respect she enjoyed among the gang members, her name still left an unpleasant aftertaste. She was known to be a strange duck, hard as nails, unflappable, a girl who did not shrink from any violence and who always kept a cool head, even in the most perilous scrapes ... but who lost all self-control if anybody so much as dared to demonstrate any genuine affection for her. Tenderness would bring a fellow nothing but vicious truculence – or annihilation – and for that reason, Erfu, who seemed bewitched by her eccentric personality, for the most part left her alone. It was enough for him that he and Kim were shacked up together; what might be going on in her mind was beyond him – not that he wanted to know, anyway. Making a virtue out of necessity, he'd always come up with the same joke: 'My girlfriend is an angel. She commutes between Heaven and Earth, and keeps two lovers. One of them is flapping around up there, the other one is me. What a lucky devil I am!'

~

There were three weeks to go before the summer holidays. My life rippled along calmly without Kim. Lots was happening, but it all slipped past me without affecting me, like a hand trying to scratch your back through three layers of sweaters. Something had happened that had caused a big to-do throughout the school, involving the young maths teacher Mrs Xu, the one I had overheard complaining about students' treatment of her and whom Mrs Feng had been trying to console. As a token of gratitude, Xu had denounced Mrs Feng to the school authorities as a covert counter-revolutionary element. After her initial weeping spells, it seemed that Xu had come to her senses. Once she had had the chance to look around – and up – she had concluded that only those adaptable enough to smother their consciences and go along with all the Red insanity, had a chance of survival. Or better even: they could take a stab at climbing up the ladder. Opportunist that she was, she saw the light and adopted 'Director' Chen and Back-at-my-old-university as her illuminating role models. She wrote down the things Feng had said to console her, used her vivid imagination to embellish it here and there in order to bring out the reactionary nature of Feng's words, and added some proletarian, gunpowder-pungent criticisms of her own.

Chen praised Xu's conduct to the heavens, because slowly but surely he had managed to back himself into a somewhat isolated corner – having mown down all his colleagues except the Deputy Headmistress, he had no supporters left standing to help carry the Huangshuai Movement forward. In this young snitch he recognised a great opportunity: he would recruit to his side a number of instructors who lacked the spine or integrity to resist. He gave Xu the most important post in the school after the two directorships: Head of the Secretariat. And so she was now walking around with her nose in the air and was happily barking out orders.

Feng had been locked up in a makeshift solitary-confinement cell in one of the school's outbuildings, and from there was soon sent away to a re-education camp in Heilong Jiang Province – in the northernmost reaches of China – so that the informer would not have to face either her victim or her own conscience.

I, meanwhile, had become so inured to machinations of this sort, all carried out in the name of the Revolution, that when I heard this story

I didn't even raise an eyebrow. I had kept myself removed from any involvement in politics, which in my eyes was nothing but a wrestling match between two opposing parties – those that were more skilled at the art of lying and bluffing threw their opponents in jail.

The only thing that really interested me now was the pursuit of the Art of True Love, to put into practice what I had learned from the banned romances that were still being passed clandestinely from hand to hand. I already knew what it was like to go into raptures over some phantom dreamboat, but was beginning to look around to see if I couldn't spot the real thing. The boys my age didn't attract me, perhaps because, like me, they were too self-involved, in search of their own identities. They just didn't have it in them to pay enough attention to their girlfriends, no matter how they swore high and low that they loved them. Anyhow, the boys had a look in their eyes that I didn't particularly appreciate. To a boy, a cute girl was a lollipop that existed only to satisfy his sweet tooth. No, I was more interested in the teachers.

The man who taught physics to the seniors, Mr Gong Wei, was the one I fancied the most. Even though I had never sat in his class, I had heard enough flattering things about him to know that he was not only an excellent teacher thoroughly versed in his subject, but a very likable sort besides. Also, over the past three months I had been seeing quite a lot of him – at the special denunciation meetings the whole school was required to attend. At such gatherings, only the most criminal elements, in other words the cream of the faculty, were put through the wringer. Their hands were tied behind their backs with thick rope; they had to bow down so that their head hung between their knees. Every few minutes, when a few lines from a denunciation article had been read, these teachers would have their faces slapped, their hair pulled and – if the paragraph in question contained some particularly important political lesson – their groins viciously kicked. In view of the fact that with their hands lashed behind their backs it was hard for the teachers to keep their balance, they often fell down and hurt themselves. They would groan piteously as the students hauled them upright like sacks of garbage and tried to steady them back on their feet. Gong Wei invariably retained his dignity during this kind of episode, no matter how grotesquely he was mistreated; even if he got his nose rammed into the ground, he never complained. One day a student grabbed him so roughly that she yanked a handful of hair right out of his head. Startled, she jumped back, let the tuft of hair flutter to the floor, and burst into tears in the middle of the stage, in full view of hundreds of participants. Gong Wei looked up at her with compassion and tried to reassure her with a friendly smile as the blood dripped down his head.

The girl had been trailing him wherever he went ever since. This in itself wasn't too difficult to do – he had been assigned a new job, together with a number of his colleagues: mopping the bathroom, corridor and classroom floors. He also had to sweep the streets around the school. Whenever this girl caught up with him, she would offer him a glass of water, for his thirst, or a towel to wipe his sweat. But he pretended not to see her, because he knew people were beginning to notice her misplaced sympathy for a reactionary element – an offence that could get her into serious trouble. He was trying to save her by giving her the brush-off. Such a fine, caring man – his concern made my heart beat faster . . .

Alas, as if fate wanted to play a trick on me, Gong Wei didn't take the slightest bit of notice of me, whereas 'Director' Chen, the conniving sneak I detested with all my heart, was paying a little more attention to me than he should.

A SUGGESTIVE ANTHOLOGY

In the middle of July, ten students of different levels were summoned to the Headquarters of the Huangshuai Movement. I was one of them. What we had in common was that we had all received high marks in writing and composition. We were each given a week to complete five denunciation articles, which were to be assembled into a pamphlet; the idea was that the students would take this anthology home, to study it during the vacation. I was given the additional job of editing the articles. Naturally, Chen was the editor-in-chief. Since I reported directly to him, I often had to go and ask him for guidance. The odd thing was that he didn't roar at me like a bear that's undergoing castration, as he tended to do when delivering the incendiary revolutionary speeches I heard over the loudspeakers every morning. On the contrary, in my presence he would loll back in his desk chair, completely relaxed, twirling a pen between his thumb and forefinger and rolling his eyes left, right, up and down. He never said anything overtly flirtatious, but still he managed to give me the message that he was coming on to me.

Thus one afternoon, after a quick look at the draft I'd written of the anthology's table of contents, he said, in a deliberately deep voice, 'It's just – beautiful!' But he wasn't looking at the sheets of paper in his hands; his eyes were like a two-way escalator, roving from my face down to my breasts and back up again. He slobbered over the word 'beautiful' in such a way that even the back end of a pig wouldn't be fooled into thinking he was referring to the table of contents. What was worse, it kindled my vanity, and I promptly fell under the spell of his flattery, even though common sense told me I ought to despise the opportunistic brute. I had to give it to him: Chen, an older man, certainly seemed to have a knack for seducing young girls with his sweet-talking. Compared to this, Liqiang's awkward fumbling had been nothing. But then I glanced out the window to see the noble Mr Gong Wei sweeping the courtyard under the burning sun. I managed to keep Chen safely at arm's length, despite his manifest displeasure and barrage of sly insinuations.

RUINATION AND RESTORATION

The stories about Kim and her buddies were becoming ever more hair-raising. Their looting was getting out of hand. Whereas they used to take to their heels as soon as the driver yelled, 'That's enough now! Scram!' They had now begun molesting any truck driver who tried to defend his merchandise. Kim's mob had apparently decided they could afford to stage brazen heists in broad daylight. But the produce drivers weren't born yesterday, and they alerted the police. Now Kim and her gang had to contend with armed police officers, who were on the prowl to catch them in the act. The only way to counter that problem was to get themselves some guns; and obtaining guns was easier than you might think. During the initial phases of the Cultural Revolution, all kinds of weapons, including machine-guns, had been used in the internecine fighting to defend the purity of Mao's teachings. Despite a strict ban on gun ownership, quite a number of people still had them. Besides, the security around the arms arsenals was no longer airtight, thanks to the disruptions of the Red Revolution. The buzz was that Kim's group had managed to get its hands on hand-grenades and dozens of rifles, which they had hidden somewhere in the hills not far from the mud-house quarter. This rumour in itself was enough to douse the policemen's enthusiasm for sabotaging Kim's looting sorties. There was enough violence as it was: sabres were rattling everywhere, and the police units themselves were no exception. Even in their own ranks, the Capitalist Roaders were being hounded or sometimes clobbered to death by the radical leftists. Compared to that, the nicking of some vegetables and the mugging of a few country bumpkins wasn't even worth mentioning.

*   *   *

As the summer holidays approached, I picked up again my lukewarm, but relatively safe friendship with my fellow caste members. For a whole month I believed myself to be on the same wavelength as my girlfriends. And I did not need to feel guilty about Kim any more.

This was the month the Huangshuai and Zhang Tiesheng Movements were finally called to a halt. The *People's Daily* – the CPC's throat and tongue – claimed the reason was that the academic world had now been thoroughly purged of Revisionist elements, whereas independent reports via the gossip channel suggested it was because the Helmsman's Parkinson's Disease had taken a turn for the worse, thereby giving His opponents in the Politburo the upper hand. These reformers, who had seen themselves squelched by Him until now for being such Capitalist Roaders, made quick work of the countless campaigns that were paralysing the nation. They reactivated the education system, with the result that Huangshuai and Zhang Tiesheng were toppled from their perches.

When I walked in through the school gates on the first day back after summer holiday, I saw that the buildings had been scrubbed clean; there wasn't a scrap of wall poster left in sight. The lamp-posts, which had been swaddled for months in belligerent handbills, revealed their true nature once more: grey cement. The teachers were walking around with textbooks under their arms instead of mops or brooms. They had traded the rags they used to wear for the impeccable clothes befitting a teacher. Rushing from their offices to the classrooms, they were making final preparations for the new semester. From the cheerful expressions on their faces and the sense of authority they projected, you would never have guessed that just a few weeks ago they had been tormented and beaten as political criminals. But look closer, and you could see traces of the ravages the Huangshuai Movement had inflicted on them: grey hair and crow's feet for even the youngest teachers, and much worse for those over forty. Mr Gong Wei was walking around with his head held high, the way I remembered, but his gait was not as steady as before – his left knee had been irreparably damaged when a student had allowed himself to get a little carried away in his counter-revolutionary frenzy and had attacked it with a padlock chain.

The school administration exhibited a similar mix-up of rehabilitation and permanent damage. According to the Ministry of Education, those who had seized power during the Huangshuai Movement now had to clear the decks. Two months ago Mr Dong, the former Director, had suffered a brain haemorrhage during a denunciation session, which had left him paralysed on his left side. Since Chen already held the post of Deputy Director before the Movement was launched, he was now Deng's official successor. And seeing that Chen's own old post was now vacant, Back-at-my-old-university was able to keep her position as Deputy Directress. Only Mrs Xu, the one who had turned in her colleague and had zoomed to the top so fast, wasn't able to make her newly won status stick. Now that the normal teaching routine had been resumed, the Head of the Secretariat shouldered a heavy burden. The person who held that post had to be experienced in financial administration, as well as personnel issues, and have great co-ordination abilities to call on besides, or else the school, with its eleven hundred pupils, ninety teachers and thirty support personnel, would turn into bedlam. Chen couldn't take that risk, no matter how highly he valued the whistle-blower's erstwhile contribution to the Huangshuai Movement. Conscious of the fact that his own Director's chair was rather wobbly, he was determined to prove to his superiors that he was the man for the job. So, in order to let her down gently, Chen fobbed Xu off with the honorary title of Commissioner of Propaganda. The way things stood, propaganda was no longer relevant, now that the political cyclone had blown itself out. Still, it was a respectable demotion for a once-influential opportunist – it allowed her to step down, without loss of face, to a position more suited to her qualifications.

'On your feet!' Shunzi ordered the class when Mrs Meng entered the classroom, thus re-establishing the routine of showing a teacher respect.

'Good morning.' Mrs Meng's voice sounded feeble, weaker than the one we were used to hearing before the Huangshuai Movement. But her tone was as friendly as ever, as if she had never been cursed, humiliated, falsely accused or tormented by us. She walked to the podium and placed her textbooks and folders on the table.

Shunzi wasn't the only one who was bothered by guilt feelings that he was taking care to hide. The rest of us, too, were asking ourselves: How can Mrs Meng still be so nice to us, after all that we did to her? Doesn't she harbour any resentment towards us? Why doesn't she use her position of authority to take revenge? Also, it took some getting used to, to see our teacher standing upright; for months we hadn't seen anything of her but the top of her skull, since she had had to stand with her head pressed to her knees the whole time.

Little by little we relaxed. Mrs Meng's forgiving nature was apparent in the way she resumed her teaching, with the same combination of level-headedness and enthusiasm as always.

Kim's chair was empty. I hadn't expected otherwise; it wouldn't surprise me if Kim hadn't even taken the trouble of enrolling for the school year. Did

Kim realise what she was missing? The disorganisation of the Huangshuai Movement was over and it should be easy for her to catch up. There was no reason, then, to remain with the street gang, was there? I feared that Kim had sunk so far into the quicksand of gang life that she had lost any aspirations she might once have had to a more socially acceptable road to success.

But imagine my astonishment when the next day I saw Kim sitting in her usual place! She was wearing a brand new polyester outfit, her hair was combed and her face was slick with an almond-scented cream that had been a tad too liberally applied. She sat at her desk and obeyed all the rules, like a good girl. In maths class, she was called on and, to everyone's amazement, she got the answer right. It shouldn't have been all *that* astonishing, since while she had been playing hooky, her classmates' time had been exclusively employed in making life hell for the teachers; basically, she hadn't missed a thing.

Her presence certainly did not go unnoticed, however. The students shrank from her in fear and apprehension; the teachers did not bother to sweep their contempt and disapproval of her under the carpet. Mrs Meng, for example, said things like '*you* people' and 'your kind of crowd' whenever she addressed Kim. You couldn't help noticing that whereas the teachers harboured no hard feelings towards the students who had tormented and insulted them during the Huangshuai Movement – on the contrary, these were treated like innocent angels – their demeanour towards Kim, who hadn't uttered a nasty word nor lifted a finger against them, was rude and denigrating. Clearly the teachers considered the wholesale brutality that went hand-in-hand with political movements a freak occurrence, forgivable in light of what was going on elsewhere throughout the country. However, the caste differences were an immutable fact of life which they must never, under any circumstances, forget.

And so Kim's resolve to be a model pupil and create a place for herself in 'decent' society was nipped in the bud. She became more and more impossible for the teachers to control. But she never skipped school any more; in fact, her punctuality was just one more thorn in the side of the instructors, who looked down on her as nothing but scum. Kim's rigidly pursed lips and the fire in her eyes were not good signs. Our classmates and teachers were intent on freezing Kim out, and Kim was doing everything she could to worm her way back inside.

TO MIRU

The autumn break was the perfect occasion for a school camping trip. It had been years since my school had arranged any kind of outing. But this year, to prove to us and our teachers that the Huangshuai Movement was definitely over, that the school's return to normality was for real, and perhaps even to compensate in some small measure for the ravages wrought by the political insanity, Chen was organising a very special camping expedition.

He had truly outdone himself. Through all sorts of second- and third-hand connections, he had managed to rent a pint-sized island for two weeks. It was called Miru, and it was situated about eighty miles offshore. The island came with a five-storeyed dormitory building, a canteen and a little ferryboat that provided transportation to and from the island, and which could also be used for excursions along the coast.

We couldn't concentrate on our lessons any more – all worked up, we maintained an incessant chatter. The water would be warm enough to go swimming, there would be wild animals to see – Miru was a nature reserve – and there would be unusual shells to find on the beach.

The formalities required in preparation for the trip were less fun, however. We all had to go to the doctor for a written affidavit of good health. That meant waiting in line for hours, filling in forms in quadruplicate and having blood drawn for blood tests. 'You see,' said Mrs Meng, 'we can't afford the risk of having anyone infected with a chronic or contagious disease come along. Miru is so far from the inhabited world; if anyone gets sick, help will be hard to come by.' Our parents were also asked for their written consent, because the school was not inclined to ship some mama's boy or girl all the way out to the island only to have them bawl their eyes out with homesickness once they got there.

We had to be divided into bunkmate-groupings, like last year. This should have been a pretty straightforward procedure; we had become used, through the years, to being sorted according to caste, as simple as that. Kim, however, posed an unexpected obstacle. At the time of the Learn from the Peasants internship, it hadn't been *such* a terrible calamity for her fellow caste-members to be assigned Kim as their room-mate, but now that she was an outlaw, everyone jumped out of her way as if she were a bucket of spitting sulphuric acid. From Mrs Meng, Kim could expect no sympathy, far from it: what she got instead was a trenchant raising of the eyebrows connoting downright antipathy and abomination. After a lot of sparring among the third-caste groups, which laid into each other viciously in the hope of proving that the rival sisterhood was more suited to Kim's company, the umpire, Mrs Meng, stepped into the ring to halt the bout: 'Stop your squabbling! You have all won, the lot of you. Kim doesn't have to bunk with any of you. I'm going to see the Director, to ask for a solution acceptable to all parties involved.'

While her caste-mates' bickering had been going on, Kim's face had first turned red with anger, then pale with indifference. But by the end, when Mrs Meng intervened, a cryptic grin had slowly but surely crept across her face. She folded her arms across her chest and sat there calmly observing her fellow students flying at each other's throats over where she ought to sleep, as if they were fighting about someone else.

Three days later Director Chen did indeed come up with a solution: he assigned Kim to the broom closet that was situated somewhere on the ground floor; the buckets, dustpans, brooms and mops would be cleared out to make room for a straw pallet for Kim.

'Gee! A room all to myself! Just for me alone! What a lucky dog I am!' It was the first time since the autumn camping trip had been announced that Kim had actually opened her mouth. She laughed so hard that her whole body shook, and for one long minute her classmates cowered in their seats. Kim's eyes were spewing sniper-fire, the way they had done on the day she tossed chairs and desks around to clear a path to get at Wudong.

The three senior years, including my class, would occupy the island the first week. After the week was over we would leave, to make room for the juniors moving in. Kim sat there taking it all in with an inscrutable grin.

Monday, 20th October 1974: the big day, finally. After a three-hour bus ride, we boarded the boat, which was bobbing impatiently at the dock. On deck, I allowed my eyes free rein. It took some getting used to, to see only one colour everywhere one looked. The familiar brownness of the earth slipped out of sight, and with it went the comforting sense of being at one with my surroundings. I was tickled by a mild curiosity and vague apprehension. I combed my fingers through my hair, tousled by the salty wind, and admitted the generous sea air deep into my lungs and my being.

All the passengers were huddled together on deck, pressed against the railings. We weren't all chattering for once. Impressed by the immense expanse of water, we were silent, lost in our own thoughts. I had always assumed that man was the ruler of the universe. After all, mankind could employ its technological wizardry to change a green meadow into a grey factory or a white skyscraper at the drop of a hat; similarly, with a flick of a switch it could transform respected academics into bourgeois-sympathising cow-devils and snake-demons overnight; it could even use political propaganda to whip up a peacefully co-existing population into a rabble of revolutionary warmongers who couldn't wait to fly at each other's throats, in just a matter of hours. But the sea – the sea was worlds removed from man's terror and machinations. Should the Almighty Helmsman try to roar at the sea, to intimidate her by calling her a 'Capitalist roader', it wouldn't make a speck of difference to the sea; she would not be even the slightest bit ruffled.

As we drew nearer to the distant little speck in the water, it grew larger and clearer, until it assumed the shape of a molehill. Miru was in sight.

⌒

My dream was like a painting. A pale golden beach, orange coral reefs, dark-green scrub, the brown earth and the biscuit-coloured building that was our abode. The dominating hue, however, was that of the sea, which, aside from being so immense, was such a saturated blue that I felt that my own body would turn blue too if I gazed at it long enough. I saw Kim standing all by herself in the stern, while the prow and sides were so jam-packed with fellow students that they threatened to burst – literally, since the metal railings were bulging dangerously from the crush of the crowd: no one wanted to miss out on getting the best view of the endlessly fascinating sea. It was a chilling contrast: the emptiness around Kim, and the bustling scene just a few feet away from her.

But now the miserable expression slithered off Kim's face; a grimace appeared in its stead. She stuck her index finger into her mouth and let out a piercing whistle. At her feet the deck split in two, and out leaped five boys with long hair that stuck straight up from their heads, which made them look as if they'd been electrocuted. Sinking deferentially to their knees before Kim, they were all ears, awaiting her command.

Kim's lips moved. She spoke . . .

I struggled with all my might to open my eyes. I didn't want to hear the order Kim was giving them. But the nightmare galloped on.

When I finally awoke with a start, I told myself to forget my dream, to refuse to acknowledge what I had heard or seen. Fortunately the beach was littered with shells – beachcombing would take my mind off it.

⌒

The next day there was a swimming session. We discovered, to our pleasant surprise, that our swimming performance had improved all around, even though it didn't *feel* as if we had exerted ourselves more than we would in the pool. Mr Gong Wei explained that the water here was thirty per cent salt, which made us more buoyant. I knew this in theory, from my physics lessons, but I would never have guessed that it could have anything to do with real life.

In the afternoon, we were given a tour of the wooded hill straddling the centre of the island. Our biology teachers were going to point out and explain a few things. Never had we seen such dense undergrowth! We became even more excited when our teachers warned us to keep to the footpath or run the risk of landing in a swamp or quicksand – or of startling the wild animals that lived in the forest. We were tickled to death when we spotted an iguana – well, his tail anyway, which – *zoom!* – scooted under a rock as soon as it heard our cries of astonishment. While one of the teachers chronicled the anatomy and feeding habits of the lizard family, we eagerly stopped to pick the exotic fruits and berries proffered by the underbrush. We listened respectfully, with only half an ear, to the 'lesson'; we felt sorry for our instructors who couldn't help practising their profession, even while on holiday. We hitched up our overloaded trouser pockets with smugness. Mmmm! What a treat we were in for tonight, feasting on the fruit that hadn't cost us a fen!

POWER CUT

At nine thirty that evening, my forty dorm-mates and I were crowded into a tiny bathroom meant for no more than six people. We were getting ourselves ready for bed. Naturally, there was some pushing and shoving at the sink. My shoulders were wedged between five or so sturdy girls; even if I gave up on trying to wash myself, I'd never be able to squeeze myself out of this impossibly crowded cubicle. As if that wasn't bad enough, the power suddenly went out. With toothbrush in hand and foaming mouths, dozens of us barged into each other, getting increasingly panicked the longer the impenetrable darkness held. All semblance of reason evaporated. Instead of staying calm and requesting those nearest the door to leave first, we got into each other's way, trying to claw a passage out of the claustrophobic hole. The result was that no one could budge, neither forwards nor backwards; we were all trapped.

Mrs Meng hurried towards us, stumbling over obstacles. I could hear her feet colliding with benches and tripping over the water basins, backpacks and shoes that lay scattered on the floor.

Mrs Meng's firm, reassuring voice could be heard over our screeching: 'Director Chen and Mr Gong Wei are on their way down to the cupboard housing the circuit breakers. It's probably just a blown fuse, they'll have it fixed in no time, so don't be scared.'

But as the darkness pressed in on us further, Mrs Meng's words lost their soothing effect. The whimpered wailing, grumbling and swearing drowned everything else in an ocean of noise.

In the midst of this din I could hear a tiny little sound, like an unsightly giggle, coming from very far away. The sound of someone laughing, somewhere.

Was I imagining it? How on earth could I detect something like that in this chaos – it was impossible, wasn't it?

After about fifteen minutes, a lightbulb finally flickered on, banishing the gloom. We managed to get a grip on ourselves eventually, though it wasn't easy: it took us another ten minutes to leave the room completely. Only a handful of us had any interest in continuing our night-time ablutions. We had the entire bathroom all to ourselves.

~

The third morning was one with a 'news from the homefront' theme. The one and only boat, which for reasons of economy made just one trip to the mainland every three days, brought us sacks full of mail.

The letter from my parents read more like a questionnaire:

What are the sleeping arrangements like on Miru?
Are you eating healthy food?
Are the clothes you packed warm enough for the windy weather at the seashore?
What is the water temperature?
Isn't it too cold to go swimming?

Their fretting was understandable. After all, I was seldom away from home these days, and it was too bad that the one time I did finally go somewhere, it had to be to a desert island, eighty miles removed from the mainland.

The boat held quite a different significance for Director Chen, since it was the only link between Miru and the civilised world across the water. Weather advisories alerting us to potential storms and cyclones, orders from his superiors, as well as the latest political news, were all dependent on this ship. The island had never merited an underwater telephone cable link; the same went for a radio transmitter. The canteen staff, too, always greeted the arrival of the boat with joy, for the food supplies and drinking water needed replenishing every three days.

That evening, at nine-thirty on the button, the power went out again. This time there was no panic – we now accepted it as part of the price of living in such primitive conditions. We simply waited, some more patiently than others, for the current to be restored. Through the grapevine, I heard that Director Chen and Mr Gong Wei were puzzled as to how the power cut might have come about, since the fuses had been intact both times. It looked as if someone had deliberately pulled the switch. Still, that was probably a little far-fetched. It was more likely that Miru's generator was simply beginning to show its age, and was ready for an overhaul. Mr Gong Wei had promised to give the entire apparatus a thorough inspection the following morning.

HAUNTED HOUSE

At nine the next morning, armed with the compulsory life jackets, we were neatly drawn up on the dock. We were about to set out on a reconnoitring expedition along the coast, to try and find some thimble-sized coral islands that were indicated only on the detailed maritime charts Chen was now studying.

Too – tooo . . . ffshooo. The boat inhaled once, twice, then breathed its last, with a sob. A few minutes later the skipper dashed out of the vessel, his face running with sweat and his arms spread despairingly up to the sky: the boat could not be sweet-talked into starting, come hell or high water.

'Oooh-noooo . . .' was our cry when Chen told us the excursion would have to be postponed until the next day.

Our disappointment was just a flea bite compared to the Director's own chagrin. He threw his weight around, cursing, pleading one moment, bullying the next – he tried everything in the book to convince the ferryman he had better fix the thing in a hurry, and yesterday wasn't soon enough. The man in the blue overalls shook his head with an emphatic no; he refused to give Chen any sort of guarantee as to when the boat would be repaired . . .

'Mr Director, I have been sailing this ferry for ten years. You don't have to tell *me* how sorely the old tub needs an overhaul. And I am all too aware of the problem of the food supplies, the drinking water tank and the communications with the mainland. When the boat's on the blink, Miru becomes a prison. In just a few days we'll be without food or water. Five years ago I experienced a calamity like that, and I said to myself at the time: I won't survive this a second time. So, Mr Director, you understand that, as I live, I will do everything in my power to fix the ferry. But give you my promise? That I can't do.'

I overheard this conversation, since I was standing close by. I interpreted it, however, as merely the sort of flap you could expect from two grown-ups impressed with their own importance – a tempest in a teapot. Who cared if we had to spend another day on the island? We would have a ball! My heart was entranced by the celestial blue waves, still enveloped in the white morning mist, slowly being spray-painted orange by the rising sun.

First we collected shells, then we played basketball on the golden sand and after lunch, when it got warmer, we plunged into the sea. Picking fruit to feast on at dinnertime rounded out our wonderful day. If it were up to us, we would spend *weeks* out here.

But that night for the third time in a row the power went out again – at exactly the same time as before. The passivity with which we had accepted it yesterday now made way for fear. Though most might not want to admit it, from the bewildered expressions I could tell that the others' misgivings mirrored mine: this house was haunted! How in Heaven's name could there be a power cut every night at nine thirty on the dot, when Chen and Gong Wei hadn't been able to discover anything wrong with the fuse box or generator? But no one said anything, naturally. Who wanted to see the older students mock us for being silly, superstitious little kids!

SAND IN THE RICE

The fifth day. We were acting like a flock of sheep abandoned by its shepherd. All our teachers had been summoned to an emergency meeting. Rumours were flying: not only had the boat been declared beyond repair, but it turned out that the diesel fuel tank had run dry as well. The childish insouciance with which we had first greeted the news that the ferryboat wouldn't start was rinsed away like a layer of sand. Finally we were forced to face the facts. Some of us even declared that we were doubly doomed. 'You see, even if, wonder of wonders, the boat is fixed, then we still can't get off the island – we have no fuel left. There are two inflatable rubber dinghies, true, but who can say for sure that on our way to the mainland we won't have any humongous waves crashing on our heads, not to mention the likelihood of a storm?'

Oh Buddha! My heart leapt into my throat and I wanted to yell out: quick, hide the dinghies! I had a horrible premonition that unless they were promptly secured, by the next morning those rickety rowboats would be just the latest two casualties in the string of mysterious accidents. I bit back my words with difficulty. My common sense was wagging its finger at my instinct: *Lian, have you totally gone off your rocker? Where did you get the idea that there's something shady going on? Any boat can come down with mechanical problems, any rusty tank can spring a leak, any generator can suffer a malfunction that makes it break down at times . . . Stop seeing ghosts everywhere!*

The next day the dinghies had vanished without a trace.

The faculty kept having meetings and we were slowly beginning to lose our appreciation of the cursed island's gorgeous views. Since yesterday, meal portions had been cut in half. Our stomachs rumbled all day long and disturbed our sleep at night. Washing ourselves was out of the question, and for brushing our teeth we were each given half a cup of water. There was enough drinking water for the time being, but according to Director Chen in his morning address, tomorrow might be a different story. If the boat remained out of commission, food and water supplies could not be replenished. After breakfast we crept back into bed, not just out of boredom, but also on the advice of our biology teachers. Since we were dizzy with hunger and thirst, getting increasingly upset over it, said our teachers, would only make our bodies burn more calories. Staying in bed, the biologists maintained, would prevent our blood-sugar levels from dropping too precipitously.

My stomach grumbled, but my head was remarkably clear. All the bewildering thoughts that had clouded my mind over the past days had evaporated. I now knew the root cause of the trouble on Miru. After kidding myself for days, half-unconsciously and half-deliberately, today I finally plucked up the courage to face the facts.

The broom closet where Kim slept was next door to the fuse box, on the ground floor. No one else slept down there, and hardly anyone ever went there, especially at night. Every evening at nine thirty, Kim stole to the meter cupboard and pulled the switch. Then she would sneak back to her little room, laughing like a hyena, while we on the floors above screamed and ploughed into each other like a pack of blind mice.

A NEW TERROR

Director Chen's face was as white as chalk; our teachers walked around as if they had lost it. I heard that Miru's underground diesel tank, which was there to provide the ferryboat with emergency fuel, was also empty. I hadn't been aware that such a tank existed. And besides, why go to the trouble of emptying the tank as well? Haven't you already wrecked the one and only boat?

I was startled. I'd been having an imaginary chat with Kim! Biting my lip, I glanced around cagily. No one had noticed, luckily.

It was said that knowledge is power. Stuff and nonsense! The knowledge I had about the source of Miru's troubles placed me in a weaker, not stronger, position. On the one hand, I felt obliged to inform the Director of my suspicions, so that we could muster all our resources to launch a lightning strike against the root cause of our problems; on the other hand, I couldn't help wanting to protect the girl who used to be my best friend. To justify my silence, I pictured to myself how they would jump on Kim and seize her, lock her up and put her through the wringer. If I didn't spill the beans, I would just be one of the six hundred other anxious students. But if I told on Kim, I would be left to face my conscience alone. If Kim's terrorist activities ever did come to light, Kim's life wouldn't be worth a dime. With the same stubbornness with which I had always clung to my love for Kim, I now put Kim's wellbeing ahead of that of the rest of the world. My own included.

I joined my fellow-sufferers' chorus of lamentation, groaning 'in despair' every time another dismaying fact came to light. And there seemed to be no end to it for now: the first-aid kit was approaching rock bottom; more and more students were getting sick; we had almost run out of medicines.

I shuddered. Had I made the right choice? I was sick with worry: what was Kim trying to achieve with her terrorist acts? Was she just determined to teach the uppity and cruel first-casters a lesson, to show them they couldn't humiliate a third-caster without getting their comeuppance? And, if they did end up taking this 'lesson' to heart, would Kim then back off? Or was she intending to settle the score with her enemies once and for all? If that was the case, then our hours were numbered. Knowing what Kim was capable of, her ingenuity and doggedness, I estimated our chances of surviving Kim's murderous plans to be just about nil.

Only one last straw remained for me to clutch at: that the Deputy

Headmistress would be competent enough to bail us out. The arrangement had been that Back-at-my-old-university would come to Miru that very afternoon with the remaining half of the school, once the older students had returned to the mainland. But that was the problem, of course. The Headmistress would not be able to leave for the coast with the other five hundred students until the rest were back in Beijing – there was nowhere for them to sleep otherwise. If Back-at-my-old-university had any sense at all, of course, she would be wondering by now why the ferry had failed to make any roundtrips in the last few days for food and water. Surely a light would come on in her head, now that she hadn't heard a word from Chen about how things were going and when he would return? Even if the headmistress was unable to travel to Miru herself, she could at the very least alert the coastguard or harbour police. Or was she simply asleep at the switch, and leaving it up to Director Chen to decide to return with his six hundred pupils whenever he felt like it?

A number of the teachers and a few strapping boys from the sixth year took turns keeping watch on the beach, craning their necks and peering at every little speck on the horizon that might signal a vessel approaching. At every change of the watch, our mood sank another mile or so below sea level.

But before Back-at-my-old-university figured out something was wrong, a new threat appeared out of the blue. On the eighth day of our confinement on Miru, Chen discovered a note on his 'desk' in the bedroom that also functioned as his office.

> DON'T YOU GUYS GET IT YET?
> SIX HUNDRED NUMBSKULLS!
> YOUR HOURS ARE NUMBERED
>
> MIRU

Until this moment, no matter how odd Chen might have found the recent series of mishaps, he had merely ascribed them to a fluke set of coincidences. Only now did it truly hit home that a human hand lay behind all these incidents, and he finally took full measure of the gravity of our situation. But who was passing him or herself off as *Miru*? He had never given the meaning of the name any thought before. *Mi*, 'secret', and *Ru*, 'like' . . . Like a secret? What did it mean? He shivered. He stuffed the note into his pocket instinctively, as if that might make the looming catastrophe disappear. He sank down on his bed and gave his brain free rein, setting it trundling like a treadmill.

Chen ran down the list of co-workers he had thrown to the lions during the Huangshuai Movement, and trembled from head to toe. Of the twelve teachers who had come to Miru, he could not think of a single one who had not been crucified by him, directly or indirectly. Each one of them had more reason than not to want to pay him back . . .

He swallowed a gulp of icy air, slapped himself on the cheeks and mumbled, 'Xingshun Chen, you grandpa of all idiots! How could you be such a dunce, to think that with all your sins you could get off scot-free! The time of final reckoning is here. You're all washed up, not a doubt about it – only . . .' The pouches under his slanty eyes suddenly began a shifty dance. Why had the note-writer referred to 'you guys'? This might be just an ordinary criminal, after all, to whom vandalism was simply second nature . . . and yet, whatever was he doing it *for*, if not to punish Chen for his bestial behaviour during the Huangshuai Movement? Yet – on the other hand, hadn't the students participated just as avidly as he in the persecutions?

The first line of Chen's reasoning had now come full circle. By the twentieth or so time round, he felt as limp as a cowpat.

INQUISITION

At three in the afternoon Chen summoned all of Miru's residents to a meeting. He read the threatening note aloud to us thirteen times – as often as was necessary to achieve the desired effect. The students were in a total state of panic by then, ready to give their all to what Chen was telling them to do – which was, to help him lure the hidden terrorist from his lair. Screaming bloody murder, they were like sponges sucking up the Director's orders. 'Divide each class into four groups and make note of any suspicious movements or behaviour by each and every one of you over the past five days. For example, was this one or that one always in the bathroom just before or after the power cut? Was he seen washing his hands with unusual frequency, to get rid of the smell of gasoline perhaps? If so, write his name down on a blacklist. It doesn't matter how long the list gets. Better that a few innocent people be accused than that the guilty party be allowed to slip through the net. Trust me, your Director. I'll know how to sniff the suspect out.'

The teachers' actions, too, had to be gone over with a fine-tooth comb. They were the ones Chen had it in for, basically. This wasn't easy for us; it cost Chen gallons of fast-talking liar's-spit to convince us that we had a duty to suspect our teachers of terrorist activities. Why, didn't everybody *know* that spies from the Capitalist West were trying to infiltrate our Communist State, cloaked as intellectuals or business people? Who knew – there might be a US secret agent hidden among the teachers! What if he was plotting to murder the proletarian-minded students on Miru, as part of a heinous conspiracy to throw all Communist China into utter chaos?

Chen had set off a witch-hunt. He folded his arms over his chest, observed the groups hotly arguing amongst themselves and kept a close eye on his colleagues' reactions to his call to arms.

To his surprise and disappointment, his colleagues appeared just as alarmed as himself, and seemed to be just as befuddled as he when it came to fingering the miscreant. He realised that neither political foul play nor mass manipulation would dig him out of deep trouble this time. There was something fatally amiss here, and there was nothing that even he, the consummate schemer, could do about it. His one consolation was that this sleuthing proved that Chen couldn't possibly be the only one the sociopath had it in for.

Dozens of students were hauled up front to 'confess' before the maddened, terrified crowd that they were the guilty ones. Mr Gong Wei, too, was dragged up on to the podium. He was a suspect because at every incident, he had always been first on the scene, supposedly to check the fuses and, 'after much fiddling about', declare them intact. How could the power have gone out if there weren't any blown fuses? When the ferryboat's engine had given up the ghost, it was Gong Wei who had gone onboard, ostensibly to examine the machinery, only to give up on trying to repair it 'after a lot of monkeying around'; in his informed opinion, there was nothing wrong with the motor. The further the crowd pursued this false lead, the more convinced they grew that Gong Wei's behaviour showed him to be the culprit. But dread of the looming catastrophe had blinded everyone to one important fact. Gong Wei was the only physics teacher on Miru; he was an engineer by trade and thus the obvious one to turn to if there were any technical malfunctions. Now Mrs Meng, of course, had never been present at the scene of any of the crimes; but that was only because she didn't know her arse from her elbow when it came to machines. In this mass panic, a scapegoat *had* to be found and offered up so that everyone else's life might be spared. And so, for the second time this year, Gong Wei became the scapegoat and sacrificial lamb of choice.

While my fellow students were beating Gong Wei to coerce a confession out of him, I couldn't help sneaking a look at Kim. There she sat in the middle of the audience, one leg flung over the other like a pig in clover – a broad grin splayed across her face. She was obviously enjoying the spectacle. How *could* Kim gaze on so calmly as dozens of innocent people were put through the meat grinder, and revel in it to boot?

Of course it was true that the roles were normally reversed: the horde could always be counted on to gloat at the sight of Kim getting slapped around and eating humble pie. Why should *that* be considered fair game, and not this?

I was beginning to wonder if it was worth it to continue protecting Kim at the expense of Gong Wei and those who shared his fate. Where did my responsibility lie? Could I keep my mouth shut with impunity, and allow Kim to put the fear of God into the island's six hundred denizens, set them up against each other and threaten them with total extinction?

The deciding factor, however, was my own preference for staying alive. The chorus of yammering all around me and the sword hanging over my head settled it: my attitude towards my former best friend did an abrupt hundred-and-eighty-degree flip. Suddenly I felt a kinship, not with Kim, but with Kim's persecutors. No matter how much I used to despise some of them for always giving Kim such a hard time, right now I was in the same boat as the rest of them – the boat that Kim was trying to sink.

BETRAYAL

After the assembly, I decided to inform Director Chen of my suspicions.

Standing before the door to Chen's room, I lost my resolve again. How was I to explain to him what lay behind Kim's acts of revenge? The only thing he knew about Kim was that she was one of the leaders of the largest street gang in the district. If he had ever been offered any concrete proof of her delinquency, he would have expelled her from school long ago. To him, there was a straightforward parallel to be drawn between assaults on innocent people and a criminal pattern of behaviour. He had never seen Kim up close and would never believe she had once been an innocent victim herself, that she had been picked on for years by her heartless schoolmates, the very same ones she was menacing now. It was inevitable, then, that he would deal harshly with Kim and show her no mercy; he was likely, in the interest of safety, to have her thrown in the slammer, or even have her put to death.

The Director was on his way out of his 'office' when he found me standing outside his door. Delighted, he invited me into his room at once. As usual, a smile that was meant to be irresistibly seductive crept over his face. He pushed the only chair in the room towards me and went and sat down on a shaky little stool. His eyes sparkled suggestively, as if they were trying to send me a message: Lian, since the disbanding of our little editorial team of the denunciation anthology, I've missed you *ever* so much. I told you back then that you could always look me up for help with your studies or work. But you have kept me waiting and waiting, until today . . .

Little by little he inched his stool nearer to me. I could practically feel his hot breath.

The Director looked at me expectantly and said, 'Lian, you know how delighted I am to see you, but I have only five minutes to give you. I must find a way to warn the harbour police, or else we are staring death right in the eye.'

Of course! It was what I had come here for. In one breath I told him what I thought I knew. How the power cuts, the crippling of the ferryboat, the emptying of the fuel tank and the disappearance of the rubber dinghies were all connected, and why I was sure that Kim was behind it all.

As my tale progressed, the slimy smile on his face began drying up visibly, until it slithered off his face like a snake. The stool he was sitting on creaked and seemed about to collapse under his weight. He stood up, shaken. Blowing hot and cold, he paced up and down the little room like a caged bear and finally let himself fall on to the bed. He was white as a sheet.

'Tell me how did such a proper, good-looking young lady as yourself end up with a mobster lowlife for a bosom friend?! Had all the nice first-caste girls died out, then, when you were looking for a buddy? Why didn't you come to me earlier, if you'd known all along who was behind this terrible business? Don't you realise you can be charged as an accomplice?!'

Tears welled up in my eyes.

'If, as you just said, you "know Kim as well as you know your other half", then could you, by any chance, explain to me what she means by YOUR HOURS ARE NUMBERED?'

In a flash, I suddenly saw it all. 'Director Chen! Could it be that she didn't just let the fuel in the diesel tank empty out, but that she siphoned it into barrels?'

Chen blinked his eyelids rapidly. He shook me roughly. 'What did you say?! Siphoned it into barrels? What for?!'

We faced each other in silence.

The man drew his fingers through his hair and berated himself out loud for being fool enough to allow a criminal element to come with us to this deserted island. Three, four times he said the same thing.

'But she isn't a criminal at all!' I tried to cut him short.

'Oh shut up! Are you feeling sorry for that piece of scum now?'

Never before had he spoken to me so roughly, in the same bloodthirsty voice that used to screech over the loudspeakers during the Huangshuai Movement. My head spun. My feet suddenly felt strangely light . . .

Before I had a chance to collapse, he had clasped me by the arms and pressed me up against himself savagely. I almost threw up. Never had I been touched like this by a man – and by such an opportunistic sneak, too! Fear paralysed me. Numbly I looked the other way as his breath exploded in my right ear. His limbs were wrapped around my body like boa constrictors. *Ehnn* . . . he sighed, entreating me with his eyes.

He dragged me over to the bed and pushed me down by the shoulders. Every muscle in my body cramped up; I gritted my teeth. Don't feel a thing, don't feel a thing, I told myself over and over again, clenching my fists. He grasped my hands, peeled my fingers apart and slapped them to his groin. I tore myself free, scrambled to my feet, shuddering, and clamped my eyes shut. I couldn't bear looking at the man.

Three fingers are coming nearer. My one and only eyeball. The fingers twist, twist. A sudden stab of pain.

I don't need to see any more.

'I thought you were in such a hurry!' I croaked. 'Weren't you on your way to warn the harbour police?'

He glanced at his watch. Frowning, he smoothed out his clothes. 'I have to go. Don't be afraid. Don't tell anyone what you have told me. I am going to gather a group together – some of the teachers and a bunch of strong sixth formers. We'll throw Kim into solitary for now – we'll rig a cell up for her. And then we shall see if your theory holds. We've got nothing to lose. If the reign of terror stops, the mountains will shout Long Live Mao! And if it doesn't, then at least we shall have given it our all. In the meantime, we'll light campfires everywhere and pray that any ships or planes in the area will discover us and come to our rescue.'

The magnitude of what I had done took my breath away. I was a traitor.

DEAD TWIGS

Kim would not have been Kim if she hadn't been able to smell the approaching danger.

By five thirty Chen and his cohorts had combed the building from cellar to attic, but of course Kim was nowhere to be found. Seeing that the members of the search party weren't exactly careful to keep their burning desire to get their hands on the miscreant to themselves, the curiosity of the rest of the students was ignited; so Chen felt obliged to explain what they were up to. Besides, the fury of the mob could be put to use: they could all pitch in and help track Kim down. He informed them of Kim's plans to annihilate them all. The doubts he had earlier expressed to me were history, now that it appeared that Kim had vanished without a trace.

The floodgates had been opened: it was no holds barred, now. My classmates and contemporaries were especially vociferous; their yelling set the ceiling rattling. 'Hah! See? We always said she was a sleazeball, the worst trash of the human race, a criminal from birth, and, and, and . . .' They bared their fangs and strained at the leash, they just couldn't wait to catch her, skin her alive and rip her to bloody shreds. Spurred on by days of discomfort, hunger, thirst, uncertainty, panic and fear, they were beset by a fury that knew no limits. Kim needn't count on any clemency; she would never be allowed to leave the autumn-camp all in one piece . . . *if* they ever managed to catch her, that is.

The thirty-odd students who had been held under suspicion, along with Mr Gong Wei, were released with wagonloads of apologies. As if they were all of one mind, the residents of Miru raced outside helter-skelter to hunt down the culprit, who they knew must still be roaming out there somewhere on two hind legs. Their hatred for the despised third-caste underdog and feared gang leader had increased to epic proportions.

But of the youthful terrorist – not a trace.

Evening fell and everyone hurried to the canteen. The meal was more dismal than ever. Everyone got half a bowl of corn porridge. It was so watery you could use it as a looking glass to admire your gaunt face. Big strapping seniors eagerly licked their bowls clean; I was afraid that their maddening hunger might drive them to chomp on the crockery itself. Before the events of the afternoon, the seething anger in the dining hall hadn't been aimed at anyone in particular, but now all expletives were forwarded to Kim's address. It was revolting to have to listen to.

What if they did manage to capture Kim? The thought alone made me dizzy. Yet . . . what if they *couldn't* find Kim, and she went her merry way and carried out her sweet revenge unimpeded – what then?

When Chen had made my suspicions public, he had left out part of my story. He didn't think it wise to reveal that Kim might have stored the stolen diesel oil in order to set the building on fire. He didn't want to add fuel to our emotional and physical burnout by giving us even more sleepless nights. He did put together a squadron of night watchmen, who were charged with reporting any and all suspicious movements to the Central Security Command Post, consisting of Chen and four male colleagues.

Aside from fifty or so students fainting from hunger and dehydration, nothing untoward happened for the next three nights. But the more drawn-out the wait, the wilder the speculation over the impending disaster.

$$\sim$$

On the twelfth day of our imprisonment on the island, Chen discovered, at the exact same time as four days earlier, another note on his 'desk':

YOUR MINUTES ARE NUMBERED

MIRU

I was in the middle of giving Qianyun, Liru and Feiwen a pep talk in their dorm: 'Believe me, I *know* they will arrest that lowlife very soon, and then we can all go home.' My own words shocked me: was I now calling my 'best friend' a 'lowlife'? Just four days ago, I had wanted to snap the Director's head off for using those very words about Kim! Even when Kim, in front of fifty of her classmates, had called me an 'arse-licker' just for attempting to talk to her, it hadn't made a dent in my conviction that my love for Kim would last for ever. And now? Now I was firmly on the side of classmates I had once hated from the bottom of my heart. We all had but one wish: to capture Kim and de-fang her. How *could* my feelings have made such a complete U-turn, in so short a time? Was it because my own life was suddenly on the line? Was I wishing Kim the worst – imprisonment and death – just so that I would live? I had always thought of my devotion to Kim as holy: that, if called upon, I would gladly lay down my life for it.

Chen came storming into the dormitory, dragged me back to his office and, with trembling hands, showed me the second anonymous threat. What did it mean – YOUR MINUTES ARE NUMBERED? The previous note had said: YOUR HOURS ARE NUMBERED. Hours, minutes, then seconds. Did this mean that we had a little time left to prevent the final onslaught? Or did Kim's concept of time end at minutes, not seconds?

Chen proposed that he would ask for four volunteers to swim to the mainland. 'I'll be one of the four,' he said, swaggering, and pressed me against himself.

I don't need to see any more.

I pushed him off me. 'Are you out of your mind? Eighty miles! That's downright suicide!' With a shock I realised that I was talking to him using the familiar form of address. Chen sank to his knees. He was now at shoulder-level with me. 'Let *me* try to find Kim,' I beseeched him. 'I'll talk to her. I can't promise anything, but I'll do my best to get her to give up on her murderous intentions. But there is one condition. Don't use me as bait. Don't even think of following me. Or it'll be all over for me. And for the rest of you, too. I know Kim: she will not tolerate a traitor. And anyone who forces me into the role of traitor will find no mercy in her eyes.'

Now that I had come to a decision about Kim, I began chewing on a plan. How to go about finding her? I was anxious to go to her broom closet right away, to figure it out. I already had my hand on the doorknob.

The man made a grab for me. He sniffed at me, leaving no place untainted. The blood vessels in his neck looked like they were about to blow a gasket. His eyes drilled through my blouse like laser beams piercing a steel plate. He had developed a raging dislike for the buttons on my clothes. 'Don't,' I begged. But he had already bared my shoulders; I felt his wet mouth on my breast. I was terrified that he might actually devour me. I tried jabbing him away with my knees. But that only goaded him into playing rougher with me.

My neck. Those hands on my fur. The pain is death. I am wrenched in two. I snap.

No need to see any more.

❧

It was four p.m., but I crawled into bed, warning my bunkmates: 'Don't disturb me. I'm going to sleep. I didn't sleep a wink last night.' I fell asleep and immediately became enmeshed in a nightmarish tangle of dreams.

Once again I was pacing the deck of the emptied ferryboat. But where the bridge once stood there now towered a huge figure of Buddha. The statue began to speak, first in the voice of Grandpapa in Qingdao, then in Uncle Changshan's. Somewhere behind me sat Kim, all by herself, watching me. I could not see her, but I knew that she was there. Buddha's prophecy, or Grandpa's, or Cannibal's, cut through me like a knife. I tried to understand what he was on about, but I could not concentrate properly – Kim's eyes were piercing into my back. The voice sounded familiar, and I tried to catch the words, crackling as if they came from a badly-tuned radio. '. . . dead twigs . . . crickets . . . behind the barracks . . .' I turned around to face Kim. My friend was almost as huge as the Buddha. The boat was staggering dangerously under all the weight. Behind Kim I spied an island. The sun was sinking into a bath of orange light – no, it was the moon, vast, oval and red . . . The sea was in flames. '. . . down at the lake, Lian . . . save us . . . it is so quiet here . . .'

Far away, high above the fiery glow, twinkled twin stars.

I woke up in a sweat. I jumped out of bed.

THE GREATEST GIFT

The moonlight painted everything silver in the clear autumn night: the beach, the sea, the red, yellow and orange berries in the bushes, the brown earth. Crickets chirped and frogs croaked. The evening smelled fresh as a lemon. Peace lapped at the island, the peace that nature always offers mankind on a fine silver tray after the sun has set.

The building was in an uproar. Even out here on the beach, I could hear the residents wailing. Yet I felt remarkably calm, like a Buddhist who is following the course his destiny has laid out for him. The moonlight rinsed the terror from my being like a grain of sand.

It was as if I were on my way to the Lily Theatre. Not, this time, to confide my history stories to the crickets and the frogs, or to suck in the wisdom of my mentors – Qin and Cannibal – but to meet with Kim in the stillness behind the barracks. Kim – who had once been my friend, into whom I had poured so much effort, but had now lost across an unbridgeable chasm. Qin was far away, in the camp, he had let me go, some way back in the grisly past. And Cannibal was possibly even further away, an evanescent wisp on that distant horizon he called the White Luck . . . But those two still seemed infinitely closer to me than my best friend, who had been reincarnated as a terrorist and was putting my life on the line.

I wondered how Kim was making out, after hiding out in the bushes for four long days. Only Buddha could tell how she had managed to keep herself alive. And only Buddha would know, too, what was going on inside her head.

After following the shore for a while, I cut into the interior, trusting my innate secret compass. I veered away from the path, something the naturalists had sternly warned us against because of the considerable risk of landing in a swamp or quicksand. Or of wandering into some neck of the woods infested with snakes or foxes. It was odd, I had jumped from being a hopeless scaredy-cat to a reckless daredevil. Hopping over one puddle after another, I crooned the ditty Kim had always been so crazy about:

> *Butterflies love flowers*
> *Flowers like nothing better*
> *than to be touched by butterflies*

More than the desire to live, I felt a deep need for some sort of clarity. I wanted an explanation: what had this three-year-long friendship meant to Kim, what had been the point of all our hard-won achievements, which had brought us such pain and anguish, yet so much hope and satisfaction? And most of all: How had I lost my friend?

I dived into a forest of reeds and slashed my way through tall grasses. I could practically smell Kim. I never hesitated even a single second over the direction I was taking, as if I had had the path to Kim mapped out for me minutely, down to the last foot, in my dreams.

A deep, still quiet muffled everything. Suddenly I saw the moon lying flat on the ground! I had come to a lagoon in the middle of the forest. The moon floated on top of the glassy surface, meticulously etched, down to the finest detail. The croaking of the frogs broke the silence. Even the crickets had come over for the occasion, and heralded my arrival with a serenade.

At the far side of the lagoon grew a massive jujube bush, impenetrably dense. Excitement shot up the marrow of my spine. Kim's hiding place! I was sure of it! Even though I had never been here before, every twig around me was familiar. I had seen all this before, in my dreams.

The scorching desire to see Kim was like a shot of courage injected straight into my arteries. I plunged my left foot into the water. What was there to be afraid of? Drowning? What a joke! Whether I went up in flames without warning, along with the rest of them, or perished here in the lagoon, it really didn't make a difference.

'Watch out!' I nearly jumped out of my skin on hearing that familiar voice slash through the silence of the somnolent hill. 'The water is deep.'

I stood frozen like a statue, gawking at the bushman masquerading as my friend Kim. Her hair looked practically blonde, because of all the straw in it. The once-stylish polyester blouse was no better than a floor mop, torn to shreds by the thorns. Her trousers were like a failed painting – a hotch-potch of motley colours spilling into muddy brown.

Impulsively, I started to wade over to Kim.

'Stay right where you are!'

Good advice, probably: the water was already up to my knees.

Kim was standing in front of the jujube bush on the opposite shore of the lagoon. It was the rough belligerence in her voice that brought me down to earth with a bang, rubbing my nose into the cold hard facts. I was dealing with a terrorist here, not with the friend I had missed so very much.

'Are you alone?'

'Yes. I wanted to talk to you in private.'

The bushman studied the ruched collar of reeds behind me warily and it was only when she was satisfied there was no suspicious rustling to be detected anywhere that the mistrust faded from the green, brown and yellow camouflage of her face. She aimed a savage kick at the base of a dead tree, which promptly, with a compliant *yeeayow*, splashed into the dark water. The top branches landed on my side. Once the water had settled down, I stepped on to the floating pontoon, my legs shaking with trepidation as well as with eagerness.

When I was almost halfway across, I heard Kim command, 'Stop!'

Obediently I stood stock-still, balancing myself on the floating tree bobbing in the middle of the pond. I had long since resigned myself to the role of Kim's helpless victim.

Kim nimbly ran up to me as if the narrow tree trunk were a wide asphalt carriage-way. She came to a halt just a hair's breadth from me. It totally slipped my mind that I had come here for anything but this. How wonderful, to be close to Kim once more, and not to have to worry about making a fool of myself!

Kim smiled at me. She whispered into my ear: 'I knew you'd come. I knew you would know how to find me.'

At this even the last remaining shadow of my original resolve melted away. I blushed at Kim's honeyed words, falling once more under the spell of my fondness for my best friend.

Kim crossed her arms, stoically waiting for my sermon. 'Go on, you might as well start now. Go ahead – tell me that you have to be more beastly than a brute to scare the pants off hundreds of people with underhanded sabotage and anonymous threats. Don't tell me you hadn't got it figured out yet, you know I was the one who trashed the boat and stole the diesel oil, didn't you! Well? What did they do to you, cut out your tongue? Aren't you supposed to warn me that there's going to be a heavy price to pay, that I'd better give myself up or else?'

These last words startled me from my daze. I nodded enthusiastically.

'Give myself up? Who to? To that bunch of cowardly morons who haven't even realised yet that the building's completely encircled with oil drums that I've filled up with diesel fuel? That the whole place can go up in a sea of flames any time, whenever I say so?'

'So it's *true*, you really do want to burn the building down?' I said, stating the obvious.

'Does anyone else know of my plan?'

'Only Director Chen and a few of the teachers.'

'Do they know at what time?'

The world was spinning around again. I just managed to keep myself from toppling into the water. 'What . . . what do you mean? Is it supposed to happen today, then?!'

Kim looked at me with a mocking smirk. 'I thought you knew me so well! So how come you haven't figured out yet what time I am making my move?'

Now I remembered a scene from my nightmare: the glow of the *sunrise* blending with the blaze of an inferno.

'Come on, Kim, can't you spare our lives?'

'Why should I?'

Tears seeped into my eyes. 'Have you completely forgotten the wonderful times we had together? The training for the 1500-metres race, doing our homework together, the medicinal herbs you picked to cure my vitiligo, the New Year's party, the sleepover at my house . . .' Deep in my heart, I was ashamed of the way I was going about trying to win over Kim – what a low-down creep I was, to bring up our past like that.

But Kim had already begun finishing my litany for me: '. . . and the fiasco of the exam-results announcement, and spending my hard-earned fen on a blouse that was really a raincoat, and being made the laughing stock over my silly crush on Wudong, that out-to-lunch eunuch!' She stamped her feet on the tree trunk beneath our feet as if she was going totally berserk. The surface of the water fractured into a thousand splinters. I slipped. But Kim caught me just in time. And as soon as I felt Kim's strong arms envelop me, I felt as safe as a baby snuggling up against its mother's cushiony breasts.

I started pleading again; I was so desperate by now that I knew no shame: 'I didn't want to say this at first, but couldn't you, couldn't you . . . can't you just cancel your plans to destroy us all . . . for *my* sake?'

'For *your* sake? And why on earth should I do that?'

I was floored. I did not know how to answer that one.

'All right then,' smirked Kim, 'my heart isn't made of granite. And it's true that you *are* the only one I'll miss when I'm merrily scribbling graffiti on the walls of my jail cell, or on the day that I get to pose for the firing squad.'

I wobbled again, out of joy – I almost lost my footing. Or perhaps it was just that I wanted to be held by Kim one more time. I had had Kim figured right, after all! Kim cared for me deeply enough to think of me when push came to shove.

But Kim would not stop grinning. She fumbled in her trouser pocket and pulled out a long knife. She blew on it, and the razor-sharp murder weapon sang out a fine note – *phweee!* She turned the knife around and around in her hands, her eyes flashing with pride, as if she had never seen it before. The blinding moonlight that glanced off it severed her final link with me.

'I'll do it real quick. You won't feel any pain. I've butchered lots of chickens in my time. Believe me, it's the greatest gift I could ever give you. It's got to be a billion times better than getting roasted to a crisp inside a burning building like a Peking Duck, I should think. Hey, say something, why don't you! What do you think of the special favour I'm prepared to do for you?' The knife flashed in the moonlight.

For an instant I thought it had already happened. The log under my feet felt as if it was sliding into quicksand. I had lost my footing, my very last grip. I turned and ran as fast as I could. It didn't even sink in properly that I was bolting across an alarmingly teetering tree trunk. Before I knew it, I had reached firm ground.

But Kim was close on my heels, and caught up with me soon enough. She pinched my arm. 'Lian, if you are fool enough to even *think* of returning to that building that's about to become history, with the intention of warning Chen, you'll be giving up the greatest gift I have to offer you.'

'Let me go-o-o-o!' I *hated* Kim suddenly, with all my heart and soul. I screamed, 'You ungrateful third-caste piece of shit! It's true you were born for a fen and will never amount to a kuai!

Phweee . . . Kim whipped the knife out of its scabbard again and pressed the tip of the weapon against the underside of my chin. 'As long as you're at it, tell Chen I have some secret helpers here among the students, and they'll see to it that no matter where he goes with his pack of little scaredy-cats, my plan will be executed *precisely* as scheduled, not a second later and not one iota different!'

Struggling like mad, I yanked my sleeves out of Kim's grip, and bolted.

I did not need the moon to light the way. When I finally looked over my shoulder, I had long since reached the beach. Kim had not followed me.

HOMEWARD

The teachers and the strongest boys of the sixth year were rounded up and informed of Kim's plans. They helped Chen evacuate the building. The six hundred students huddled together on the beach, wrapped in blankets, and tried to catch a few winks, in spite of the cold, the discomfort, the foreboding and the dread. Our stomachs were growling madly and we were too sluggish to stay awake . . .

P-phoooo-p-phoooo! Towards dawn a familiar sound reached us on the chilly beach. We craned our necks and it was Qianyun who called out first, 'Papa! My Papa is here!'

We all thought she'd gone stark raving mad from hunger and fear, but when a gleaming patrol boat came into sight, we were only too happy to concede that she was right. There, standing on the deck, surrounded by four armed soldiers, was, indeed, Qianyung's father. A cheer went up for the rescuers, though it took our last ounce of strength.

It was hard to say who was more nonplussed, the rescuers or the students. Qianyun's father, shouting across the water, rolled out an endless train of questions: 'What's going on here? Why hasn't anyone heard from you? Two weeks! Don't you realise your parents are dying of worry? Qianyun, where are you? Let your father see you. If I don't bring you back safe and sound, your mother will murder me!'

When the boat was moored, it was the turn of Chen and his cronies to shake the old general and demand an explanation: 'How come *you* have come? Where is that Deputy Headmistress? Sitting on her lazy arse, while we've been staring death in the face?'

After a lot of shouting back and forth, Chen found out that Qianyun's father had commandeered a naval patrol boat – not too difficult a feat for someone in his position. Then it was the General's turn to hear the whole story.

'Who's responsible?' The war veteran's eyebrows sank into a frown. Yet it was clear that the peril of our predicament had perked him up considerably; his military instincts, long dormant, were re-awakened, and made him quite chipper. 'What? A student at your school? Just a scrawny little girl? Is *that* what's been making you pee in your pants for over a week?'

With a number of teachers and self-important boys chiming in, Chen gave a blow-by-blow account of the terrifying events on the island.

The sardonic grin left the General's face. It wasn't just that Chen was able to persuade him of the gravity of the situation, but he had finally noticed the students sprawled higgledy-piggledy all over the place, every one pale as a ghost and skinny as a skeleton from hunger and dehydration. He radioed back a report on Miru's plight to the harbour police and the Beijing security forces, with an urgent request for reinforcements. When he was done, he asked Chen, 'Haven't you any idea where that little terrorist of yours is hiding?'

With probing eyes, Chen scoured the group of students among whom I was sitting. I understood at once what was up. What should I do? Lead them to the lagoon and have Kim arrested? Or pretend that I hadn't paid attention in the dark last night and could not remember the way to Kim's hideout? My fond memories of our friendship were battling it out with the nightmare recollection of the knife held to my throat, and of Kim's plot to set six hundred people on fire like so many matchsticks.

The Director called me over to him and began blackmailing me: 'Tell this gentleman the truth, or I'll tell him about your fishy secret relationship with that gang leader!' As he said this, he put his hands on my shoulders.

I screamed, 'Let me *go-o-o-o*!'

'She must be hiding somewhere in the forest, over there on that hill,' said Chen. I had involuntarily dropped the hint last night that that was the direction I was going to go looking in.

'Fetch the megaphone from the bridge,' Qianyun's father barked to one of his men, 'and yell at that – what's the name of that piece of scum again, Pang, Bang, Zhang? – that she has got to give herself up. Or else we'll find other ways to fix her!'

The Beijing police arrived before noon. I was interrogated as if *I* was the terrorist. Then I was locked up in a little room. The police didn't want to let their one and only potential informant wander about freely.

The whole thing made me sick. I kept having to throw up. I banged my head against the wall until everything went black.

When I opened my eyes, I saw Chen's hateful face hovering over my bed. In a voice sweet as treacle, he wheedled, 'Lian, I had no choice. The lives of six hundred people are at stake!' He leered down my blouse.

I spat in the man's face.

The man tightened his fists around the bars of the bed. 'Come on, Lian, don't torture me so . . . Do me a favour, open your eyes! Look at me! Will you listen to me? I've got some good news for you: it isn't necessary for you to lead the police to Kim any more. They were just given the go-ahead to blow up the hill.'

I sprang bolt upright. 'But it's against the law to kill someone in such a . . . such a horribly gruesome way!' Auwah! My head was so sore!

Chen laughed. 'Against the *law*? If it were up to the police, Kim would be torn limb from limb! Terrorising six hundred people out of their wits and plotting to burn them alive; screwing up a million-kuai ferryboat and stealing the contents of an entire fuel tank – do you understand what the penalty is, for all that?'

'I will lead the police to Kim!' I didn't understand it myself. Why was I taking Kim's side again?

'It is too late for that. They are already on their way.'

'Come on, quick, I want to go to Kim! She'll listen to me.'

'But they have left already,' Chen repeated.

I shuddered.

Hong-hong . . . donnnnnng!

Giant bursts of fire and waves of heat rocked the island off its moorings.

White steam escaping from red chalices. Thousands of cinders swirling in a blaze of glorious gold. A never-ending streak, a sigh, a comet returning home.

EPILOGUE

Years went by, political movements came and went, and I no longer hunched my back in order to hide my breasts. Quite the contrary. I did remain partial, however, to the chirping of crickets and the croaking of frogs. Every time it rained, I would stare at the puddles in the bare fields devoid of grass, and pretend that what I saw was a lake – the lake where I could pour my own interpretation of Chinese history into a patient ear. Then the faces of Uncle Cannibal and Uncle Qin would come swimming to the water's surface and I would start to cry. I wept about my time in the re-education camp, when I had felt so terribly lonely, and about the loneliness that had drawn the two sweetest men in the world into the kingdom of my heart. When would I ever attain such happiness again?

But the crickets and frogs weren't the end of it. In fact, all that chirping and croaking was threatening to blast my ears off any minute, just like – just like the hill that had exploded by the lake on Miru, when Kim had gone up in ashes in a whirling nirvana of liberation. And older men weren't necessarily kind and wise, either: Director Chen's harsh voice still bored its way into my eardrums at the slightest provocation. Then I would remember as if it had been only yesterday how that seedy man had tweaked my little buds and how he'd leered at me with teeth full of plaque.

My heart had more room in it now, however: in it the Lily Theatre and the island Miru that had been the death of Kim coexisted peacefully side by side, as did Qin, Cannibal and Director Chen. There was a piece of me in all of them. No, Kim wasn't dead, neither was Cannibal, nor Qin, no more than ever-regenerating nature.

It was only when I got married and had children of my own that I finally began to appreciate Father and Mother. I too tore a strip off my children for their own protection: I might have regretted it later, but at least I understood why Mother had pulled my underpants down around my ankles and smacked me in full sight of the university's dismayed party chairman. How else would I have come to know Qin and Cannibal, if it hadn't been for Mother's spanking me? Hadn't that been my ticket to the re-education camp? How could I have mourned Kim all these years if I hadn't ever known how blissfully happy our friendship had made me feel? How could the Lily Theatre glitter in all its glory, if it weren't for the darkness surrounding it?

GLOSSARY

Bapao – A steamed bun stuffed with a leek-and-meat filling, made tasty with garlic, ginger, sesame oil, MSG and salt.

Bok choy – a vegetable commonly eaten in China.

Business of the rain and clouds – Sexual intercourse: the clouds represent the woman's bodily fluids and the rain stands for the man's seed. A mingling of rain and clouds means orgasm.

Capitalist Roader – one who follows the Capitalist, instead of the Communist, way.

Caste – A concept here borrowed from India to explain the differences in social groupings. In the People's Republic of China, the highest caste was composed of party officials, civil servants, intellectuals, prominent actors, dancers, athletes etc. The workers made up the middle, or second, caste; peasants were relegated to the lowest caste. Even though the word 'caste' as such was never used by the leadership, the symptoms of this stratification played an essential role in everyday affairs. The term 'class', on the other hand, was one that was consistently employed by the Party in its quest to 'correct' the unequal relationships between social groupings. During the Cultural Revolution especially, a new hierarchy was assiduously promoted, in which the lowest classes were upgraded and the highest were booted down to the lowest rung on the political ladder. Slogans like *'Workers, peasants and soldiers are the leaders of the land'* were posted at every street corner and blared from loudspeakers all over China. To the annoyance of the Helmsman, the class system was a flop: the traditional caste system remained in place, and never stopped being the decisive factor in almost every aspect of human relations.

Chihuo – 'Greedy pig'; someone whose only talent lies in making a pig of himself.

Dao – 'I have come'; 'present'.

Daonian – To talk about someone with great love and concern.

Dui – 'That's right!', 'sure enough', 'indeed'.

Erhoe – Chinese violin, a musical instrument with two strings.

Fen – Chinese coin (a hundreth of a *yuan* or *kuai* and a tenth of a *yiao* or *mao*).

Foehn (or föhn) – (German) A hot dry wind coming down from the mountains.

Fuwuyuan – Member of the service staff in the hotel, restaurant and retail sector.

Gai – The sound of a Chinese sigh. Instructions: Suck in a deep breath, allowing a strong current of air to bounce off the soft palate. For a sigh to turn out well, one must sense the roof of the mouth vibrating. An expression of hopelessness, helplessness, grief, or false modesty.

Gall (dog's bile, bear's gall, etc.) – The gall bladder is associated with daring, guts, and impertinence. Based on the belief that eating a certain animal organ will strengthen and heal the corresponding organ in one's own body, one might say of someone who is daring or impudent that he has swallowed a fair quantity of gall, or bile. The larger or more dangerous the animal whose gall is sampled, the braver or more brazen the person who has partaken of it.

This is also the reason that the so-called 'liquor of eight lashes' is so popular among Chinese men. This drink has eight preserved pizzles floating around in it, preferably culled from wild animals. Fortified with even just one sip of this drink, a man can go at it again with rockhard firmness – or is convinced that he can.

Grenade throw – Instead of the discus, javelin or shotput, schoolchildren were taught from the age of six to throw objects resembling hand grenades in physical education class. This was viewed by the Party as an essential step towards military readiness.

Hesong – A tree whose roots are thought to have healing and purifying powers.

Huangjiang sauce – Black bean sauce, made of fermented soy beans.

Jimu – (*ji* = collecting, building and *mu* = wood) Building blocks; Chinese equivalent of Lego

Kang – Traditional family bed, made of stone; usually with built-in stove

Ki – Breath; spirit of life. *Not having the ki going your way:* things are not going well for you. If someone is unlucky, he will say, 'The *ki*, the breath that is in me and all around me, has grown murky'.

Kowtow – (*kow* = to hit something hard with something soft; *tow* = head) A way of greeting or begging, wherein one kneels down, with both hands on the ground and the head lowered to or touching the floor. The harder the head is tapped or banged against the floor, the greater the reverence or despair its owner wishes to convey.

Kuai – Chinese currency, approximately fifty pence at the time of the Cultural Revolution. This is the informal term; *yuan* is a fancier name for the same thing.

Kwalá – An onomatopaeic exclamation reproducing the sound of a wooden garden door opening on rusty hinges.

Liangshang junzi – Literally, 'roof gent': robber. In the past, thieves usually broke into their victims' homes via the roof. This feat was carried out, very simply, by pushing a few roof tiles out of the way, installing oneself on a crossbeam, and waiting patiently until the residents left the house. At this point the miscreant would slide down a vertical beam, thus gaining entrance to the residence and the freedom to help himself to its contents. Seeing that this profession demanded a certain acrobatic proficiency as well as a fair deal of patience and tact on the part of the practitioner, he was referred to, respectfully, as 'the gentleman on the roof'. Another explanation is to be found in a story from the Han Dynasty in which a wise man catches a thief in flagrante delicto and says, 'Even though you occupy yourself with criminal activities, I am sure that the core of your being is whole, and that inside you are a true gentleman'.

Mao – Informal name for *yiao* coin, worth ten fen.

My Ought-To-Be-Lynched-With-A-Thousand-Stab-Wounds – My darling; sweetheart. The Chinese are frugal with endearments, especially when it comes to their spouses. One of the most fervent expressions of love a young woman could shower on her beloved went as follows: 'Roll the hell out of here and hide your pig snout over there in the corner!' The young man, if he was sufficiently on his toes, would respond with: 'So? Are you coming with me, you old sow, or not?'

Another explanation for why married couples gave each other such names can be found in the ancient tradition of arranged marriages. Most youngsters met their spouse for the first time on the day of their wedding. Over time, one learned to adapt to one another and in the most fortunate cases one might even begin to love each other. One was well advised to do so, too, since divorce was to all intents and purposes just as much out of the question as marrying of one's own free will. It was inevitable, naturally, that there would be a number of marriages in which the partners would nurse a lifelong hatred for each other. Seeing that there was no physical escape from this hell, compensation was sought in the form of creative verbal abuse. *Gaiside*, 'he/she who would be wise to drop dead on the spot', and *laobusi*, 'he/she who simply refuses to breathe his/her last breath' are two examples of the many variations on 'my love'.

Ning – To take hold of an exposed portion of the skin between the thumb and forefinger, making sure that it is firmly pinched between the fingernails, and then to twist in in clockwise fashion; the pinched skin is ready to be released only when the victim's cries become too much to listen to any more.

Pink incident – An affair that scandalizes everyone. Since the colour red symbolizes the love sanctioned by society, it is the lighter variation of that colour which serves to indicate love that is beyond the pale.

Row-houses – Barrack-like, single-room houses.

Seven feelings and six desires – A Buddhist concept. The feelings and desires in question must be transcended in order to attain Nirvana; the word 'desire' here means not only 'desire for' but also 'the manner in which this desire manifests or expresses itself'.

The seven feelings are: happiness, anger, worry, fear, love, hate and longing.

The six desires are:
    —colours and sex
    —form and expression
    —a proud bearing and an attractive demeanour

—words, speech and sound
—smoothness and delicacy of the skin
—the human appearance

Son of the Dragon – The emperor. The head of state was not human, but the offspring of a dragon. Only this reptilian species was blessed with the heavenly mandate to lord it over the nation.

Tongxinglian – (*tong* = the same; *xing* = sex; *lian* = to love) Homosexuality. But *xing* also has another meaning, 'surname', which explains why Lian mistakenly interprets the idiom to mean 'people with the same surname who love each other'.

Wangshi bukan huishou – 'Don't turn around, because behind you lies the dreadful past'.

Wenyan – Written Chinese language that was in general use until the Fourth of May Movement of 1919. It was so different from the spoken language that a blacksmith needed an interpreter to understand what even the lowliest civil servant had written to him.

Yaojing – A witch who could take on different shapes: seductive young woman, innocent ingenue, bitch-on-wheels, murderess, etc., according to the wishes of the one calling her into being.

Yuan – The formal name for *kuai*, Chinese currency.

Zuojia – Writer; also means 'to be at home', whence the alternate meaning, 'homebody'.

ACKNOWLEDGEMENTS

This book is like a watermelon. To whom or what does the fruit owe thanks for its ripening? To the wind that spread the seed over the fertile ground; to the rain that sprinkled it; to the sun that prepared a warm bed for the seed; or to the minerals and other nutrients that fed the young shoot?

The wind that wafted me to the place I now call home – The Netherlands – is the 'Opening and Reform Policy' of my native country (the People's Republic of China); the rain that irrigated my determination to keep writing is the person who first discovered me, Nol van Dijk; the sunbeams that shone on me and gave me strength during the long and difficult writing process are my friends, including Marlies Roemen, Jan Klerkx and Jeanne Holierhoek; the nutrients my manuscript required in order to grow, blossom and bear fruit were provided by my publisher Oscar van Gelderen, the second person to 'discover' me, as well as by my dedicated editor, Adriaan Krabbendam. Oscar's rock-solid belief in me was the kiss that awakened my slumbering self-confidence, giving me leave to continue with determination and devotion; Adriaan not only gave the manuscript the benefit of a very professional editing job, he also cherished every word, every sentence and every passage.

Also in the category of wind, rain, sun and nutrients is Lex Spaans, Uitgeverij Vassallucci's co-publisher, who created the necessary conditions for the publication of this book, and introduced me to my literary agent Linda Michaels. Linda – my third discoverer – immediately made my work known to many publishers all over the globe.

Next I'd like to thank Elsbeth van den Berg, August Hans den Boef, Chaja Polak, Ton Servais, Renée J. Lenders-Stam, Joan van de Ven, Jos Versteegen and Michèle Zwarts for their indispensable contributions to the genesis of this book.

No effort, however, can be matched by that of my dear friend Will, who, in the seven years during which I worked on this book, gave me all the love, attention, support and priceless advice that I so deeply craved.

Nor can I thank my parents enough, who not only brought me into this world, but also had a hand in making me the person I am. They had so many dreams for me, which have come true, one by one, in quite unexpected ways.

Mutely, the watermelon thanks the Creator by ripening into an edible fruit. I fervently hope that this book will be of service to my readers by offering them love, joy and friendship.

Lulu Wang
Maastricht, February 1997

The Tempest
JUAN MANUEL DE PRADA

Alejandro Ballesteros, a young Spanish art historian, arrives in a wintry Venice to study Giorgione's painting *The Tempest*. But on his first day there, he witnesses a murder and is propelled into a dangerous web connecting the city's rarified academic circles with a master forger. Exploring the boundaries between art and reality, intellect and passion, this is a mesmerising and thought-provoking novel by one of Spain's most celebrated new writers.

'This richly decadent novel is an homage to the treacherous landscapes of its Venetian setting. Like Thomas Mann's *Death in Venice*, it evokes how the city is both an invitation to mystery as well as the threat of the unknown ... Here is a place that serves as a graveyard to the monuments of its own desires, and in de Prada there is a voice that is equal to such a haunting lament'
Graham Caveney, *Sunday Express*

'I loved it'
Brian Davis, *Time Out*

'de Prada has weaved a unique murder story shot through with poetic fetishism. The eroticism that permeates de Prada's Venetian journey makes this book a high contender for potential cult status. Quite a read'
David Diebold, *Dublin Evening Herald*

'Works as a thriller, and a discussion of art, academia and emotion ... *The Tempest* defies categorisation and should enjoy broad appeal'
Joanna Clarke-Jones, *Financial Times*

SCEPTRE

The Snake in Sydney
MICHAEL LARSEN

When a young woman is rushed to a Sydney hospital suffering from a snakebite, she's lucky to be treated by Annika Niebuhr, a doctor whose fascination with serpents began with the Norse myths of her Danish childhood. Annika recognises the bite of a taipan – the world's most poisonous snake, but not one native to Sydney – and realises it can only have been planted.

Inadvertently, or so she believes, Annika is drawn into an investigation that becomes increasingly outlandish. A miraculous recovery, a clairvoyant schizophrenic, the apparent suicide of a close friend – none makes sense to a rational medic. Yet for all her scepticism, Annika begins to realise that she must use her instincts and imagination if she's to survive.

'A remarkable attempt to pinpoint and grasp the reality we take so much for granted'
Weekendavisen

'An unusual thriller, bursting with information about poisonous snakes, jellyfish, comets and other aspects of the natural world'
Good Book Guide

'What makes the book remarkable is the means by which Larsen builds tension. For the expository passages between each plot development, normally descriptive or mood building, here constitute, more often than not, a debate about the nature of knowledge'
Tangled Web

'This book takes on no less than the biggest questions posed by the theories of cognition, the secrets of life and creation'
Jyllands-Posten

'A hugely talented and well-written thriller, bulging with knowledge'
De Tri Stiftstidender

SCEPTRE

Conditions of Faith
ALEX MILLER

Impulsive, idealistic and restless, Emily Stanton finds herself, with university behind her, on the threshold of life in 1920s Melbourne. When she is introduced to a Franco-Scottish engineer whose Paris home promises the exotic, she chooses against academia and leaves Australia as his wife. But marriage and the prospect of motherhood soon fail to provide sufficient fulfilment and she embarks on a journey of self-questioning and intellectual reawakening that takes her as far as Tunisia, and towards a crossroads in her life.

'This is an amazing book . . . No paraphrase can do justice to this novel'
Carolyn See, *Washington Post*

'I think we will see few finer or richer novels this year . . . a singular achievement'
Andrew Reimer, *Australian Book Review*

'Ambitious and convincing . . . explores the psyche of a woman torn between family and career with subtlety and grace'
William Ferguson, *New York Times Book Review*

'Interesting and thoughtful . . . Miller has a considerable talent for the evocation of a vivid range of atmospheres and emotions'
Jane Shilling, *The Times*

'A mesmerising story of dreams and obsessions . . . thought provoking and eloquent'
Grania McFadden, *Belfast Telegraph*

'A fine, engrossing novel'
Michael Fitzgerald, *Time*

SCEPTRE

Confessions of a
Lapsed Standard-Bearer

ANDREI MAKINE

'An evocation of a Russian childhood in a little town near Leningrd after the war. Alyosha, the narrator, and his friend Arkady march joyfully through the forests, leading their Young Pioneer troop with drum and trumpet towards the 'radiant horizon' in which they have been taught to believe. They do not know about the watchtowers and prison camps behind the trees. Back home, in the flats where they live, their life is happy, too. Then one day, on parade, they rebel. After that, the blinkers start to fall from their eyes ... Alyosha finally leaves Russia for Paris and becomes a writer, while Arkady goes to America and prospers. Alyosha feels they have both betrayed their childhood and all it meant to them. But in this book, with its wonderfully sharp, sensuous imagery and delicate delineation of feeling, that childhood comes alive again. It is a moving and gripping story'

Derwent May, *The Times*

'Makine has Chekhov's tender humanity and wonderful ability to evoke states of feeling by description of wealth, landscape, buildings, etc. ... He cannot fail to arouse in the reader a wistful nostalgia. There is beauty in the world he makes for us, beauty and courage and goodness flowering, despite the harsh wintry reality of deprivation. His is a superb achievement ... He is a wonderful writer'

Alan Massie, *Scotsman*

'A glory and a dream'

Gary Atkinson, *Glasgow Herald*

'Stunning ... the lasting impression from this excellent novel is one of hope'

Sam Phipps, *Scotland on Sunday*

SCEPTRE

Fred and Edie
JILL DAWSON

Shortlisted for the Whitbread Novel of the Year Award

Set in the early nineteen twenties, this mesmerising tale is based on the true story of Edith Thompson, an attractive, ambitious woman who was charged with conspiring to murder her husband. Drawing on newspaper reports of the time as well as letters by Edie to her young lover Fred, the novel creates an intimate, tantalising voice for Edie as the story unfolds of how she came to be on trial for her life at the Old Bailey. Was Edie simply ahead of her time or did she collude in her own fate? Teasing out answers to a compelling mystery, this is a novel of entrancing imagination, sensitivity and grace.

'A captivating account of a strangely impassioned, and compelling, love affair'
Caryl Phillips

'It will captivate readers . . . Edie is so wonderful, so bitterly honest about herself, especially her understanding of her own sensual nature. And the sex is beautifully written about. Jill Dawson magnificently gets into a woman's skin and makes the whole act sublime'
Margaret Forster

'Jill Dawson's novel about the famous Thompson and Bywaters murder trial makes compelling reading . . . Edie, as envisaged here, is a latter-day Emma Bovary, whose passionate wish to live life to full leads in the end to her destruction. Dawson has given her a hauntingly authentic voice, and imparted an edgy, contemporary resonance to her story'
Christina Koning, *The Times*

SCEPTRE

A selection of other books from Sceptre

The Tempest	Juan Manuel de Prada	0 340 75023 5	£6.99	☐
The Snake in Sydney	Michael Larsen	0 340 74884 2	£6.99	☐
Conditions of Faith	Alex Miller	0 340 76667 0	£6.99	☐
Confessions of a Lapsed Standard-Bearer	Andreï Makine	0 340 72809 4	£6.99	☐
Fred and Edie	Jill Dawson	0 340 75167 3	£6.99	☐

All Hodder & Stoughton books are available from your local bookshop or newsagent, or can be ordered direct from the publisher. Just tick the titles you want and fill in the form below. Prices and availability subject to change without notice.

Hodder & Stoughton Books, Cash Sales Department, Bookpoint, 39 Milton Park, Abingdon, OXON, OX14 4TD, UK. E-mail address: order@bookpoint.co.uk. If you have a credit card you may order by telephone – (01235) 400414.

Please enclose a cheque or postal order made payable to Bookpoint Ltd to the value of the cover price and allow the following for postage and packing:
UK & BFPO – £1.00 for the first book, 50p for the second book, and 30p for each additional book ordered up to a maximum charge of £3.00.
OVERSEAS & EIRE – £2.00 for the first book, £1.00 for the second book, and 50p for each additional book.

Name_____

Address_____

_____

_____

If you would prefer to pay by credit card, please complete:
Please debit my Visa/Access/Diner's Card/American Express (delete as applicable) card no:

Signature_____

Expiry Date_____

If you would NOT like to receive further information on our products please tick the box. ☐